The OPEN Toolbox
of Techniques

This book was written with contributions from other members of the OPEN Consortium, in alphabetical order: Simon Brown, Wayne Butcher, Danni Fowler, Ian Graham, Wayne Harridge, Peter Horan, Steve Howard, Maksim Lin, Graham Low, Marco Scheurer, and Bhuvan Unhelkar.

The OPEN Series

Consulting Editor: Brian Henderson-Sellers

Related titles

The OPEN Process Specification *Ian Graham, Brian Henderson-Sellers and Houman Younessi*
Documenting a complete Java application using OPEN *Donald G Firesmith, Greg Hendley, Scott Krutsch and Marshall Stowe*

ACM PRESS BOOKS

This book is published as part of ACM Press Books – a collaboration between the Association for Computing (ACM) and Addison Wesley Longman Limited. ACM is the oldest and largest educational and scientific society in the information technology field. Through its high-quality publications and services, ACM is a major force in advancing the skills and knowledge of IT professionals throughout the world. For further information about ACM, contact:

ACM Member Services	**ACM European Service Center**
1515 Broadway, 17th Floor	108 Cowley Road
New York, NY 10036-5701	Oxford OX4 1JF
Phone: 1-212-626-0500	United Kingdom
Fax: 1-212-944-1318	Phone: +44-1865-382388
E-mail: `acmhelp@acm.org`	Fax: +44-1865-381388
	E-mail: `acm_europe@acm.org`
	URL: `http://www.acm.org`

Selected ACM titles

Component Software: Beyond Object-Oriented Programming *Clemens Szyperski*

The Object Advantage: Business Process Reengineering with Object Technology (2nd edn) *Ivar Jacobson, Maria Ericsson, Agneta Jacobson, Gunnar Magnusson*

Object-Oriented Software Engineering: A Use Case Driven Approach *Ivar Jacobson, Magnus Christerson, Patrik Jonsson, Gunnar Overgaard*

Software for Use: A Practical Guide to the Models and Methods of Usage Centered Design *Larry L Constantine, Lucy A D Lockwood*

Bringing Design to Software: Expanding Software Development to Include Design *Terry Winograd, John Bennett, Laura de Young, Bradley Hartfield*

CORBA Distributed Objects: Using Orbix *Sean Baker*

Software Requirements and Specifications: A Lexicon of Software Practice, Principles and Prejudices *Michael Jackson*

Business Process Implementation: Building Workflow Systems *Michael Jackson, Graham Twaddle*

Interacting Processes: A Multiparty Approach to Coordinated Distributed Programming *Nissim Francez, Ira Forman*

Design Patterns for Object-Oriented Software Development *Wolfgang Pree*

The OPEN Toolbox of Techniques

Brian Henderson-Sellers
Anthony Simons
Houman Younessi

ACM Press
New York

 Addison-Wesley

Harlow, England • Reading, Massachusetts
Menlo Park, California • New York
Don Mills, Ontario • Amsterdam • Bonn
Sydney • Singapore • Tokyo • Madrid
San Juan • Milan • Mexico City • Seoul • Taipei

© 1998 Brian Henderson-Sellers, Anthony Simons and Houman Younessi

Addison Wesley Longman Limited
Edinburgh Gate
Harlow
Essex CM20 2JE
England

and Associated Companies throughout the World.

The rights of Brian Henderson-Sellers, Anthony Simons and Houman Younessi to be identified as authors of this Work have been asserted by them in accordance with the Copyright, Designs and Patents Act 1988.

All rights reserved. No part of this publication may be reproduced, stored in a retrieval system, or transmitted in any form or by any means, electronic, mechanical, photocopying, recording or otherwise, without either the prior written permission of the publisher or a licence permitting restricted copying in the United Kingdom issued by the Copyright Licensing Agency Ltd, 90 Tottenham Court Road, London W1P 9HE.

Many of the designations used by manufacturers and sellers to distinguish their products are claimed as trademarks. Addison Wesley Longman Limited has made every attempt to supply trademark information about manufacturers and their products mentioned in this book. A list of the trademark designations and their owners appears on page xviii.

Cover designed by Senate
Typeset in Computer Modern by 56
Printed and bound in The United States of America

First printed 1998

ISBN 0-201-33134-9

British Library Cataloguing-in-Publication Data
A catalogue record for this book is available from the British Library

Library of Congress Cataloging-in-Publication Data
Henderson-Sellers, Brian.
    The OPEN toolbox of techniques / Brian Henderson-Sellers, Anthony Simons, Houman Younessi.
        p. cm. – (The OPEN series)
    Includes bibliographical references and index.
    ISBN 0-201-33134-9 (hardcover)
    1. Object-oriented programming. 2. Computer software–Development. I. Simons, Anthony, II. Younessi, Houman. III. Title. IV. Series.
QA76.64.H48   1998
005.1'17–dc21   98-34616
                                                                                                        CIP

Contents

Foreword		xiii
Preface		xv
List of abbreviations		xix

1 Overview of OPEN — 1
- 1.1 What is OPEN? — 1
- 1.2 OPEN's overall architecture — 3
- 1.3 OPEN's contract-driven lifecycle: two examples — 8
- 1.4 OPEN's tasks — 12
- 1.5 OPEN's techniques — 15
- 1.6 Products, deliverables and modeling language — 18
- 1.7 Further information — 19
- 1.8 About this book — 19

2 OPEN concepts, notations and deliverables — 21
- 2.1 Overview: modeling languages — 21
- 2.2 OPEN concepts — 22
  - 2.2.1 Basic relationships — 24
- 2.3 Notations for OPEN — 30
  - 2.3.1 OPEN's preferred notation: COMN — 30
  - 2.3.2 UML notation — 36
  - 2.3.3 Other notations — 45
- 2.4 Diagram types — 47
- 2.5 OPEN deliverables — 52

3 OPEN techniques — 57
- 3.1 Techniques selection criteria — 57
- 3.2 Techniques relating to user requirements — 58
- 3.3 Project management and quality assurance techniques — 67
- 3.4 Modeling techniques for seamless analysis and design — 69
- 3.5 Techniques for database design and construction — 78
- 3.6 Techniques for distributed architectures — 79
- 3.7 Techniques for user interface design — 79
- 3.8 Reuse strategies and supporting techniques — 80

3.9	Coding styles and implementation techniques	81
3.10	Some useful techniques in training and education	83

4 The future of OOAD and OPEN 85
4.1	OOAD in the future: towards convergence	85
4.2	OPEN-ing the dOOr to the future	86
4.3	Final summary	86

Appendices 89

Details of the OPEN techniques (in alphabetical order) 89
Technique: <Name> 89

A Core techniques 91

Abstract class identification	91
Abstraction utilization	92
Acceptance testing	95
Access analysis	98
Access path optimization	99
Active listening	99
Activity grid construction	103
Agents	105
Aggregation	105
Analysis of judgements	105
Analysis patterns	107
Application scavenging	107
Approval gaining	110
Assertions	111
Associations	111
Audit requirements (a.k.a. data security)	111
Beta testing	112
Blackboarding	114
Brainstorming	116
Business process modeling	117
CIRT indexing	119
Class internal design	121
Class naming	127
Clustering (DB)	129
Clusters	131
Cluster testing	131
Code/document inspections	132
Cohesion measurement	132
Collaborations analysis	133
Collapsing of classes	140
Completion of abstractions	142
Complexity measurement	143
Composition structures	144

Computer-based training	144
Concept maps	145
Configuration management	147
Containment	151
Context modeling	151
Contract specification	153
Cost–benefit analysis (CBA)	154
Cost estimation	155
Coupling measurement	157
CPM charts	157
CRC card modeling	159
Creation charts	160
Critical success factors (CSFs)	161
Customer (on-site) training	163
Database authorization	166
Database fragmentation	167
DBMS product selection	168
DBMS type selection	169
DCS classification	172
DCS optimization	173
Defect detection (a.k.a. defect identification)	175
Delegation analysis	177
Dependency	178
Dependency-based testing	179
Design by contract	180
Design patterns	180
Design templates	180
Dialog design in UI	182
Distributed systems partitioning and allocation	188
Domain analysis	190
Envisioning	192
Event modeling	193
Exception handling	194
Expected value analysis	199
Fagan's inspections	200
Finite state machines	200
Framework creation	200
Games	203
Gantt charts	207
Generalization and inheritance identification	208
Generalization for reuse	210
Genericity specification	210
GQM	212
Granularity	214
Group problem solving	215
Hierarchical task analysis	217

Hotspot identification	219
Impact analysis	219
Impact estimation table	220
Implementation inheritance	222
Implementation of distributed aspects of system	222
Implementation of rules	222
Implementation of services	224
Implementation of structure	226
Indexing	227
Inspections	228
Integration testing	234
Intelligent agent identification	236
Interaction modeling	237
Interfacing to relational DBMS and legacy code	238
Internet and web technology	239
Interviewing	240
JAD	245
Kelly grids	246
Layering (using aggregations)	248
Lectures	248
Library class incorporation	250
Library management	252
Mapping to RDB	254
Mechanisms	254
Membership	254
Mentoring	254
Mixins (take care)	256
Multiple inheritance	257
Object lifecycle histories	257
Object replication	258
Object retention requirements	259
Package construction	260
Package coordination	261
Package and subsystem testing	263
Partitioning and allocation	264
Path navigation	264
Pattern recognition	267
Peer review	268
PERT charts	268
Pistols at dawn	269
Power analysis (a.k.a. political systems analysis)	269
Priority setting	271
Process modeling	272
Protocol analysis	272
Prototyping	274
Quality templates	275

Query optimization	275
Questionnaires	278
RAD	280
RAD workshops	280
Record and playback	281
Redundant associations	282
Refactoring	282
Refinement	283
Regression testing	284
Relationship modeling	287
Reliability requirements	291
Repertory grids	291
Responsibility identification	291
Reuse measurement	292
Reverse engineering	293
Reviews	294
Revision of inheritance hierarchies	296
Rich pictures	297
Risk analysis	298
Role assignment	303
Role modeling	307
Roleplay	308
Rule modeling	309
Scenario classes	310
Scenario development	310
Screen painting	313
Screen scraping	314
Scripting	316
Security requirements (DBMS)	316
Service identification	316
Simulation	318
SMART goals	319
Social systems analysis	320
Specialization inheritance	321
Specification inheritance	321
Standards compliance	322
State modeling	323
State transition diagrams (STDs)	324
Statistical analysis of data	324
Stereotyping	325
Storage of derived properties	327
Storyboarding	327
Subclassing	328
Subsystems	328
Subsystem coordination	328
Subsystem identification	328

x   CONTENTS

    Subsystem testing 328
    Subtyping 328
    System event modeling 329
    Systems audit 329
    Task analysis 330
    Task decomposition 330
    Task modeling 330
    Team building 330
    Textual analysis 331
    Thresholds 332
    Throwaway prototyping 334
    Timeboxing 335
    Time-threads 336
    Train the trainers 336
    Transformations of the object model 338
    Tuning of database 341
    Unit testing 342
    Usability measurement 343
    Usability testing 346
    Usage 348
    Use case modeling 348
    V&V 348
    Versioning (DBMS) 348
    Videotaping 349
    Viewpoints 350
    Visibility analysis 352
    Visioning (for BPR) 355
    Volume analysis 355
    Walkthroughs 356
    Web technology 357
    Workflow analysis 357
    Workshops 358

B Suites of techniques   **361**
    Action research 361
    BPR 363
    Formal methods 366
    Metrics collection 368
    Soft systems analysis 373
    System acceptance 376
    TQM 381
    Visualization techniques 384

References   **391**

Index   **421**

CD Contents

C More experimental techniques
Connascence
Event charts
Fuzzy logic and fuzzy modeling
Hypergenericity
Law of Demeter
Literate programming
Ownership modeling
PLanguage
PSP
PS–PPS
Qua-types
Repeated inheritance
Task points
Variant analysis
Zachman frameworks

D Non-OO/traditional techniques with limited utility in OPEN
Dataflow modeling (dangerous)
ER modeling (but take care)
Function points
Information engineering (but take care)
Normalization
Petri nets

E Supporting reference material – concepts, artifacts and theory
Abstract and deferred classes
Abstraction
Access paths
Aggregation, membership and containment
Assertion language
Associations, dependency and usage
BNF lifecycle specification
BPR theory
Classification and partitions

Cohesion, coupling and connascence
Collaborations
Color in UIs
Complex adaptive systems (cas) theory
Complexity measures
Containment
Contracting
Cost estimation models
CRC cards
Delegation
Discriminant
Distributed systems
Encapsulation and information hiding
Generalization, inheritance and polymorphism
Genericity
Idioms, patterns and frameworks
Implementation using an oopl
Intelligent agents
Interaction diagrams
MVC framework
Naming conventions
Object-z
Packages
Partitions
Power types
Prototypes
Relational databases
Responsibilities and responsibility-driven design
Reuse metrics
Roles
Rules
Scenarios, task scripts and use cases
Services
Stereotypes
Team structures
Traits
Usability
Visibility
Wrappers

Foreword

When I first began using object technology in 1985, object-oriented programming languages were just coming into vogue. At that time, functionally modest applications were the focus of attention. The small teams of talented people that developed such applications usually succeeded without employing a well defined software development process. However, as the 1980s came to an end, use of object technology began to shift towards the development of increasingly larger and more sophisticated applications, utilizing larger and more diverse teams. Software development organizations began to demand better defined development approaches for creating object systems. The work of pioneering methodologists, practitioners and academicians yielded many sound analysis-and-design techniques.

The early 1990s could be characterized as the evolution of analysis-and-design methodologies and their attendant graphical notations. Although necessary and important, these methodologies and notations did not specify the overall process model – the organization of project activities along with a prescription of where and when to use specific techniques. Initial attempts to reuse well known, highly structured process models such as Waterfall met with limited success. In attempts to imitate the perceived benefits of having a singular model such as Waterfall, many object methodologists, corporate developers, and academicians began to search for the one, unified software development process model that could be used on all object projects.

As Adele Goldberg and I assert in our book, *Succeeding with Objects: Decision Frameworks for Project Management*, there is no one single software process model that can be used on all projects. Rather, different types of projects, e.g., first-of-a-kind, variation-on-a-theme, maintenance, re-engineering and so on, all require their own specific process model. Many people found this denouncement of the singular process model quite disturbing. The question we heard most frequently was: How can we ever achieve highly repeatable processes if we use a different process model on each project? The assumption underlying this question was that repeatability must occur at the most aggregate level – the entire process model. In practice, tangible reuse of a specific process model may occur across substantially similar projects. However, what is much more common is the reuse of individual techniques across many or all projects, and reuse of process model subparts across multiple classes of projects.

The best process model approach is a framework and set of strategies for creating specific process model instances. This approach is exemplified in the work of the OPEN Consortium. Their earlier book, *The OPEN Process Specification*, provides a methodological framework from which specific process model instances may be created to meet the individual needs of an object project. Other books produced by the OPEN Consortium, including this one, provide more details on how to implement the different stages of the process model – what to do and when to do it.

To execute the tasks of a specific project using a process model instance, we still need a description of the techniques that describe how to carry out each task. This book, *The OPEN Toolbox of Techniques*, provides a complete compendium (or toolbox) of the techniques that can be reused across many or all instances of the methodological framework. The techniques described in this book support tasks in diverse areas such as: business goals and power structures, requirements engineering, analysis and design, implementation and testing, frameworks and libraries, databases and distribution. The authors link each technique with one or more process tasks for which it is suitable. They provide alternative techniques for completing the same process task, and indicate how some techniques may be grouped into useful sequences. Furthermore, they illustrate the benefits and point out the pitfalls of using each technique. The result is a comprehensive, dictionary-style reference manual that provides cogent descriptions of a broad range of techniques.

This book makes a statement about how far we have come as community. The ability to create such a book presumes the existence of a substantial body of best-practice techniques. The authors have undertaken the prodigious task of aggregating and organizing both their unique contributions as well as best practices from methodologists, practitioners and academicians around the world. If you are interested in establishing repeatable software development practices, regardless of whether you are an avid user of the OPEN process framework or some other process, you will find this book to be an essential desktop reference. Indeed we have come a long way since 1985.

Kenneth S. Rubin
President, Innolution
June 1998

Preface

Is object technology (OT) right for you? Now – or at some time in the future?

Taking a decision to migrate to a new technology is always a risk – a risk that you may be unsuccessful because of a lack of skill, a lack of resources or any one of a myriad of difficulties; a risk that the technology may be just a 'fad' (a particular worry in computing); a risk that you may not be able to find the right people, perhaps because the new technology is not taught sufficiently widely in schools and universities; a risk that it may not be appropriate for your particular domain.

All the signs are that object technology is not just a fad, that it is to be the underpinning of industrial software development for sufficient time to come to make a major investment worthwhile. In a very down-to-earth book about how to use object techniques to their fullest, Baudoin and Hollowell (1996) use the analogy of surfing. Since a number of the authors of this OPEN Techniques book hail from the mecca of surfing, Australia, this seems an appropriate metaphor. Choosing a wave (in the sea or in technology) that has already peaked means that you will be quickly beached with little profit to show. Swimming out further to catch a wave just forming may be exhausting and there is a higher risk of the wave petering out before it becomes really useful (or exciting). The trick is to catch the wave at just the right time, between these two extremes. Baudoin and Hollowell are convinced that the OO wave is one worth catching *now* – as are we. It is still in its prime, neither exhausted nor still in diapers, and has clearly demonstrated its capabilities in a number of domains, as witness the increasing number of papers and books on how to use OT in different commercial areas.

This book describes the techniques supported by OPEN in creating the process-focused, third-generation OO methodological framework described in the companion volume, '*The OPEN Process Specification*'[†]. We do *not* discuss basic OO concepts, ideas and modeling techniques. Instead we target the users wishing

---

† The observant reader will note that the techniques listed are not absolutely identical to those foreshadowed in the Process Specification book – well, times change and OT moves on at full steam.

to deploy an OO methodology in their organization (be it commercial software development, business and enterprise modeling and re-engineering or in a university or other teaching environment). Readers may thus be system architects, developers, managers or educators. Each will approach this text from a different viewpoint.

The structure of the book is simple: the first chapter describes the OPEN methodological framework together with a brief description of two possible instantiations of it. The second chapter discusses metamodels and notations (collectively referred to as a modeling language) together with OPEN's deliverables. The third chapter gives an overview of the various techniques, logically grouped.

The meat of the book, however, is in the full descriptions for each of the numerous OO techniques which form part of the OPEN Toolbox (Appendix A). Since these will be required on an 'as-needed' basis and, once utilized will frequently become second nature, the format is that of a dictionary in which the techniques are listed alphabetically. Here is where you will find the main description of a single technique: Chapter 3 offers the underpinning synergy between the techniques, the tasks and the process lifecycle of OPEN. Any repetition between the book itself and Appendix A is intended so that each part (either the chapters of the book or the appendices) can be studied relatively independently.

In the book itself, we include only those key, mainstream OPEN techniques (Appendix A) and suites of techniques (Appendix B). Accompanying the book you will find a CD which contains further related information in the form of more experimental techniques (Appendix C) and some non-OO/traditional techniques (Appendix D). We also include, on this CD, a number of essays on various aspects of the underpinning ideas of object technology (Appendix E). Some of our supporting CASE tool vendors have kindly agreed also to allow us to include on the CD versions of their tool.

As well as our colleagues in the OPEN Consortium (who are all listed in Table 1.1), we would also like to thank especially, for their constructive review comments on all or parts of earlier drafts, Ishbel Duncan, Don Firesmith, Juhani Iivari, Paul Strooper, Raj Vasa and the students of the Class of '97 studying Object Technology 1 (IT921) at Swinburne University of Technology. Also thanks to Rob Allen for supplying some paragraphs on Java; Larry Constantine for assisting with usability metrics and Mike Creek for preparing the CD. For supplying full or partial entries in the appendices, we are most grateful to (in alphabetical order) Simon Brown, Wayne Butcher, Danni Fowler, Ian Graham, Wayne Harridge, Peter Horan, Steve Howard, Maksim Lin, Graham Low, M. Scheurer and Bhuvan Unhelkar.

Individually, the authors would like to dedicate this book: (BH-S) to Ann, with thanks for continued tolerance when he is in the throes of book-writing; (AJHS) to John and Elinor, for setting him on the right track; and (HY) to (the late) His Excellency Dr M.A. Modjtahedi – a master architect of many intellects and personalities.

If you require local support for OPEN, contacts are given below. For more up-to-date information, consult the OPEN web site or the Addison-Wesley catalog entry for this book.

North America
    Genesis Development Corporation: http://www.gendev.com
    Knowledge Systems Corporation (KSC): http://www.ksccary.com/
    Thomsen Dué: http://ourworld.compuserve.com:80/homepages/rtdue/
    Tower Technology Corporation: http://www.twr.com

South America
    Intuitive Technology: http://www.intuitive.com.br

Europe and Middle East
    Bezant: bezant@compuserve.com
    Object House: steif@objectus.co.il
    OIG Ltd.: http://www.oig.co.uk
    Sen:te: http://www.sente.ch/
    Wayland Informatics: http://www.wayland-informatics.co.uk

India
    Fourfront: rajeshp@giaspn01.vsnl.net.in

Australasia
    COTAR: http://www.csse.swin.edu.au/cotar/ and brian@csse.swin.edu.au

In addition, we wish to acknowledge the following copyright holders for permission to reproduce copyright material in the book or on the CD: ACM for Table A.3 and Figures B.7 and E.24; Addison Wesley Longman for Tables 1.2, A.2, A.5–11, A.14, A.15, A.17, A.20, A.23, E.2, E.7–8, E.10, E.12 and Figures 1.3–5, 1.10, 2.14, A.30, A.38, A.48, C.3, E.14, E.69 and E.80; American Meterological Society for Figures A.52 and E.21; ACS Inc. (The Australian Computer Society) for Figures A.29 and E.54; Cambridge University Press for Table E.11 and Figure A.17; IEEE for Table A.13, part of Table A.19 and Figures A.45–7; Information Technology Institute of Singapore for Figure B.9; J.C. Baltzer Science Publishers BV, for Table A.4; Manning Publications co. for Figures E.55–6; Microsoft Corporation for Figures A.61–2; Object Management Group for Figures 2.21, 2.29–30 (parts), 2.31–2, 3.4 and E.11; Plenum Press for Figure B.1; Prentice Hall for Table A.19 (part) and Figures A.34, B.3, E.30, E.52–3 and E.65; Routledge Ltd for Table B.1; SIGS Publications Inc. for Tables A.16, A.21, A.27 and Figures 2.3–4, 2.7, 2.9, 2.15–6, 2.36–8, A.7, A.18, A.40, A.49, A.56, E.1, E.4–9, E.41–2, E.46–7, E.60, E.62, E.64, E.68 and E.70–1; Springer Verlag for Figures A.6 and E.61; and John Wiley and Sons for Figure A.44(b).

We would also like to thank (in alphabetical order) the following people for supplying diagrammatic material: Tina Case for Tables A.1, A.25 and Figures A.2, A.3, A.23, A.55; Phil Haynes for Table A.22; Peter Horan for Figures A.41, A.42, E.38, E.39; Ying Leung for Figure B.8; Mark Ratjens for Table A.28, A.29 and Figure A.31; and Rebecca Wirfs-Brock for Table A.24.

Trademark notice

Apple and MacApp are trademarks of Apple Computer Inc.

C++ and Unix are trademarks of AT&T

CORBA is the trademark of the Object Management Group

Eiffel is the trademark of the Non-Profit International Consortium for Eiffel

fsbp and Future Strategy Business Planning are registered trademarks of Future Strategies Inc.

IBM is a trademark of International Business Machines, Inc.

Java and Open Look are trademarks of Sun Microsystems Incorporated

Motif is a trademark of OSF

MS Windows, Windows 95, Visual Basic and Foundation Classes are all trademarks of Microsoft Corporation

NeXT is the trademark of NeXT Computer

Objective-C is a trademark of Productivity Products International

Objectory is the trademark of Objective Systems and Rational Software Corporation

ROSE is the trademark of Rational Software Corporation

Smalltalk is a trademark of ParcPlace Systems Inc.

SOMATiK is the trademark of Bezant Ltd

List of abbreviations

a.k.a.	also known as
ADT	Abstract Data Type
API	Application Program Interface
ASD	Adaptive Software Development
BDC	Business Domain Classes
BNF	Backus–Naur Form
BOM	Business Object Model
BON	Business Object Notation
BPR	Business Process Re-engineering
CAS	Complex Adaptive Systems
CASE	Computer Assisted Software Engineering
CBA	Computer-Based Assessment
CBA	Cost–Benefit Analysis
CBO	Coupling Between Objects
CBT	Computer-Based Training
CEO	Chief Executive Officer
CI	Configuration Item
CIRT	Class, Instance, Role or Type
CLOS	Common Lisp Object System
CML	Computer Managed Learning
CMM	Capability Maturity Model
CODASYL	COnference on DAta SYstems and Languages
COM	Common Object Model
COMMA	Common Object Methodology Metamodel Architecture
COMN	Common Object Modeling Notation
CORBA	Common Object Request Broker Architecture
CPM	Critical Path Method
CRC	Class, Responsibility, and Collaborations (cards)
CSF	Critical Success Factor
DAC	Data Abstraction Coupling
DB	Database
DBMS	DataBase Management System
DCOM	Distributed Common Object Model

DCS	Distributed Computing System
DDD	Data-Driven Design
DFD	Data Flow Diagram
DIT	Depth of Inheritance Tree
DOS	Disk Operating System
ER	Entity Relationship (modeling)
ERA	Entity Relationship Attribute (modeling)
FFT	Fast Fourier Transform
GPS	Group Problem Solving
GQM	Goal Quality Metric
GUI	Graphical User Interface
HCI	Human–Computer Interface
ICM	Idealized Cognitive Model
IDL	Interface Definition Language
IEEE	Institute of Electrical and Electronics Engineers
I/O	Input/Output
IOM	Implementation Object Model
ISO	International Organization for Standardization
ITT	Invitation To Tender
JAD	Joint Application Development
JIT	Just In Time
JSP	Jackson Structured Programming
KWIC	Key Word In Context
LCOM	Lack of Cohesion Of Methods
LDC	Logical Dialog Controls
LDD	Logical Dialog Design
LDO	Logical Dialog Outline
LOC	Lines of Code
MBO	Management By Objectives
MI	Multiple Inheritance
MOSES	Methodology for Object-oriented Software Engineering of Systems
MPC	Message Passing Coupling
MVC	Model View Controller
NIH	Not Invented Here
NLM	Number of Local Methods
NOC	Number of Children
NRM	Number of Remote Methods
OADF	Object Analysis and Design Facility
OADTF	Object-oriented Analysis and Design Task Force (of the OMG)
OB	ObjectBase
OBA	Object Behavior Analysis
OID	Object IDentifier
OMG	Object Management Group
OML	Object Modeling Language
OMT	Object Modeling Technique
OO	Object-Oriented

OOAD	Object-Oriented Analysis and Design
OOPL	Object-Oriented Programming Language
OOPSLA	Object-Oriented Programming, Systems, Languages and Applications
OOSE	Object-Oriented Software Engineering (Jacobson et al., 1992)
OPEN	Object-oriented Process, Environment and Notation
ORB	Object Request Broker
OT	Object Technology
PERT	Program Evaluation and Review Technique
PL	Programming Language
PM	Project Management
PSP	Personal Software Process
RAD	Rapid Application Development
RCS	Revision Control System
RDB	Relational DataBase
RDD	Responsibility-Driven Design
RE	Risk Exposure
RE	Requirements Engineering
RFC	Response For Class
RMI	Remote Method Invocation
ROOM	Realtime Object-Oriented Methodology
RRL	Risk Reduction Leverage
SBM	State Behavior Modeling
SCCS	Source Code Control System
SCM	Software Configuration Management
SDLC	Software Development Life Cycle
SEP	Software Engineering Process
SEPA	Software Engineering Process Architecture
SM	System Meter
SMART	Specific, Measurable, Attainable, Relevant, Trackable
SOM	System Object Model
SOMA	Semantic Object Modeling Approach
SSADM	Structured Systems Analysis and Design Method
SSM	Soft Systems Methodology
STD	State Transition Diagram
SVDPI	Subject/Verb/Direct.Object/Preposition/Indirect.Object
TBD	To Be Decided
TOM	Task Object Model
TQM	Total Quality Management
UI	User Interface
UML	Unified Modeling Language
UON	Uniform Object Notation
VC	Visual Coherence
V&V	Verification and Validation

Chapter 1
Overview of OPEN

1.1 What is OPEN?

OPEN is an acronym for Object-oriented Process, Environment and Notation. OPEN is a *process-focused*, 'third-generation'[†], full lifecycle object-oriented (OO) method (or methodology). It was initially created by a merger of three second-generation methods (MOSES, SOMA and the Firesmith method) commencing at the end of 1994 when it became clear that (a) there were too many first- and second-generation methods in the marketplace and their scopes were too limited; and (b) the concepts underlying these three methods were almost completely compatible. In 1997, the Synthesis methodology was the last methodology to be merged into OPEN.

The OPEN method is developed and maintained by the 30+ members of the OPEN Consortium – a non-profit grouping comprising the original authors of the methods cited above together with other members drawn from the OO methodology, research and training communities worldwide (see Table 1.1). (Other early influences and participants in the development of OPEN were the Responsibility-Driven Design (RDD) method and Jim Odell.)

OPEN is essentially a *framework* for third-generation object-oriented software development methods, providing strong support for process modeling by using a tailorable, objectified lifecycle (Graham, 1995b; Graham *et al.*, 1997b). It has an embedded project management and reuse framework. It supports business process modeling and offers guidelines on migration strategies. A prime concern of OPEN is software quality and the use of metrics.

OPEN thus provides a methodological framework which can be tailored[‡]

[†] First-generation OO methods originated in the early 1990s. They were devised by individuals or small groups working alone. Second-generation methods, from the mid-1990s, were still authored by small groups but borrowed extensively from other authors. Third-generation methods are under the guidance of larger, collaborative groups and have a wider software development process focus to them.

[‡] Thomsett (1992) identifies four stages of evolution of the IT profession (dark age, tokenism, get even, mutual respect). Godfrey (1998) equates the last two to 'user seduction' in which marketing is the sole driver and 'user co-operation' in which user-focused tailoring dominates. OPEN clearly meets the fourth stage criteria.

OVERVIEW OF OPEN

Table 1.1 The members of the OPEN Consortium in alphabetical order.

Dinu Anastasiu
Colin Atkinson
Jean Bézivin
Ed Colbert
Philippe Desfray
Richard Dué
Daniel Duffy
Roger Duke
Don Firesmith
Yossi Gil
Ian Graham
Brian Henderson-Sellers
Kitty Hung
Graham Low
Jim McKim
Daniela Mehandjiska-Stavrova
Simon Moser
Kinh Nguyen
Alan O'Callaghan
Meilir Page-Jones
Dilip Patel
Rajesh Pradhan
Dan Rawsthorne
Tony Simons
Madhu Singh
Paul Swatman
Bhuvan Unhelkar
Katharine Whitehead
Alan Wills
Russel Winder
Houman Younessi
Ed Yourdon
Hadar Ziv

---

either

(1) as OPEN/Firesmith, OPEN/SOMA etc. – public domain standardized methods; or

(2) by individual organizations for their own internal use – OPEN/'your company'; or

(3) embodied in a commercial, Level 3 (Henderson-Sellers and Edwards, 1994b) proprietary method.

The heart of both public domain and commercial instantiations of OPEN is the metalevel process description, a formulation which, it is anticipated, will form the kernel of a proposal to the Object Management Group (OMG) in 1998/9.

In addition to synthesizing the best ideas and practices from MOSES, SOMA, Firesmith and Synthesis, OPEN also utilizes concepts from BON[†], Discovery, Mainstream Objects, Martin/Odell, OBA, RDD, ROOM, Syntropy, UML and others. Its metamodel and notation are largely compliant with emerging (late 1997) OMG standards and each offers value-added extensions to the corresponding elements in UML Version 1.1 (OMG, 1997a, b).

OPEN also offers a set of principles (see below) for modeling all aspects of software development, across the lifecycle. Individual methods may conform to the OPEN methodological framework (e.g. Firesmith *et al.*, 1998; Simons, 1999) by applying its principles and adopting all or part of the OPEN framework specification: lifecycle, tasks, techniques and modeling language (metamodel plus notation). OPEN will continue to evolve as new techniques are developed and enhanced by working methodologists, users and researchers.

In summary, OPEN extends the notion of a methodology not only by including a process model (Graham *et al.*, 1997b) but also by providing guidelines for constructing versions of this model tailored to the needs of different industry domains, individual organizations and problem types. The process model is described in part by an object model and, as such, is adaptable. One sample realization of this object model was discussed in Graham *et al.* (1997b) – a book which described the *process* underpinning the OPEN methodological framework. Further instantiations are described by, for example, Firesmith *et al.* (1998) and Simons (1998b, 1999).

1.2 OPEN's overall architecture

As a third-generation OO method, OPEN encapsulates business issues, quality issues, modeling issues and reuse issues within its end-to-end lifecycle process support for software development using the object-oriented paradigm. The technical issues of object model building are relatively well understood, in that OPEN leverages off existing methodological modeling techniques as found in, for example, MOSES, SOMA, Firesmith, Synthesis, RDD, BON and UML. However, the more important process issues still provide a challenge both to the methodology developer (as described here) and the users of those methodological ideas.

Underpinning any methodology must be a lifecycle process. The lifecycle process is essentially one component of the methodology, the key elements of which (Figure 1.1) can probably best be grouped into

- lifecycle process
- techniques

[†] Method names and other acronyms are defined in the List of abbreviations (page xix).

4 OVERVIEW OF OPEN

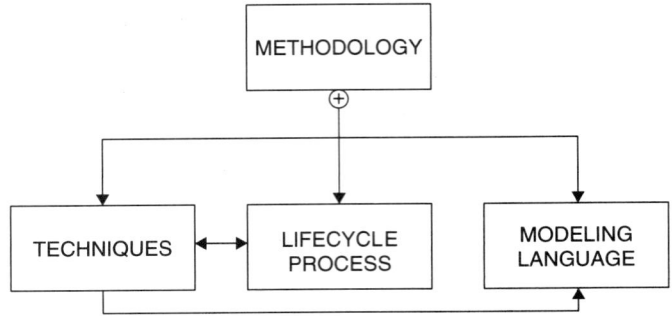

Figure 1.1 A method (or methodology) is an aggregation of many elements, the three primary ones being lifecycle process, techniques and representation.

- representation (using a modeling language).

Thus, as Younessi and Henderson-Sellers (1997) point out, 'methodology' includes (lifecycle) process. However, at a larger granularity, the (software engineering) process must include not only a methodology but also consideration of the people/organizational culture and also the tools/technology which are available (Figure 1.2). Yet, it is generally believed that, however hard we seek it, a single, generally applicable process will remain an unattainable and illusory Holy Grail of software engineering. Rather, different organizations, different development styles and different development domains will require their own specialized lifecycle process (e.g. Daniels, 1997). Each of these software engineering processes (or SEPs) will be highly relevant under specific constraints and, as such, fairly widely useful. Generification of these SEPs permits us to seek an underlying architecture, the SEPA (software engineering process architecture) (Edwards and Henderson-Sellers, 1996). A SEPA for object-oriented development, which as we shall see is embodied within OPEN, thus provides an integrating framework. No one project will ever use this framework unaltered; rather, each will instantiate a particular part of the framework for their own circumstances. This 'tailoring of the process' is in fact a major task[†] within the overall OPEN architecture. The SEPA is described by a set of objects. Any type of interaction is possible within these objects in true object-oriented fashion if the messages sent between these reifications of OPEN activities meet the client object's contract. The activities trigger or enable each other by message passing. The messages are guarded by pre- and post-conditions representing tests. The 'methods' of an activity are its *tasks*. Tasks can also be considered the smallest unit of work within OPEN (Figure 1.3). Tasks are carried out by actors (people) using techniques. Two example SEPs, based on the contract-driven lifecycle process architecture, are described briefly below (Section 1.3).

---

† OPEN tasks are covered in the companion volume, *The OPEN Process Specification* (Graham *et al.*, 1997b).

OPEN'S OVERALL ARCHITECTURE 5

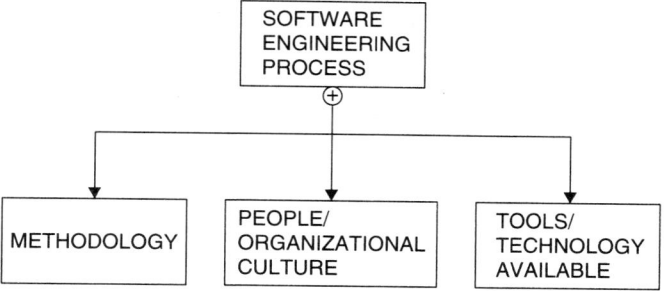

Figure 1.2 A software engineering process encompasses methodology (see Figure 1.1), people/organizational culture and tools and technology available.

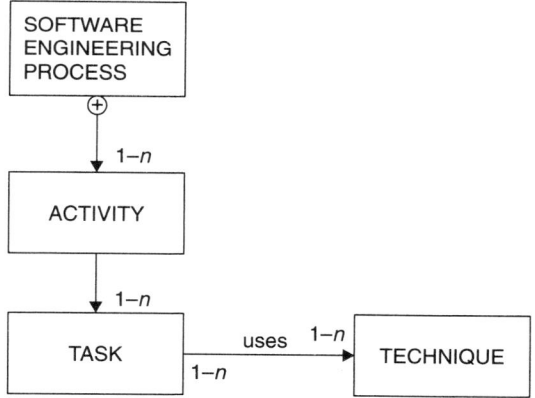

Figure 1.3 Activities (with possibly sub-activities) have tasks which are realized by the use of one or more techniques (after Graham *et al.*, 1997b).

A two-dimensional matrix then links the task (which provides the statement of goals, i.e. the 'what') to the *techniques* (which provide the way the goal can be achieved, i.e. the 'how'). Techniques range across project management through to detailed theories and practices for requirements engineering and system modeling. *OPEN techniques are the focus of this book.* OPEN provides a large repository of well-matched techniques taken from existing methods as well as from its progenitors.

This approach is not unlike the one proposed by Daniels (1997). He clearly distinguishes between the project management/business perspective, which he calls the 'lifecycle', and the software developer's viewpoint: the development process. Daniels argues that much of the failure that has occurred in software development has been the result of force-fitting the 'lifecycle' and the 'design process' together as a single tool for both development and management. Thus progress, from a project management viewpoint, he argues, has typically been measured in developers' units (e.g. five DFDs have been fully coded) rather than in users' units (e.g. three of the main goals of the accounts-receivable subsystem can now be attained).

Thus, any given project has a lifecycle and a design process (which should each be chosen from a suite available at the organizational level); the development process then consisting of *activities*, delivering 'products' (deliverables in OPEN) by means of task completion.

One of the greatest technical advantage of an OO lifecycle process is that of (almost) seamlessness. 'Objects'[†] are used as the basic concept and unit of consideration during requirements engineering and design as well as in the OO programming language and future maintenance. 'Objects' are the common language of users as well as technical developers. This helps cognitively in terms of learning, remembering and decision making since cognitive translations and recasting from one world view to another are minimized if not eliminated by this use of a single (OO) mindset. Of course, the notion of seamlessness causes concern for project managers who have previously been accustomed to the analysis and design phases having clearly defined boundaries. In addition, an over-emphasis on use cases (which are a functional not an OO description) can thwart seamlessness.

Secondly, through seamlessness, object-oriented systems provide good traceability through the software development lifecycle – an advantage for project management. Traceability requires business objects to be identified and tracked right through into code. This is in stark contrast to structured entities which are torn apart in the normalization process into multiple relational tables or during entity relationship modeling. In addition, functions provide a major focus of modularization in traditional software development. Adding new data elements often causes major restructuring of these functions. These structured techniques thus tend to fragment the design and code and traceability is thwarted.

In this seamless, iterative lifecycle, incremental delivery is the norm. This is, of course, highly advantageous in keeping the user 'in the loop' providing immediate feedback – always a currently viable version of the developing work product (e.g. design, software) for use and evaluation; thus assisting in producing higher quality software. The elements which comprise this iterative, incremental and parallel lifecycle describe the high-level activities which must be undertaken in order to produce the software product(s). The activities, outlined below, are linked together in an organization's tailoring of the contract-driven lifecycle – which produces their specific SEP. The way in which they are linked together depends on the organization and the problem. Case study example SEPs are to be discussed in a future OPEN book: *Tailoring the OPEN Lifecycle – Case Studies*.

Finally, OPEN embodies a set of (object-oriented) principles. It permits enhanced semantics for object models based on the contributions of methods

---

† At this stage, we do not want to enter into any arguments regarding the use of the words object, type, class, role and instance, collectively called CIRT (see Chapter 2) in OPEN, and will for the present just use 'object' in a truly generic and formally undefined sense.

such as SOMA, RDD, BON, etc. Furthermore, OPEN is fully object-oriented in that encapsulation is a basic principle. Thus, since bi-directional associations violate encapsulation (Graham et al., 1997a), they are strongly discouraged. In addition, there is ambiguity in whether such a relationship, as advocated in UML for instance, represents a true bi-directional relationship or merely one with directionality yet to be decided (e.g. Fowler and Scott, 1997, page 62). It is a logical consequence of the use in OPEN of one-way associations as default that class invariants are not an optional extra in the modeling semantics. Furthermore, rulesets (which generalize class invariants) can also be used to model intelligent agents as objects.

In OPEN, OO principles are basic and should be adhered to. These include:

- object modeling as a very general technique for knowledge representation (not just programming)
- encapsulation
- polymorphism

together with

- a focus on responsibilities and Meyer's (1988) 'design by contract'
- clear, jargon-free and well-founded definitions of all terms, and
- extensive use of abstraction techniques, a foundation for semantically cohesive and encapsulated 'objects'.

Design by contract, or 'contracting', is embodied not only in the analysis and design techniques as described in this volume, but also in the lifecycle model used in OPEN. This lifecycle model, known as the contract-driven lifecycle, is a fully object-oriented description of the OPEN process framework (Graham et al., 1997b). In it, process elements, or activities, are represented by objects which interact *only if* the pre- and post-conditions of the contract between any pair of activities is met (see further details below in Section 1.3).

In OPEN, process is a major focus and support for the full lifecycle is a major strength. Another major strength of OPEN is in the area of notation and semantics. During 1995, the call from OMG for a standardized metamodel and notation led some members of the OPEN Consortium to invest additional effort in these directions. Thus was created the OPEN Modeling Language or OML. OML is the name for the combination of metamodel and notation (Figure 1.4), in parallel to a similar combination created by Rational methodologists, known as UML (Unified Modeling Language). Furthermore, OML provides an OMG-compliant extension to the UML notation and metamodel (see Chapter 2). Both OML and UML are useful over a wide spectrum of situations (Whitehead, 1997) and, indeed, either notation can be used in conjunction with the OPEN methodology (see Section 2.3). The OML metamodel (Firesmith et al., 1997) is derived from the work of the metamodeling COMMA project (Henderson-Sellers and Bulthuis, 1997) which itself has provided valuable input to the OMG

8 OVERVIEW OF OPEN

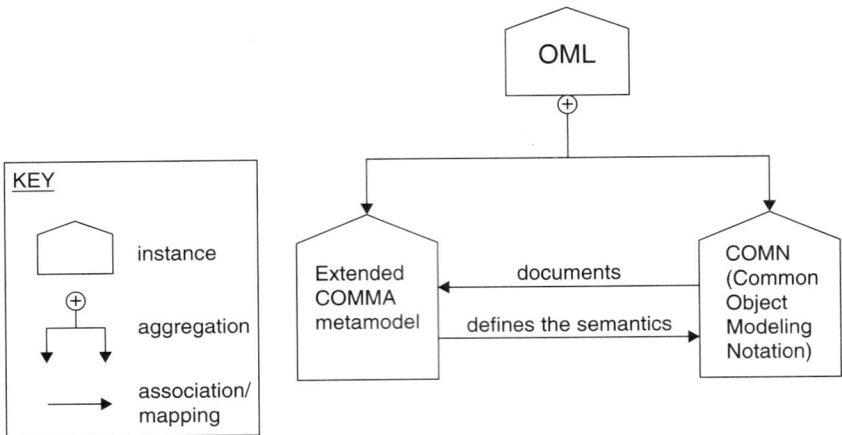

Figure 1.4 OML (OPEN Modeling Language) has two parts: the metamodel, derived as an extended version of the COMMA metamodel of Henderson-Sellers and Firesmith (1997a) and the notation, COMN (Common Object Modeling Notation) (after Graham *et al.*, 1997b).

metamodeling effort. The notational element of OML also has its own name: COMN or Common Object Modeling Notation (see Section 2.3.1). Whilst it was designed for use in OPEN, COMN is not so restricted and can be used in conjunction with other OO methods. Consequently, we have published the COMN notational standard (Firesmith *et al.*, 1997) and the process description (Graham *et al.*, 1997b) in two other volumes, thus separating two of the major elements of a methodology noted above: process and the representation of its products. Indeed, we go further and keep the techniques separate again. The overview/catalog of these techniques is contained in this volume, whilst others (such as requirements engineering and application to financial software) will be explored in detail in other books written by members of the OPEN Consortium.

1.3 OPEN's contract-driven lifecycle: two examples

The contract-driven lifecycle, as used in OPEN, is shown in one instantiation in Figure 1.5. The model is, in essence, very simple. In summary, a development program may be decomposed into a network of projects that produce deliverable, working software products. Projects are composed of activities (as detailed in Graham *et al.*, 1997b). The activities in OPEN permit a largescale temporal structuring of the project management for an OO product development and necessarily including schedules for builds and releases. Each activity has a set of goals and, in truly object-oriented fashion, has an interface consisting of methods which are the selected tasks, internal state and external services, and has pre- and post-conditions to satisfy all contractual obligations. Each OPEN activity is shown as a box, either with rounded corners (an unbounded activity) or with rectangular corners (the latter represent activities tightly bound in time, i.e. the ideas of timeboxing are applied – see Section 4.1 of Graham et al., 1997b). Since we are modeling these activities as objects, we can associate contracts with each activity object (hence the lifecycle name of 'contract-driven'). These are expressed primarily by pre- and post-conditions; in other words, constraints that have to be met before an activity can be commenced and final conditions that have to be met (and signed off) before the activity is complete and another activity can be initiated (triggered). Testing is an integral part of these exit conditions. Testing should deliver test results against both use cases or task scripts (a higher form of use cases – see Graham, 1997a) and a technical test plan of the normal kind – for example, tests that answer the questions: Does an enhancement leave previous things that worked working? Does the system work well under stress and high volume I/O?

The contract-driven lifecycle allows the developer to move from activity to activity in any order so long as all the pre- and post-conditions are met. This does not, however, lead to anarchy. Rather, it supports flexibility so that different organizations can choose their own tailored lifecycle process model from the OPEN activities. Secondly, within a single organization, individual projects may have different foci, which require different configurations of this highly flexible lifecycle process. Thus, an individually chosen lifecycle can be created for projects and/or organizations, whilst remaining 'OPEN-compliant'. The developers still speak the same language and can still talk to each other!

The progression order is neither prescriptive nor deterministic. Rather, the contract-driven lifecycle permits (1) ordering in an iterative, incremental and parallel fashion and (2) the tailoring by a given organization to its own internal standards and culture. Different configurations, chosen to reflect the needs of different problems and different organizations, can be constructed from this flexible framework. We indicate in Figure 1.5 some of the likely routes between activity objects for an MIS project – other variations are discussed in Graham et al. (1997b). But remember, the main governing constraint on the routes are whether you do or do not meet the pre-conditions of the activity to which you wish to transition.

The first example here is one that is typical of MIS systems development and one that is central to OPEN/SOMA (Graham, 1995a). Each combination of activities and interconnecting paths defines a software engineering process (or SEP). Once chosen, the lifecycle process is fixed – although still, at least in an OO project, highly iterative, incremental, parallel and flexible and with a high degree of seamlessness.

A second example is shown in Figure 1.6 which shows the activities of the OPEN/Firesmith method (Firesmith et al., 1998). The Initial Planning and Development activity has tasks which include Document the Background, Initial Training, Tailor the Method, Model the Context, Capture the Initial Requirements, Create the Initial Architecture, Document the Initial Products, Scope

10 OVERVIEW OF OPEN

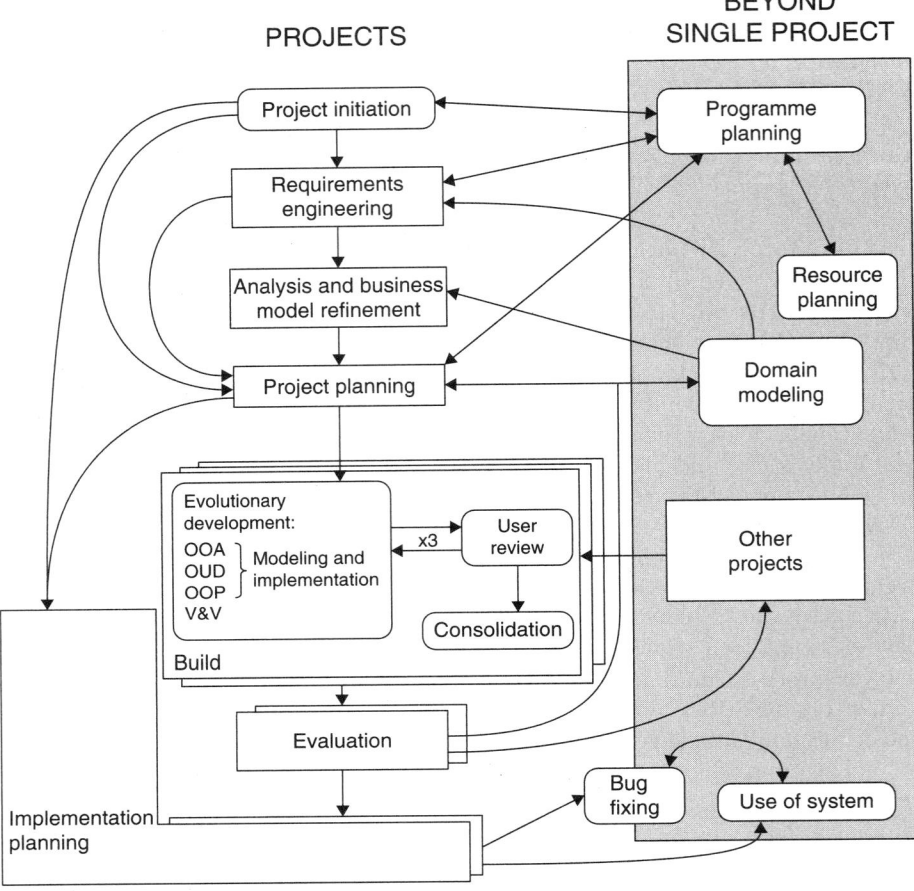

Figure 1.5 Contract-driven lifecycle process model – one example instantiation (revised from Graham et al., 1997b).

the Application and Plan Build Development. While there is a rough ordering of these tasks, there is also significant temporal overlap.

In the OPEN/Firesmith instantiation, the second major activity is Build Development. In parallel with the Build activity of Figure 1.5, this also has subactivities and is the focus of the technical part of software development. Following Build Preparation, Requirements Analysis and Package Development proceed in parallel. Build Acceptance Testing then completes the activity. The task: Verify the Packages and Use Cases can be useful throughout, noting that 'due to the functional nature of use case modeling, use cases should be used more for verification purposes than for requirements analysis purposes' (Firesmith et al., 1998).

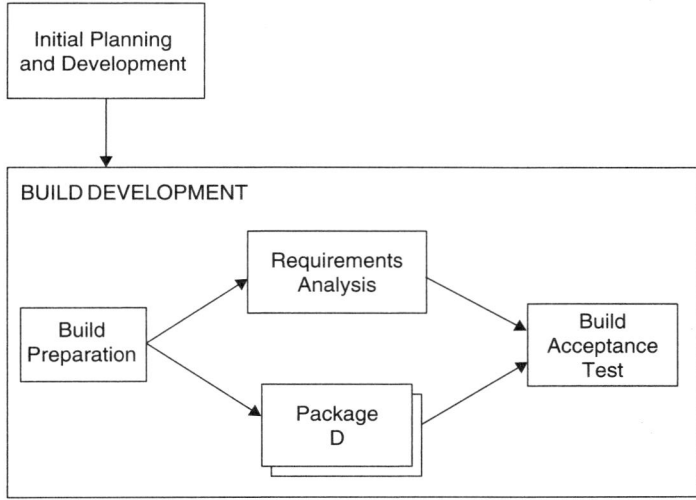

Figure 1.6 The Firesmith instantiation of OPEN: Planning and Build Development.

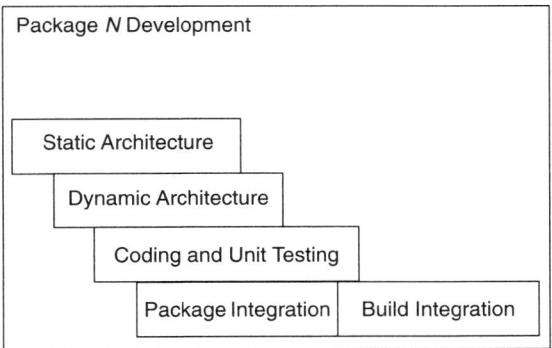

Figure 1.7 The Firesmith instantiation of OPEN: Cluster N Development.

Requirements Engineering and Package Development proceed in parallel. The tasks associated with the former include Requirements Elicitation, together with Requirements Analysis and Specification. Package Development is highly iterative and for each iteration has several tasks (Figure 1.7) which are performed in a highly iterative, incremental and parallel fashion. Different packages can be developed concurrently by assigning them to different package development teams. The appropriate tasks include Identify the Packages, Model the Package Static Architecture, Model the Package Dynamic Architecture, Coding and Unit Testing, Package Integration and Build Integration.

Details of the techniques for both these lifecycles follow the guidelines in this book. Further details of these two exemplar processes can be found in Graham *et al.* (1997b) and Firesmith *et al.* (1998), respectively.

1.4 OPEN's tasks

What activities do not do is to identify things that have to be done at a low enough resolution to match with tasks needing to be undertaken in order to meet the goals of each activity. For example, when the developer is focusing on an activity such as Evolutionary Development, there are a number of associated tasks that need to be undertaken successfully. One of these is the task: 'Structure the object model'. This is a clearly delineated goal that someone can take responsibility for (the delivery of a well-structured object model for the problem in hand). We should also note that for this particular activity, more than one task will be identified; for other activities there may be predominantly only one task required. We can think of these links (tasks to activities) in one of two ways: in a probabilistic manner or in a purer OO fashion by allocating tasks as methods of the activity objects (as noted above). At a future time, we assign, in very general terms or in more specific terms for any one, highly specific project, probabilities (or, to be more accurate, deontic[†] certainty factors), for each of these task/activity links. As the lifecycle is increasingly tailored to a specific domain, the values of the deontic factors change to a bimodal distribution (0 or 1). This thus allocates with certainty which tasks are needed for which activities. These tasks can now be more usefully modeled as methods of the activities. Thus the deontic matrix between tasks and techniques of Henderson-Sellers *et al.* (1996b) turns out to be only an unstable, transient modeling artefact.

OPEN's tasks are statements of things that need to be done. They are described as the 'smallest unit of work on a schedule which contributes to a milestone'. Tasks are either completed or not completed – they are listed in Table 1.2. From OBA, we can also delineate the information associated with a task. A figure of merit between 0 and 1 is assigned by the project manager. It indicates the importance of the task in meeting the associated milestone. For each individual milestone, the sum of all the associated tasks should be unity (Goldberg and Rubin, 1995).

However, tasks say what is to be done, but not how. The 'how' is the role of the techniques. This book is about techniques – techniques which give advice on 'how to actually *do* object-oriented development'. Many of these techniques are well known and well documented elsewhere. In this case, references to further sources of information will be given rather than trying to include the full body of knowledge for every single technique.

[†] Deontic logic is the logic of duty or obligation. It adds extra operators such as MAY, MUST and OUGHT, to ordinary first order predicate calculus.

Table 1.2 OPEN Tasks in alphabetical order. These are described in full in Graham *et al.* (1997b).

Analyze user requirements
Code
Construct the object model
Create and/or identify reusable components ('for reuse')

    Construct frameworks
    Optimize for reuse

Deliver product to customer
Design and implement physical database

    Distribution/replication design
    Operational and performance design
    Performance evaluation

Design user interface
Develop and implement resource allocation plan

    Choose hardware
    Choose project team
    Choose toolset
    Decompose programs into project
    Develop education and training plan
    Develop iteration plan
    Develop timebox plan
    Identify project roles and responsibilities
    Manage packages/subsystems
    Set up metrics collection program
    Specify individual goals
    Specify quality goals
    Use dependencies in the BOM to generate first-cut project plan

Develop business object model (BOM)
Develop software development context plans and strategies

    Develop capacity plan
    Develop contingency plan
    Develop security plan
    Establish change management strategy
    Establish data take-on strategy
    Integrate with existing, non-OO systems
    Tailor the lifecycle process

Table 1.2 (Continued.)

Evaluate quality

    Analyze metrics data
    Evaluate usability
    Review documentation

Identify CIRTs

    Determine initial class list
    Identify persistent classes
    Identify roles
    Refine class list

Identify context

Identify source(s) of requirements

Identify user requirements

    Define problem and establish mission and objectives
    Establish user requirements for distributed systems
    Establish user DB requirements

Maintain trace between requirements and design

Manage library of reusable components

Map logical database schema

Map roles on to classes

Model and re-engineer business process(es)

    Build context (i.e. business process) model
    Build task object model
    Convert task object model to business object model
    Do user training
    Prepare ITT

Obtain business approval

Optimize reuse ('with reuse')

Optimize the design

Test

    Perform acceptance testing
    Perform class testing
    Perform package/cluster testing
    Perform regression testing

Table 1.2 (Continued.)

Undertake architectural design

> Develop layer design
> Establish distributed systems strategy
> Select database/storage strategy

Undertake feasibility study

Undertake in-process review

Undertake post-implementation review

Undertake usability design

Write manual(s) and prepare other documentation

1.5 OPEN's techniques

Knowing that the task: 'Structure the object model' is one of several tasks that the developer can undertake in order to complete the activity does not tell the developer *how* to accomplish the task(s). The task is the goal, the what; the how is described by one or more techniques. Indeed, the developer may have to choose between several possible techniques, some of which may be always useful, some possibly useful, whilst other techniques should be avoided altogether. The principles associated with technique selection are exemplified in the 'Discovery' method (Simons, 1998a, b), one of the contributing influences to OPEN. Discovery recognizes the cognitive bias that each modeling technique brings; and so tries to preserve the plasticity of early models while alternative concepts are still being tried. Each technique is recognized as having a single focus, or purpose; so, for example, ER modeling is only used for back-end database table design and not especially for object identification, which is carried out using a responsibility-driven approach (Figure 1.8). Models are chosen for their effectiveness in communicating with the client. Techniques are sequenced so that the output deliverables from one clearly serve as input to the next (as part of the contract). The deliverables must overlap, so that cross-checking may be carried out. The mutual influence of the current emerging design and existing design patterns and frameworks is properly handled (Figure 1.9). Discovery also provides a number of techniques for transforming the system model during the subsystem identification stage (see OPEN Technique: Collaborations analysis). Discovery may be regarded as a particular configuration of OPEN techniques, since it mandates a particular sequence of development for the Build task.

The project manager/developer is at liberty to accomplish an OPEN task with whichever compatible OO techniques and tools he or she is familiar – OPEN only recommends, it does not mandate. However, in order to aid the developer, OPEN does suggest a large range of techniques which have been found to

16   OVERVIEW OF OPEN

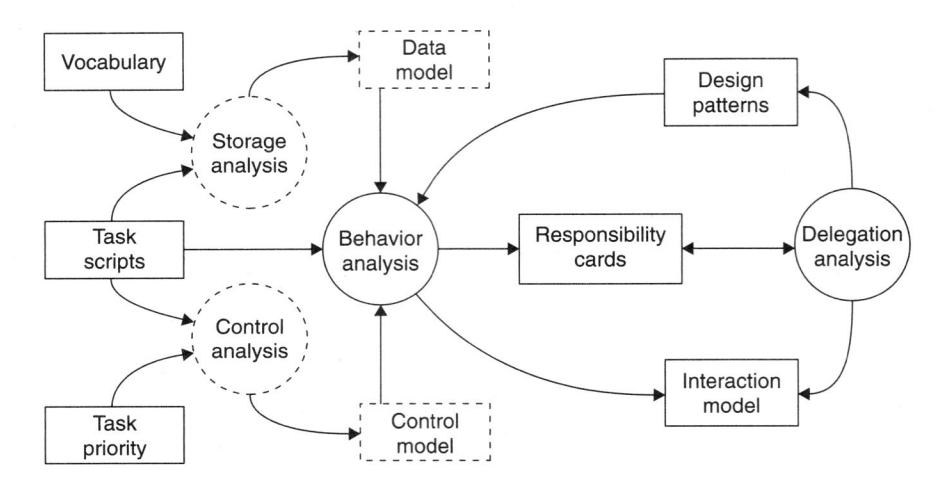

Figure 1.8 Object modeling in OPEN/Discovery at the metalevel. [Key: A rectangle represents a model to be delivered; a circle is the process of applying a technique; an arrow indicates the direction of information flow; and a dotted outline indicates optionality.]

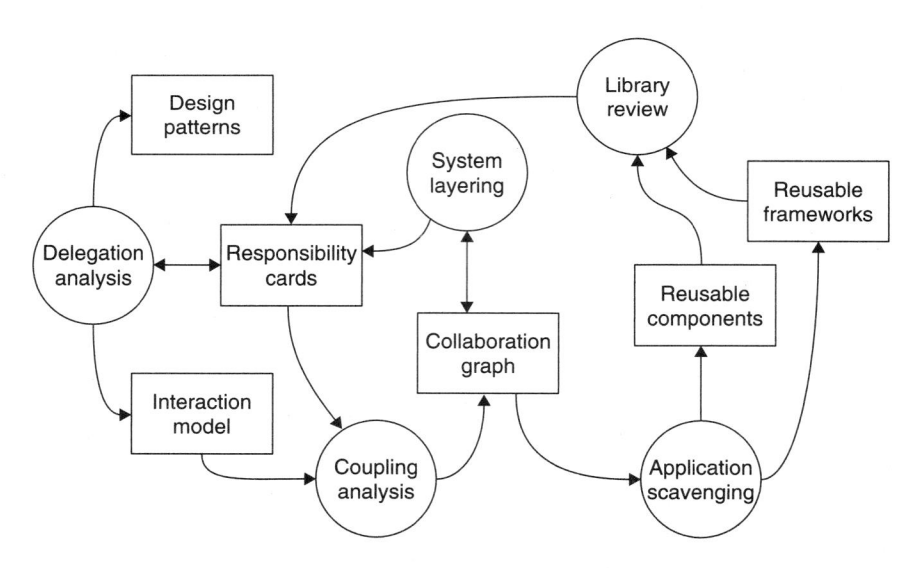

Figure 1.9 System modeling in OPEN/Discovery at the metalevel. [Key is as Figure 1.8.]

Tasks

Techniques				
M	D	F	F	F
D	D	F	F	D
D	D	O	O	D
F	O	O	O	F
F	M	O	D	F
R	R	M	R	O
D	R	F	M	O
D	F	M	D	D
R	R	D	R	R
O	D	O	O	R
F	M	O	F	D

For each task/technique combination we will recommend five levels of probability from Always to Never

M = mandatory
R = recommended
O = optional
D = discouraged
F = forbidden

Figure 1.10 The core of OPEN is a two-dimensional relationship between tasks and techniques. For each task, a number of techniques may be useful. For each combination of task and technique, an assessment can be made of the likelihood of the occurrence of that combination. Some combinations can be identified as mandatory (M), others that are recommended (R), some as being optional (O), some are discouraged (D) but may be used with care and other combinations that are strictly verboten (F = forbidden) (after Graham *et al.*, 1997b).

be appropriate – the OPEN 'Techniques Toolbox' documented here (especially Chapter 3 and Appendices A and B, and C and D on the CD). There is a fuzzy nature to the linkage of techniques and tasks – represented most successfully by a deontic matrix (Figure 1.10). In OPEN, an overall recommendation is made in terms of M (= mandatory), R (recommended) O (= optional), D (= discouraged) and F (= forbidden). For instance, some tasks are clearly best accomplished with a single, specific technique – a technique applicable to that task and nothing else (for example, implementation of services which supports the coding task). Other techniques will be found useful in a range of tasks (for example, contract specification). And finally, for some tasks there may be a choice that the project manager has to make with technical guidance provided by others. For example, there are many ways of identifying classes, instances, roles and types, collectively called CIRTs, from their initial letters. These include interactive techniques such as the use of CRC cards to identify responsibilities; scenarios/task models/scripts/use cases to focus on functionality delivered as a prelude to finding CIRTs within these scripts; textual analysis, in which nouns in the requirements analysis have the potential to be realized as CIRTs; simulation which focuses on the objects within the modeling exercise; and even (for some skilled[†] people), the use of ER

[†] We say skilled not to disparage ER but rather to stress that it is our experience that good OO designers can make good use of ER since they have the OO mindset; but that novices or

diagrams as a basis for a CIRT structure diagram.

These deontic links are illustrated best in a two-dimensional matrix in which the actual pattern of M/R/O/D/F values should be determined as part of the initial planning activity. This two-dimensional matrix also offers the project manager significant flexibility. If new ideas/tasks are developed in a particular context, then incorporating them into this framework is extremely easy. It only requires the addition of a single line in the matrix and the identification of the M/R/O/D/F nature of the interaction between this new technique and the tasks within the chosen lifecycle process (Graham *et al.*, 1997b).

1.6 Products, deliverables and modeling language

An important component of a methodology is the products produced. This is often done by using a set of graphical models which is developed using a chosen notation. Depending upon the notation used and the domain of application (MIS, real-time etc.), these may have different weights and frequency of utilization. Graphical models of the static architecture go by different names in their depiction of classes, objects, packages, roles and/or types. They are also used at various degrees of granularities, from context level down to the depiction of the internal 'guts' of an object's method. In OPEN's preferred notation, COMN (Section 2.3.1), there are six types of semantic net which are used to describe and document the static aspects of the system. *Context diagrams* are low granular relating the proposed system to the environment and externals. *Layer diagrams* depict the layered architecture. *Configuration diagrams* show the overall structure, visibility and semantically important relationships. *Package diagrams* are the nearest to the 'class diagram' of, for example, Booch, OMT or UML. However, they show not only classes, but also types, roles and packages (at a higher level) and objects (particularly in real-time applications). Both OPEN and Fusion (Coleman *et al.*, 1994) urge the creation of independent *inheritance diagrams* to document all such network structures. Finally, the COMN and UML *deployment diagram* allocates software processes to processors, particularly important in distributed applications, perhaps based on ORBs.

These static diagrams are complemented by various dynamic views. These are fairly traditional in OPEN and other approaches. *State transition diagrams* are used to show the states and inter-state transitions for individual classes. *Interaction diagrams* show either object interactions in (a) a *collaboration diagram*, which resembles a semantic net focused on instances and which may or may not have exceptions and message passing sequences annotated with sequence numbers; or (b) a *sequence diagram* (a.k.a. 'fence diagram') which shows, for each object, its interactions and collaborations in a time-focused sequence. Migration diagrams are also available in OML Version 1.1 (see Henderson-Sellers and

---

poor designers use ER as a crutch to stay within the information engineering/data modeling paradigm whilst fooling themselves, and probably their managers, that they are doing OO design.

Firesmith, 1998a). These are analogous to a collaboration diagram but for a distributed systems, showing movement of software (distribution units, classes, packages or objects) rather than messages along the arcs.

Another version of dynamism is the functionality of the system which is typically shown using a non-OO approach based on use cases. In COMN, we support not only this approach (the *use case diagram*) but also the more business-focused *task script diagram*, both types of *scenario class diagram*.

A full description of notational possibilities is deferred until Chapter 2.

1.7 Further information

For more information, the OPEN home page is located at URL:

http://www.csse.swin.edu.au/cotar/OPEN/

with mirrors at

USA: http://www.markv.com/OPEN
UK: http://www.scism.sbu.ac.uk/cios/mirrors/OPEN/
Israel: http://oop.cs.technion.ac.il/OPEN

1.8 About this book

This book describes the techniques found useful in support of the OPEN process. The process itself is described in detail in Graham *et al.* (1997b). The techniques described here are the 'tools of the OO trade'. If you are well versed in OO ideas, you will find here much you are familiar with – those well-accepted tips and techniques; but we hope you will also find some new ideas you can apply and add to your personal toolbox of techniques. If you are relatively new to object technology, then this book will provide you with a comprehensive set of ideas, guidelines, tips and techniques which you will need in your everyday work as a member of an object-oriented software development team. Readers are thus likely to be developers, project managers, business managers or educators. Each will approach this text from a different viewpoint.

The structure of the book is as a sequence of four chapters which paint the overall picture of an OO software development. The major chapter is the third, which brings together ranges of techniques which are focused on a particular area in software development – such as database or modeling. Preceding that are two overview chapters. Chapter 1 describes the overall architecture of OPEN. Chapter 2 discusses modeling languages (based on and extending the emerging OMG metamodel facility) and recommended notation together with several other acceptable notations as well as the deliverables, both project management focused and technical. As a prelude to the discussion of the technical deliverables, we need to ensure that all the technical terms are understood so we describe the basic concepts and theories on which OT is built – but only to the extent that you will need to appreciate them as a practising software developer.

The final chapter gives our glimpse of the future: the direction in which standards are likely to evolve; what will be the likely role of object technology in mainstream software development; and what part OPEN might play in those future developments.

Most types of reader will benefit from reading the overview chapters (Chapters 1–3). However, they are still very much summary in nature. The full detail has been put in the reference sections (appendices) at the end of the book and on the CD. The first four appendicies fully document the techniques of OPEN (a similar full documentation of the OPEN tasks is in Graham *et al.*, 1997b), Appendix A describing the core techniques accompanied by three subsidiary appendices describing (B) suites of techniques, and, on the CD, (C) more experimental techniques and (D) non-OO and traditional techniques which might be useful in OPEN if treated with care and expertise. Appendix E contains background information on concepts (complementing Chapter 2.1), underpinning theory and short descriptions of some of the commonly used deliverables.

In these appendices is to be found a dictionary-type listing – one which is to be dipped into as necessary and not designed to be read sequentially. This reference portion of the book is described alphabetically, as you might expect. Any repetition between the book itself and the appendices is intentional so that that each part (either the chapters of the book or the appendices) can be studied relatively independently.

In summary, the OPEN methodology will facilitate widespread adoption of object technology; it provides a standard, compatible with but significantly extending the OMG's OADTF metamodel standard, that is flexible enough to be useful to small, medium and large enterprises; a standard that can be used for different vertical markets – from MIS to hard real-time; a standard that therefore has a common core with modular extensions. It is *imperative* that this standard is of the highest quality, transcending the vested interests of individuals and individual companies.

OPEN already has users worldwide, consultants and universities teaching it and CASE vendors supporting its notation and process. As our name suggests, we are open to further collaboration and all major methodologists have been invited to join and contribute to the work of the OPEN Consortium.

Chapter 2
OPEN concepts, notations and deliverables

2.1 Overview: modeling languages

A modeling language is to OOAD what an implementation (programming) language is to coding. A modeling language has two components: a metamodel and a notation (Figure 1.4). This chapter discusses the concepts and metamodel of the OPEN Modeling Language (OML) and then the preferred OML notation, called COMN (Common Object Modeling Notation) as well as other alternative notations.

The OPEN Modeling Language (OML) was created to support a pure, responsibility-driven way of developing OO systems. In addition, its notation utilizes modern ideas from semiotics (the science of signs and symbols) in order that the symbols are highly usable and, as far as possible, easily intuitive.

As the OMG process for metamodel standardization proceeded during 1995–7, the authors of OML remained in close contact with this process so that, following the endorsement of OMG's UML standard in late 1997, only minor adjustments to OML Version 1.0 (which had been published in March 1997: Firesmith *et al.*, 1997) were required in order to create Version 1.1 (Firesmith and Henderson-Sellers, 1998b; Henderson-Sellers and Firesmith, 1998a). Version 1.1 can in many ways be regarded as a superset of UML since it offers additional support for OO modeling (e.g. full and integrated support for responsibilities, scenario classes and aggregations).

The metamodel embodies the *rules* of the modeling language. Metamodel fragments are explained in Section 2.2 wherever they help in understanding the underlying *concepts* embodied in OPEN and in OO in general. In the spirit of encouraging convergence in concepts, we will not undertake any direct comparison here between OML and the OMG/UML standard (but see, e.g., Henderson-Sellers and Firesmith, 1997b for a comparison of OML Version 1.0 and UML Version 1.0); rather, we shall only draw the reader's attention to areas in the OML metamodel which enhance the OMG standard.

A notation, on the other hand, is merely a way of communicating those concepts and rules to other people. Obviously, a notation which can easily represent all the rules is clearly preferable to one that cannot. OPEN's preferred nota-

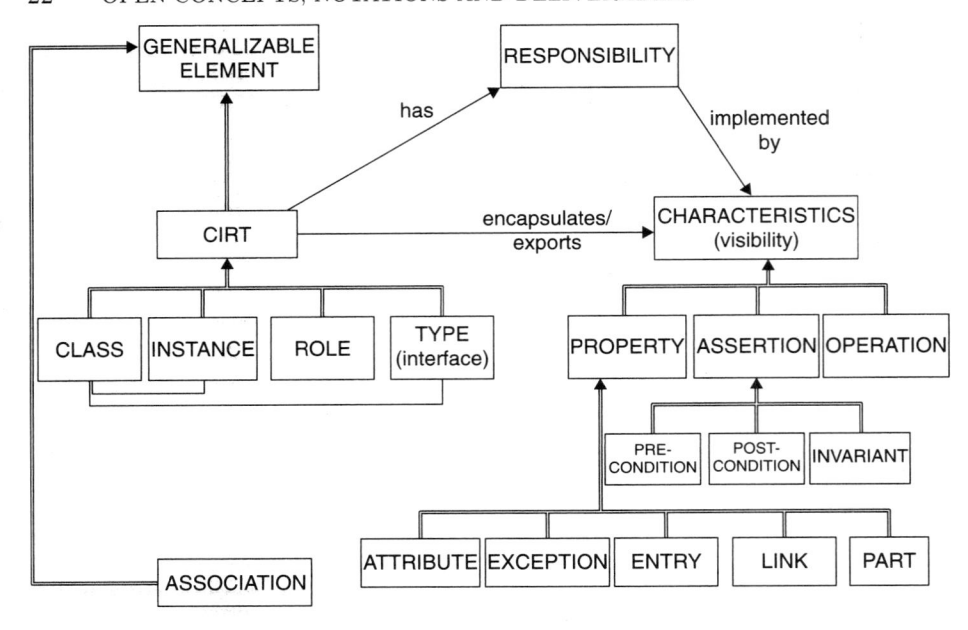

Figure 2.1 The static metamodel for OML Version 1.1.

tion, COMN, is described in Section 2.3.1 and other notations in Sections 2.3.2 and 2.3.3.

Notational elements are not used alone; they are grouped on diagrams which emphasize certain aspects/views of the software system. The suite of diagrams discussed in Section 2.4 provides this complementarity and facilitates a full description of the software being built. Finally in this chapter, we describe the OPEN deliverables (Section 2.5).

2.2 OPEN concepts

In this section, we describe, in brief, the underpinning concepts of OT and especially of OPEN. For some of the key concepts, such as Abstraction and Classification, there are longer essays in CD: Appendix E. Here, we concentrate instead on the modeling concepts as depicted in the metamodel underpinning OPEN. The book you are reading utilizes Version 1.1, which provides slightly more features and more clarity than Version 1.0 as described in Firesmith et al. (1997).

The static metamodel from Version 1.1 of OML is shown in Figure 2.1. Here, only the major elements are shown. As peers, OML supports CLASS, INSTANCE, ROLE and TYPE. (Their interconnexions are shown in more detail in Figure 2.2.) Together these four concepts are grouped together as CIRT (from

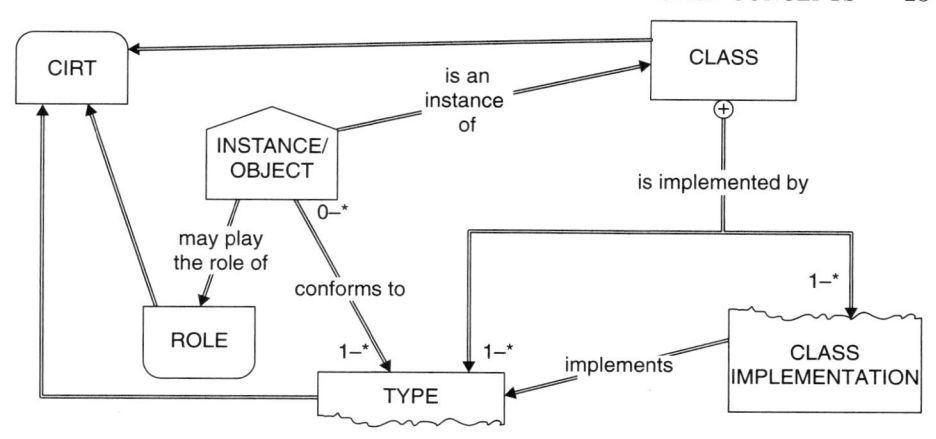

Figure 2.2 Metamodel and notation for Object, Class, Type, Role and Implementation. The Class icon is 'torn apart' into the Type (external/interface) and the Class Implementation (internals). All icons can have a drop-down box in which information pertinent to the lifecycle stage is displayed (updated from Henderson-Sellers *et al.*, 1997b).

the initial letters). The rationale is that in the seamless nature of OOAD, it can often be ambiguous as to whether we are dealing with a class or its instance or its interface or perhaps we want to emphasize the role-playing nature of the object – we are neither sure nor categoric. CIRTs permit flexibility in modeling and are used frequently in the MIS world. CIRTs can be generalized and thus inherit (using specialization inheritance) from the GENERALIZABLE_ELEMENT metaclass (newly introduced in Version 1.1 of OML to conform to the OMG standard). ASSOCIATIONs are also generalizable and thus shown on this diagram, although there is much greater detail on associations later in this chapter and in the Appendices.

CIRTs have RESPONSIBILITYs, which are at a high level of abstraction, supporting Wirfs-Brock *et al.*'s (1990) ideas and enhancing the OMG metamodel in this area by linking responsibilities to characteristics which implement them (in the OMG metamodel responsibilities are simply tagged values, i.e. strings). Characteristics can be divided into PROPERTYs, ASSERTIONs and OPERATIONs. In fact, each of these three implement a specific kind of responsibility: respectively, a responsibility for knowing, a responsibility for enforcing and a responsibility for doing (see Figure 2.3 which shows the metamodel structure for visibility = YES in Figure 2.1 – see attributes on CHARACTERISTICs).

OPERATIONs are implemented by METHODs. ASSERTIONs, which are treated as full metaclasses in OML (an enhancement to the OMG/UML), can be either PRE-CONDITIONs, POST-CONDITIONs or INVARIANTs (Figure 2.3). The third characteristic, PROPERTY, has six subtypes (five more than UML) but only three (EXCEPTION, PART and MEMBER) are visible (Figure 2.3)

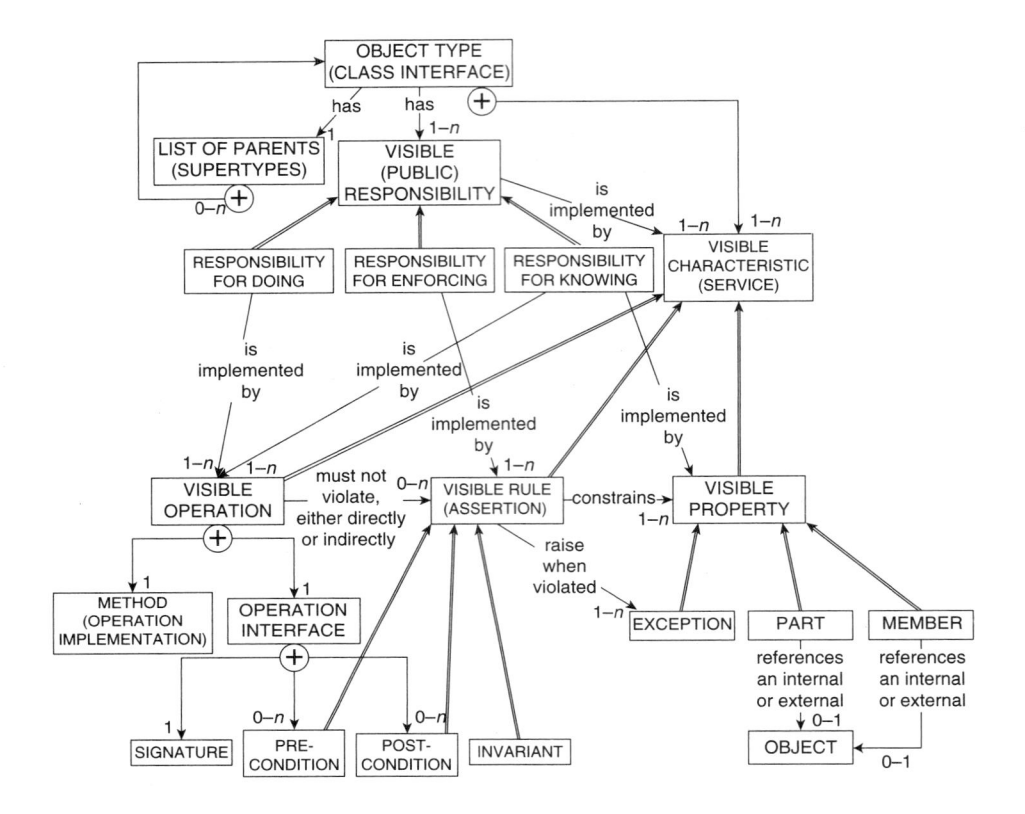

Figure 2.3 OML's metamodel for Visible Responsibilities. An OBJECT TYPE has VISIBLE RESPONSIBILITYs. These can be subdivided into responsibilities for knowing, doing and enforcing which are then implemented by VISIBLE OPERATIONs, RULEs and PROPERTYs (after Henderson-Sellers and Firesmith, 1997a).

whereas all six are part of the metamodel which focuses on the internal or 'hidden' responsibilities and characteristics (Figure 2.4).

2.2.1 Basic relationships

The second major part of the static metamodel describes relationships between CIRTs. There are a number of relationships generally agreed upon although their details differ. Work to converge these various views is presented in Henderson-Sellers (1997b, 1998) and Firesmith and Henderson-Sellers (1998b) and synopsized here.

In OML Version 1.1, one pleasing aspect of the relationship model is its carefully structured metamodel (Figure 2.5). All relationships are binary, uni-

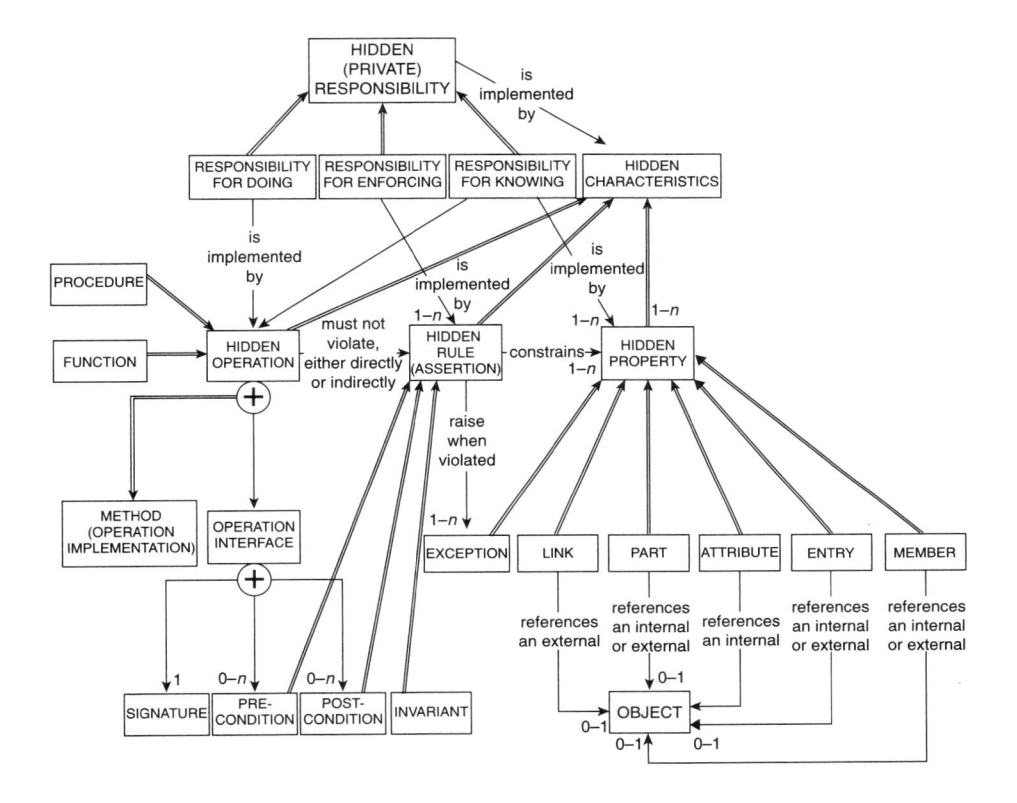

Figure 2.4 OML's metamodel for Hidden Responsibilities. CLASS IMPLEMENTATION consists of HIDDEN RESPONSIBILITYs which are implemented by HIDDEN CHARACTERISTICs (OPERATIONs, RULEs, ATTRIBUTEs, PARTs, LINKs, EXCEPTIONs, ENTRYs and MEMBERs) (after Henderson-Sellers and Firesmith, 1997a).

directional dependencies or mappings. These can be of two static types and two dynamic types. The two static relationship types are referential (in which one thing 'knows about' another) and definitional (in which one thing is defined by relationship to another); the dynamic groups being scenario relationships and transitional relationships. This grouping also creates a structure for the development of a consistent notational set (Section 2.3.1) by insisting that each branch of Figure 2.5 has its own unambiguous notational arrow 'style'.

Referential relationships focus on various types of association including dependency, usage and aggregation. There are various flavors of association in the literature, e.g. whether they are bi-directional, uni-directional or non-specific in their direction. A uni-directional association could be regarded as a TBD (To Be Decided) association augmented by one-way navigability and, consequently,

26   OPEN CONCEPTS, NOTATIONS AND DELIVERABLES

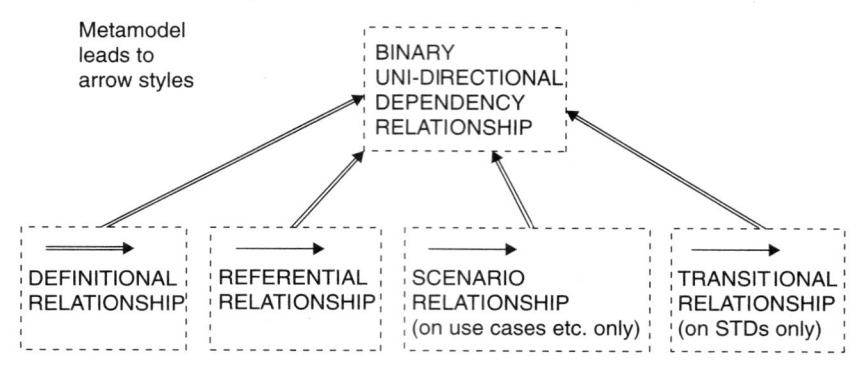

Figure 2.5 Metamodel architecture for relationships in OML Version 1.1 (based on information in Firesmith *et al.*, 1997). Only the four main groupings of relationships are shown: definitional, referential, scenario and transitional. Note that all five metaclasses are abstract classes, as shown by a dashed line in OML.

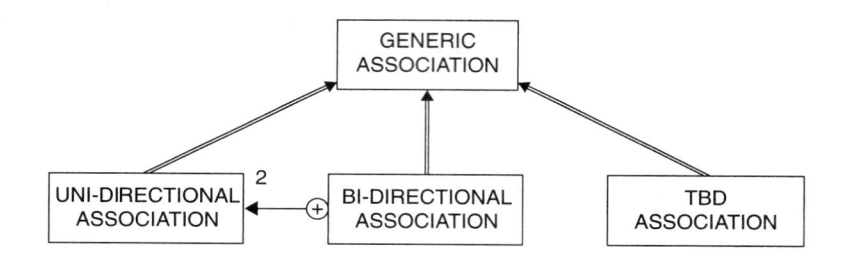

Figure 2.6 Three subtypes of generic association.

a bi-directional association as a pair of uni-directional mappings (e.g. Cook and Daniels, 1994, page 34; Graham *et al.*, 1997a; Henderson-Sellers, 1997b) – actually between power sets. This suggests a metamodel for associations as shown in Figure 2.6.

Aggregations are often regarded as a special form of association. Based on earlier work on aggregations by Winston *et al.* (1987) and Odell (1994a), Henderson-Sellers (1997a) derived a combination of these two previous models to identify seven kinds of whole–part (or meronymic) relationship which fall naturally into two groups (Figure 2.7): aggregation (a configurational relationship) and membership (the three non-configurational relationships identified previously as useful in object modeling). This, then, suggests an elaboration of the metamodel hierarchy as shown in Figure 2.8. [It should be noted that there is an error in the OML metamodel in Firesmith *et al.* (1997) where it is stated that CONTAINMENT is a subtype of WHOLE–PART RELATIONSHIP. As seen here and in Henderson-Sellers (1997a), this is incorrect and CONTAINMENT needs to be a direct subtype of REFERENTIAL RELATIONSHIP.]

OPEN CONCEPTS 27

		Configurational	Homeomerous	Invariance
Aggregation	Component–integral object	yes	no	no
	Material–object	yes	no	yes
	Place–area	yes	no	yes
	Feature–activity	yes	no	yes
Membership	Portion–object	no	yes	no (or yes)
	Member–bunch	no	no	no
	Member–partnership	no	no	yes

- Configurational – when the parts bear a particular functional or structural relationship to one another or to the object they constitute
- Homeomerous – when the parts are the same kind of thing as the whole
- Invariance – when the parts cannot be separated from the whole without destroying the whole

Figure 2.7 Seven subtypes of aggregation proposed by Henderson-Sellers (1997a) based on earlier work of Winston *et al.* (1987) and Odell (1994a) (after Henderson-Sellers, 1997a).

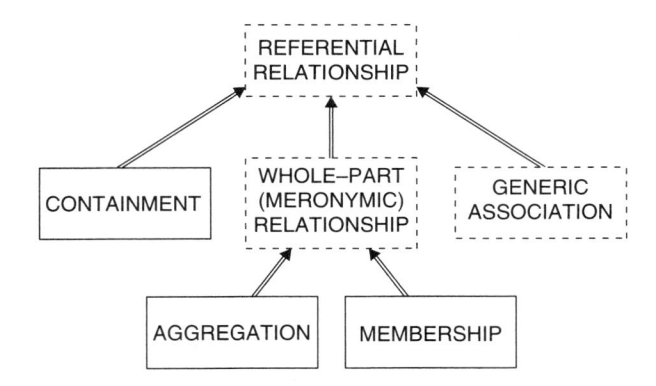

Figure 2.8 Further elaboration on the referential relationship 'branch' of Figure 2.5.

```
                    ┌─────────────┐
                    │  AGGREGATE  │
                    └─────────────┘
                           │
                          (+)
                           │
                      {by-value,
                       constant}
                           │
                        ■ ↓ 0–2
                    ┌─────────────┐
                    │  COMPONENT  │
                    └─────────────┘
```

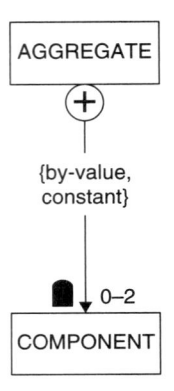

Figure 2.9 Example of a whole–part, referential relationship showing the use of stereotypes and tombstone annotation (after Firesmith and Henderson-Sellers, 1998a).

As well as a configurational/non-configurational characteristic, there are (at least) three other important[†] characteristics of aggregation that are particularly relevant in physical design/implementation:

- by value vs by reference
- variable vs constant
- mandatory vs optional.

In OML Version 1.1, as described here and in Firesmith and Henderson-Sellers (1998a), the above three characteristics are kept distinct, resulting in eight possible combinations. By-value or by-reference is indicated by a stereotype; variable or constant by a black tombstone at the part end to indicate that the lifetimes of the whole and of the parts are intrinsically bound together; and the use of multiplicity for mandatory versus optional (Figure 2.9).

In OML Version 1.0, metamodel diagrams were drawn separately for associations (class level) and links (instance level) – compare Figures 3.55 and 3.56 of Firesmith *et al.* (1997), for example. In Version 1.1 (here), an additional partition of ASSOCIATION/LINK permits the full information at both class and instance level to be captured in a single metalevel diagram.

Definitional relationships (Figure 2.10) include those for classification, implementation and inheritance. This branch (of Figure 2.5) is only explicitly discussed in Firesmith *et al.* (1997). The most important part is probably the inheritance strand in which specialization or the is-a-kind-of relationship is the

---

† There are several other stereotypes applied to REFERENTIAL RELATIONSHIP. These are not part of COMN Light and a full description can be found in Firesmith and Henderson-Sellers (1998a, b). See also brief description in CD: Appendix E and, in particular, Figure E.10.

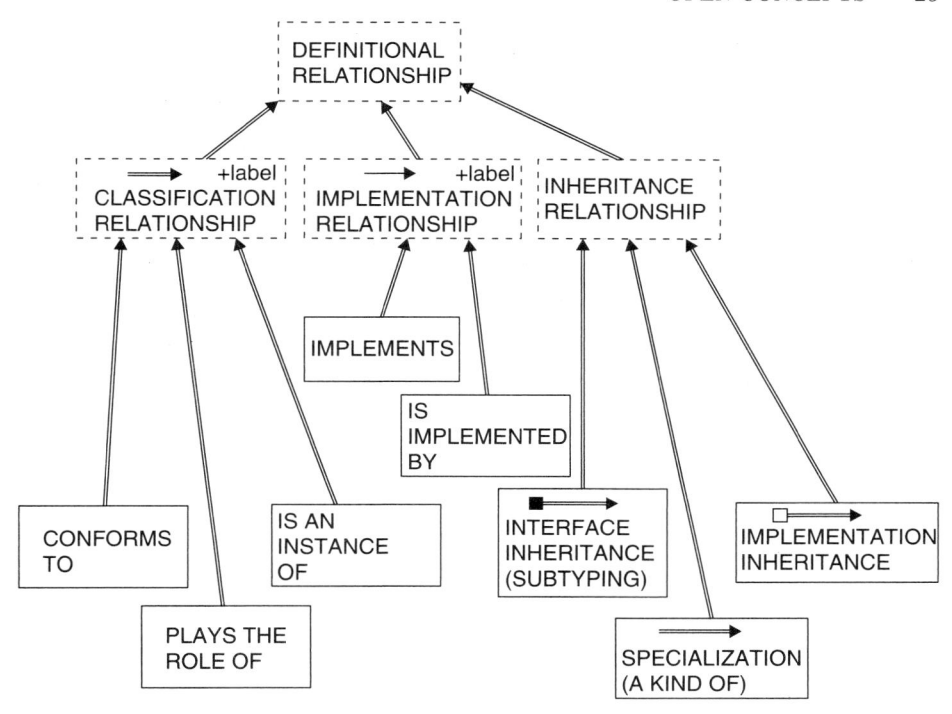

Figure 2.10 Further detail on the definitional relationships of Figure 2.5 (based on information in Firesmith *et al.*, 1997).

most used. It is good for both knowledge representation (in, say, user requirements/analysis) and in support of polymorphism, through dynamic substitutability. Since simple subtyping (specification or interface inheritance) should be used less than specialization inheritance and given that we positively discourage the use of implementation inheritance, they are represented as adornments (see Section 2.3.1). Such differentiation is explicitly not supported in UML which purposefully confounds subtyping and subclassing (OMG, 1997a, page 41).

Finally, the scenario and transition branches of Figure 2.5 each have a full metamodel (see, e.g., Firesmith *et al.*, 1997; OMG, 1997a) – but are not discussed any further here since their uses are somewhat more specialized and notationally specific.

Stereotypes

A stereotype is a user-defined subtype in the metamodel. This corresponds to defining a partitioning of the elements of the class defined by the metatype into subsets (defined by the metasubtype). An example will no doubt help here. CLASS is a metatype. We, the user, may choose to define in this metamodel two

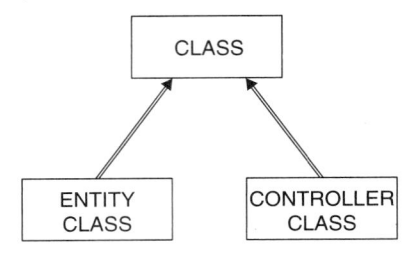

Figure 2.11 The metatype CLASS has to sub(meta) types: ENTITY CLASS and CONTROLLER CLASS.

subtypes of CONTROLLER_CLASS and ENTITY_CLASS (i.e. the stereotype names of 'controller' and 'entity') (Figure 2.11). Now consider all the instances (set elements) of the *STATIONERY* class (which is one particular instance or the CLASS metatype). These, shown in Figure 2.12, are divided into two groups or partitions (which, for simplicity, we will assume do not overlap): stationery items which can be classified as entity objects (e.g. pen objects) and those which can be described as being controller objects (e.g. pen tracker objects). Thus, the pen tracker objects can themselves be described by the class *PEN_TRACKER* which may have the *controller* stereotype attached to it.

2.3 Notations for OPEN

OPEN is process-focused and, as such, invites support from one or more notations. Whilst the preferred notation is COMN (Section 2.3.1), we realize that some developers may choose to use other notations such as UML (Section 2.3.1) to describe the OPEN deliverables, particularly those technically-focused ones created as part of the modeling activities.

2.3.1 OPEN's preferred notation: COMN

A methodology needs to include a means for representing the generated artefacts – it needs to contain a notation. Whilst only a small part of a methodology, it is, however, the most obvious part. Since choosing a methodology also implies choosing a CASE tool, it is a component of the methodology which often surfaces first and, not prevented, can take over the whole mindset. OPEN's deliverables *can* be represented by any notation (e.g. UML, BON, Coad and Yourdon – some of these are discussed below in Section 2.3.2 and 2.3.3) although there are a number of aspects of the OPEN approach in which some things that can be expressed readily in COMN cannot be expressed or will not be properly expressible within the semantics of UML (e.g. responsibilities, rulesets, exceptions, package encapsulation). Furthermore, as we described in a previous article (Henderson-Sellers

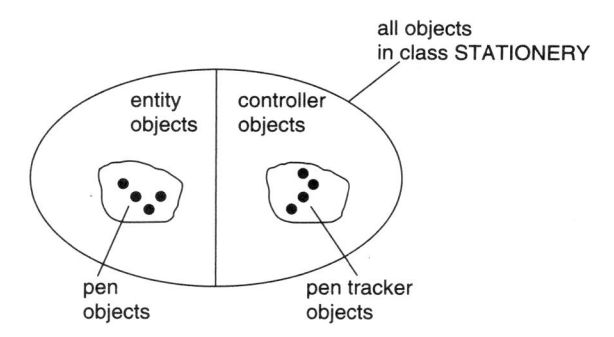

Figure 2.12 The two metatypes in Figure 2.11 correspond to a partition of all objects in a selected class into those which are entity objects and those which can be described as controller objects.

et al., 1997a), some common UML practices (bi-directional associations) violate OPEN principles; for example, that of supporting true object orientation with a responsibility-driven flavor.

Three typical examples of OPEN's emphasis on pure object-orientation are:

(1) OML emphasizes objects, types, classes, and their responsibilities rather than the early identification of properties as do some data-driven notations strongly based on entity relationship attribute (ERA) relational database modeling techniques (e.g., OMT, UML, Shlaer/Mellor, Coad, Fusion).

(2) OML emphasizes uni-directional relationships over bi-directional relationships because uni-directional relationships are the default in the object paradigm (e.g., objects use internal properties to reference other objects). When needed, bi-directional associations are derived from two uni-directional relationships that are semi-strong inverses of one another and require all of the additional operations to ensure referential integrity (Graham *et al.*, 1997a).

(3) COMN draws aggregation arcs from the aggregate to the part (because that is how aggregate objects are defined and reference their parts in the object-oriented world) rather than from the part to the aggregate (which is how relational database tables mimic aggregation by joins via foreign keys – a JOIN operation corresponding to a generic bi-directional association).

The full documentation of COMN Version 1.0 is available in Firesmith *et al.* (1997) and a Light version is described in Appendix B of Graham *et al.* (1997b). COMN Light is summarized here together with some small improvements which were added in Version 1.1 (Firesmith and Henderson-Sellers, 1998b; Henderson-Sellers and Firesmith, 1998a) in order to provide a tighter coupling to the OMG OADTF standard. A simplified introduction to OML Version 1.1 is also included in the book by Henderson-Sellers and Firesmith (1998b).

For many of us, once we have learned a notation we find no barriers – we can use the notation easily and fluently. It is like learning a programming language or learning a natural language. Some natural languages are harder to learn than others. It is generally appreciated that Chinese and English (for non-native speakers) can present almost insurmountable problems. For a francophone, on the other hand, learning Italian is relatively easy. Even becoming fluent with the basic alphabet (choose from Roman, Japanese, Cyrillic, Arabic, Hebrew and many others) can be a challenge for adults with no previous exposure. So, an interface, here the alphabet, that is unfamiliar or does not include easy-to-intuit symbols (arguably Chinese is easier here because of its ideographic heredity) makes the syntax and semantics hard to learn. So it is with an OOAD notation.

The OPEN preferred notation (known as COMN, standing for Common Object Modeling Notation) has been designed with intuition and usability in mind. Granted we cannot find internationally recognizable symbols amenable to all types of novice in every country; however, if we assume we are trying to describe pictographically the main, commonly understood elements of object technology such as encapsulation, interfaces, blackbox and whitebox inheritance, a discrimination between objects, classes and types, then designing a broadly acceptable and *internally consistent* notation becomes possible.

Semiotics is the study of signs and symbols. Those semiotic ideas were built into the MOSES notation (Henderson-Sellers and Edwards, 1994a) and into UON (Page-Jones *et al.*, 1990) both of which have had influences on the COMN notation as well as more recent studies in interface design and notational design (see discussions in Constantine and Henderson-Sellers, 1995a, b). Unlike UML, OPEN has no hereditary biases from an earlier, data-modeling history. OPEN's notation has been designed from the bottom up by a small team of methodologists who have worked on these issues over the last decade.

The COMN notation provides support for both the novice and the sophisticate. Here we describe only those elements necessary for beginning and, indeed, which will be found in around 80 per cent of all applications. In a nutshell, we need to have symbols for:

- instance versus class versus type versus role versus implementation together with the supertype of CIRT. All icons have optional drop-down boxes for information relevant to the particular activity or task of the lifecycle (see below for details)
- basic relationships of association/mapping/using, aggregation, containment, membership and inheritance.

We also need to build not just a static model, utilizing these chosen symbols, but also:

- a state-transition model (dynamics of individual objects and classes)
- an interaction model
- a use case model (or an extension thereof).

Different models (semantic, interaction, state, scenario) provide different views of a single overall model and are thus tightly interconnected.

Henderson-Sellers and Firesmith (1997a) were the first to introduce into an OO notation the well-understood notion that a class is composed of an interface plus an implementation. Graphically we 'tear apart' the class icon to get the two complementary icons: the type(s) and the class implementation (Figure 2.2). An object is an instance of a class as well as conforming to its type(s). Both class and object are similar; however, the mnemonic is that the class is the blueprint (house blueprints are on rectangular sheets of paper), whereas the instantiation of the blueprint is the house†. The CIRT icon is the old MOSES/UON tablet icon, used initially to represent class in Version 1.0 of COMN (Firesmith *et al.*, 1997) – in Version 1.1, we elevate the tablet to be the CIRT icon and introduce a rectangle, in conformance with the OMG notational standard. In this document (OMG, 1997b), options are given to either use stereotypes for all classifier concepts except object and class or to use graphical icons for each of these stereotypes. In OML, we choose the latter option to add visual clues beyond those given in a textual stereotypical label.

The CIRT icon itself is also unmistakable and cannot be confused. In MIS systems, we usually use CIRT icons since we usually have one concept (e.g. bank account) with very many instantiations. Our diagrams might equally represent types, classes or their instances – so the CIRT icon is most applicable. We tend to only use object icons for specific message-passing sequences (on collaboration diagrams). On the other hand, in real-time systems it is usually object icons that are most prevalent since there is frequently only a single occurrence of a class and the control features dominate. Another sign used is that of a dotted line to indicate a more ethereal notion. Abstract/deferred classes or CIRTs are more ethereal than classes or CIRTs so they get a dotted outline. [An alternative is to label it as an abstract stereotype.] The icon for role in COMN is that for a CIRT but inverted and was chosen to be reminiscent of the Greek tragedy role player's mask.

The other interesting item here is how to design a notation that will be appropriate throughout the lifecycle. The answer we have come up with is 'drop-down boxes' (Figure 2.13(a)). These are attached below the icons (for all icons) and can contain information relevant to the particular activity/task of the lifecycle. They can document traits of various kinds (Figure 2.13(b)): descriptions, responsibilities, characteristics (e.g. operations, properties) etc. Although drop-down boxes are primarily designed as a way of dynamically providing flexibility when using an upper CASE tool, they can and are drawn statically on white-boards and paper.

---

† Another way of remembering this is that an object is 'more real' than a class so the icon is represented by a sharper icon whereas the class icon is more regular. We note that in coding, the reverse is probably true – a run-time object is more ethereal than a compile time class. However, while OT is about both the modeling of business problems and provision of modular and reusable solutions, we believe the need for cognitive notational assistance is more urgent during problem modeling, as this is inherently more complicated, error prone and difficult, with greater consequences if an error is made that in the detailed design or implementation.

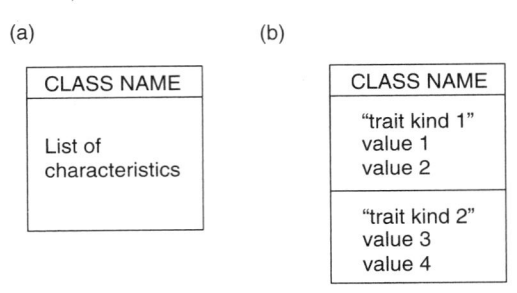

Figure 2.13 OML's drop-down boxes permit the inclusion of a variety of information pertinent to progression through the lifecycle. These characteristics can be collected together by trait kind.

Notation for relationships

In Figure 2.14 we see the notation for major relationships illustrated: specialization, uni-directional associations (mappings), various aggregations and containment. All relationships are uni-directional – as indicated by the arrowhead. Again the icons chosen are self-explanatory. We use a double arrow for the tighter, more strongly coupled definitional relationship. The default definitional node, the easiest to draw, is the is-a-kind-of which thus gets an unadorned double arrow. It is also less common than an association/linkage which therefore is allocated the easiest arrow to draw (single thickness – see below). A label can be used to indicate the discriminator used for the subclassing. Specialization, the default, is the is-a-kind-of relationship. Other types of 'inheritance' (blackbox and whitebox) can be shown but the basic, encouraged is-a-kind-of gets the easiest-to-draw line. All other definitional relationships (also with double arrow) carry a textual label. These can be grouped into classification relationships (conforms-to, is-an-instance-of, plays-the-role-of) and implementation relationships (implements, is-implemented-by) – see Figure 2.10.

An association is always, by default, uni-directional and is represented by a plain one-way arrow (which contrasts with the (usual but not mandatory) bi-directional focus in UML). If no decision has yet been made, the arrowhead may be left off (TBD association) until a later decision adds it. This is more reasonable than permitting an unarrowed line to mean bi-directional. Leaving off arrowheads may be carelessness rather than a design decision! Semantically, mappings as used here do not break encapsulation; whereas bi-directional associations do (Graham et al., 1997a) – if needed these are represented by double-headed arrows as a shorthand for a pair of uni-directional associations which are semi-strong inverses of one another. We believe in supporting a true object-oriented paradigm as default. Uni-directional associations minimize coupling and thus enhance reuse as well as simplifying forward and reverse engineering.

The remaining arrows in Figure 2.14 all relate to aggregation-like connexions. Aggregation is a whole–part relationship (see above and Henderson-Sellers,

NOTATIONS FOR OPEN   35

⟹ definitional (classification, implementation or inheritance) – unlabeled default is specialization (a kind of)

■⟶ subtyping (blackbox inheritance)

□⟶ subclassing (whitebox inheritance)

⟶ association/mapping

⊕⟶ aggregation

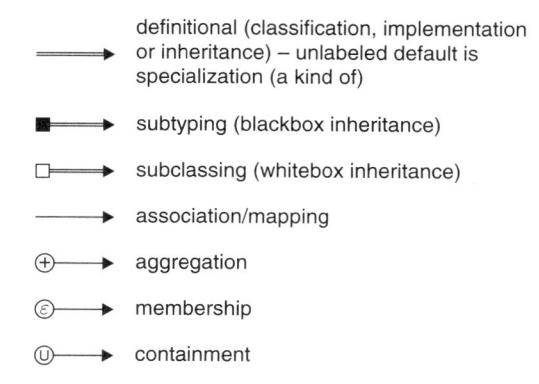

ε⟶ membership

Ⓤ⟶ containment

Figure 2.14 Relationships are indicated by arrows, some with adornments. The major relationships are illustrated here and form part of the COMN Light notation (adapted from Graham *et al.*, 1997b). The arrowhead style is not meaningful – we use both white and black in this book as confirmation.

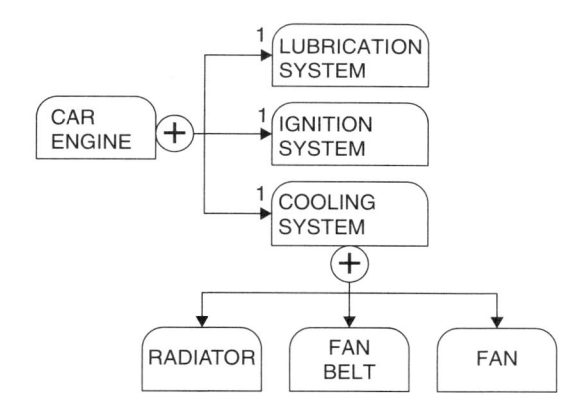

Figure 2.15 Example of an aggregation relationship (after Henderson-Sellers *et al.*, 1997b).

1997a) in which the parts bear a functional or structural relationship to each other or to the object they constitute (Figure 2.7). This is denoted in COMN by a plus sign which represents the fact that the aggregate (the car engine in Figure 2.15) is (usually more than) the sum of its parts – an aggregate has at least one emergent property (Kilov and Ross, 1994, page 112). The other three categories in Figure 2.7 are non-configurational. These are grouped together in OPEN as the 'membership' relationship (a subtype of whole–part relationship) and represented by a ∈ or set membership symbol (Figure 2.14).

Often confused with aggregation is the looser containment concept. A good example here is what you store in the trunk of your car (Figure 2.16). The items

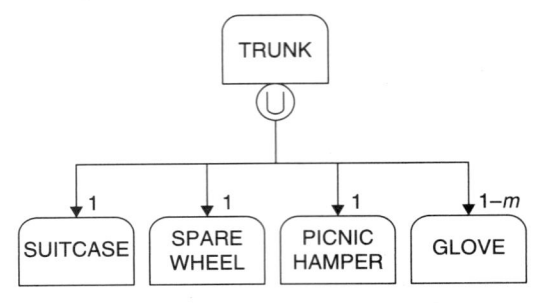

Figure 2.16 Example of containment relationship (after Henderson-Sellers *et al.*, 1997b).

are connected with trunk, but that connexion may be highly temporary. We replace the plus symbol with a cup symbol to give the visual clue suggested by this icon of a cup and its contents. An aggregation results in a structure having relationships between parts whereas when using containment there is no such inter-part relationship.

There are in fact two further types of relationship: transitional and scenario. These are more advanced features, not part of COMN Light and thus not discussed here (see *OPEN Modeling Language (OML) Reference Manual* by Firesmith *et al.* (1997). Transitional relationships are not used in the static model (semantic net or class models) but only in dynamic models, and scenario relationships only in use case/task script models. Beginners can use any state-transition model they choose before investigating the OML state-transition model. Similarly, although we prefer a task script/use case model for large systems, any version of this to help gain understanding of user requirements will be satisfactory for learning the overall OPEN approach. Interconnexions between diagrams are likewise reserved for discussion of the full notation.

Notation for stereotypes

In OML, the stereotype name is a label enclosed in braces (e.g. {*control*}) placed below the class name (Figure 2.17). The rationale for the positioning is that the stereotype qualifies the class name yet is subordinate to it (cf. UML when the stereotype name is *above* the class name – Section 2.3.2 and Figure 2.31).

2.3.2 UML notation

Perhaps the most likely alternative notation is the UML notation created by members of Rational Software Corporation, the latest version of which (Version 1.1) having recently been endorsed by the Object Management Group (November 1997). It is that version (Version 1.1) that is described here (OMG, 1997a). Figure 2.18 shows the basic icons for class and object. The icon shape is

NOTATIONS FOR OPEN   37

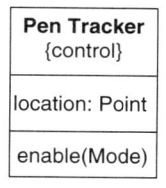

Figure 2.17 OML's stereotype notation.

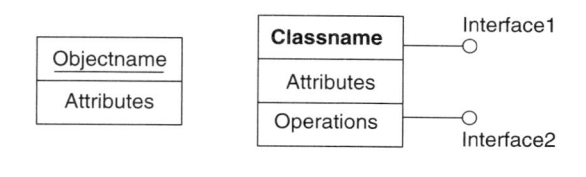

Figure 2.18 Class, interfaces and objects in UML.

the same for both these metatypes: a rectangle. The differentiation is created by underlining the name of the object. UML's equivalent of the drop-down box of Figure 2.13 is the box(es) attached beneath this rectangle. As seen in Figure 2.18 the normal usage is for there to be one box for an object and two for a class. For a class, attributes are shown in the upper box and operations in the lower. It is argued that an object only has attributes, since at runtime the operations are actually stored centrally and are not part of the object image in memory. Consequently, only attributes need to be shown in analysis and design. However, further boxes can be added as required, e.g. to show responsibilities, as in OML (see above – Figure 2.13).

Interfaces (which demonstrate the type aspect of a CIRT[†]) are shown as circles on the ends of lines ('lollipops'). Thus a class can have several interfaces. UML interfaces show the visible operations of a class, i.e. those operations which can be accessed by a client class (Figure 2.19) with a dependency which has been stereotyped to become a 'uses' dependency. Since it is impossible to show an interface's operations using the lollipop style of representation for the interface, an alternative is offered (left-hand side of Figure 2.19): the class is shown with a dependency to its interface object. This interface is represented by a class icon named Set with an interface stereotype (≪interface≫ on class Set). Now the attached operations box can show the list of appropriate public operations available in the interface. (Note that in this case the attribute box is of no interest and has been omitted).

---

† There is no notation in UML for a CIRT.

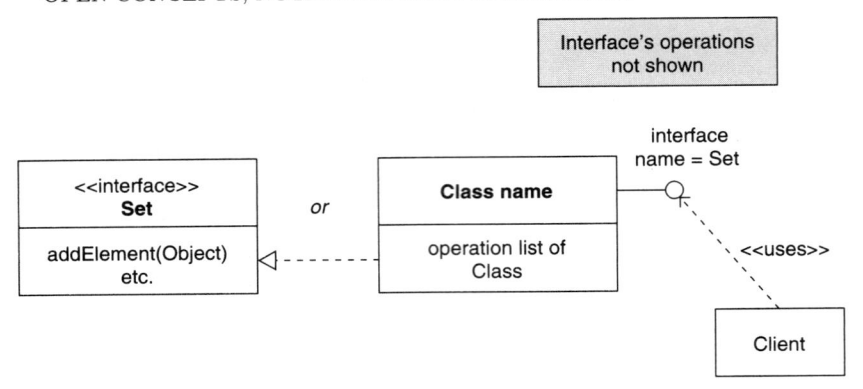

Figure 2.19 UML interfaces show visible operations of a class.

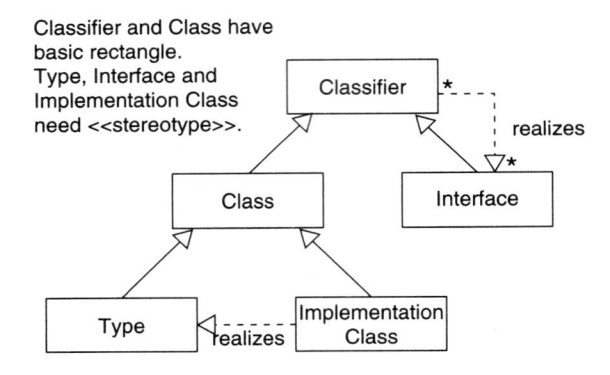

Figure 2.20 Notation and stereotype in the Classifier hierarchy.

The notation for class and object has been seen to be a rectangle. So too is (a) the UML Type; (b) the UML ImplementationClass; and (c) a supertype of Class and Interface in the metamodel called Classifier (Figure 2.20). Both Classifier and Class have the basic, unadorned rectangle whereas Interface, Type and ImplementationClass require an appropriate «stereotype» placed above the class name (see example above – Figure 2.19). In addition, in the metamodel of Figure 2.20 we also see that a Classifier realizes an Interface and an ImplementationClass realizes a Type.

There are several stylistic recommendations made in UML. For components of the class icon:

- class name: bold, centered
- class name for abstract class: bold and italic, centered
- stereotype name: plain font in guillemets above class name, centered

NOTATIONS FOR OPEN 39

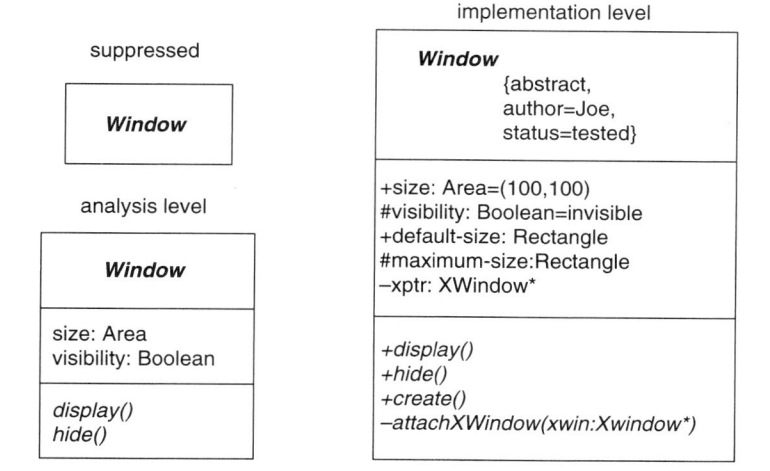

Figure 2.21 Three levels of suppression of information in the UML class icon (copyright OMG, 1997b).

- class names begin with upper case
- attributes and operations left justified, plain font unless abstract when they are italic. Lowercase initial letter.

And for the level of detail of the components in a class icon (Figure 2.21):

- everything except the class name can be suppressed leaving a plain rectangle with the class name, or
- showing the two standard (attribute and operation) boxes, at the analysis level, with names and types but no visibility information, or
- showing the two standard (attribute and operation) boxes, at the implementation level, with full details of visibility, initial values (see size:Area = (100, 100) in Figure 2.21) and hidden details not shown in the analysis level version. Visibility markers, as seen here, are + for public, − for private (hidden) and # for protected. At this (implementation) level, additional information can be added to the name segment within braces (e.g. abstract class constraint, authorship, status). [Also seen in this figure are the results of the application of the style guidelines above for bold and italic names.]

In UML Version 1.1, the relationships can be summarized (Figure 2.22) as

- generalization
- dependency, including usage

40 OPEN CONCEPTS, NOTATIONS AND DELIVERABLES

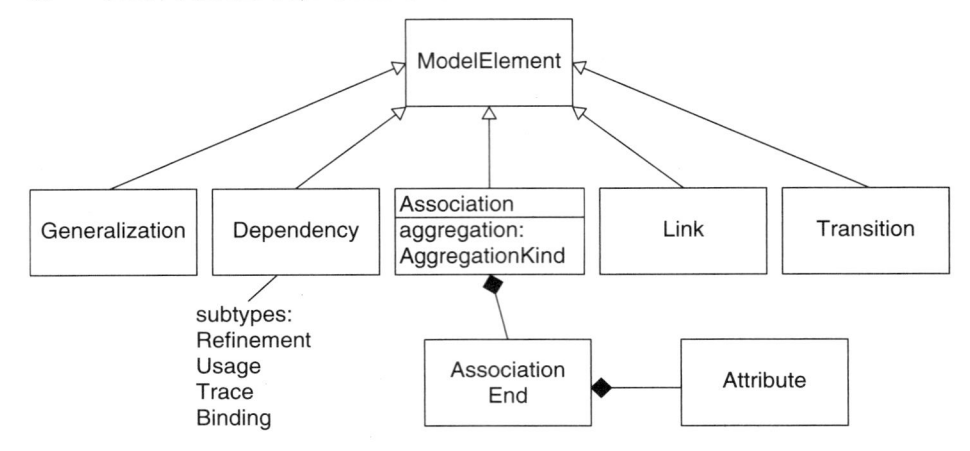

Figure 2.22 The metamodel for relationships in UML Version 1.1 (based on information in OMG, 1997a, b). (Robert Martin states that an Association is a type of Dependency, but not shown as such in UML documentation.)

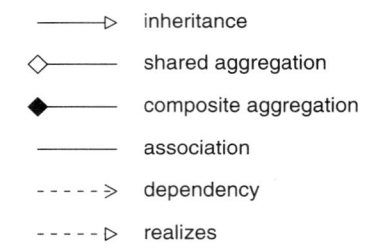

Figure 2.23 Notation for the major relationships in UML summarized.

- association
- link (an instance of an association)
- transition (relevant to STDs only).

Notation for the most frequently occurring relationships in the class diagrams is shown in Figure 2.23. UML strongly prefers the use of bi-directional associations – although this has been slightly weakened in the Version 1.1 metamodel as compared to the Version 1.0 metamodel. Nevertheless, the UML preferred rationale is that a single, unarrowed line (Figure 2.24) should represent bi-directionality (although the documentation permits other interpretations, e.g. the one used in OML and preferred by Fowler and Scott, 1997, page 62) and that on the (rarer) occasions when uni-directionality is required, this should be shown by an open arrowhead. Thus the refinement process that occurs removes/negates information – a poor practice in knowledge representation according to Brach-

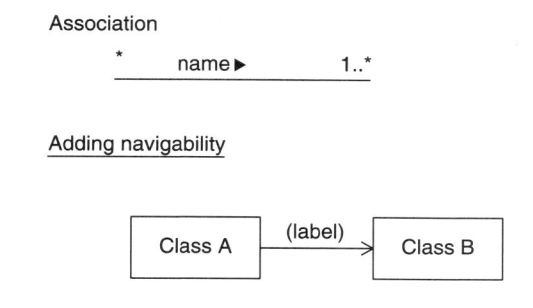

Figure 2.24 UML associations.

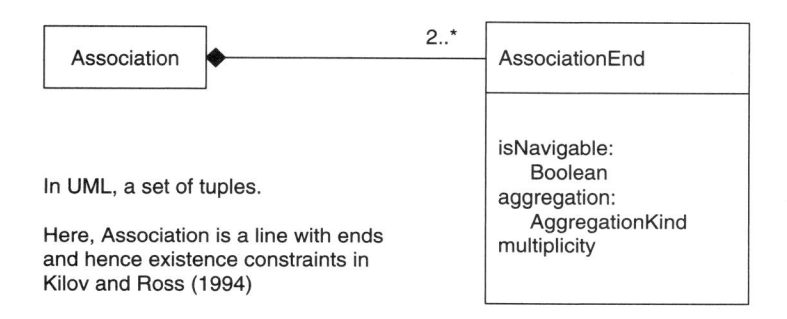

Figure 2.25 In UML, Association consists of two or more AssociationEnds which themselves have attributes including isNavigable, aggregation and multiplicity.

man (1985). There is also no way in UML to show undecided (TBD) directionality on associations.

UML associations usually have a name with a solid black triangle indicating in which direction the name should be read. The association line has two ends (called association ends and represented as concepts in the metamodel). Attributes of AssociationEnd include multiplicity, ordering labels, qualifier, navigability, interface specifier, changeability, visibility and an aggregation indicator (shared, composite or none) (Figure 2.25).

UML's aggregation is most interesting. Whilst there is a notation for aggregation (actually two 'flavors'), there is no corresponding metatype (of Aggregation) in the UML metamodel. Rather, it is an enumerated type (aggregation:AggregationKind) represented as an attribute in the AssociationEnd metatype. In other words, you take a UML association, change the AggregationKind attribute on AssociationEnd from none to either composite (composite aggregation) or aggregate (shared aggregation) to create those two aggregation relationships. The first (composite) is represented as a black diamond on the aggregate end of the relationship and the second (aggregate) is a white diamond. The black diamond depicts a strong aggregation in which lifetime dependencies are linked and there is a configurational, non-invariant relationship. This

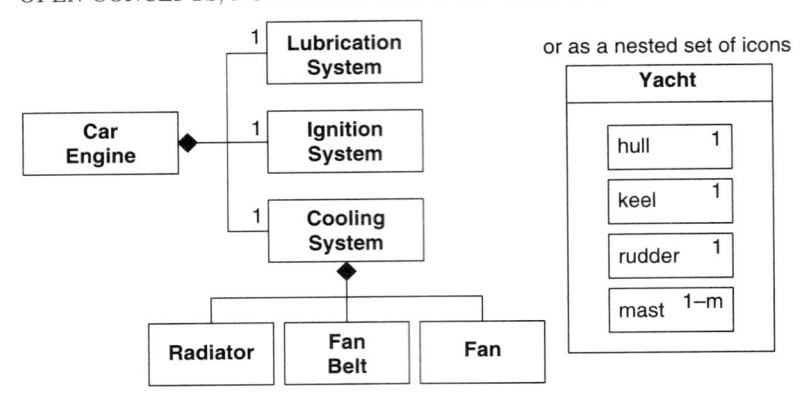

Figure 2.26 Representing aggregation in UML.

is a combination of the first line of Figure 2.7 and the tombstone (stereotype) of OML (Figure 2.9). The use of this is shown in Figure 2.26 which depicts the same example as that shown in COMN in Figure 2.15. An alternative depiction is also shown in Figure 2.26 as a set of nested icons which is visually more appealing whilst not really scaling well. The white diamond is purposefully loosely defined (OMG, 1997a, page 40) and is intended to indicate that the 'part object' may belong to two or more aggregates concurrently – in other words, that there must be at least *two* white diamonds in any shared aggregation structure. However, sharing is actually a characteristic of the class not of the relationship, aggregation or otherwise (Firesmith and Henderson-Sellers, 1998a).

Generalization/inheritance in UML has only one type, ostensibly representing specification and specialization inheritance (is-a-kind-of) and shown by a directed line from subtype to supertype with a white arrowhead at the supertype end (Figure 2.27). A discriminator can be used, as in COMN. However, here the discriminator name is repeated for each separate generalization connexion and the relationships which are grouped together (shown by a yoke in OML) are connected via a dotted line.

Finally, a dependency is a relationship where one class depends upon another in such a way that should the interface of the server CIRT change, then it is possible that the client CIRT may also need to change. Dependencies can arise from many sources, a common one being the addition of navigability to an association (Fowler, 1997, personal communication). Dependencies also occur when objects are passed as arguments to messages and when packages are reliant on each other.

In UML Version 1.1, Dependency and Association are separate and have no connexion – they are merely both types of ModelElement. Discussion in the OTUG newsgroup in late 1997 suggested that perhaps an Association should be re-modeled in UML as a subtype of Dependency (at the metalevel). This led, in

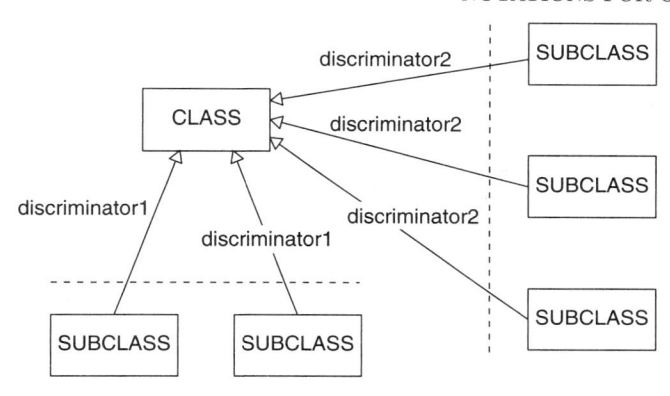

Figure 2.27 Representing generalization in UML including the use of discriminators.

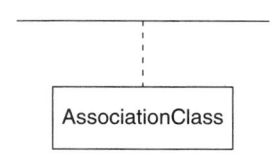

Figure 2.28 UML association class. It is also possible to have an association class which inherits from Class and Association.

part, to a re-analysis by Henderson-Sellers (1997b) which led to the suggestion that Dependency and Usage might be the dynamic counterparts of Association.

Inheriting qualifiers from OMT as it does, UML similarly inherits the notion of an AssociationClass. This is essentially the reification of the association to a first-class citizen: a class (Figure 2.28). It is shown in the notation as a class icon (rectangle) attached to the association line by a dotted line. In the metamodel, an AssociationClass inherits multiply from Association and Class. Kilov and Ross (1994) note that this type of association is observed to be relatively uncommon in commercial systems designs.

Associations in UML can also show an 'or' constraint. Figure 2.29 shows that an Account may be held by either a Person or a Company. Whilst this might be useful as a first draft, it is more than likely indicative of a missing concept/CIRT – here the notion of *ACCOUNT_HOLDER* (lower part of Figure 2.29, depicted in COMN by a role). A second constraint between associations becomes possible since, in the metamodel, Association inherits from the metatype of GeneralizableElement. An example of the use of this is shown in Figure 2.30. Again, useful initially, the occurrence of such a constraint could indicate a missing class and a simpler, more straightforward and more readily implementable design such as that shown (in OML notation) in the lower part of Figure 2.30 might be preferable.

Finally, stereotypes in UML are depicted using guillemets, with the stereo-

44   OPEN CONCEPTS, NOTATIONS AND DELIVERABLES

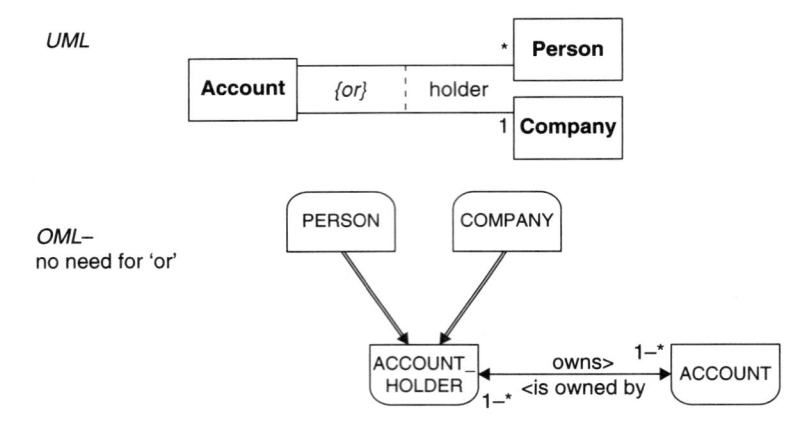

Figure 2.29 The use of a constraint in UML to depict an 'or' situation (after OMG, 1997b) and an alternative using an additional CIRT in OML notation.

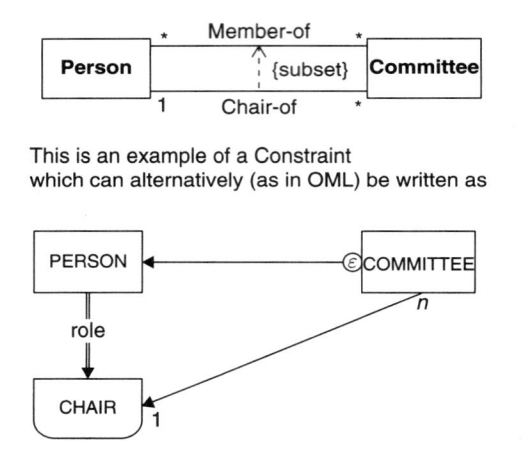

Figure 2.30 The use of a constraint on a UML association (after OMG, 1997b) and an alternative using an additional CIRT in OML notation.

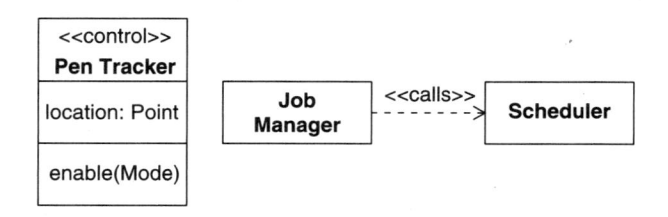

Figure 2.31 Stereotypes in UML (after OMG, 1997b).

NOTATIONS FOR OPEN   45

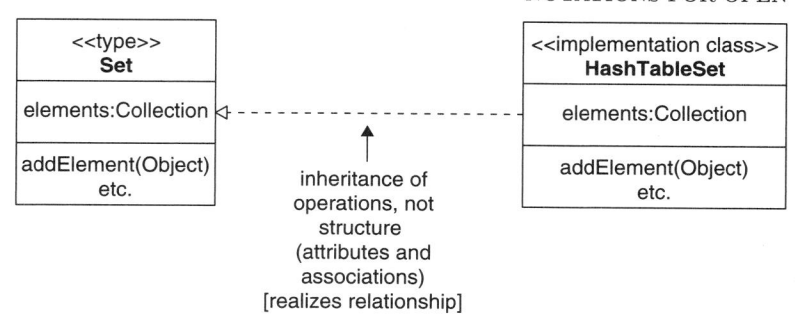

```
┌─────────────────────┐                              ┌──────────────────────────────┐
│      <<type>>       │                              │  <<implementation class>>    │
│        Set          │                              │        HashTableSet          │
├─────────────────────┤◁- - - - - - - - - - - - - - -├──────────────────────────────┤
│ elements:Collection │              ↑               │     elements:Collection      │
├─────────────────────┤      inheritance of          ├──────────────────────────────┤
│  addElement(Object) │      operations, not         │      addElement(Object)      │
│        etc.         │         structure            │             etc.             │
└─────────────────────┘      (attributes and         └──────────────────────────────┘
                              associations)
                          [realizes relationship]
```

Figure 2.32 The use of stereotypes in UML to create Types or Implementation Classes (adapted from OMG, 1997b).

type name *above* the class name (as seen above) or above the relationship name (Figure 2.31). Stereotypes are used widely in UML – although OMG (1997b) documentation notes that users may prefer to turn them into specific icons. [This is effectively what OML does.] A major use (as inferred from Figure 2.20) is to change a regular class into either a Type (role) or an Implementation Class (Figure 2.32). When doing so, the dependency relationship has the semantics of operation inheritance but not structure (attributes and association) inheritance.

2.3.3 Other notations

Coad and Yourdon

The Coad and Yourdon notation also offers compatible if not complete support for OPEN's modeling techniques. The object/class icon is a rounded rectangle. Used with a double border it describes classes and their objects (Coad and Yourdon, 1991), used with a single border it represents just the class, i.e. an abstract or deferred class (Figure 2.33). These icons have typically three compartments when used in architectural diagrams: class name, attributes and services (here the term service describes purely the behavioral aspect of an object/class).

Generalization relationships are shown by an undirected arc with a semicircle and aggregation by a white triangle. It should also be noted that the multiplicities are reversed to other notations. In Figure 2.33, class 4 consists of $1-n$ instances of class 5 and 2 instances of class 6. Relationships relevant to object connexions join the outer rounded rectangles; the relationships relevant to class–class connexions join the inner (class) rounded rectangle. Instance level message connexions are a uni-directional thick, grey-shaded arrow from 'sender' to 'receiver' (i.e. from client to server).

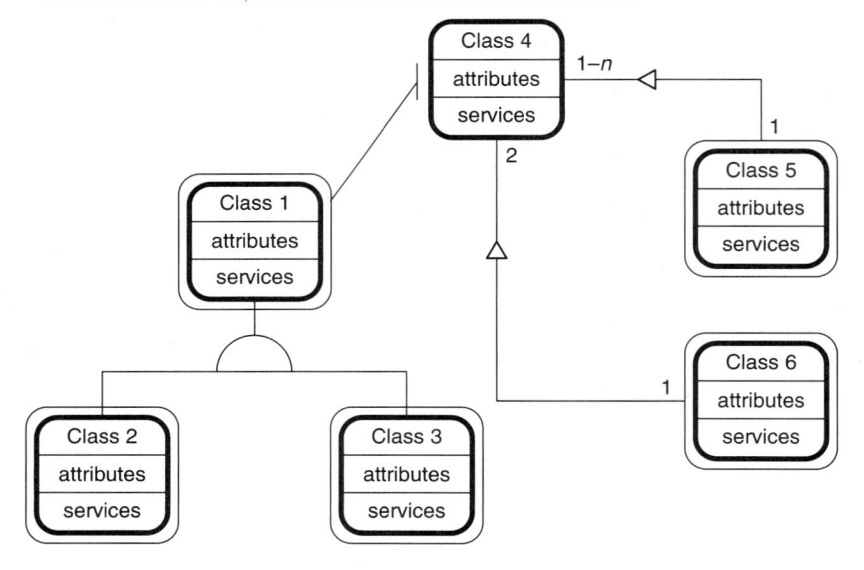

Figure 2.33 Class, object and relationship icons from the Coad and Yourdon notation.

BON

BON has a slightly different look to its notation but has a highly compatible set of concepts to OPEN's. The class icon is a rounded rectangle with six compartments (Figure 2.34). In addition to the normal class name, and public features (a.k.a. services), there is space for indexing information, superclasses, features with restricted visibility and invariants. There is also a 'shortened form' of an ellipse. There are a wide range of annotations to the class name to represent

- reused class (name underlined)
- persistent class (black circle)
- parameterized class (parameters in [ ])
- deferred class (asterisk)
- effective class (plus sign)
- interfaced class (black triangle)
- root class (double ellipse).

Objects are represented by a rectangle and 'clusters' (packages in UML and OML) by a dotted rounded rectangle (as in OML).

Relationships are divided into static links and dynamic links (Figure 2.35). Features have signatures which can be of several kinds. The symbols used for describing assertions form a complete language (see CD: Appendix E) using formal mathematics.

```
┌─────────────────────────┐
│      CLASS_NAME         │
├─────────────────────────┤
│  indexing information   │
├─────────────────────────┤
│  Inherits: PARENT       │
│            CLASSES      │
├─────────────────────────┤
│    Public features      │
│ ───── A, B, C ─────     │
│ Features only visible   │
│ to classes A, B, C      │
├─────────────────────────┤
│ ───── Invariant ─────   │
│    Class invariant      │
└─────────────────────────┘
```

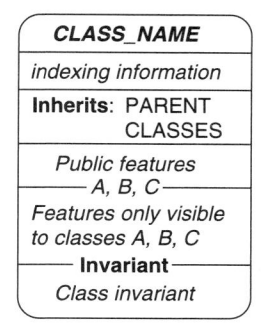

Figure 2.34 Class interface details for the BON notation (after Waldén and Nerson, 1995).

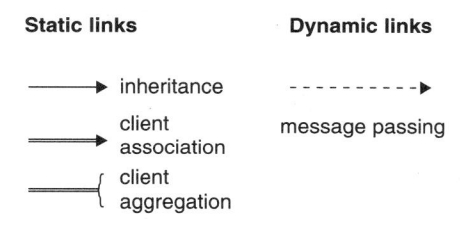

Figure 2.35 Static and dynamic links in BON (after Waldén and Nerson, 1995).

2.4 Diagram types

Since a notation is used to model business domains and applications with a great deal of inherent complexity, no single view or diagram type is adequate to capture all important aspects of the resulting model. COMN and UML therefore offer a set of diagram types (Table 2.1) that provide relatively orthogonal views of the *single underlying model*. Some diagrams document static architecture, whereas others document dynamic behavior. Some diagrams view the model at a very high, blackbox level of abstraction, whereas others open up the blackbox to display encapsulated details. The OML metamodel (Firesmith *et al.*, 1997) provides a way to capture the single underlying model and check for consistency. It is critical that changes made to one diagram are synchronized across and reflected in appropriate changes being made to all the other diagrams, probably by using an automated CASE tool.

These views are relatively orthogonal in that each diagram provides a view of the underlying model that can be understood and studied separately. However, these diagrams are related to each other in interesting and useful ways because they provide views of a single underlying model, and this allows CASE tool vendors to provide coherent cross-referencing and consistency checking.

There are four main kinds of diagram types in both COMN and UML

48 OPEN CONCEPTS, NOTATIONS AND DELIVERABLES

Table 2.1 Comparison of main diagram types (COMN and UML).

COMN	UML
Semantic nets	Static structure diagrams
Scenario class diagram	Use case diagram
Interaction diagram	Interaction diagram
STDs	Statechart diagrams
(Activity diagram not used)	Activity diagrams
(type of semantic net)	Implementation diagram

(Table 2.1): semantic nets, scenario class diagrams, interaction diagrams and state transition diagrams. In addition, UML supports implementation diagrams (seen as a type of semantic net in COMN) and activity diagrams (not seen as relevant in COMN).

Semantic nets

The semantic net, of which there are six subtypes in OML (Table 2.2), is the most important and most widely used diagram type in the OPEN method. OPEN uses semantic nets instead of extended entity relationship diagrams because:

- semantic nets from the artificial intelligence community are designed to document static architecture in terms of modeling elements and the semantically important relationships among them
- semantic nets naturally capture classification (is-a), specialization (a-kind-of)[†], and aggregation (has-part) relationships
- These diagrams primarily document objects and classes, rather than relational database tables. Entity relationship diagrams from data models are therefore misleading
- These diagrams should not be called class diagrams (as they are by UML) because they document internal and external objects, types, roles and packages as well as classes (e.g. Figure 2.36).

Semantic nets are mirrored in UML by class diagrams, component diagrams and deployment diagrams (Table 2.3).

Scenario class diagrams

Scenario class diagrams may be used for (1) task scripts, (2) use cases or (3) mechanisms. All three are supported in COMN to document a set of collaborating scenario classes and the invocation and precedes relationships between them. In

---

[†] The AI community also does not confuse is-a and a-kind-of relationships, a confusion which is, unfortunately, common in the object community.

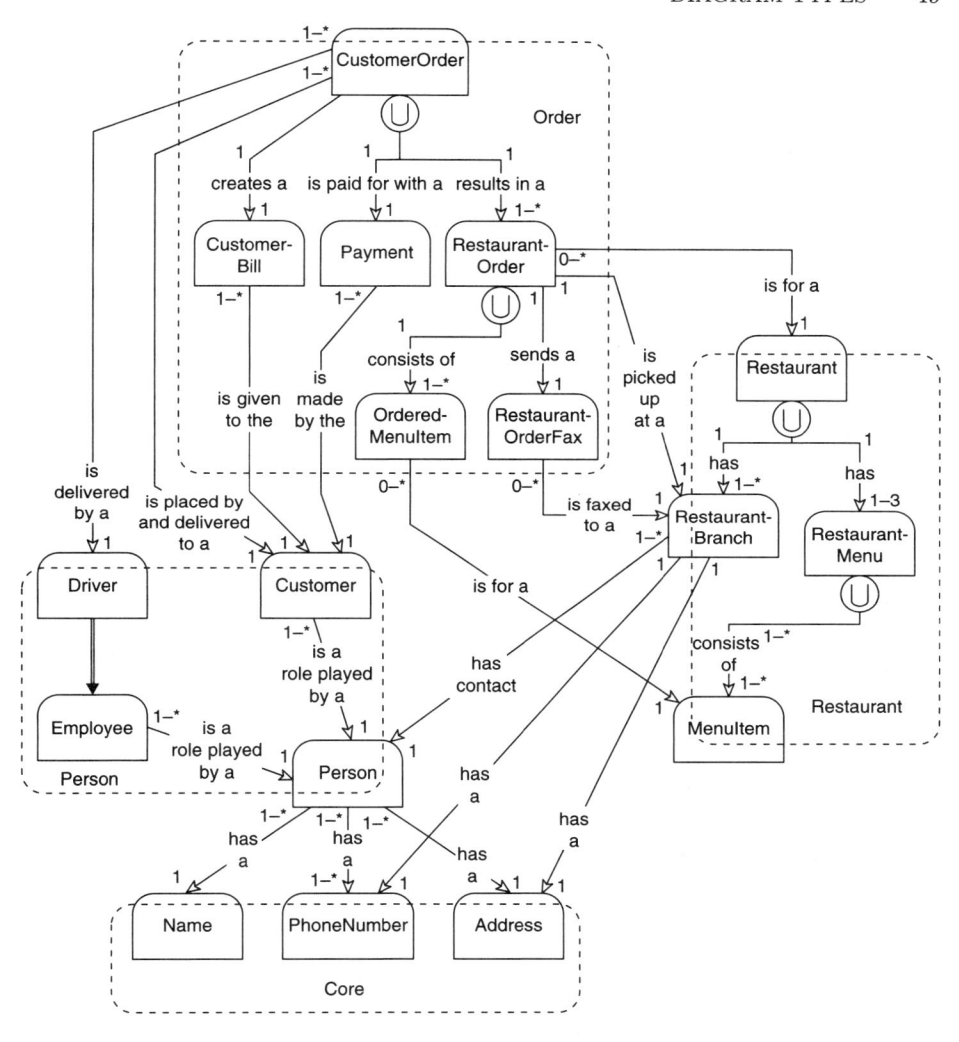

Figure 2.36 Cluster diagram showing classes for a good delivery order entry application (after Firesmith et al., 1997).

contrast, in UML use cases hold a pre-eminent place although their metamodel is not yet well connected to the static architecture metamodel.

Interaction diagrams

Interaction diagrams show interactions (message passing and exception raising) and may be either collaboration or sequence diagrams and are fairly standard in OO notations. Collaboration diagrams have a graph structure similar to semantic

Table 2.2 Six subtypes of OML semantic net.

	Diagram type	Purpose

1.	Context diagrams:
	     System context diagrams
	     Software context diagrams
		Depicts scope and environment

2.	Layer diagrams	Depicts the overall architecture in terms of layers
3.	Configuration diagrams	Depicts the overall architecture in terms of packages
4.	Package diagrams	Describes the elements comprising each package
5.	Inheritance diagrams	Depicts all or part of an inheritance graph
6.	Deployment diagrams	Depicts the allocation of software to hardware in a distributed system

Table 2.3 Comparison of semantic nets in OML and UML.

OML	UML

• Context diagrams
     System context diagrams
     Software context diagrams	

• Configuration diagrams	• Class diagrams
• Package (cluster) diagrams	and
• Inheritance diagrams	object diagrams
• Layer diagrams	• Component diagrams
• Deployment diagrams	• Deployment diagrams

nets (Figure 2.37). They may be shown with or without messages (respectively showing interactions and collaborations) and are typically used to provide summary information, particularly in terms of coupling. On the other hand, sequence diagrams use the standard fence notation and are used to show sequencing. Major advantages of COMN over UML interaction diagrams are the ability to handle exceptions and the availability of logic boxes to handle branching, looping, critical regions and interleaving due to concurrency, thereby greatly decreasing the number of diagrams that need to be developed and maintained.

State transition diagrams

Whilst state transition diagrams may have many flavors, the underlying concepts are usually credited to Harel (1987). The details of the COMN STD are in Firesmith *et al.* (1997). COMN STDs were developed from Harel statecharts incorporating later work from Embley *et al.* (1992), Firesmith (1993) and Selic *et*

DIAGRAM TYPES 51

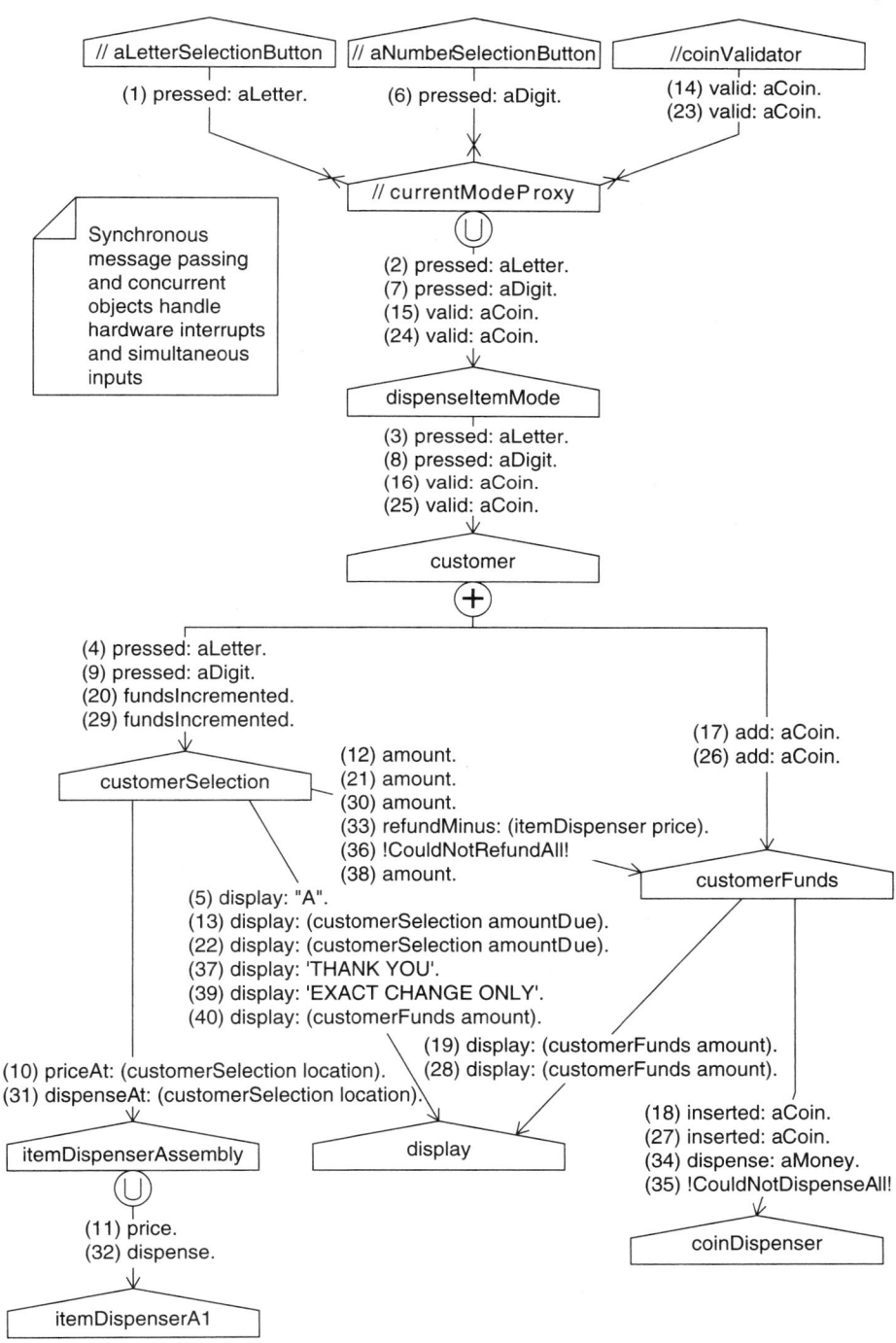

// aLetterSelectionButton
(1) pressed: aLetter.

// aNumberSelectionButton
(6) pressed: aDigit.

// coinValidator
(14) valid: aCoin.
(23) valid: aCoin.

// currentModeProxy
(2) pressed: aLetter.
(7) pressed: aDigit.
(15) valid: aCoin.
(24) valid: aCoin.

Synchronous message passing and concurrent objects handle hardware interrupts and simultaneous inputs

dispenseItemMode
(3) pressed: aLetter.
(8) pressed: aDigit.
(16) valid: aCoin.
(25) valid: aCoin.

customer

(4) pressed: aLetter.
(9) pressed: aDigit.
(20) fundsIncremented.
(29) fundsIncremented.

(17) add: aCoin.
(26) add: aCoin.

customerSelection

(12) amount.
(21) amount.
(30) amount.
(33) refundMinus: (itemDispenser price).
(36) !CouldNotRefundAll!
(38) amount.

customerFunds

(5) display: "A".
(13) display: (customerSelection amountDue).
(22) display: (customerSelection amountDue).
(37) display: 'THANK YOU'.
(39) display: 'EXACT CHANGE ONLY'.
(40) display: (customerFunds amount).

(19) display: (customerFunds amount).
(28) display: (customerFunds amount).

(10) priceAt: (customerSelection location).
(31) dispenseAt: (customerSelection location).

(18) inserted: aCoin.
(27) inserted: aCoin.
(34) dispense: aMoney.
(35) !CouldNotDispenseAll!

itemDispenserAssembly

display

coinDispenser

(11) price.
(32) dispense.

itemDispenserA1

Figure 2.37 Scenario collaboration diagram for a vending machine application (after Firesmith *et al.*, 1997).

al. (1994). States and transitions are represented with events triggering changes between states. Guards decide whether any particular event will trigger an event change or whether the state remains unchanged.

In addition, *creation charts* (q.v.), derived from the BON method, may be found useful. These are charts with essentially two columns labeled 'Class' and 'Creates instances of' which show classes which create instances of other classes. This amplifies the information in a collaboration diagram in which, for instance, a class may act as a server to several classes but it is ambiguous as to which of these several classes can create instances of the server class. Other ways of identifying such creation responsibilities are to rely on layering techniques as advocated strongly in OPEN/Discovery, to use the Object Interaction Graph of Fusion or the {new} constraint of UML.

2.5 OPEN deliverables

OPEN deliverables are part of the post-condition for each activity and are described in Chapter 5 of Graham *et al.* (1997b). For convenience, they are also summarized here.

The *project proposal* is a short document (typically only one page) stating the business requirement, scope, justification, sponsor, constraints, completion criteria, project costs etc. Based on the project proposal, requirements are elicited from the users resulting in a *users requirements statement* which represents the shared understanding of the users and developers. It represents the results of the collaborative requirements engineering process and any additional technical constraints. Users review this document and sign it off before further work commences (one iteration in many). From this document, the analysts can identify, iteratively with the users, the tasks that are necessary and build a task object model of these tasks. Appropriate metrics, reuse possibilities and business process definitions are all likely to be included in the resultant users requirement specification which is business/user focused. From this, analysts then create a software-focused version in terms of a *systems analysis report*. It may be supplemented by physical and paper-based prototypes. Prototypes are needed for the *user interface* and for the *model code*.

Before the product is constructed, it is necessary to undertake serious planning and this will result in a number of documents as deliverables. For example, there should be an overall *project plan*, perhaps in the form of a Gantt chart. The *quality plan* should also be a prime focus. Other important deliverables here are a *disaster recovery plan*, a *security plan*, a *configuration management and version control plan*, a set of *test plans* and a *training requirements report*.

Once the software development lifecycle is entered for the first of its planned iterations, the deliverables switch focus from the users and project management to technical, object-oriented models of the system as it is first conceived and ultimately evolves towards the deliverable product. A range of deliverables are built up during the evolutionary development activity. These include CRC cards,

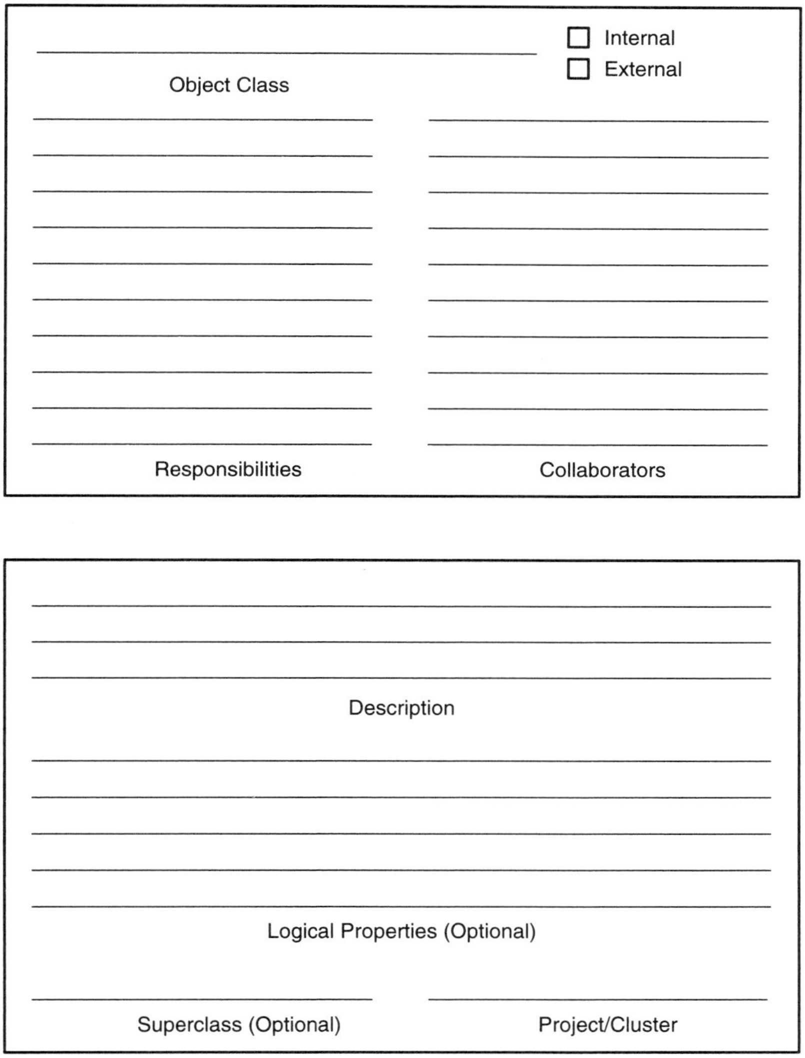

Figure 2.38 Example object CRC card as used in COMN (after Firesmith et al., 1997).

class cards, a range of graphical models (actually complementary views), test cases and code.

Early in the analysis, *CRC cards* and/or *class cards* have been found to be a good way of both 'getting the discussion going' and encouraging 'object think'. The class CRC card, as used in COMN, is shown in Figure 2.38 (see also Firesmith et al., 1997). CRC cards can also be written at the object, package and role levels. These COMN-style CRC cards stick closely to those originally proposed by Beck and Cunningham (1989). (For more details on the Build Activity graphical models, see Section 2.4.)

As part of the iterative lifecycle and, in particular, the evolutionary development activity within the build activity, testing is a major feature, i.e. in OPEN it is *not* a post-hoc activity. This means that fairly early in development, often in parallel, *test harnesses* should be designed and built. Some authorities suggest that as much as 50 per cent of the overall system development work should be on testing so this is a critical feature of the OO software development lifecycle. Testing plans need to be documented, at a minimum, as (a) *class test cases*, (b) *package test cases* and (c) *acceptance test cases*.

CIRT specifications present the completed details of the interface for an individual object class. This is basically the full design as seen from outside the class. With fully specified contracts, the use that can be made of this class by others is now finalized and irrevocable. From this specification, the coding can now be undertaken.

Source code is also a form of documentation and certainly a deliverable[†]. Code is needed not just for classes (assuming implementation in a class-based OOPL such as Eiffel or Java) but also for packages. Code can also be regarded, from a deliverable viewpoint, as internal (to the development team) and also as *release code*. As the degree of sophistication and the number of iterations increases, a report on the *potentially reusable components* and on *frameworks* will become possible.

In principle at least, fully working code can be generated from a detailed design. Any code so generated should either be maintained through the design or, if done at the code level (which is probably more likely), lead to an automatic update of the design documentation and also, when necessary, the analysis diagrams. In practice, whilst some tools are capable of realizing full code generation and perhaps some reverse engineering (so that OOAD diagrams can be updated automatically following a code change), other OO tools seem to generate, for example in C++, only the header files and not the methods. Whilst helpful, such a tool has more affinity to a structured editor than a code generator.

At the completion of all the iterative cycles, summary reports are required. Typically there are the *system design report*, an *integration test plan* and an *acceptance test plan*. The system design report may be fairly comprehensive including, *inter alia*, a copy of the user specification for review purposes; a full description of the implementation object model (viz. the detailed design and implemented code); a *database design* where needed; an *impact analysis*, a statement on *backup and recovery requirements*; a description of the *audit, security and control requirements* and a statement on the *interfaces with system software and reusable components*. In addition, the report should contain the test plan and the *results of the testing program*. The results of the test plan are then reported independently against the integration test plan and the acceptance test plan (*system test reports*). Finally, all the technical and users' documentation

---

[†] Some seem to think the only deliverable!

should have been prepared so that the *users' manual* is ready for delivery to the customer along with the software itself.

Designs, code, other products and the process should all be measured and the *metrics* reports tabled. The role of metrics in OPEN is critical in monitoring, providing feedback and for process improvement. Consequently the metrics reports are endemic to the whole of the development process. They will tend to be used in the various review and consolidation activities. Indeed, the modular nature of the architecture of OPEN, in conjunction with this measurement focus, sets the foundation for comparability between distinct applications of each technique and, eventually, comparability at higher levels. It also has a positive influence on the ease and quality of decision making for reuse.

The main deliverable from the user review activity within the build activity is the agreement (written or verbal) to proceed to the next iteration with proposed modifications or to the consolidation activity.

In the consolidation activity within the build activity, the main deliverables are *a full set of the technical documentation* documenting all design decisions and describing interfaces to any other systems. A *report on operational implications and required actions* is also required. Also at this stage it is necessary to delimit the mode of implementing the product and undertaking the conversion. This *implementation and conversion plan* will outline the steps to be followed in moving to the new system involving technical and end-users' roles and responsibilities in the change process.

In the evaluation activity, the pre-release product is evaluated by a direct comparison between the current status and the planned status. A suite of reports is required: a full *design report* evaluating the technical aspects; an *acceptance document* from the users as fulfilling the requirements document; reports for *bugs/faults*; results of the testing harness runs in a *test report*; together with a *traceability report* and an overall *review report*.

In the broader scope of the overall programme, the potentially reusable classes identified earlier are listed as candidate reusable classes.

Once the system is ready for implementation at the users' site, then a switch-over plan, known as a *system conversion plan*, has to be created. This plan should also include a contingency plan in the event of problems with regard to the old versus the new system.

Once the system has been installed, acceptance tests are undertaken resulting in an *assessment of implementation process* report and an *assessment of systems acceptance test*. This leads to a full *post-implementation review* which must be appropriately documented.

Other documents that are needed but may be only needed to be created once, or even acquired from a third party are standards and guidelines documents. Coding and design guidelines are available now and will become increasingly common.

Chapter 3
OPEN techniques

3.1 Techniques selection criteria

In OPEN, tasks are accomplished by the use of one or more techniques. The task is the statement of the unit of work required, the what; the how is described by the technique. This is similar to saying that I want to hang a picture on my living room wall. This is today's task. But how do I do that? I use some technique – but often I have a choice between techniques; and furthermore I may use not just one but several techniques to accomplish my task. In this case I have a choice between using (a) a hammer to knock a nail into the wall or (b) a screwdriver[†] and a screw *together with* (for either option) a piece of string and knowledge of how to tie an appropriate (reef) knot.

OPEN techniques are thus ways of doing things. They include ways that have been tried and tested over (at least) the last decade; but also may include new techniques that are more experimental. Some indication on the level of maturity of the individual technique is thus given as part of its full specification, using a star rating on the entries in Appendices A and B, and C and D on the CD.

Remember, the techniques you use are your choice – within the constraints of being effective and efficient in accomplishing the task and being compatible with the OO mindset. In other words, the developer chooses the appropriate technique(s) from those described in OPEN or from their own experience, sometimes selecting between two (or more) competing alternatives. Thus, for example, in order to find objects, the choice may be between, say, using use cases, using noun analysis, identifying concepts and their responsibilities, using CRC cards, etc. In reality, many tasks are best accomplished by a mixture of techniques rather than just one. There are too many cases of the use of a single technique being taken to an extreme. For example, at one conference, a story of noun analysis being used for a 300-page requirements specification rightly created disbelief in the audience at such a gross misapplication of the technique.

Our own recommendations are based on both theory and practice; although we fully realize the need to permit individual managers and project team mem-

---

† We would prefer a power screwdriver; or a hook for the picture rail (reuse!).

bers not to feel bound in a straitjacket – we therefore recommend, we do not mandate. Our own 'toolbox' collection of techniques, which you are free to borrow, is described in detail in this book; whilst other OPEN books are planned by the OPEN Consortium members which will present details of some pre-tailored SEPs appropriate for specific domains such as MIS, finance, embedded systems. OPEN's techniques number well over 100 and are (a) listed alphabetically in the appendices and (b) discussed in groups in the subsequent sections of this chapter.

Choice of techniques is assisted by a deontic matrix linking techniques to tasks. In OPEN we aim to give our overall recommendations in terms of M (= mandatory), R (recommended) O (= optional), D (= discouraged) and F (= forbidden). However, it should be remembered that these values will be assigned from study across a large number of contrasting projects. For your own project, you will be able to tailor the OPEN lifecycle process: one significant element of this is refining these probabilities – preferably until they (almost) all fall into either the M or F categories.

In this way, techniques are intrinsically orthogonal to the notion of tasks. They can only be grouped together very roughly (Table 3.1). They are akin to the tools of the tradesperson – a carpenter's toolbox contains many tools, some of which have superficial resemblances but may have operational affinity to tools of different outward appearance.

In the following sections, we outline the OPEN techniques in these loose groupings; a full description, technique by technique, is to be found in the appendices which, together, essentially provide a reference manual or dictionary for all the recommended OO techniques.

3.2 Techniques relating to user requirements

The general area of requirements engineering is a nexus between social science and (computer) technology. It bridges between the user(s) and their requirements and the ability of the software engineer to construct a design that is both implementable in a language suitable for computation and also understandable (and therefore endorsable) by the end-user.

The first steps in requirements engineering are identification of the source or sources of the requirements (e.g. people, paper-based files, electronic databases) and then the elicitation of the particular requirements (for this particular project) from those sources. This is perhaps most difficult when the source is human since there is much sociological understanding necessary for (and often foreign to) the requirements engineer, whose mindset is often science/technology-focused. Many of the OPEN techniques involve traditional people interaction and problem-solving techniques such as brainstorming sessions, active listening, interviewing and questionnaires. Indeed, there are a myriad such techniques for gaining information and it is certainly not the intention that you should use *all* of them on each particular project. Choose the one that suits the skills of the

Table 3.1 OPEN techniques in logical/temporal groupings.

(1) *User requirements*
Action research
Active listening
Activity grid construction
Analysis of judgements
Brainstorming
Concept maps
Context modeling
CRC card modeling
Domain analysis
Expected value analysis
Interviewing
JAD
Kelly grids
Power analysis
Questionnaires
RAD
Record and playback
Rich pictures
Roleplay
Scenario development
Simulation
Social systems analysis
Soft systems analysis
Storyboarding
Throwaway prototyping
Videotaping
Workshops

(2) *Project management and business issues*
Approval gaining
BPR
Business process modeling
Configuration management

Table 3.1 (Continued.)

Cost–benefit analysis
Cost estimation
CPM charts
Critical success factors
Customer (on-site) training
Envisioning
Gantt charts
Hierarchical task analysis
Impact analysis
Impact estimation table
Library management
Package construction
Package coordination
PERT charts
Pistols at dawn
PLanguage
Priority setting
Project planning
Prototyping
PSP
Risk analysis
Role assignment
Scenario development
Simulation
SMART goals
Social systems analysis
Systems acceptance
Systems audit
Team building
Throwaway prototyping
Timeboxing
TQM
Versioning (DBMS)
Walkthroughs

Table 3.1 (Continued.)

Workflow analysis

(2a) *Quality*

Testing
Acceptance testing
Beta testing
Dependency-based testing
Integration testing
Package and subsystem testing
Regression testing
System acceptance
Unit testing
Usability testing

Inspections
Defect detection
Inspections
Reviews
Walkthroughs

Metrics
Cohesion measurement
Complexity measurement
Cost estimation
Coupling measurement
Function points
Law of Demeter
Metrics collection
Reuse measurement
Statistical analysis of data
Task points
Thresholds

Table 3.1 (Continued.)

Other
CIRT indexing
Class naming
Contract specification
Exception handling
Formal methods
GQM
Hierarchical task analysis
Literate programming
Quality templates
Refactoring
Rule modeling
Standards compliance

(3) *Modeling techniques*

Concepts/philosophy
Abstraction
Classification
Encapsulation and information hiding
Generalization (see also Classification)
Responsibilities and responsibility-driven design

Technical/low-level OOA/D
Abstract class identification
Class internal design
Class naming
Collaborations analysis
Contract specification
Creation charts
Delegation analysis
Design templates
Event modeling
Generalization and inheritance identification

Table 3.1 (Continued.)

Genericity specification
Granularity
Hierarchical task analysis
Interaction modeling
Layering
Mixins
Petri nets
Qua-types
Refactoring
Relationship modeling
Responsibility identification
Rule modeling
Scenario development
Service identification
State modeling
Stereotyping
Time-threads
Visibility analysis

Other
Abstraction utilization
Application scavenging
Blackboarding
Business process modeling
Completion of abstractions
Connascence
CRC card modeling
Dataflow modeling
ER modeling
Event charts
Exception handling
Formal methods
Function points
Fuzzy logic and fuzzy modeling

Table 3.1 (Continued.)

Hierarchical task analysis
Hotspot identification
Hypergenericity
Information engineering
Intelligent agent identification
Object lifecycle histories
Ownership modeling
Pattern recognition
Protocol analysis
PS–PPS
Refinement
Reverse engineering
Revision of inheritance hierarchies
Role modeling
Roleplay
Screen scraping
Simulation
Textual analysis
Transformations of the object model
Viewpoints
Visualization techniques
Zachman frameworks

(4) *Database*
Access analysis
Audit requirements
Clustering (DB)
Collapsing of classes
Database authorization
Database fragmentation
DBMS product selection
DBMS type selection
Indexing

Table 3.1 (Continued.)

Interfacing to relational DBMS and legacy code
Mapping to RDB
Normalization
Object replication
Object retention requirements
Path navigation
Query optimization
Reliability requirements
Storage of derived properties
Tuning of database
Versioning (DBMS)
Volume analysis

(5) *DCS*
DCS classification
DCS optimization
Distributed system partitioning and allocation
Implementation of distributed aspects of system
Scenario development

(6) *User interface*
Dialog design in UI
Screen painting
Usability testing

(7) *Reuse*
Access analysis
Application scavenging
CIRT indexing
Collaborations analysis
Completion of abstractions
Framework creation
Genericity specification

Table 3.1 (Continued.)

Granularity
Layering
Library class incorporation
Library management
Pattern recognition
Reuse measurement
Revision of inheritance hierarchies
Scenario development
Variant analysis

(8) *Coding*
Class internal design
Creation charts
Generalization and inheritance identification
Inspections
Implementation of distributed aspects of system
Implementation of rules
Implementation of services
Implementation of structure
Law of Demeter
Mixins
Screen scraping
Storage of derived properties
Wrappers

(9) *Training and education*
Computer-based training
Games
Group problem solving
Internet and web technology
Lectures
Roleplay
Simulation

Table 3.1 (Continued.)

Train the trainer
Videotaping
Workshops

requirements engineer and the culture of the end-user. For many organizations, a well-structured approach will be appreciated; perhaps a highly structured questionnaire. For more creative environments or ones in which the requirements are perhaps not well understood by the potential users, roleplay, storyboarding and rich pictures may prove helpful.

One important area is to find out what assumptions are in the end-user's mind. What functionality of the proposed system is so 'obvious' that it will never be stated? A simple example here would be an undo facility, a consistency of location for the exit function on the menu and so on. It is important to ascertain what presuppositions the user has in these particular areas before progressing to the specific functionality of the software to be constructed. In addition, what *non-functional requirements* are implicit, hidden or forgotten?

When more than a single user is involved (as is usual), more extensive techniques are required. Here, RAD and JAD, and their associated workshops, have been found most beneficial. Whilst it is important to ensure that the adoption of RAD/JAD is *not* seen as a permissible reason/excuse to prototype rapidly ('hack'), such workshops can bring together in a highly productive environment system analysts and users. Good sources of reference here are Graham (1995a, 1996d).

Following elicitation is a process of understanding, in conjunction with users, exactly what the implications (in terms of software) are for the satisfaction of those requirements. Here problem-solving skills are to the fore. Techniques such as simulation and CRC cards can be most useful.

Many of the techniques included in OPEN's requirements engineering group of techniques have little historical base in OT. Rather, what is needed is an interviewer/requirements engineer who has an OO mindset and can tailor questions and lines of enquiries that will permit the discovery of CIRTs with the greatest facility. Discussions should focus on responsibilities, some scenarios and concepts in the business domain. It may be dangerous to focus on data, particularly if the interviewees have been educated/trained in entity relationship modeling.

3.3 Project management and quality assurance techniques

OPEN has a significant focus (and therefore a large number of techniques) on project management and quality (testing and metrics). Project management

(PM) is, in many ways, an overlay to the whole process of building software, encompassing also business issues such as approval gaining. In this business context, before any software is even contemplated, there are a number of business decisions that have to be made. An assessment of the business problem and its likely feasible solutions (OPEN Task: Undertake feasibility study) will use techniques such as cost–benefit analysis, simulations, critical success factors, impact analysis, business process modeling and so on.

Once approval has been given for the construction of a software solution to the business domain problem, PM techniques begin to focus on planning techniques such as package (subsystem/cluster) identification and coordination together with traditional planning tools such as CPM and Gantt charts, perhaps as implemented in one of the shrink-wrapped project management software tools.

At the personal level, there are a number of techniques that have been found to enhance personal productivity in certain cases. For many software developers, an awareness of their own work strategies for success has been engendered by the application of the PSP technique, perhaps linked to SMART goals. This may also be enhanced if the organization supports the goals of an organizational quality scheme such as TQM.

PM also extends to the deployment of the software at the customer site. Here techniques such as customer (on-site) training and standard cut-over strategies need to be planned and actioned.

Under the PM umbrella are also placed V&V and metrics. In OPEN, testing is seen as an integral part of the activity objects (Graham et al., 1997b) being part of the post-condition. This means that not only software artefacts but also process elements are evaluated en route rather than post facto. Testing can, however, still be implemented at several levels: including unit (class) testing, package testing, integration testing. It can be done internally (alpha tests) or externally (beta tests) or on-site (acceptance tests). Increasingly, it is important to include specific testing strategies to address usability (OPEN Technique: Usability testing). They can be 'failure based' or 'defect based' – for example, code unit dynamic testing and code unit inspections, respectively.

As well as formal testing techniques, defect detection techniques are also advocated, based primarily on some form of static evaluation of the work product (e.g. walkthrough) which is generally highly efficacious in detecting errors at a relatively early stage. As in any teaching environment, if you are able to successfully explain your design/code/thoughts/ideas etc. to someone else, in such a manner that they fully understand (much like writing this book really!), then you can claim some sort of success. In the software context, successful acceptance by a third party suggests the artefact has good quality; errors are often discovered by the originator in the course of their explanation rather than being found by the observer. Inspections are a good example of such a technique.

Object-oriented metrics are fully supported in OPEN although we fully realize that the industry understanding of metrics and their utility is often woefully deficient. As well as advising on metrics collection programs, OPEN specifically supports as individual techniques: coupling and cohesion, complexity, connascence, reuse metrics and task points.

Other quality-focused techniques in OPEN include class naming standards, exception handling techniques, the use of formal methods, the background architecture of the GQM model (for metrics usage), rule modeling and standards compliance.

3.4 Modeling techniques for seamless analysis and design

Modeling techniques form the largest grouping of OPEN techniques. They also provide the most object-oriented flavor – many are new to OT in comparison with PM or UI techniques, for instance, which have an obvious heredity outside of OT. In this section, we 'weave together' a number of these modeling-focused tools from the OPEN Toolbox – full details are to be found in the appendices.

Modeling is representing someone's perception of a situation which can be external (a problem) or internal or conceived (a solution or design) as a system. In object modeling, we first model a business system and then a software system, at a given level of abstraction. The use of abstraction is not only one of the most central tenets of OT, but also for many one of the most difficult (Swatman, 1992). Abstraction requires the capturing of the essence of a problem and its elements – in terms of types, objects, relationships etc. – at a given level of detail or granularity.

An abstraction mindset leads to the successful introduction and use of classification. It is natural for people to group together common items in their everyday world in order to impose a cognitive or mental model of the external 'real world' in which we all exist. Indeed, some philosophers argue that since the only reality is our own cognitive perception of the world around us – and each of us constructs our cognitive map independently and differently – then the real world has no unique (or 'real') meaning or existence! Children classify objects into the same class – for instance my left black sock and my right black sock are both classified correctly as sock. Only after the age of three years (Lakoff, 1987) does it become possible to make the next step of classifying socks, trousers, vests etc. as items of clothing. A parallel skill is then to be able to answer correctly the question: 'Which is the odd item out of the list: Stephen Hawking, Alfred Nobel, Isaac Newton and Albert Einstein?'[†].

This skill of classification to a higher abstraction level leads to the notion of generalization – identifying a superclass or supertype, which may often be an abstract class in OO jargon (i.e. one with no instances), but which captures the essence of a shared concept. As noted in Martin and Odell (1992), only *shared* concepts have value – in life or in OO – a 'concept' unique to an individual is no concept.

[†] This was asked of a team on the Good News Week TV quiz show in Australia to celebrate 1997 Science Week. The 'answer on the card' turned out to be Newton as the other three were concerned with 'big bangs'. Of course this answer is incorrect as all Trekkies know – only Nobel did not appear in the Star Trek episode 'Descent, part 1'.

Concepts and abstractions focus on the external view – how an object is seen, what it is responsible for knowing and how it behaves. Responsibilities, introduced by Wirfs-Brock *et al.* (1990), represent high level abstractions of integrated state and behavior. As illustration, consider the CIRT to represent a horse. This can be done by using:

- the *data-driven* approach which describes a horse in terms of its parts: head, tail, body, leg(4)
- the *procedural* approach which describes a horse in terms of operations it can perform: walk, run, trot, bite, eat, neigh
- the *responsibility-driven* approach which describes a horse in terms of its responsibilities: communicate, carry things, maintain its living systems.

A data-driven approach tends to be very evolutionary, as exemplified in methods such as OMT and Fusion. Whilst OMT does not prevent the developer from identifying 'behavior' during analysis, all examples are data-focused. The Coad and Yourdon methodology has a similar data-driven focus. Fusion, on the other hand, *does* mandate that only data are considered during analysis. The use of a data-driven ('OO') methodology such as these may, if used by an unskilled developer, lead to traditional entity-relationship models rather than true object models. In a true object model, behavior (as exemplified by responsibilities) tends to be more equally distributed among CIRTs – this was amply demonstrated in a recent metrics study (Sharble and Cohen, 1993) in which the data-driven design (DDD) was shown to be of a lower quality (as measured by their set of metrics) than the responsibility-driven design (RDD).

Methods, other than OPEN, which have a responsibility focus include RDD, OBA, MOSES, SOMA and BON. These are all well supported by the contracting metaphor, as used in RDD, BON and OPEN.

Whilst both a DDD and a RDD approach can work, particularly in the hands of a skilled developer, we have generally found that novices prefer a RDD. Indeed, it has been found that a responsibility-driven approach is more than useful in teaching undergraduate students the OO paradigm. Whilst permitting DDD, we strongly recommend a RDD focus to your development strategy. Whilst a responsibility-driven design focuses on an holistic approach at the model building level, a contract-driven approach takes that one level higher and applies those ideas to the lifecycle process itself. The objects representing activities have both responsibilities and contracts: pre- and post-conditions controlling the overall development process (Chapter 1).

Responsibilities can be identified from requirements, elicited by techniques such as CRC or roleplays and can be categorized[†] as either (a) responsibilities for knowing; (b) responsibilities for doing; and (c) responsibilities for enforcing. These are then implemented by one or more operations in the CIRT interface

---

† We guess stereotyped is the current jargon word for this!

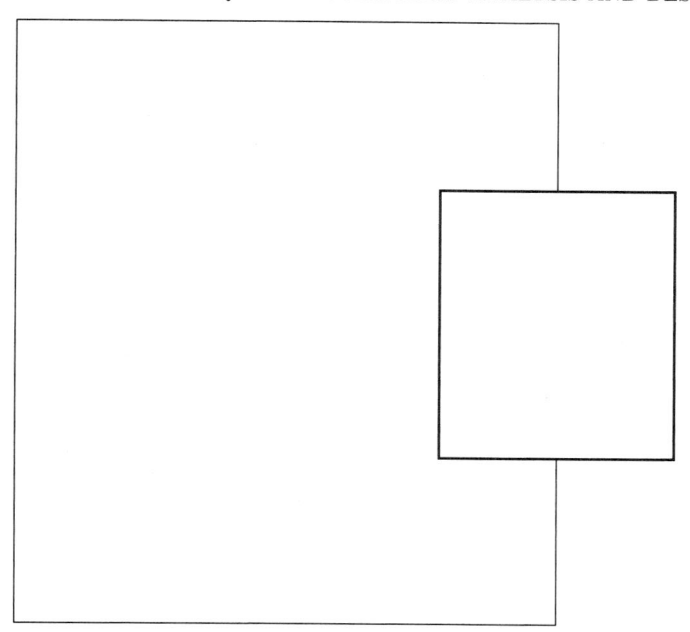

Figure 3.1 Icons straddling a boundary give a visual representation of public availability.

(see Figure 2.3 in Chapter 2). Operations in the interface then link smoothly across to one or more (often only one) methods in the code (Figure 2.4).

By focusing on the interface, as should all good application developers, we are also focusing on another key element of object technology: encapsulation/information hiding. Encapsulation is a boundary – it may be transparent, translucent or opaque. Information hiding requires an opaque encapsulation in which only those details of the coded class which are reflected in the externally available services (operations and (logical) attributes) or, at a higher level, external responsibilities can be seen from outside the class. These details, together with the class name, constitute the interface. They should be supplemented by responsibilities for enforcing linked to internal rulesets. This is well depicted in the old Booch icon, used today only for component and deployment diagrams in UML, often known as the 'Gradygram' (Figure 3.1). The visual representation of 'information' straddling a CIRT's boundary, providing a window or conduit to the inside, is readily comprehensible. This visualization was also used in UON (Page-Jones *et al.*, 1990) and MOSES (Henderson-Sellers and Edwards, 1994a) and is used in various diagram types in COMN (Firesmith *et al.*, 1997).

Good OO design is thus highly modular. CIRTs have restricted interfaces detailed by their responsibilities – data (attributes) and methods are coding decisions, not of OOAD concern. Each CIRT thus identifies, encapsulates and fully represents a single concept in the domain *at the current abstraction level*. As abstraction levels change during the OPEN process as more and more detail is added†, more CIRTs will be identified, some CIRTs will be found to be aggregates and thus decomposable into their parts.

CIRT identification may rely on any one (or in fact more than one) of several techniques including textual analysis, task analysis, use case evaluation, from state transition diagrams or CRC roleplay exercises. It is rare for anyone to be able to identify concepts alone. Our view of the world is interactive and dynamic; our design of the software system is also implicitly dynamic. Simply offering services or declaring responsibilities reminds us of John Donne's 'No CIRT is an island'‡. CIRTs are only of value if they interact. Thus in identifying concepts it is almost inevitable that we concurrently think about how they interact.

In OT, the most frequent interactions to be modeled are binary – they involve only two CIRTs. In OOAD, relationships are usually established between classes or types although these relationships are (except for generalization/inheritance) actually surrogates for instance–instance links. In early stages of building the object model, the emphasis will be on mappings/associations some of which may be usefully modeled as aggregations (composition structures) or containment. Later, as knowledge is gained and refined, generalization/specialization will be used increasingly to create inheritance structures. Also, usage structures are elaborated as inter-object communication patterns unfold.

Some associations will be explicitly represented as mappings (OPEN default is a one-way mapping); others will be better represented as properties or attributes. Indeed, associations and attributes are virtually interchangeable (see OPEN Technique: Transformations of the object model) – at least during the modeling activity in which the object model is constructed. In OOAD, aggregations model whether the relationship is configurational, homeomerous and invariant (Odell, 1994a). Whilst seven commonly occurring combinations with these binary characteristics occur, four can be grouped into a configurational aggregate (whole–part) and three into membership (Henderson-Sellers, 1997a).

An additional relationship of topological inclusion (Odell, 1994a) or containment (Firesmith *et al.*, 1997; Henderson-Sellers, 1997a) reflects elements in a container which bear no whole–part connotations. The seven (stereotyped§ to two) whole–part relationships (aggregation or composition) say nothing about ownership, lifetime dependency and the like. These characteristics are certainly relevant in coding (see Firesmith and Henderson-Sellers, 1998a) – here aggregations reflect asymmetrical, whole–part usually configurational connexions which support method propagation and exhibit one or more emergent properties (Parsons and Wand, 1997a).

In all interactions, particularly associations and aggregations, the responsibility is a high-level statement related to the service(s) that is to be provided.

---

† OPEN is an elaborational method, along with Booch, OMT, OOSE, RDD etc.
‡ Sorry for the misquote, but the real phrase is too gender specific!
§ We just love that word! [Don't check it in a dictionary or you'll be confused.]

This must be supplemented by a set of rules which govern that service provision. This is known as 'software contracting' (e.g. Meyer, 1988, 1992c).

The objective is to clearly document the meaning of services and responsibilities. A contract may be specified at two levels (Low *et al.*, 1995): at the 'method' level following Meyer or at a higher level following RDD – in which a contract is regarded as a 'set of related responsibilities' (e.g. Wirfs-Brock and McKean, 1996). Contracts and responsibilities are thus *not* synonyms – although they are often confused (e.g. Rational, 1997a).

Contracts were a focus of MOSES and in BON these ideas were stressed even more forcefully. OPEN consolidates these ideas and confirms the value of contracts, not only in building the object model but also as an important and integral part of the lifecycle model.

Contracts are realized in terms of pre-conditions, post-conditions and invariants. These may be specified at any time in OOAD. Quite often they are application specific and are clarified late in the software development lifecycle (SDLC); sometimes they are the most obviously identified characteristics and provide the nucleus for the CIRT derivation. Sometimes, invariants will be appropriate for general CIRTs but it is important for the designer to question the specificity of the constraint at all times. One technique is to develop an abstract class, with more general invariants, and a subclass for the more specific application invariants. In this way, the general pattern of CIRT relationships is available for reuse in other applications.

Invariants may appear directly in the requirements document where property values are limited to certain ranges or as invariants on relationships. Alternatively, the use of STDs may highlight further invariants, especially upon the operations. Invariants are useful for ensuring that parameter values in a model are reasonable and that relationships are realistic – further support for ensuring the production of high quality software.

Invariants can thus be viewed as post-conditions of all services of a CIRT. A request for a value of a property must occur when the invariant is satisfied and, since properties do not change the state of an object, only report it, the invariant must also be satisfied after the request. During implementation, properties may be viewed as queries on the state that simply report the value of the physical attributes. They do not, therefore, change the state of the CIRT.

The invariants describe, or constrain, the CIRT properties to be of certain values. Constraints on the properties can always be modeled by defining a separate CIRT which constrains all its instances to be in the defined state. For example, a property that returns an *INTEGER* value may be constrained to values between 10 and 20. This constraint could be modeled by a separate CIRT called, for example, *CONSTRAINED_INTEGER* which only returned values of between 10 and 20. The property of the original CIRT could, instead of being modeled as a CIRT *INTEGER*, be modeled as a CIRT *CONSTRAINED_INTEGER*. The decision on whether to introduce a separate CIRT to describe this constraint is in the hands of the modeler and will depend upon issues such as understandability, complexity and reusability. Constraints on the properties, although redundant in some sense, are useful elements that can be employed effectively in modeling

CIRTs.

Although the idea of an invariant was originally introduced into the OO community by Meyer (1988) in his description of the language Eiffel, it provides significantly more than a language feature, being an important way of specifying constraints on classes rather than individual operations (e.g. Masotti, 1991; Kilov, 1992). Invariants should therefore be declared explicitly rather than hidden within operation definitions. The constraint clause may become quite large and may be hidden at various resolutions by a suitable tool for simplicity of presentation. Its presence, however, is important in that it provides a way of specifying important semantic constraints on the class.

Good OO design focuses on associations, mappings, dependencies and usage (depending upon your choice of metamodel). Good OO design adds detail, as the process continues, by means of aggregations, transformations (e.g. attributes to associations) etc. A good designer will defer his/her use of generalization – unless the domain is well understood and a knowledge hierarchy easily and safely constructed. We have seen too many poor designs result from premature use of inheritance.

Generalization is the safest and most useful form of inheritance since it supports polymorphism and design reuse. It maps to specialization inheritance in the working system. On the other hand, a second 'flavor' of inheritance, specification inheritance, supports type substitutability but is weaker than the is-a-kind-of specialization inheritance in the context of design reuse (knowledge representation). Finally, implementation inheritance should only be used in the context of optimization of design/code since it mitigates strongly against reuse at the application developers' level.

Inheritance structures may also include multiple specializations. This network structure is harder to maintain and understand and multiple inheritance should only be used when necessary. [The analogy we like to use is that of a chainsaw – great for sawing down trees (the difficult jobs) but highly dangerous if used for more mundane tasks such as pencil sharpening.] Indeed, we would go even further and suggest that inheritance itself (as single inheritance), whilst being a 'trademark' of an OO system, should be used sparingly. There are many cases when it is the first, unthinking modeling option. In reality, reuse is better served in many of these cases by delegation/subcontracting/collaborations. Some useful reminders of this necessary balance in using different techniques for different jobs are given in texts by Page-Jones (1995) and Riel (1996).

Finally, when using inheritance to represent partitioning, it is all too easy to use multiple partitioning criteria simultaneously. This can lead to true specialization relationships when viewed singly, but that any one instance *must* belong to more than one subclass (Figure 3.2). In this case, the use of discriminators (q.v.) is suggested – although it should be noted that this is a modeling technique that translates poorly into code. This problem occurs when it is assumed implicitly that *all* classes must be related by an inheritance relationship. Sensible use of collaborations and properties (attributes, associations etc.) would often provide a better object model (Figure 3.3).

One frequent error is the use of inheritance to represent an apparent

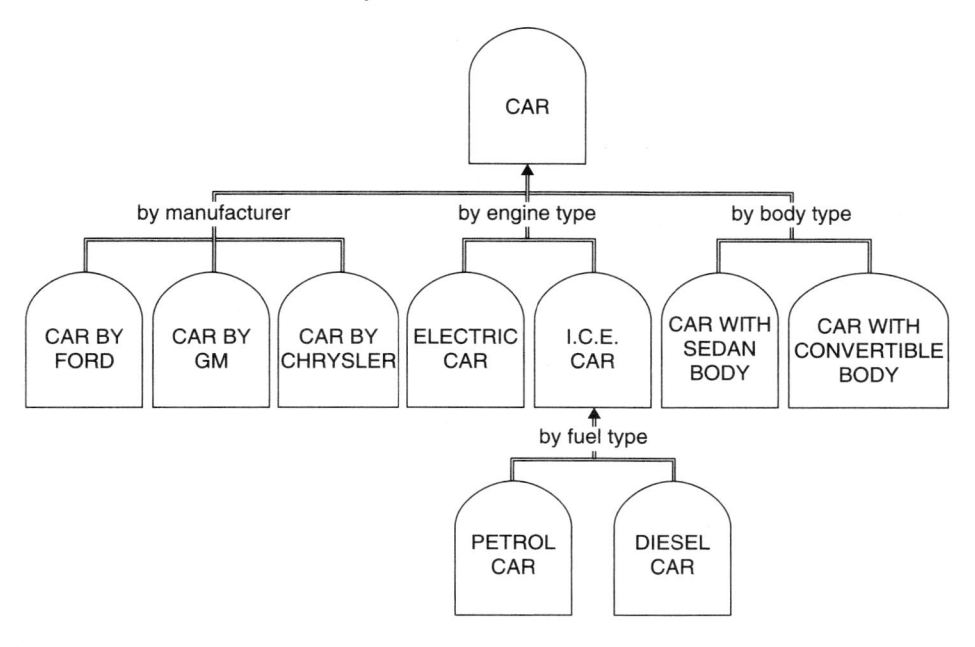

Figure 3.2 Explicit depiction of multidimensional classification/specialization criteria being used to classify the hierarchical model (adapted from McGregor and Korson, 1993).

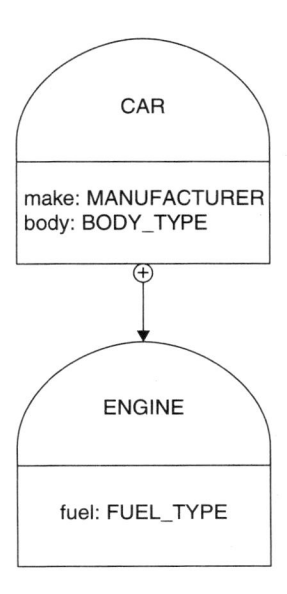

Figure 3.3 Remodeling the hierarchy by use of aggregation rather than inheritance. Here the connexion between *CAR* and *ENGINE* is shown.

is-a-kind-of knowledge structure (specialization inheritance) when a more appropriate modeling technique would be that of roles. Discussed initially by, for example, Reenskaug *et al.* (1992), Renouf and Henderson-Sellers (1995), Wieringa *et al.* (1995), the important role of roles has been recognized in the publication of the OOram method (Reenskaug *et al.*, 1996) and the incorporation into the UML and OML metamodels. Essentially, a role is a temporary object classification in the sense of an instance, say of type *PERSON*, temporarily adding an additional classification, say *EMPLOYEE* and *COMMUTER*. Consider an instance of type *PERSON*, Margaret. Between 8 and 9 a.m., she is a commuter, between 9 and 5 an employee and between 5 and 5.45 a commuter again. Yet all the day she remains a person. Using subtypes to model this would be inappropriate since it would lead to an instance of subtype *COMMUTER* (the instance Margaret in fact) moving, at 9 o'clock, to become an instance of subtype *EMPLOYEE*. Such temporary migration between subclasses can be indicative of the need for role modeling.

Furthermore, since Margaret is a commuter for only a short period of time and then stops being a commuter, it is reasonable to say that for each instance of person, there are two instances of commuter during the day. So roles are temporary reclassification but, perhaps more importantly, are additional classifications rather than a change of classification – for instance between *EMPLOYEE* and *RETIRED*. Roles occur frequently in real life. Role modeling is a software technique of representing that reality in the software design.

The dynamic side of OO modeling may be seen in user interactions with the system (use cases), in the state–transition descriptions of how a single class (or more strictly interfaces belonging to a single class) handles events or in the way that a small group of CIRTs may collaborate together to fulfil a single service request by delegation, subcontracting and inter-CIRT collaborations. Indeed, many such designs could be regarded as patterns, a topic of immense value to realize a component software industry.

Collaborations may be documented by collaboration diagrams which show sequences of message sends (service invocations) laid out in a similar visualization to a class diagram/semantic net. The same diagram types can also be used to document use cases, scenarios and task scripts. Whilst no unique[†] definition of use cases exists, they can be understood as describing how a system functions from the (external) user's viewpoint.

Use cases (and their variants) have many uses. They may be useful in eliciting and describing user requirements; they may help in the identification of CIRTs or, conversely, be identified from the CIRTs and the semantic net and collaboration diagrams; they may be useful in directing the testing program.

Whilst it is generally (and loosely) agreed that a scenario is an instance of a use case and that a use case is an instance of an essential use case, it is also proposed that a task script is a generified use case (Graham, 1997a). OML suggests an abstract metatype of SCENARIO_CLASS with subtypes of TASK_SCRIPTS, USE_CASE and MECHANISM. Exact definitions are cur-

---

† Cockburn (1997a) identifies 24 commonly used variants.

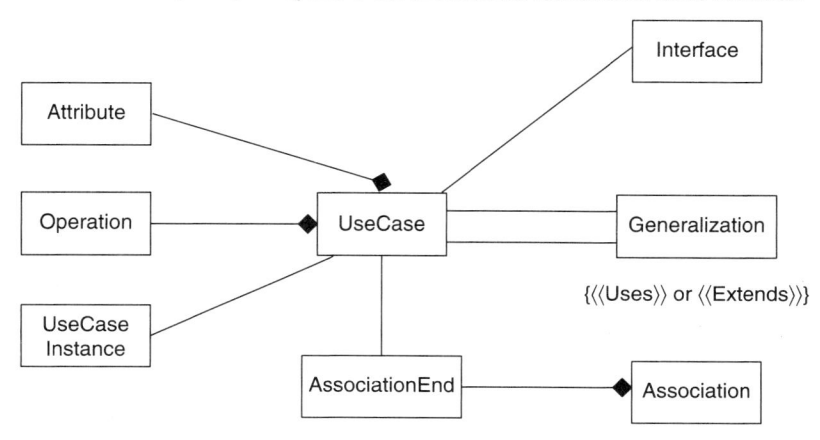

Figure 3.4 OMG/UML Version 1.1 metamodel for use cases (after OMG, 1997a).

rently being sought, although the current metamodels (OMG, 1997a; Firesmith *et al.*, 1997) and discussions (e.g. Graham, 1997a; Cockburn, 1997a) do not promise to offer conclusive agreement immediately. Indeed, UML Version 1.1 (OMG, 1997a) provides yet another take on this. In the metamodel shown in Figure 3.4, we see a UseCase modeled as an object with attributes and operations and association to AssociationEnds.

Whilst many authors have embraced use cases as part of their methods, it must be remembered that

- they show functionality. Decomposition could too easily lead, not to objects, but to detailed DFDs (e.g. Firesmith, 1995b). Decomposition of task scripts is argued (e.g. Graham, 1995a, 1996c) to lead to an identifiable end-point in the *atomic task script*, thus providing a more reliable modeling technique
- there is no obvious way to 'find the object' directly from a use case. Techniques for converting use cases to objects are little different to those aimed at finding objects directly from the requirements documents. Whilst this is not surprising, care is required
- there are still many 'dialects' which foils inter-communication between development groups.

Some methodologists advocate that their methods should be totally usecase driven (e.g. Jacobson, 1996). We beg to differ. Use cases (and their alternatives) need to be an integral part of a method – as they were in MOSES, SOMA and Firesmith and continue to be in OPEN. In fact, one software tool supporting SOMA, SOMATiK, *generates* use cases.

Finally, a word on stereotypes might be apposite. The word, in a linguistic sense, suggests something representative – sometimes pejoratively. In OT, its meaning has been changed to mean a temporary metalevel subclassification.

In OOSE (Jacobson *et al.*, 1992), CIRTs are either controller objects, entity objects or interface objects. These stereotype labels indicate the superset to which the object belongs. This approach is merely a convenient way of dividing up objects following a 'divide and conquer' style. There is nothing sacrosanct in these classification categories and no impact on the semantics or implementation styles implied. Following Wirfs-Brock's (1994) discussion on OO stereotypes[†], the concept has been embodied in the UML approach to modeling. Stereotypes are applied liberally as means of extending the concepts as portrayed in the UML metamodel.

Whilst providing much-vaunted extensibility (an important aim of the metamodel), excessive use of stereotyping runs the risk of different developers producing overlapping or ill-defined classifications. In fact, this leads to the identical problem observed by McGregor and Korson (1993) in their introduction of the discriminant – used later in MOSES, OML and UML (see discussion above regarding Figures 3.2 and 3.3).

As well as classes, some relationships are suggested as ripe for stereotyping. OMG (1997a) encourages the use of the ≪uses≫ and ≪extends≫ stereotypes on the dependency relationship between use cases. Such predetermination probably offers more advantages than the unstructured stereotypes of classes. Indeed, in UML (but not in OML), the implementation face of a class (the internal view), an abstract class, an interface and a 'type' are all presented as stereotypes on CLASS (in the metamodel). In the OML metamodel extension to this pending OMG standard, each of these is represented by a concept, i.e. by a metatype in the metamodel (Figure 2.2).

3.5 Techniques for database design and construction

Many of the OPEN database techniques have roots in traditional database (Case *et al.*, 1996). Establishing requirements for reliability, transactions and storage volumes, clustering, access analysis and audit requirements are similar. There is some slight dependency here on the type of database chosen. We assume that the choice to be made is between a relational database (RDB), an object relational database and an objectbase (OB) – OPEN technique: DBMS type selection. In the latter case, the mapping of the design model to the database itself is clear. Objects created in the application are smoothly mapped into the objectbase and, in reverse, are readily restored from database to memory.

Object-relational database systems combine the advantages of object-oriented programming languages with relational programming features (Chamberlin, 1996) such as views and high-level procedural languages. Whilst significant progress has been made in implementing such systems, features such as inheritance, polymorphism and extensibility of interfaces are not always supported

---

† Whilst this paper introduced the term 'stereotype', the idea of grouping objects into a small number of classifications is seen in much earlier works (e.g. Budd, 1991, page 23; Jacobson *et al.*, 1992, page 134).

in current releases of object-relational databases. Object-relational databases have the advantage that existing corporate data continue to be directly accessible whilst supporting the OO paradigm.

Where objects can be stored directly in an object-relational database, consideration should be given to implementing OO features currently not supported by the database. Technique: Mapping to RDB provides guidance in the event that it is decided to utilize an RDB or the relational side of an object-relational database.

3.6 Techniques for distributed architectures

Many contemporary systems are built to operate in a distributed or client–server (hardware) environment where the hardware nodes are physically disparate. There are many support issues such as the acquisition of an appropriate bandwidth and connectivity, probably using an Object Request Broker (ORB) architecture.

Specific OOAD techniques, as exemplified in OPEN and first discussed in Low *et al.* (1996), focus on ways to add distribution to the design. The basic idea is that in documenting such issues of distribution, the notation for DCS can be regarded very much as an overlay on to the existing design. This notation then adds information about virtual and actual nodes, migration between nodes and so on. One of the major areas of concern is that of partitioning and allocation (Low and Rasmussen, 1998). Partitioning refers to the division of the system into logical groupings or partitions and allocation is the technique of allocating these partitions to specific hardware nodes.

The OPEN Technique: Implementation of distributed aspects of system then offers support for the coding side of a distributed system.

3.7 Techniques for user interface design

User interface (design for usability, usability testing and coding techniques) has been sadly neglected in the OO literature. Since this text is not an HCI text (see, for example, Cooper, 1995), it mainly discusses issues to be drawn to the developer's attention. It is clear that these issues are at the same time (a) important and (b) often ignored for expediency. OT is a technology that can bring benefits of quality to the software industry. A major component of quality, at least as far as the user is concerned, is usability. For a successful software industry, it is thus crucial to focus on the quality of the user interface. Here we discuss mainly issues of the use of color, the presentation of different dialog options and the technique of screen painting. Testing, as with all other elements of OPEN, is an integral part of the OPEN framework – hence the specific inclusion of a technique: Usability testing.

3.8 Reuse strategies and supporting techniques

Reuse is an integral part of OPEN. There are issues of technical concern and issues of managerial concern. It has been argued that many of the technical issues are solved and it is really the NIH[†] syndrome that is the problem.

CIRTs designed for a single project tend not to represent the totality of the concept they are modeling. The characteristics included will be those pertinent to the current project rather than to the intension. For reuse, classes (and other artefacts) need to be complete, highly tested and robust (among other things). Techniques such as Completion of abstractions and Revision of inheritance hierarchies are relevant here. These focus on, firstly, creating a full and complete specification of the concept and secondly on the likely modifications to the inheritance hierarchy to permit a more flexible representation of concepts in the problem domain. Addition of genericity (Technique: Genericity specification) can also be useful here.

Reuse is not merely at the class level; indeed some observers are now claiming that class reuse is all but irrelevant and that the only realistic level for reuse is via patterns, mechanisms, components and frameworks.

Creation of reusable artefacts is one thing (OPEN Task: Create and/or identify reusable components ('for reuse')); finding existing components requires a totally different set of techniques (OPEN Task: Optimize reuse ('with reuse') and Task: Manage library of reusable components). If developers cannot identify an appropriate artefact *rapidly*, then they will not reuse it but will redevelop it from scratch. Thus it is important that artefacts are not only well cataloged (OPEN Technique: CIRT indexing) but that tools exist to locate these stored artefacts (for one example, see Thorne, 1997).

On the PM side of reuse, we need to consider how the quality of reusable artefacts destined for storage in the company library can be assessed. Quality metrics (coupling, cohesion, complexity etc.) are available and new reuse metrics have been proposed but not yet tested (OPEN Technique: Reuse measurement). Another important element is a person responsible for the quality of the library. This important role necessitates both a reactive and a proactive response: accepting and checking artefacts proposed for inclusion in the library together with the active encouragement of the provision of such classes and encouragement to (re)use them in later projects.

The hardest part seems to be how to implement a 'rewards' strategy that will encourage a reuse mindset. Many obvious such strategies are open to abuse. For instance, 'royalty' payments to developers may be made on the basis of how often a class they have contributed is used by others (friends can easily be cajoled/entreated to use these 'as a favor') or on the extent to which the classes in the current project have been extracted from the library (ditto). Some newer ideas are currently being investigated as a subproject under the 'OPEN banner'.

[†] Not Invented Here.

3.9 Coding styles and implementation techniques

OOAD produces a design that is essentially programming language independent. Detailed design, particularly of the internal implementation design of operations (as methods), and the ensuing coding into the chosen language, are all issues of 'coding' (a.k.a. implementation). There are a number of OPEN techniques which give advice on coding issues.

When coding, the focus of the development team switches from consideration of the interface (the type aspect of the CIRT) to the internal viewpoint (the class implementation). Operations in the interface are now implemented or realized by a method (member function in C++, for example) in the code. Firstly, it may be necessary to design the way that a particular method is to be constructed. Since C++, Eiffel and Java (and less so, Smalltalk) are essentially object-oriented *procedural* programming languages, then the way in which the code is structured internally to a method is indeed procedural in nature. Consequently, it is generally believed that designing such methods simply requires the application of traditional structured design techniques *but at a much smaller scale* than occurs in a traditional, structured programming development environment. Thus, one might anticipate seeing structures such as loops, if/then/else, case/switch statements and linear series of assignment statements. *However*, whilst conventional wisdom suggests that in C++ (for instance) such a piece of procedural code to implement a single method may be 20–30 lines long, more recent evidence (Haynes and Henderson-Sellers, 1996, 1997) shows that in *all* OOPLs, the typical method size in well-written OO code is 2–3 lines long only. In other words, good C++ style should be not 'C style' but 'Smalltalk style'. If this observation is repeated and upheld, then the OPEN Technique: Class internal design will fade into insignificance.

Implementation (coding) of services (or characteristics) and structure is in terms of methods, properties (exceptions, links, parts, attributes, entries and members) and assertions (pre-conditions, post-conditions and invariants) – Figure 2.4. Some of these are truly hidden or private; whilst others cross the boundary and are, in fact, public operations (there should be no public properties: Wirfs-Brock and Wilkerson, 1989a). It is important to note that the `public` section of a class should include only those methods which provide its interface – and this should be minimal, according to the purpose of the abstraction. Data attributes should never be `public` (in C++, it is possible to provide inlined `public` methods to access attributes, in any case). In C++ in particular, there is a third category of visibility: `protected`. Whether to mark attributes as `private` or `protected` is a difficult decision. There are two common coding practices:

(1) in systems that rely more on composition than inheritance, make all data attributes `private`

(2) in systems that rely heavily on inheritance, make all data attributes `protected`, so that descendants may easily access them.

In the first style, data are strongly encapsulated, so that only the declaring class may access them directly. This means that any descendant, although it inherits the data attribute, cannot access it. If the descendant needs access, it is common to define **protected** access methods in the original class. If systems make heavy use of inheritance, this can lead to code-bloat, with many internal access methods. In this case, it is more sensible to decide to make all data **protected** (the second style).

The notion of visibility relates both to what features are seen as part of the class interface, i.e. what are external responsibilities or external services; and also the extent to which other classes are permitted to see, and hence have access rights to, this particular class. Objects are visible to each other when they are in the same scope, i.e. within the same namespace. Fusion (Coleman *et al.*, 1994) contains a richer family of visibility relationships: reference lifetime, server visibility, server binding and reference mutability. These may be useful for detailed design decisions but are not formally part of OPEN.

Finally, it is sometimes the case that several public methods rely on a common algorithm – for example, insertion, removal and membership testing in a **Set** class may involve a common searching operation. This may be made into a **private** (or **protected**) internal method, reducing the size of the code overall. However, a review should be conducted of classes that acquire too many internal methods of this kind. Often this indicates a class hiding a functional abstraction, which should really be conceived differently, with the behavior distributed over several objects.

Related to the same encapsulation theme are the notions of **friends** in C++ (Stroustrup, 1991) and selective exporting in Eiffel (Meyer, 1992a; 1997). C++ originally provided the **friend** mechanism to allow a class to break its own encapsulation selectively, for the sake of efficiency. A class may declare another class, a method, or a global function to be a **friend**, meaning that this program component is trusted and has privileged access rights to the internals of the declaring class. In principle, **friend** declarations should only be used as a last resort. However, certain language limitations in C++ have led to **friend** declarations being commonly used in three identifiable situations:

(1) to circumvent bounds-checks in operations involving two different class abstractions, e.g. multiplication of a **Vector** and a **Matrix**

(2) to extend the interface of library classes not available to the developer, e.g. overloading **operator >>** and **operator <<**, conceptually members of the **iostream** classes, to read and write new user-defined classes

(3) to enable automatic type conversion, by replacing binary methods, which normally block type conversion, with global friend functions, e.g. global overloads of **operator +**, **operator -**, which access inside **Vector** and **Matrix**.

Eiffel provides a flexible export mechanism which is the dual of friends – instead of breaking encapsulation, it offers selective interfaces to different clients.

By default, every feature is public; however,

feature{*NONE*}

makes the following declarations secret (equivalent to protected), and

feature{*CLASSA, CLASSB*}

makes the following declarations accessible only to the named classes.

Stylistic guidelines for different languages are emerging. These are often referred to as the 'idioms' of that particular language. Some more general guidelines for 'good coding' are to be found in the Law of Demeter which is aimed at the preservation of encapsulation. It was formulated by Lieberherr *et al.* (1988) and later revised by Lieberherr and Holland (1989) and is a form of voluntary design restriction, which prohibits the sending of messages to certain categories of objects from within methods. The need for such a law arises mostly in languages which pass objects by reference, such as Smalltalk, Eiffel or Java. In these languages, it is possible, by some combination of message expressions, for an object to obtain access to part of another object (a sub-object) and cause this to be altered, without the permission of the owning object. The intent of the law is to force all messages to sub-objects to pass through the interface of the owning object first, which then delegates the request to the sub-object (see Technique: Delegation).

Other design/coding decisions include whether to store information or to recalculate it on each method invocation. As an example, consider the characteristic/property of a class which gives an enquirer the current balance of a bank account. The value of the balance object to be returned to the client object could be stored as an attribute of the bank account object. Alternatively, what is stored may be a transaction history, probably since the last bank statement was issued. The current balance is thus calculated anew each time the *balance* operation/service is requested as *previous balance* $+ \sum$ *recent transactions*.

The use of a distributed system also forces certain coding decisions. For instance, using an ORB focuses attention closely on the interface and possibly on IDL considerations – inheritance is no longer as important since what is important is the interface and services provided by the CIRT in question. Design decisions regarding virtual and actual nodes need to be implemented, as does code to implement asynchronous or synchronous message passing sequences. It is likely that concurrent threads will be created and coded.

3.10 Some useful techniques in training and education

For someone embroiled in education on a day-to-day basis, many of the OPEN techniques will be obvious. They are not specific to OT but to adult learning. They include those with a technology focus, for example computer- and WWW-based self-training courses, through traditional lectures to more interactive elements such as workshops, group problem solving and roleplay.

Perhaps the most crucial element, as observed by almost all writers, is that the investment in training should not be skimped. Goldberg and Rubin (1995) suggest that the training investment needs to be around 40 days per year and that it takes a typical developer around 18 months to migrate their mindset from a traditional one to an object-oriented one. Of course, as more universities teach object concepts from day one, this training curve will be alleviated and only specifics (e.g. a specific methodology, specific tool or specific programming language) will need to be learned on the job. However, at least for the next few years, education and training are needed to assist in migrating existing (often very successful) software development shops from a structured (e.g. COBOL) and/or 4GL programming environment into an OO environment in which not only is an OO language used but so, most importantly, is a process-focused, full lifecycle OO methodology which integrates business issues with technology and project management issues[†].

Finally, until the dearth of good OO developers and consultants is alleviated, one important element of training is a 'train the trainer' program.

---

† As you might have guessed, we think that OPEN is a prime candidate here!

Chapter 4
The future of OOAD and OPEN

4.1 OOAD in the future: towards convergence

Many of the ideas underpinning object-oriented analysis and design are stabilizing rapidly. At the same time, increasing use of OT will identify problems that users need to solve that are not currently supported in any OOAD approach. The field of OOAD must therefore still grow. New relationships will be identified, evaluated for usefulness and either accepted or rejected. For instance, proposals have been made for relationships of ownership (Yang et al., 1995) and for assimilation (Kathuria and Subramaniam, 1996). Only time will tell if these have real usefulness for the industry.

In addition, the plethora of OO methodologies in the early 1990s is beginning to shrink to a small number – perhaps three or four. Many will simply be tailored versions of de facto standards. For instance, as we have discussed in this book, OPEN is a tailorable framework standard within which customized versions will exist for your individual industry or as provided by international methodologists in book form (see other titles in the OPEN Series of books).

There will be an increasing emphasis on process – if we didn't believe this we wouldn't have needed to write these books on OPEN! OPEN will continue to provide the most comprehensive, industry/business-focused OO process. Members of the OPEN Consortium will also be leaders in any initiative of the Object Management Group in the process area. Whilst this seems inevitable to many of us, both within and outside the Consortium, the likely timescale is far from clear.

There is likely to be a wider adoption of OT from hitherto untouched industry sectors. More applications will be critical to the mainstream core business and no longer small, stand-alone, value-added systems. This means that the twin issues of legacy code (mostly COBOL in the business domain) and relational databases will need to be addressed more seriously, along with the use of 4GLs. The problem of integrating so-called legacy systems into an OO future will be further exacerbated by the need to re-engineer early legacy OO systems (Casais, 1998).

At a more prosaic level, the OPEN Consortium, in its further evolution of the metamodel and notational elements (OML), will accept, endorse and improve

86   THE FUTURE OF OOAD AND OPEN

the OMG metamodel as far as is possible but if the product (currently called UML) fails in any areas (as the current version does in its support for a truly responsibility-driven approach), we will continue to forge ahead with full support for quality OO ideas, inside or outside of the 'industry standard' that the OMG is trying to promulgate.

Whilst no-one can predict the future, we anticipate both parallel and collaborative development of OML and OMG/UML in the metamodel and notation arena. We expect a small number of groupings of real methods. Obviously there will be a group focused on UML-compatible tasks and techniques, particularly those with a use-case-driven process flavor. OPEN will continue to offer full process support and will look for opportunities to work with other non-aligned methodologists who are currently remaining independent of these two large groupings (OPEN Consortium and the UML Partners). The transformational approach advocated by Sally Shlaer and Steve Mellor will probably continue to market itself as a distinct alternative to both a UML/use-case-driven and an OPEN focus – but could merge itself into one of these two mainstream approaches.

4.2   OPEN-ing the dOOr to the future

The creation of OPEN as a collaborative, process-focused third-generation OO methodology is one element towards quality industry support for 'real' OO software engineering. It opens a door to the future for software developers who are concerned with increasing the maturity of their software development environment – perhaps by focusing on their ascendance through the five levels of the Capability Maturity Model (CMM). After all, CMM level 3 accords with the use of a process. Further sophistication requires the use of that methodology to monitor and control the development process. OPEN offers the methodological support to enable an industry to move to these higher CMM levels.

Further work on OPEN will focus on further improvements to the process methodological framework and, in particular, the construction of 'pre-packaged advice' on tailoring the process to particular industry domains. There still needs to be an even greater emphasis on usability and user-interface design, on requirements engineering and on the liaison between OO requirements engineers and OO software builders. Finally, there will be investigations on whether a formal underpinning using, say, Object-Z will provide benefit to the industry.

4.3   Final summary

Perhaps the hardest challenge for an OO software engineer is to make the right choices. In terms of process, clearly the OPEN process framework is a suitable choice for many, primarily because of its flexibility and tailorability. However, having selected process in terms of activities and tasks, there is the important concern about which techniques are most useful. In this book we have described not only all the available OO techniques but have also given advice on their pluses and minuses, where and when they do work and don't work. Some techniques may be more useful only to the sophisticated designer, some are more experimental. We have indicated some of these rankings throughout the book, particularly in terms of our 'star rating' on techniques and also the collection of some of the more experimental techniques in one place (CD: Appendix C).

We hope you will choose wisely – and have success (and fun!) in developing OO software solutions to your business problems.

Appendices

Details of the OPEN techniques (in alphabetical order)

These appendices form a reference section and should be treated as such. Ordering is alphabetical, as in any dictionary or reference tome. Each technique is described in a logical way, laid out under identical headings of:

Technique: <Name>   Star rating <*/**/***>

Focus:
Typical tasks for which this is needed: [in alphabetical order]
Related techniques: [in alphabetical order]
Input (pre-condition):
Underpinning concepts: [entries here are either references to entries in Appendix E on the CD (lead caps) or plain text explanations (lead lower case)]

Technique description

Technique usage [not relevant in Appendix D]

Deliverables and outputs (post-condition)

Individual techniques appear in Appendix A and groups of techniques in Appendix B. We give each technique a 'star rating' which expresses (roughly) the industry's 'level of confidence' in the knowledge represented:

    *** well-tried

    ** reasonably well validated

    * experimental or not well understood

Those *really* experimental techniques are doubly highlighted by being placed in a separate section on the CD (Appendix C). These should not be regarded in any way as of secondary importance; rather they are not at present 'mainstream

OPEN', not being quite as well tested. Appendix D lists those techniques which are more appropriate in a non-OO environment but which can, with care, be used successfully for OO development.

Finally, Appendix E provides backup material on concepts, artefacts and theory. It is placed on the CD since it is reference material to be consulted if and when required.

Enjoy!

Appendix A
Core techniques

Abstract class identification   Star rating ***

Focus: Design and reuse
Typical tasks for which this is needed: Construct the object model, create and/or identify reusable components ('for reuse'), optimize the design
Related techniques: Revision of inheritance hierarchies
Input (pre-condition): Design documents and diagrams
Underpinning concepts: Abstract and Deferred Classes; Abstraction; Generalization, Inheritance and Polymorphism

Technique description

Abstract and deferred classes are classes that are designed never to be instantiated. It is not possible for them to have instances because some part of them is incomplete. It is the job of their descendants to complete the details in order to create an effective class with instances.

A typical abstract/deferred class might be *VEHICLE* – you never see an instance of a vehicle on the roads; but you do see instances of automobiles, trucks, motorbikes, all of which are subtypes (and subclasses) of vehicles. However, this all depends on what abstraction level is the focus of your attention. An alternative viewpoint might be that, in fact, you don't see instances even of *AUTOMOBILE* on the road, but instances of *FORD_CAR*, *TOYOTA_CAR*, *PONTIAC_CAR*. Nevertheless, even in this scenario, *VEHICLE* would remain an abstract class.

The purpose of introducing deferred classes into a design is to increase the amount of code that can be reused through inheritance (see Technique: Generalization and inheritance identification) and to reduce the inter-class coupling in a design (see Responsibility-Driven Design in CD: Appendix E and Technique: Collaborations analysis). Sometimes, the need for a deferred class becomes apparent at a later stage, when incorporating a new class into an existing library (see Technique: Application scavenging; Technique: Library management). The purpose of introducing fully abstract classes into a design is to increase the 'plug-in' compatibility of code components, fostering reuse by composition (see

Technique: Framework creation). Another important use is to maintain a fully connected class hierarchy which makes navigating, hierarchy maintenance, further inheritance and instantiation easier.

Another advantage of deferred classes is that the pre- and post-conditions of the feature can be specified in the parent class. This assists quality during polymorphic calls since the rules relating the strength of these assertions between subclass and parent are very clearly delineated (see Technique: Contract specification).

Technique usage

Deferred and abstract classes may emerge during an initial domain analysis. However, it is usually possible to suggest a huge variety of alternative intermediate classes: for example, should collections be partitioned according to whether they are fixed-size and variable-size; or whether they contain unique, versus duplicated, elements; or whether they are externally indexed or keyed? For this reason, initial intuitions about the cogency of particular intermediate classes in a given domain may prove to be wrong. What we want to do is to identify just those primary methods that are implemented differently in each descendant class, and construct deferred classes retrospectively, based on grouping the shared secondary methods that use the small set of primary methods. This is much easier to do when all the required behaviors of each descendant are known, rather than by imposing some abstract domain classification on the problem. The above approach is bottom-up, based on method composition analysis (see Technique: Generalization). An alternative approach, based on inter-class couplings, is top-down (see Responsibility-Driven Design in CD: Appendix E and Technique: Collaborations analysis).

It is generally recommended that deferred classes should not inherit from effective classes (de Paula and Nelson, 1991); although exceptions to this rule do exist. Another heuristic (Grosberg, 1993) is to construct an inheritance hierarchy using the rule that no effective classes should have subclasses. With this strategy, for example, the hierarchy of Figure A.1(a) would be revised to that shown in Figure A.1(b).

Responsibilities which are inherited by subclasses may be renamed and/or redefined and these should be shown in the detailed design, prior to coding.

Deliverables and outputs (post-condition)

Contribution to the ongoing development of the semantic nets/class diagrams.

Abstraction utilization Star rating ***

Focus: Modeling
Typical tasks for which this is needed: Analyze user requirements, construct the object model, create and/or identify reusable components, develop business

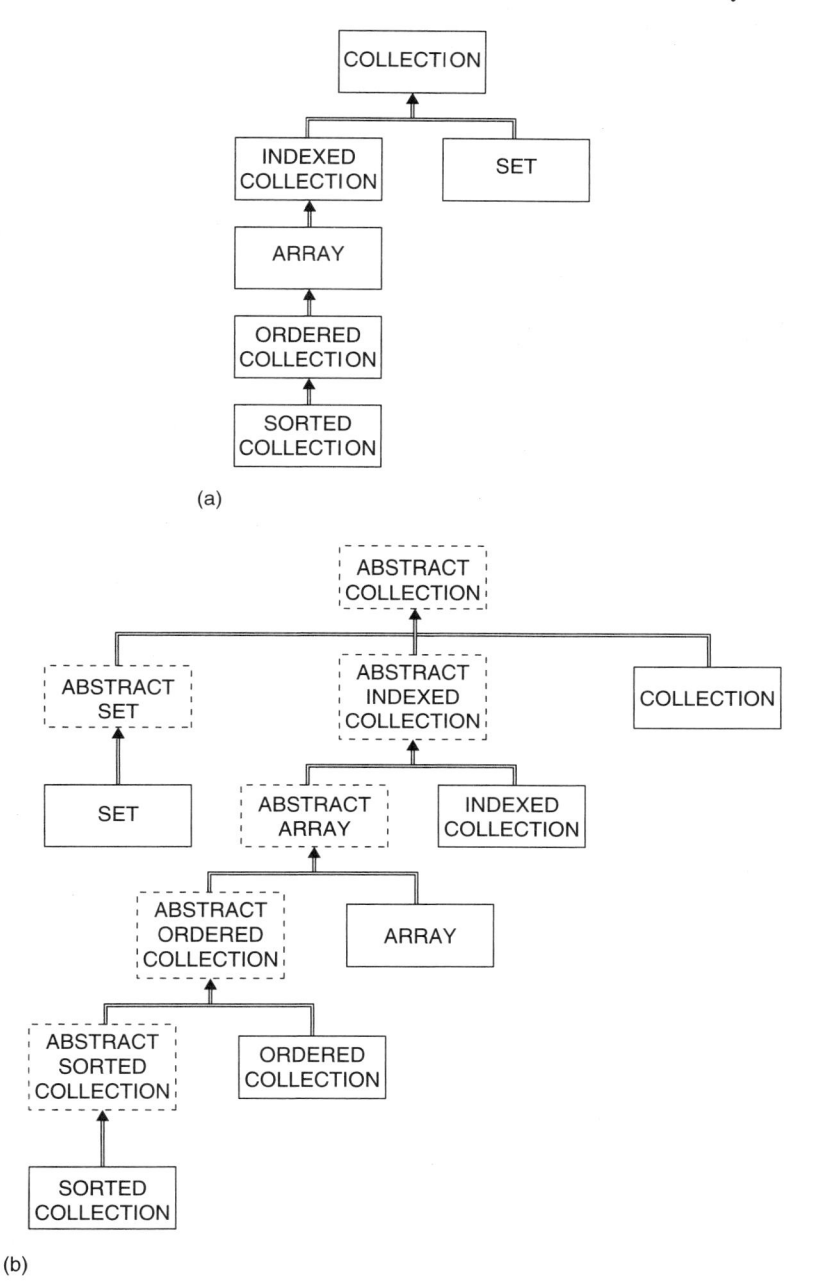

Figure A.1 (a) Simple inheritance hierarchy in which each subclass is instantiable and (b) revised hierarchy in which classes are either instantiable or inheritable from, but never both (redrawn in COMN from Henderson-Sellers and Edwards, 1994a).

94   CORE TECHNIQUES

object model, identify CIRTs, identify user requirements, undertake architectural design
Related techniques: Granularity, revision of inheritance hierarchies
Input (pre-condition): Requirements
Underpinning concepts: Abstraction; Classification and Partitions; Generalization, Inheritance and Polymorphism

Technique description

Abstraction (see CD: Appendix E) is the principle of concentrating on the most important or essential capabilities for the problem being investigated at a particular scale or granularity and consequently temporarily suppressing or ignoring less important, immaterial or diversionary detail – Koenig (1994) aptly describes it as 'selective ignorance'. The use of abstraction assists in managing complexity and thus in promoting understandability and, consequently (in a software product), maintainability, extensibility, correctness and reusability. Psychological studies (Miller, 1956) have shown that there are limits to the number of concepts ('chunks of information') that an individual person can retain in their short-term memory. This is known as the Miller limit with a value of 7 ± 2. Thus by thinking of concepts at a higher level of granularity (q.v.), we can, in essence, remember more because we are chunking at that higher level of abstraction.

Typically, a person will focus on two, at most three, abstraction levels simultaneously – and only then when they are conscious of their use of abstraction. For example, consider an abstraction hierarchy of

- city
- precinct
- building
- room
- furniture
- chair
- chair leg
- wooden leg (properties of the material of which it is made)
- atoms
- electrons.

Our cognitive focus may be architectural (city, precinct) or chemical (atoms, electrons) but never the two at the same time. Furthermore, in our normal cognition of the real world *one* of these abstraction levels can be regarded as basic (Lakoff, 1987, page 46). Typically, this is in the middle of the taxonomic hierarchy – in the example above it would be chair.

Technique usage

Abstraction can be used to both decompose a complex system into its component parts or to compose a complex system out of its component parts. Both produce architectures that are hierarchical in terms of their abstraction level. Each abstraction level should be understandable as a whole without regard to its lower level abstractions. Each abstraction level thus should contain approximately 7 ± 2 items.

Abstraction utilization is reflected in a mindset or awareness of the potential of humans to conceptualize or model at different levels of detail (abstraction levels). Optimal utilization needs a mind trained to focus on the essence of the model at the chosen abstraction level, to suppress detail whilst identifying the key characteristics.

- Select a purpose for the concept that is to be modeled (i.e. purpose of the system)
- Identify the purpose to which the model when constructed will be put (i.e. purpose of the model)
- Work back to one (several) acceptable ways of achieving the goals keeping in mind the purpose of the model (its utility)
- Identify the main transformations and structures that together achieve the system purpose in a way consistent with the purpose of the model
- Use the language (implied level of granularity) of the description of the main transformation or structure to arrive at the 'objects' that compose our 'system'. This gives you one particular level of abstraction
- Having identified one level of abstraction, go up to compose higher ones, or down to create lower ones, or both. This can be done by considering the structures, transformations or causal relationships (or some or all of the above) that coherently can be identified as together forming the elements of the current level. Do this in full consideration of the purpose of the model
- Do not go more than two levels up and two levels down (four levels in total in any one model).

Deliverables and outputs (post-condition)

Models with improved semantic architecture.

Acceptance testing   Star rating **

Focus: Testing
Typical tasks for which this is needed: Test
Related techniques: Integration testing, regression testing, reviews, usability testing

96   CORE TECHNIQUES

Input (pre-condition): Untested system, test cases
Underpinning concepts: That failures are related to defects in the system

Technique description

Acceptance testing must not be confused with the more general technique of system acceptance (q.v.). Whereas the latter is the technique by which the suitability of a product is determined, the former is one mechanism by which information to arrive at such determination may be obtained.

In other words, system acceptance is a process by which it is determined if the product meets all the required quality characteristics that it should possess, and includes the plans and procedures by which such determination is made. A system acceptance decision is made against many criteria including those of functionality, reliability, usability, maintainability, reuse, correctness, etc., not all of which can be determined through testing procedures (see below).

Acceptance testing, on the other hand, implies the activity of 'testing'. Testing or dynamic defect management (as distinct from static defect management that includes techniques such as inspection) requires the execution of the software in order to locate operational failures. Once these operational failures have been identified, a root cause analysis procedure is followed in order to pinpoint the defect(s) that cause such failure. As such, acceptance testing might be capable of uncovering many functionality, reliability and usability problems but is far less effective in uncovering problems of maintainability, reuse and correctness. These latter problems, being of a structural nature, relate to the source code and are best investigated at that level rather than through exercising the executable. Techniques such as inspections, formal proofs, static analysis and application of reuse metrics are therefore more appropriate tools.

It is also noteworthy that whilst acceptance testing uncovers some systems failures, it does nothing with regards to evaluating whether such levels of failure that have been uncovered indicate that the system is now acceptable or not. It is the role of the 'systems acceptance procedure' of which acceptance testing is only a part to define such levels of acceptability.

Technique usage

First, it needs to be decided:

- how should user acceptance testing be carried out?
- who should be the test users/ how are they selected (experience levels, etc.)?
- how do we know when enough testing has been done?
- what measures can be used to log quantitative test results?

As mentioned above, acceptance testing is a form of testing which is applied to the entire system being evaluated for acceptance. Similarly to all other forms of testing, therefore, it requires the generation of test data that are capable of providing good functional coverage. Unfortunately, this is where most acceptance testing stops. However, it is essential that other operational aspects of the system are also tested. These include:

- system reliability
- system performance (response time, etc.)
- system behavior under heavy load (stress testing)
- system usability (learnability, user friendliness, ...)
- system recoverability.

One effective way of organizing such acceptance testing is to conduct well designed beta tests. To do so, the system should be installed and run with real data at a number of customer locations. With bespoke systems, this should be the client site. With systems for general distribution, a number of sites should be selected in such a way that gives a statistically significant distribution of the general user profile. The following tests then have to be run as a minimum:

- functional tests with good path coverage
- functional tests with good function point coverage
- functional tests of typical applications, runs or transactions
- functional tests of 'typical' exceptional situations
- tests of system reliability under normal situations
- tests of system reliability under typical exceptional situations
- tests of system reliability under stress (data volume)
- tests of system reliability under stress (transaction volume)
- system usability tests
- system recovery tests.

Specific descriptions of these tests appear in the general testing literature which must be consulted in order to design effective acceptance test sets.

Deliverables and outputs (post-condition)

Acceptance testing results (Seidewitz and Stark, 1995, page 12) in the production of

- a delivered release
- an acceptance test report
- final versions of system documentation.

98   CORE TECHNIQUES

Please note that these are only raw results and must not be confused with a recommendation whether to accept the product or not, which is the output of the system acceptance technique.

Access analysis   Star rating **
(including contribution from Peter Horan)

Focus: Database access constraints, optimizing implementation, database search path
Typical tasks for which this is needed: Identify user DB requirements, code, optimize design
Related techniques: Indexing, normalization, path navigation, query optimization
Input (pre-condition): User database requirements
Underpinning concepts: Access Paths

Technique description

Access analysis is the technique which considers how data stored in a database are most likely to be searched, with a view to planning ahead for a more efficient implementation of access functions (see also Technique: Query optimization). The technique is most applicable when databases are going to be searched many more times than they are updated. The optimization strategy involves storing redundant linkages between the types of data items held. These links are in the form of index tables, or access support relations, in the relational model, and memory caches and set-valued attributes in the object-oriented model. The tables or caches provide for faster access to distantly related data, but they must be flushed if update or delete operations are performed on the database (see Access Paths in CD: Appendix E).

In order to decide which kinds of index tables or object caches are required, the data manager must first consider the following issues. For all access operations, information is required on

- access paths (the flow between objects, properties, operations and relationships) which can be derived from the entity-relationship models, object models or collaboration diagrams (q.v.)
- the type of access (create, retrieve, update, delete)
- the frequency of access, particularly during peak loads and accounting for seasonal fluctuations
- the time of access
- the location at which access entry points occur
- the need for concurrent access and
- the response time performance requirement.

Technique usage

Information in the above categories should be collected and tabulated in a suitable format. From this information, together with a notional time-cost C for each direct data access, it is possible to estimate the average and peak load response times for each kind of query. The optimal notional cost of a query is the sum of the direct access paths that have to be traversed, times C. By analyzing the frequency with which particular direct access paths are traversed, it is possible to weight C by an availability factor F, which fluctuates between average and peak load times. F is different for each direct access path, since each path may be part of many indirect query paths and therefore its availability may be restricted by different numbers of concurrent attempts to access it.

Table A.1 tabulates the peak load times and the average frequency with which particular access paths are traversed, for a database whose access paths are based on the CIRT model described in Figure A.2. The first query event in Table A.1 corresponds to the execution of the operation traced in the collaboration diagram in Figure A.3, in which all the *SALE*s for a particular *SHOP* are retrieved. From this information, predicted average and peak load response times for each query may be calculated. These figures can be compared against the required performance figures for mean and peak load times.

Deliverables and outputs (post-condition)

A set of tables estimating the statistical frequency of different kinds of query at average and peak load times; a set of tables in which typical query operations are costed for their average and peak-load response times.

Access path optimization – see Path navigation

Active listening Star rating **

Focus: User requirements
Typical tasks for which this is needed: Analyze user requirements, identify user requirements
Related techniques: Brainstorming, interviewing
Input (pre-condition): Availability of user and interviewer
Underpinning concepts: Need to get accurate user requirements

Technique description

Active listening is a style of interviewing which, like non-directive interviewing, seeks to minimize the impact of the developer's views on the client. The role of the developer is mostly to listen to the client's expressed wishes and views, prompting where necessary, and reflecting the client's statements back to the

Table A.1 Access paths for events (after Case, 1993).

Event	Access path	Type of access	Time of access	Frequency of access per time period	Peak time of access	Frequency of access at peak time
Find all sales for a given shop	*Sequential access* Shop *Association* Shop & Sale *Aggregation* Sale & Customer Sale & Product	Retrieval	6am–8pm	3000/1 day	10am–12pm	600/1 hour
Insert a new sale	*Association* SalesPerson & Sale *Aggregation* Sale & Customer Sale & Product	Creation	6am–8pm	900/1 day	11am–12pm	300/1 hour
Select sales made by a given sales person	*Sequential access* Product *Aggregation* Product & Storage Storage & Shop	Retrieval	6am–8pm	800/1 day	10am–12pm	200/1 hour
Find quantity stored and location of a given product	*Sequential access* Product *Aggregation* Product Storage Storage & Shop	Retrieval	6am–8pm	1000/1 day	2pm–4pm	260/1 hour
Find the products and shop where they are stored that have less than a given quantity in storage	*Sequential access* Storage *Aggregation* Storage & Product Storage & Shop	Retrieval	6am–8pm	1500/1 day	2pm–4pm	400/1 hour

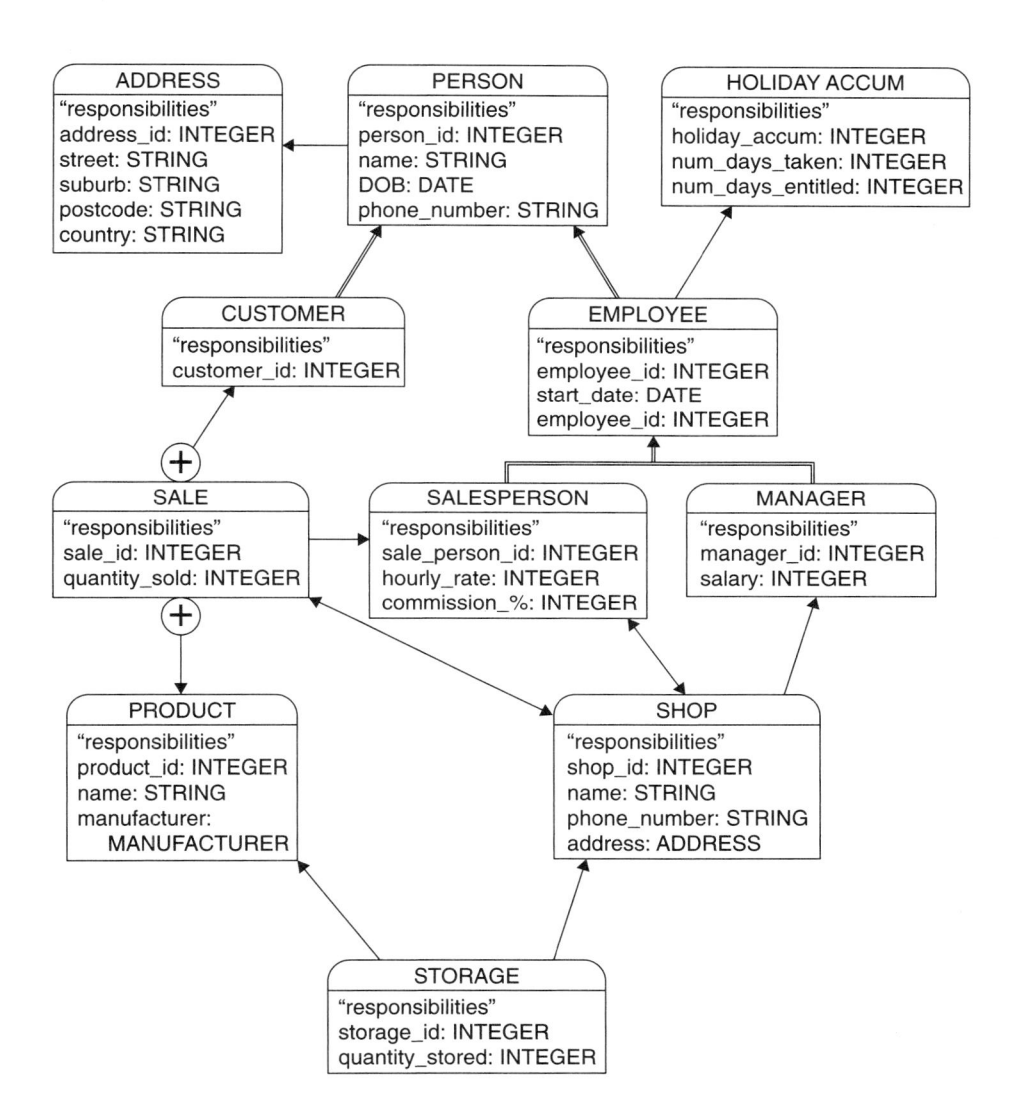

Figure A.2 Samples Sales persistent object class model (redrawn from Case, 1993).

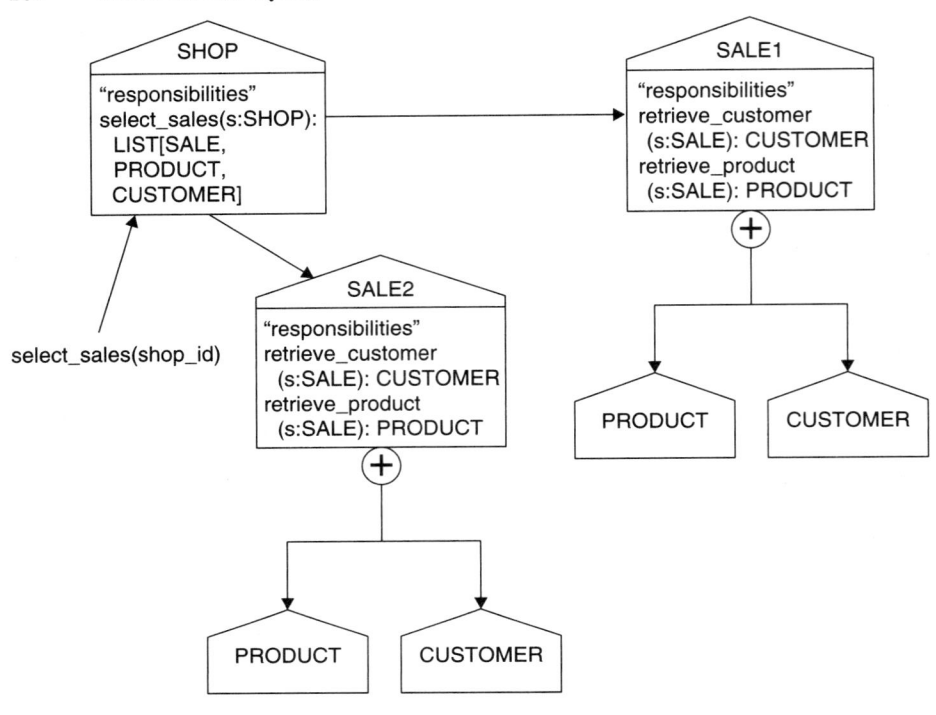

Figure A.3 Collaboration diagram from selecting sales for a shop (redrawn from Case, 1993).

client. In addition to eliciting material facts, the developer should seek to understand the feelings being expressed by the client. Focusing on points of concern about which strong feelings are expressed can lead to important discoveries about system priorities or the background social context of the client's business, or even important issues of power, ownership and control in office politics. This means that active listening can be of particular importance when social systems analysis (q.v.) and political systems analysis (q.v.) techniques are being utilized.

The basic ideas behind active listening are common sense. Research into better understanding, modeling and formalization of this approach has been carried out by scholars in educational psychology, education, and human communication. Two excellent resources for further information are Huitt (1992) and Helgesen and Brown (1995).

This technique is a generally useful human communication skill, practised by counsellors and good personnel managers. It is naturally useful during all stages of system development, but most particularly during requirements capture.

Technique usage

The following are the basic guidelines for active listening:

- listen patiently
- try to understand the feeling not just the facts
- restate the facts and feelings communicated by the speaker briefly but accurately
- allow time for discussion to continue when the point being made is of importance
- avoid confrontational questions
- use the speaker's own statements (re-iterated as a question) to elicit more information on a given point
- listen for what *isn't* said
- limit the expression of your own views
- do not make any judgements until the end.

Deliverables and outputs (post-condition)

Draft user requirements.

Activity grid construction   Star rating **

Focus: BPR, modeling
Typical tasks for which this is needed: Develop business object model; model and re-engineer business process(es)
Related techniques: BPR, RAD, workshops
Input (pre-condition): Available information on existing business processes
Underpinning concepts: Link activities to real business needs

Technique description

Activity grids originated in SOMA (Graham, 1995a; 1997a). They provide an important focus to aid in the task of Business Process Re-engineering (BPR). One problem encountered during BPR, especially where the business has a long history of incremental change and development, is the difficulty in determining which business processes are still central to the mission of the business. Many other processes may have evolved to reflect internal organizational structures, or for historical reasons as temporary work-arounds, but which were left in place. Essential core business processes may have become diluted or fragmented, hidden implicitly among several current processes. The technique of building an activity grid aims to recover the core business processes.

An important first step is to elicit the reasons for the business's existence. Other techniques (see, e.g. Technique: Workshops) help to elicit the goals of the business. Each goal is an atomic business objective, obtained by analyzing the mission statement(s) of the business. Goals shared by an organization and its

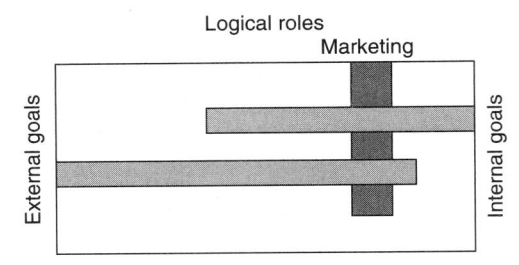

Figure A.4 Activity grid (after Graham, 1997a).

stakeholders (particularly its customers) may be *external* goals which represent shared values such as 'provide reliable product promptly' or 'give accurate advice'; or *internal* goals, such as accurate accounting practices, planned inventory levels etc. Such internal goals are shown in Figure A.4 on the right-hand side. In an activity grid (Figure A.4), the vertical (y-) axis represents the business goals, and the horizontal (x-) axis represents the organizational roles. The goals of a business must be achieved by particular departments in that business. To obtain a more logical view of the business, rather than thinking narrowly about the existing departmental structures, we identify organizational roles within the business, such as 'Marketing', 'Production', 'Sales', 'Purchasing', etc. In general, there is an $M{:}N$ relationship between departments and roles: a role may be fulfilled by several departments; or a department may fulfil several roles.

The activity grid aims to cross-reference each business goal with some business process activity, and assign it to an organizational role within the business. In this way, it is possible to justify a particular business process activity, because (a) it directly supports a goal; and (b) it is owned by a particular role. Current business processes which cannot be so inserted into the grid must be considered potentially irrelevant, since they are diluted or fragmented.

We should, however, note that activity grids consider and connect the *current* business processes with the *current* organizational units, elements or roles. Therein lies a pitfall. The business processes are pitched against their units. From this, we can identify the redundant processes and units. This may provide us with a potential process improvement. However, if the exercise stops here, as it might and indeed often does, and the option of asking the question whether the extant and deemed necessary process is indeed the best of its kind (the most effective, efficacious and efficient we can utilize) is not exercised, then the opportunity to 'radically' change a potential process is not fully realized. The BPR exercise will fall short of its potential capability and might prove to be a failure.

Technique usage

Each candidate business process activity is considered for inclusion in the grid. An activity is written horizontally against the row corresponding to the goal it supports, and vertically in the column above the organizational role which is responsible for carrying out that activity. These are written horizontally alongside the goal and thus represent a business process. Each activity is then assigned to a role (e.g. marketing in Figure A.4), hence spanning several business processes. The activity grid thus links process elements and organizational roles in a management-focused, strategic framework which is also found to be very useful as a basis for BPR (Graham, 1997a). This technique thus decomposes the business into chunks that are small enough to be modeled in detail using an object-oriented style.

When all the candidate business process activities have been considered, the activity grid is then examined to see whether there are any identified business goals which so far have no activities to support them. If so, then this should be discussed with the client. New business processes may be identified and inserted. Secondly, the grid should be examined to see if there are any organizational roles which are redundant or surplus to requirements. These are roles whose current activities do not directly support any business goals. This should also be discussed with the client; and may lead to organizational changes within the business.

Deliverables and outputs (post-condition)

Completed activity grid.

Agents – see Intelligent agent identification

Aggregation – see Relationship modeling

Analysis of judgements Star rating **

Focus: Object identification and clarification
Typical tasks for which this is needed: Evaluate quality, identify CIRTs
Related techniques: Textual analysis
Input (pre-condition): Requirements document
Underpinning concepts: Avoid proliferation of accidental objects

Technique description

The analysis of judgements technique (Graham, 1994) involves extracting and classifying 'judgements' from the text or a discussion. It is important that an object model contains only essential and not accidental objects, i.e. that identified CIRTs represent the concept 100 per cent (in the given context/domain).

Table A.2 Analysis of judgements (adapted from Graham, 1994, 1995a).

Judgement	Example	Feature
Categorical	Fred is a man	Supertype
Qualitative	This ball is red	Attribute
Reflective	This herb is medicinal	Association
Evaluative	Fred should be kind	Ruleset

Table A.2 lists the judgements useful for OOAD together with some examples and some indications as to what they refer in OT. A categorical judgement reveals genuine high-level abstractions, i.e. types and supertypes in OT. Such abstractions are called *essential*. On the other hand, a qualitative judgement may identify CIRTs of semantic relevance within the application but which, on further inspection, do not 100 per cent represent a concept – these are accidental objects. For example, nouns qualified by adjectives, such as red ball, prickly rose, rarely, if ever, define new categories (see Classification and Partitions in CD: Appendix E) but rather add descriptive information to members of existing categories. Taken to an extreme we might have a large bundle of arbitrary properties ('attributes') such as 'the large, red, rubber, sand volley-ball, signed by a famous local sportswoman'. Such accidental objects tend to be highly tailored to one particular application and are therefore unlikely to be reusable; whereas true objects are those categories recognized in cognitive linguistic theory as at a *basic* abstraction level (Lakoff, 1987, page 46) – see also OPEN Technique: Abstraction utilization for more details.

Whilst qualitative judgements reflect an object's properties or attributes, a reflective judgement is more likely to be realized as an association or usage relationship. In the example in Table A.2, we can see that a *medicinal* herb is an association between a herb and the illness being treated. Finally, evaluative[†] judgements can often reveal semantic rules. For example, we could have, at a very high business analysis level, 'employees should be rewarded for loyalty', which at a lower level would translate to a rule such as 'if five years' service then an extra three days' annual leave' (Graham, 1994, page 344).

Technique usage

List all discovered CIRTs (concepts) together with their source (probably in the requirements specification). Identify those source phrases which are adjectivally focused and, in turn, evaluate each against the judgemental criteria of Table A.2. Document the decisions taken and ratify the final list as containing only essential CIRTs and no accidental CIRTs.

---

† Evaluative judgement is our new name for Graham's (1994) value judgement since the phrase 'value judgement' is in common parlance with a somewhat looser meaning.

Deliverables and outputs (post-condition)

Improved abstractions and the likely elimination of non-essential CIRTs.

Analysis patterns – see Pattern recognition

Application scavenging Star rating **

Focus: Identify core reusable abstractions
Typical tasks for which this is needed: Create and/or identify reusable components ('for reuse')
Related techniques: Framework creation, library class incorporation, library management
Input (pre-condition): Several related applications have been built
Underpinning concepts: Abstract and Deferred Classes

Technique description

Application scavenging refers to the process of hunting through the design documents and the code of previous applications, looking for core reusable abstractions that may be incorporated into a permanent library. Although this kind of activity should be performed during all object-oriented development, the term refers most appropriately to those projects where reuse policies have been formally incorporated into the development process. Under such a process, the different members of the software house, or development team, are assigned to different roles:

- Application Developer – has the job of delivering new applications as required by the customers
- Reuse Manager – has the job of identifying in the library, and delivering to the Application Developers, appropriate software components as they are requested
- Librarian – has the job of maintaining the content of the library and the frameworks it supports, defending it from unbridled extensions suggested by the Application Scavenger, but accepting some
- Application Scavenger – has the job of searching through the latest applications delivered by the Application Developers and sifting these for reusable components which are submitted to the Librarian.

The division of responsibilities is made so that team members may concentrate on their primary goals, without distraction. An application developer should not, for example, be worrying about how to rationalize the library in the light of the current application. Too much effort is wasted on OO projects through such undisciplined redevelopment of the underlying supporting frameworks.

Application scavenging firstly has the task of identifying core reusable business object abstractions. Business objects, or domain-level objects, are those abstractions which map directly on to primary business concepts – business data or operating procedures. We distinguish such business objects from the more basic datatypes, such as *SET* and *MAP*, which we assume any object-oriented library will provide anyway. The technique proceeds by examining the CIRT descriptions for several variants of the same business object. It is likely that it will have the same, or a related, name in different applications; however, it is also possible that two completely unrelated application objects are performing the same business functions. The Application Scavenger needs to develop a good sense for minimalism and elegance, when browsing designs and code. When likely candidates for rationalization are found, the core business object concept is abstracted out. This can be done either as a base class, from which the variants used in the different applications are derived subclasses, or as a core component class, which is later enclosed by 'wrappers' (q.v.) for each particular application. The former gives rise to inheritance-based frameworks with deferred classes filling the role of the core business object; the latter gives rise to composition-based frameworks. There is a trade-off between the two approaches: the former is quicker to develop, but may be harder to maintain in the long run; the latter may require more effort, especially if the wrappers have to delegate methods to the core, but may be easier to maintain. (See the Design Patterns book (Gamma *et al.*, 1995) for a further discussion of this issue.)

Application scavenging secondly has the task of identifying novel control constructs developed for particular applications. This part of the technique feeds directly into Technique: Framework creation (q.v.) The idea is that the pattern of message passing in an application reflects an underlying control structure, which may be made explicit in a framework and later reused. Meyer (1988; 1997) gives the example of a data entry system in which different screens are displayed, requiring different kinds of input from a user, which is then processed in different ways. Generalizing from this, he designs an abstract data entry class, with a top level method which contains a loop:

> **from**
>   *init*
> **until**
>   *done*
> **repeat**
>   *display;*
>   *input;*
>   *process*
> **end;**

The particular data entry objects are then provided as effective (i.e. concrete) subclasses of the abstract data entry class – they only need to implement the deferred methods: *display*, *input* and *process*. The control logic for iteration and testing for termination is handled in one place. This kind of design arises because someone noticed the similarity between the ways in which the different data entry objects functioned. This kind of activity is harder than identifying core domain object abstractions, since it requires an appreciation of the whole application and the control strategy adopted for it.

Technique usage

Application scavenging may begin when there are three or more similar applications from which to abstract reusable components. Before this time, it is unlikely that sufficient variants of the common business objects will have been encountered for a good attempt to be made at isolating the core. A first library should be constructed from the core components, and a first control framework established.

During subsequent development, applications should be developed up to the point where high-level designs start to become available. From here on, it is possible to adopt two different strategies. The first strategy assumes *a priori* that the previously developed framework is suitable for the new application. The second strategy allows for the possibility that the existing library framework is sub-optimal for the current application.

The first approach may be taken where it is infeasible to consider reworking the current framework at this time (perhaps for reasons of time and cost). In this case, the new application's high-level control structure (in the form of a collaboration diagram) should be matched against the framework maintained by the library and, where necessary, adapted to fit the control pattern of the library framework. This will involve redeveloping the design models to include CIRTs representing the library classes supporting the framework. Application CIRTs may disappear, or be replaced by incremental 'extension' CIRTs, adding some local functionality to inherited library components. At the end of the development cycle, application scavenging may be performed on the latest application to extract the new kinds of incremental 'extension' CIRTs that could be reused; (alternatively, new kinds of 'wrapper' CIRTs, depending on whether composition is preferred over inheritance). This approach is the fastest way to develop the new application, but may result in sub-optimal performance.

The second approach should be taken, time and budget allowing, where it is clear that the natural control structure of the current application is nothing like that supported in the library. In this case, application scavenging should be performed on the new application and the current library, treated as another application, to try to identify the core components and control structures common to both. The result of this activity is a better-factored library, whose control framework can accommodate all the existing applications and the new one. The process has a greater impact on the content of the library, since it may involve breaking apart existing control abstractions and establishing different patterns of messaging – something recognized as one of the hardest parts of object-oriented design. Jacobson and others (Jacobson *et al.*, 1992, pages 135–141) advocate isolating control patterns as separate objects, as an insurance against cascading

110 CORE TECHNIQUES

updates to the library. Once the new library framework has been established, the 'extension'/'wrapper' CIRTs for the current application may be determined.

It is possible for both strategies to be carried out simultaneously in software houses which adopt the different roles described above. For the sake of the first release of new software, strategy 1 is adopted for a fast turnaround, but suboptimal performance is tolerated. As the experience of this latest application filters through the scavenging and library incorporation side, strategy 2 develops new versions of the library framework in parallel with the existing version. This new version must first be tested with all existing applications, before it goes live.

Deliverables and outputs (post-condition)

Generalized components for business objects and associated control frameworks.

Approval gaining Star rating ***

Focus: Ways to get management agreement to proceed
Typical tasks for which this is needed: Obtain business approval
Related techniques: Political systems analysis, social systems analysis
Input (pre-condition): Proposal which is completed and awaits endorsement
Underpinning concepts: Decision making

Technique description

A critical decision point is reached whenever a proposal is made to the project sponsor. The proposal may be to gain permission and/or resources to continue and the sponsor may be the team leader, a project leader or, more frequently, relatively senior management. Without this endorsement, the project is immediately terminated and any further methodological discussions become totally irrelevant. Thus approval gaining is a vital and underpinning technique.

Technique usage

There is no real guaranteed approach to gain approval – after all, even if an excellent technical case is presented (for example), there may be organizational or political constraints beyond the ken of the proposer that lead to a necessary denial. Nevertheless, there are some characteristics that can assist in gaining approval, all else being equal.

The proposal should

- be logically argued
- be presented in an orderly manner
- be carefully checked for grammatical or punctuation errors as well as for technical content

- include a management overview (1–2 page abstract)
- include a well presented development or business plan, e.g. workflow
- include a carefully thought-out budget.

Deliverables and outputs (post-condition)

An endorsed proposal.

Assertions – see Contract specification

Associations – see Relationship modeling

Audit requirements (a.k.a. data security) Star rating ***
(author G.C. Low)

Focus: DB constraints and quality assessment
Typical tasks for which this is needed: Identify user DB requirements
Related techniques: Security requirements
Input (pre-condition): Interviewee available, company audit and security policy
Underpinning concepts: Relational Databases

Technique description

Audit requirements should include the methods to detect unauthorized accesses to objects; the methods used to prevent invalid uses of the objects; and audit programs.

Technique usage

The audit requirements to be enforced by the DBMS need to be identified. Procedures need to be established to detect, report and correct invalid, unauthorized or incorrect use of the database (Case, 1993). If not provided in the database, these procedures need to be written (Martin, 1988).

The following information needs to be determined:

- methods to detect unauthorized access to objects
- methods to prevent invalid use of objects and
- audit programs.

Deliverables and outputs (post-condition)

Audit requirements section of User Database Requirements.

Beta testing Star rating ***

Focus: Tests outside development team
Typical tasks for which this is needed: Test
Related techniques: Regression testing, usability testing
Input (pre-condition): System to be tested
Underpinning concepts: Software engineers and users other than developers can find bugs faster than development team

Technique description

An effective way of ensuring that a system is going to be acceptable to the user base is to involve some of them in evaluating the system prior to its general release. This is most effective in the case of 'shrink wrapped' software, i.e. systems that are not developed for a specific client and are to be marketed to a wide customer base (e.g. Windows 95). This is called beta testing.

Beta testing is the first evaluation by users/developers outside of the development team itself. The evaluators are often end-users who volunteer to be guinea-pigs in order to (a) contribute to the quality of the product and (b) avail themselves of the facilities of the new product or new version ahead of their competitors.

Technique usage

There is more to beta testing than just putting the product out to a subset of customers who have volunteered. There are a number of important issues that have to be considered. Some of these are enumerated below:

(1) *Identify a purpose for beta testing.*
   One of the main reasons for beta test failure, or poor quality (i.e. uninterpretable) test results, is that the developer fails to make clear, in the instructions to the test subjects, what is the purpose of the test procedure. To avoid this problem, the developer should consider the following questions before designing the test instructions:

   (a) What aspects of the product are to be evaluated; or at least, is there an order of priority that should be observed?
      Not stating this requirement clearly may result in the evaluation being made in a piecemeal fashion with some important aspects having been missed or not considered to be of any consequence. For example, users may evaluate and like the user interface but never

bother to check the 'back up' facilities. If appropriate beta sites are selected (see below), then this problem will not normally arise, since personnel at a well-chosen test site will be familiar with the thorough kinds of evaluation required and will need less guidance.

  (b) What level of precision and/or detail should the test subjects apply to the product evaluation?

      Different individuals or sites may have different priorities and may evaluate the product at differing levels of criticality. This can potentially create confusion in utilizing the results of the beta test.

  (c) What feedback does the developer wish to receive from the beta testing and in what form?

      In the absence of the provision of guidelines as to what form or level of feedback is required, the developer may receive a beta test evaluation that simply says 'We liked it!' or may consist of a comprehensive, multi-volume documentation describing everything the system did and did not do!

(2) *Select your sites carefully.*

Not all volunteer organizations will provide an appropriate beta site. The following need to be taken into account:

  (a) The sites should be selected in such a way that they are statistically representative of the target market. A product developed for the 'general' market is likely to be contemplated or purchased by a wide array of potential users. These users define a spectrum of various needs and wants. During beta testing, it is important that this is taken into account in selecting appropriate beta sites. Otherwise there is a risk of losing a segment of the market or of not having certain aspects of the system adequately evaluated.

  (b) Sites should be selected that are 'capable' of beta testing the product. For a myriad of reasons ranging from lack of time to lack of expertise, some sites are not capable of adequately evaluating the product. Often, in attempting to maximize the number of participants in the beta testing exercise, developers do themselves a great disservice by including inappropriate evaluators in the test teams. Avoid wasting your time and theirs by conducting an initial screening of their abilities, commitments and, most importantly, their objectives.

(3) *Decide what to do next.*

  (a) Information from beta sites should be *used*. It is surprising how many prime developers ignore feedback from their beta sites! If sites have been selected carefully, and if the feedback data received are in a useful and statistically significant form, then they should be used.

  (b) Decide whether to enhance/modify now, to send back for more beta testing or to decide when these should be incorporated in future releases. It should also be mentioned that if site selection has been made carefully, together with specific statements of purpose, there should be no need for further beta testing.

Developers who ignore these guidelines, who forget to define a statement of purpose or who are not careful in their selection of beta sites, will usually find that they have to resubmit their produce with new instructions for another round of beta testing.

Deliverables and outputs (post-condition)

Beta-level test report.

Blackboarding   Star rating ***

Focus: Design and architecture
Typical tasks for which this is needed: Construct the object model
Related techniques: Intelligent agent identification, state modeling
Input (pre-condition): A constraint-satisfaction problem for which the ideal solution algorithm depends strongly on the distribution of data in the input space
Underpinning concepts: Intelligent agents

Technique description

A blackboard architecture is a particular system architecture used in multi-agent programming (Ermand and Lesser, 1975). It is particularly suitable for large problems of interpretation, where there is no single executive control strategy that will lead to the solution. Instead, the system functions as a society of cooperating agents, each of which is an expert in a particular sub-field of the problem to be solved. Each expert is programmed with the intelligence to recognize certain patterns in the problem space and to contribute certain results. The information is stored in a global data structure, known as a blackboard, by analogy with the way in which human experts may collaborate to solve a problem and write their contributions on a real blackboard. The blackboard data structure is perhaps more like a post-room containing a large array of pigeon-holes. Each expert agent watches particular boxes, waiting for these to be filled with the pieces of information that will trigger its behavior. Once activated, the agent will process the data received and then will post the result to another box. In this way, computation is distributed and data-driven. The path to the solution may be developed in a variety of orders, depending on the quality and distribution of the initial input data. Blackboard-based systems are sometimes called 'island-driven' systems, because the solution is developed gradually outward from islands of certainty in the input space.

One of the first systems ever with a blackboard architecture was the HEARSAY-II speech recognition system (Reddy and Newell, 1974). This used a variety of knowledge sources to process acoustic, phonetic, grammatical and semantic information. Each agent was an expert in one of these domains. Together, they built up a multi-level description of a piece of recorded speech. The blackboard contained on-going hypotheses about the content and meaning of particular parts of a spoken sentence and each agent could modify hypotheses in particular blackboard locations.

Technique usage

A blackboard architecture is suitable for data-driven problems in which the optimal order of processing cannot be determined, but many kinds of knowledge may be brought to bear in finding the solution. Problems of interpretation are particularly suited, such as visual image, speech and radar pattern recognition. A blackboard architecture is useful for preserving multiple, contradictory hypotheses until some global constraint-solving algorithm is able to find the best fitting global solution(s).

Firstly, it should be possible to index the problem space in some fashion, so that local hypotheses may be posted in locations where later processing agents may find them. Waltz's line-drawing interpretation algorithm is one example, in which the indexed 'locations' are the vertices formed by the confluence of lines in a line drawing (Winston, 1992); and Earley's chart parser is another, where the posted information are edges spanning parsed substrings of words, indexed in a chart, a well-formed substring table, by the starting and finishing node (Gazdar and Mellish, 1989). Almost any indexable data structure may be used as the blackboard, such as a two- or n-dimensional array; but one should be chosen which suits the dimensions of the problem concerned. An air-defence simulation might be based around a three-dimensional map of cells, each one corresponding to a piece of airspace over a given terrain at a particular altitude; alternatively, a two-dimensional map could be used to represent the terrain being overflown, and aircraft could carry flags representing their altitude.

Secondly, it should be possible to identify local constraints in the problem, allowing parts of the problem to be solved locally. In Waltz's algorithm, a confluence of three lines at a vertex can only be interpreted as a convex or concave corner of a box; for each of these interpretations, this restricts the number of interpretations to be given to connected vertices. In Early's algorithm, a new spanning edge is inserted into the chart every time two existing contiguous edges match the daughter-nodes of a grammar rule; the spanning edge is inserted containing the head-node of the grammar rule. In many blackboard systems, the kind of processing performed by each agent is quite different, relying on different kinds of constraint. In HEARSAY-II, the acoustic-phonetic agent would examine different acoustic signals and hypothesize different phonetic units; the lexical agent would examine different alternative paths through strings of phonetic units and hypothesize the presence of different words; the syntactical agent would then attempt to find paths through strings of contiguous words, in order to discover the most likely sentence. At each level, different constraints were exploited: acoustic-phonetic, lexical and grammatical.

116   CORE TECHNIQUES

The processing agents required by the system are then designed, according to the kinds of constraint identified above. For the Waltz algorithm, a single processing agent visits each node in a round-robin fashion, restricting the interpretation of the node in accordance with global line-labeling rules. In Earley's algorithm, a scheduler agent queues pending hypotheses, and a spanning agent selects hypotheses from the queue, adding these to the chart. This agent seeks to abut the selected edge against existing edges that start or finish at the appropriate node. If a match is found, a spanning edge is created and scheduled for addition, later. When an edge is added to the chart, a rule agent retrieves all the grammar rules associated with the grammatical category represented by edge, and generates new hypotheses involving the rule. These are handed to the scheduler for later addition. In general, any number of agents may operate concurrently. By default, each agent may simply take its turn in a round-robin fashion. However, a more intelligent strategy may be to enable or disable sets of agents, according to the state of the blackboard. This may be done through the use of meta-agents, whose job is to reflect on the current state of the solution and focus the effort of other agents where it is needed.

The blackboard architecture may be cast naturally into an object-oriented framework, with a family of CIRTs representing different kinds of blackboard, different kinds of processing agent and different kinds of control strategy. An *AGENT* and a *STRATEGY* are good candidates for abstract classes, which have multiple concrete subclasses.

Deliverables and outputs (post-condition)

A design for a solution to a data-driven problem for which no global algorithm could be found.

Brainstorming   Star rating ***

Focus: Ideas generation
Typical tasks for which this is needed: Identify user requirements
Related techniques: Workshops
Input (pre-condition): A problem
Underpinning concepts: Ego-less ideas generation

Technique description

Brainstorming is a technique for elucidating ideas on a problem without any prejudicial ego involvement.

Technique usage

The members of the brainstorm team sit around in a circle and everyone in turn either passes or throws up a single idea *without ANY comment from anyone else*. This continues with a moderator listing all the ideas until everyone passes. Then the group look for synonyms or ideas closely correlated. Only at this stage are comments requested, often for clarification. Some evaluative comment is also permissible at this stage. No-one 'owns' any of the ideas – good or bad. Then a voting process takes place until the number of ideas accepted by the group is within the predetermined tolerance.

Deliverables and outputs (post-condition)

A 'hit list' of top priority ideas (often tasks to be done).

Business process modeling   Star rating **
(including a contribution from W. Butcher)

Focus: Process, BPR
Typical tasks for which this is needed: Model and re-engineer business process(es)
Related techniques: Reverse engineering
Input (pre-condition): Business process(es)
Underpinning concepts: Understanding business process(es) can be enhanced by (formally) modeling them

Technique description

A business process is a coordinated set of techniques and methods utilized by an organization within a particular context in order to produce a predefined outcome which delivers products and services of value to its stakeholders. A business process is principally involved with the end-to-end delivery of value – intermediate products are produced only to support this end. It, therefore, tends to cross several organizational boundaries and a range of functional specialties.

Traditional business process modeling has a 'process' approach – in modeling the business, the domain is considered as a system that defines a process located in a business setting. This allows a process design approach to the problem which, by incorporating important system elements such as categories of stakeholders (e.g. customers), technologies available or attainable, and the current context of the business situation, provides a much richer picture of what there is and what is possible.

Not only does OT allow the business process modeler to capture the structural view of the situation, but also those of transformation and causality, providing a much richer, more workable model of the business. Furthermore, the seamlessness offered by object technology allows us to ensure that the 'purpose' for which the system is being constructed is preserved throughout the development. Thus the transition from a business domain to a system domain (when IT is used as a business process enabler) can be a lot smoother and much less prone to loss than taking disparate approaches to business modeling and system modeling. In other words if we utilize OT in order to model a business process, at least parts of which is subsequently implemented through software, then the chances of the success of the system development effort in meeting the 'purpose' for the development of the system is very much enhanced.

Improvement of business processes, engendered by modeling, may be incremental (e.g. TQM (q.v.)) or radical (BPR) – it is often to the latter case, BPR underpinned by OT, that business process modeling is best suited. Business process modeling may therefore be considered as forming the first stage of a TQM program (where we need to identify the problem) or the first two stages of any modern BPR exercise, namely:

- identify and state the purpose for the business engineering project
- use the purpose identified to clearly define and model the problem situation.

Several approaches to using OT as a basis for business process modeling have been proposed, often as part of proposed OO approaches (e.g. Jacobson *et al.*, 1995; Taylor, 1995; Younessi, 1998).

Technique usage

Irrespective of the specific approach being used, we need to do the following:

(1) Identify the purpose of the system which is being modeled. To do so we might, for each process, ask:

   (1.1) Is the process viewed identically by all stakeholders?
   (1.2) What value does the process deliver, and to whom?
   (1.3) How does it operate? How does it satisfy this purpose?
   (1.4) What resources are involved or required?
   (1.5) Where are its boundaries?
   (1.6) How does it interrelate with its environment?

   It is important to note of course that these questions are interrelated and must be posed iteratively. For example question 1.1 may not be answered completely until question 1.2 has been addressed, and vice versa.

(2) Having identified the purpose, we must identify the elements that form the system that delivers that purpose. These elements are the entities (objects and attributes, both of which are amongst the structural elements in the system), their static relationships with each other (associations, aggregation, specialization), activities and transformations (methods, functions or transformations), actions, events and triggers (depicting causality or the dynamic behavior of the system). These may be identified in a variety of ways including the examination of task scripts (q.v.), interviews (q.v.), study of use cases, etc.

(3) Use a conventional OO notation set (e.g. OML) to capture and communicate these elements.

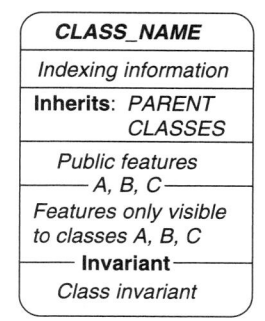

```
┌─────────────────────────┐
│      CLASS_NAME         │
├─────────────────────────┤
│  Indexing information   │
├─────────────────────────┤
│  Inherits: PARENT       │
│            CLASSES      │
├─────────────────────────┤
│   Public features       │
│   ──── A, B, C ────     │
├─────────────────────────┤
│  Features only visible  │
│  to classes A, B, C     │
├─────────────────────────┤
│   ──── Invariant ────   │
│    Class invariant      │
└─────────────────────────┘
```

Figure A.5 Class interface: expanded sections (after Waldén and Nerson, 1995).

Deliverables and outputs (post-condition)

An object model of the business process(es).

CIRT indexing Star rating **

Focus: Indexing CIRTs for future retrieval
Typical tasks for which this is needed: Code, create and/or identify reusable components ('for reuse')
Related techniques: Library class incorporation, library management
Input (pre-condition): Class descriptions
Underpinning concepts: Indexing assists in finding existing artefacts in a library/repository

Technique description

Early experiences with object technology soon highlighted the fact that if developers cannot, in about 20 minutes or less, find a class in a class library, even when they knew it exists there, then they give up and code it all again from scratch – hardly likely to support industry-wide reuse and quality assurance. However, more sophisticated software tools are needed to locate and retrieve classes than current class browsers. Suggestions have been made in the literature and there is some hope for future improvements. Henderson-Sellers and Freeman (1992) proposed that, with sufficient template-like information about the class (Table A.3), a free-text-storage and free-text-retrieval software package could be most effective in reclaiming 'lost' components from the library. Additional, more recent, discussion is found in Thorne (1997).

In the same vein, BON (Waldén and Nerson, 1995) strongly advocates including indexing information as part of the class icon (Figure A.5). They note that this should reflect information likely to be useful not only for browsing and retrieval but also for configuration management. As part of the 'comments' in

Table A.3 Description of class library database entry (after Henderson-Sellers and Freeman, 1992).

Database **Number**
Library name
    Package/Cluster or category name
      Class name
        Class **Services/Features**: state/data and behavior/functionality
      Superclass name(s)
      Classes required as **suppliers** of services to this class
      Related entries: **See-also**
      Synonyms:
    Facet Category
Language
Date originated
Version (original unless modified)
Size (in bytes)
Source (viz. author)
Vendor
Cost: $
Notes: (1) Classes required as aggregate components (included with this class as part of cost)
       (2) Other notes

> **synonyms:** car, transportation means
> **application_domains:** car rental, car lease
> **author:** John W. Smith
> **version:** 1.1
> **revision_date:** March 30, 1992
> **spec_refs:** srs.1.3.3, srs.3.4.7
> **keywords:** rental, agency, car, vehicle, automobile

Figure A.6 Indexing clause for a VEHICLE class in BON (after Waldén and Nerson, 1995).

the class itself, these data can be automatically retrieved. The indexing clause in BON, adopted here for OPEN, consists of a list of index entries where each entry is a keyword followed by a list of words. Conventions to be followed can be project specific; but if wider scale reuse is anticipated, some broader agreements on style and keyword lists are needed. A typical indexing clause is shown in Figure A.6.

Technique usage

Guidelines for indexing are given in Meyer (1994):

- keep indexing clauses short – typically 3–8 entries. Since the techniques are still immature, they need to be kept as flexible as possible

- avoid including information that can be extracted directly from the class text/code
- use a set of standardized indexes for properties that apply to many classes
- for values, define a set of standardized possibilities for common cases. For instance, we might have 'fixed', 'FIFO', 'LIFO', 'index', etc. (Waldén and Nerson, 1995, page 219)
- include only positive information. Do not include entries with null values or with N/A indications.

Keywords may be constructed individually (preferably at the organization level) or may be taken from lists such as the KWIC (Key Word In Context) lists.

Deliverables and outputs (post-condition)
Index information added to class specification.

Class internal design   Star rating **

Focus: Internal algorithm design and sequencing
Typical tasks for which this is needed: Code, construct the object model
Related techniques: Implementation of services, implementation of structure
Input (pre-condition): Design of the system in terms of interfacial detail
Underpinning concepts: Rules of OOPL being used

Technique description

Class internal design takes over when the most detailed level of object- and interaction-modeling is complete; and when the assignment of attributes to CIRTs has been decided, either by assigning data on a 'need-to-know' basis, as practised in RDD (q.v.) or by some form of entity-relationship modeling (q.v.). Furthermore, it is advisable to have decided which of your inter-object connexions are permanent and which are temporary. This can be done using the RDD 'minimization of contracts' phase, which relies on coupling measurement (q.v.), or else by using Fusion's visibility analysis (q.v.).

Technique usage

Before commencing detailed method design, you will have some form of Interaction Diagram – see Technique: Interaction modeling for more details of these approaches which in UML and OML show sequencing either as timelines or as interactions. The difference between the two is that, in a sequence diagram, the order of execution is explicit from the object timelines, whereas in the other kind of model, the order of execution is implicit. Hierarchical numbering (e.g. '3.1.1')

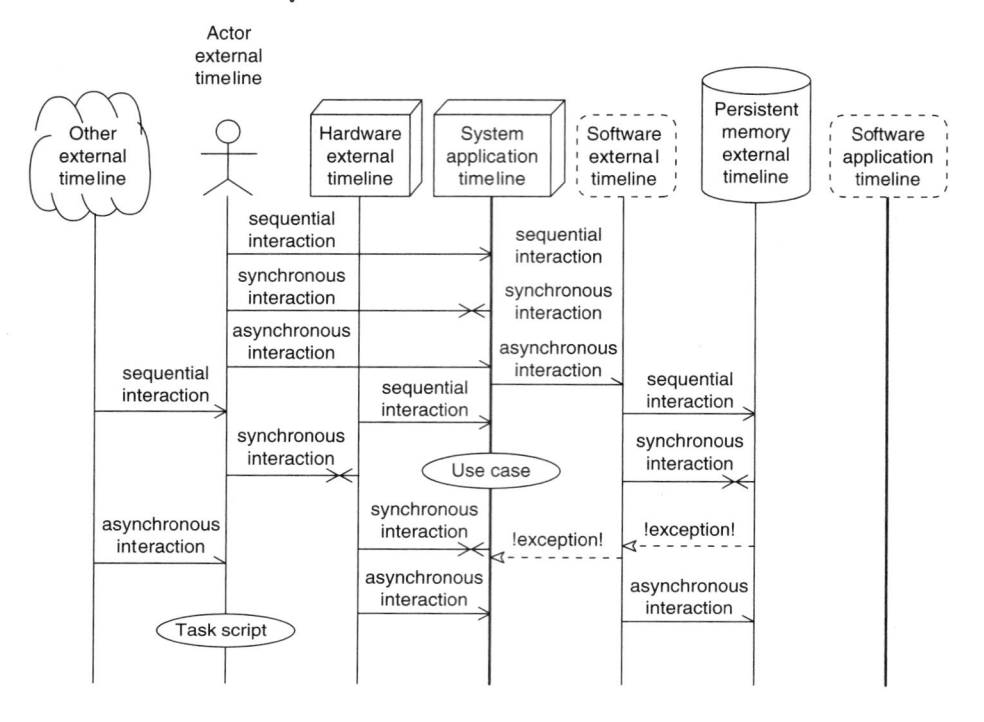

Figure A.7 Notation for blackbox sequence diagrams (after Firesmith *et al.*, 1997).

may be added to the transitions on the second kind of diagrams to indicate order of messaging, thereby making the two kinds of diagram equivalent. OML sequence diagrams also have distinct icon shapes for the CIRTs at the nodes which indicate whether the time baseline is a single, multiple CIRTs (i.e. a collection), an external etc. (Figure A.7). OML sequence diagrams can, furthermore, be blackbox (as in this diagram) or whitebox (see Firesmith *et al.*, 1997 for full details).

On some versions of sequence diagrams, a kind of structured English may be used on the left-hand side to explain the logic in the sequence diagrams. Alternatively, the traditional use of structured English alone as a documentation tool for the logic of algorithm design may be useful. Other traditional tools that might be helpful here, for internal method design in a structured OO programming language like C++ or Eiffel, are pseudocode and mini-structure charts.

FROM INTERACTION DIAGRAMS TO METHODS

Whatever style of diagram you use, it is best to have at least one diagram which illustrates the end-to-end processing initiated by each major system operation. This is extremely useful documentation for method writers and helps to counteract the 'yo-yo effect' (Taenzer *et al.*, 1989). This is the condition where system

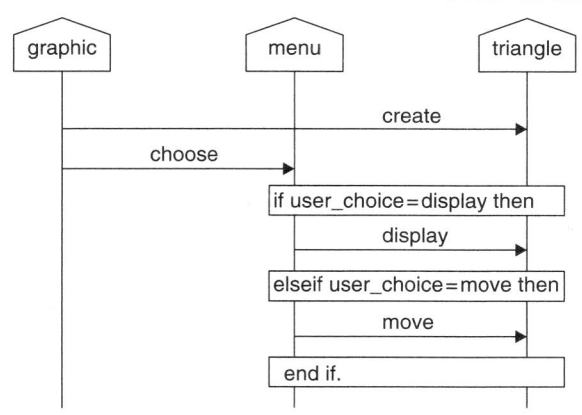

Figure A.8 Example whitebox sequence diagram.

control is so distributed as small methods in a class hierarchy that it is difficult to see how a particular system operation is provided.

Essentially, whitebox sequence diagrams may lead directly to the internal design of methods. Reading down the timeline of any individual object gives an easy rendition into code (Figure A.8). Additional annotations, as described by Baklund *et al.* (1995) can also be helpful here. The layout of the 'system structure chart' of Rist (1996) and Rist and Terwilliger (1995) appears different – essentially, the vertical columns are equivalent to the timelines of the objects in a sequence diagram and translate equally easily into code (Figure A.9). In a sense, then, these diagrams bridge between detailed design and class internal design, although detailed I/O and calls to other library classes are not shown (Figure A.10) and thus the code cannot be generated automatically from these diagrams.

Internal method/algorithmic dependencies

The internal calling sequence of methods may already be shown in a whitebox sequence diagram. However, it is appropriate to check at this stage that methods are appropriately layered. Where possible, you should ensure that common subroutines are identified and made into private (or protected) methods. For example, a *SET* class may have public *insert*, *remove* and *contains* operations. If the *SET* is implemented using a hash table, then all of these operations will necessarily use a hashing and collision-handling algorithm to find the correct table location for each element. In this case, a common *locate* method is recommended, which will return the next table index. In this way, the hashing code can be written and checked once; and the other methods may use this checked code.

What kind of techniques are appropriate for designing individual methods? Metrics studies show that for MIS applications coded using an OOPL, the size of

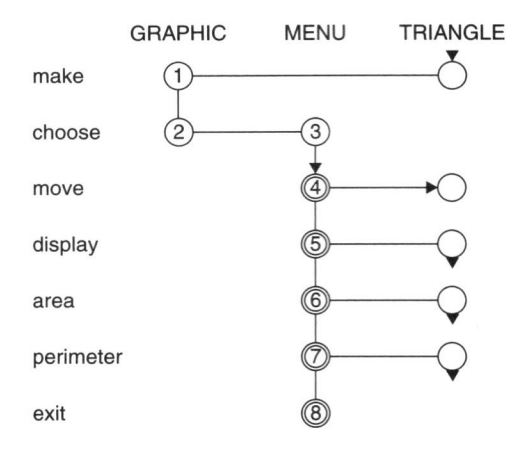

```
                    GRAPHIC    MENU    TRIANGLE
    make              ①——————————————○
    choose            ②——————③
    move                      ④————————▶○
    display                   ⑤————————○
    area                      ⑥————————○
    perimeter                 ⑦————————○
    exit                      ⑧
```

```
class GRAPHIC
creation
    make
feature
    tri: TRIANGLE
    menu: MENU
    make is
        -- create the triangle
        -- create the menu, pass the triangle as an argument
    do
        !!tri.make
        !!menu.make (tri)
    end -- make
end -- class GRAPHIC
```

KEY

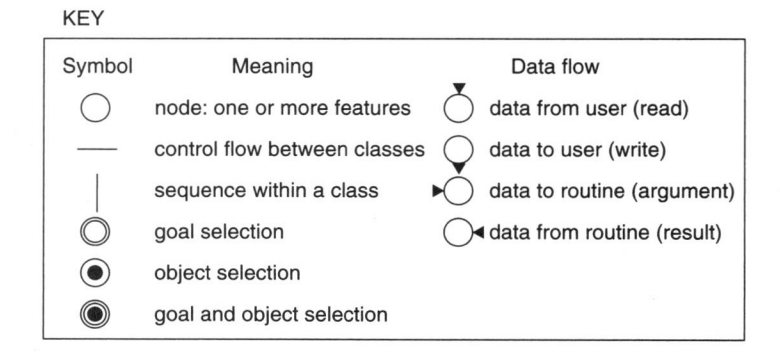

Symbol	Meaning	Data flow	
○	node: one or more features	▽	data from user (read)
—	control flow between classes	○	data to user (write)
|	sequence within a class	▶○	data to routine (argument)
◎	goal selection	○◀	data from routine (result)
●	object selection		
⦿	goal and object selection		

Figure A.9 An example of Rist's (1996) 'structure chart' for the detailed design of class internals. The graphical design is easily turned into code – here Eiffel code for the class GRAPHIC is illustrated (after Rist and Terwilliger, 1995).

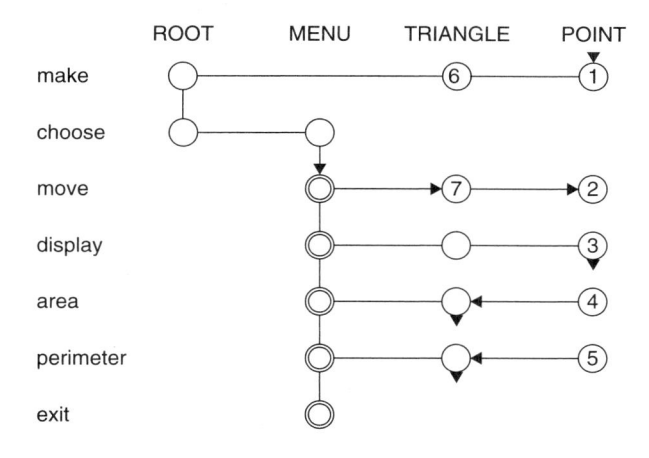

```
              ROOT      MENU    TRIANGLE    POINT

    make       ○─────────────────⑥─────────①

    choose     ○─────────○

    move                 ○────────⑦────────②

    display              ○────────○────────③

    area                 ○────────○────────④

    perimeter            ○────────○────────⑤

    exit                 ◎
```

```
class TRIANGLE
creation
    make
feature {NONE}
    top, left, right: POINT
feature {GRAPHIC}
    make is
        -- create the triangle
    do
        !!top.make
        !!left.make
        !!right.make
    end -- make
feature {MENU}
    move is
        -- get two displacements from the user, and move the triangle
    local delta_x; delta_y: REAL
    do
        io.putstring ("Enter x distance to move:")
        io.readreal
        delta_x:=io.lastreal
        io.putstring ("Enter y distance to move:")
        io.readreal
        delta_y:=io.lastreal
        top.move (delta_x, delta_y)
        left.move (delta_x, delta_y)
        right.move (delta_x, delta_y)
    end -- move
    ...
end -- class TRIANGLE
```

Figure A.10 Further details on the 'structure chart' approach of Rist (1996) showing more objects together with the code for the *TRIANGLE* class (after Rist and Terwilliger, 1995).

a method is typically two to three lines of code (Haynes and Henderson-Sellers, 1996, 1997), independent of language. It is highly unlikely that any method-level design technique will be needed for only three lines of code. On other occasions when, say for an algorithmically intensive method, a longer piece of code is necessitated[†], then any traditional (structured) design technique can be used since at that level, the main languages (e.g. C++, Java, Eiffel – but note not Smalltalk or CLOS) are traditionally procedural.

INTERNAL METHOD/ATTRIBUTE DEPENDENCIES

Typically, attributes should be secret (private/protected) and the only access to these should be granted through methods. This is always the case in Smalltalk; Eiffel treats public attributes as read-only, as though an accessor had been provided; and in C++ you should specify the access protection level desired: private, for strictly local attributes and protected for attributes that are visible in descendant classes.

Then, methods should be organized into groups according to the attributes they modify. These may correspond to stereotypes in the design documentation. Typically, for each group of attributes, there is a small group of corresponding methods that inspect/change these attributes. It is useful to cross-check the behavior of the methods with any abstract state model used to develop the behavior of the object. In particular, error transitions on the state models should correspond to pre-conditions on certain methods that protect the object from performing an operation when one of its state variables is in a boundary condition. For example, trying to pop an empty stack should be illustrated on a state diagram as an error transition, and should be caught using an exception triggered using a pre-condition in the pop method, which tests the value of the stack counter variable to determine whether this is zero.

In small objects, usually all of the methods interact with all of the state variables. Such an object is highly cohesive (a good thing). Sometimes a larger object can be partitioned into sub-objects (partitions, not subclass objects) in which different subsets of methods interact with different subsets of the state. This may indicate that the object is not atomic, and represents more than one basic object concept. However, the combination of unrelated behaviors is sometimes deliberately intended, as a result of mixin inheritance, or the use of wrappers. The check should be used to determine whether an object is unintentionally disparate.

An alternative partitioning of methods is into creators, destructors, accessors and mutators. This provides a useful indexing classification for code authors. However, organizing methods around state variables helps to maintain the correspondence between the object's abstract, or logical state (e.g. a *STACK* can be *empty*, *loaded*, or *full*) and its concrete state (i.e. the state of the *STACK*

---

† Alternatively, this may indicate poor or incomplete analysis of responsibilities i.e. a low quality design. Even large classic algorithms like the FFT can be objectified using a client–server model and several smaller part-algorithms distributed among these.

array of elements, and the integer counter showing the top index). This latter correspondence is useful for state-based testing methods (see Technique: Unit testing).

CODING STANDARDS AND BOILERPLATE

The naming conventions (see CD: Appendix E) for methods and for attributes are usually important. Class libraries usually have conventions on name length, on underscores and on capital letter usage. Where the implementation language provides further flexibility, such as `const`-protection and inlining, this should be considered. See the Techniques: Implementation of services and Implementation of structure, where these issues are discussed in more detail.

Furthermore, when designing for a library, there may be common boilerplate code that is used for every class. In C++, there might be standard sets of constructors to be provided, viz. those necessary to conform to the Orthodox Canonical Form (Coplien, 1992). There may be text substitution macros, which 'generate' a large portion of common boilerplate code, such as the `DECLARE_PERSISTENT` and `IMPLEMENT_PERSISTENT` macros used to provide type tags and object IDs for every class in the library (this is similar to the serialization protocol in the Microsoft Foundation Classes). In Eiffel, you may have to provide standard indexing information so that the class may easily be recovered for reuse (see Technique: CIRT indexing).

Deliverables and outputs (post-condition)

Detailed design documents for the internal features of each class in the system, delivered incrementally as per project plan.

Class naming Star rating **

Focus: Evaluate class abstractions and prevent name clashes
Typical tasks for which this is needed: Construct business object model, construct the object model, evaluate quality, identify user requirements
Related techniques: Library management, textual analysis
Input (pre-condition): Partial and evolving class diagram
Underpinning concepts: Naming Conventions

Technique description

Choosing names for classes is an important and influential activity. In addition to observing general guidelines on naming conventions (q.v.) to uphold consistency, brevity and clarity, you should bear in mind the following issues.

Object technology provides a good bridge between the software developer and the business client (Koontz, 1995). Thus, the names chosen for the software model of the real business problem should reflect those very entities which are part of the terminology of the business. In other words, computer jargon should be eschewed in favor of domain terminology. That way, all communication between the different parts of the business is significantly enhanced.

During the object modeling process, the choice of CIRT names has an extremely powerful influence on the way in which the model of the system develops. The kinds of CIRT you invent determines the names of the services you devise and the whole pattern of communication throughout the system. It is therefore important not to fix the model of the system too early in its development through picking out a few initial nouns and hanging all discussion about the system on these concepts. Gestalt psychology teaches that it is extremely hard to undo the effect of a first perception, so the fixing of class names should often be delayed. Foster a wide variety of terminology to describe the system and only later sift through the vocabulary to find and generalize the most cogent abstractions. A business client will tend to describe things using the conventional terminology of his/her business, which will include specific and historically-influenced terms. After logging all the client has to say, you should then sift and probe through this list of ideas. Sometimes, by simplifying the vocabulary and using more generic terminology, you may identify core concepts that are common across different departments of the client's business and so improve his/her own mental model of the way the business operates. This in turn can lead to more efficient business practices.

Technique usage

There are two competing influences upon class names: the first is to be short, terse and generic, to aid conceptual clarity and aid in identifying the class for reuse; the second is to be long, qualified and specific, to prevent name clashes in the namespaces in which the class is to be used. The latter pressure often leads to many similarly-named classes with either very long names, or qualified names reduced by abbreviation to cyphers which need an index to interpret. Furthermore, designers of particular libraries often prefix their class names with standard identifiers to prevent any clash with existing user classes, e.g. Rational's Booch components are prefixed by 'BC' and Rogue Wave's 'tools.h' library has the prefix 'RW'.

Some languages have facilities for dealing with namespaces. For example, CLOS has the notion of a package and all symbols (names) belong to a particular package (this is in the sense of a module, Ada's sense of the word). In the language, you can 'open' a package and use the names in their unqualified form; otherwise, you must use a longer qualified syntax to refer to names. The draft C++ standard has proposed something similar to this – namespaces may be 'used'; or else identifiers must be qualified. In general, current object-oriented languages offer little support for the scoping of class names, unlike the local scoping of method and local variable names, which is well supported. There is therefore little option but to introduce longer names or cypher names for classes. However, there may be ways of hiding this from the client programmer. In C++, it is possible to define type aliases using short names to stand for longer or cryptic names:

```
typedef BC_TUnboundedStack<Double> Stack;
```

or alternatively, you can define text substitution macros:

```
#define Stack(ELEMENT) BC_TUnboundedStack<ELEMENT>
```

The first solution makes 'Stack' stand for a BC_TUnboundedStack<double>, whereas the second solution gives the client programmer the freedom to specify different element-types, for example:

```
Stack(int) myStack1;
```

In C++, client programmers may therefore use generic names for the classes in applications, and alter the physical linkage to actual library classes, using a file of such name mappings.

There is still no strong agreement on whether the selected nouns, as class names, should be singular or plural. Many advocate the singular (e.g. Waldén and Nerson, 1995, page 181) on the grounds that 'since every class describes a possible set of objects, the alternative would be to *always* use the plural form. This would not make sense, since it would only yield longer names without adding any information'. The opposite view is taken in SOMA (Graham, 1995a): plural names are used for classes since a class represents an extension which is the (potentially large) number of instances. If classes are plurally-named, then the singular can be reserved for true object (i.e. instance) diagrams. On an instance diagram, such as a collaboration diagram, icons representing individuals, each with an individual, singular name are used, thus differentiating the object diagrams from the class diagrams. Inside classes, type declarations are of the form *objectname: TYPENAME*. Thus for instance, we might have *favorite_book: BOOKS* (plural class name) or *favorite_book: BOOK* (singular). The latter makes more sense intuitively for many people. In practice, it is more important to be consistent than to become embroiled in such arguments as to whether singular or plural is by some measure 'correct'.

Deliverables and outputs (post-condition)

Well-chosen names on class diagrams.

Clustering (DB)   Star rating **

Focus: DB optimization
Typical tasks for which this is needed: Access path optimization, design and implement physical database

Related techniques: Mapping to RDB, tuning of database
Input (pre-condition): Draft database design
Underpinning concepts: Aggregation, Membership and Containment; Generalization, Inheritance and Polymorphism

Technique description

Clustering is used in both objectbases and relational databases (Kim, 1990). It refers to the practice of storing objects that are logically related or commonly retrieved at the same time physically near to each other on the secondary storage medium (e.g. Hughes, 1991). This minimizes costs of retrievals since they can be moved between memory and secondary storage as a single unit (e.g. Chorafas and Steinmann, 1993, page 190).

In database technology, clustering is used to improve system performance. In the conventional approach, emphasis has focused on physical storage so that physical storage units such as pages limit the size and contiguity of the data clusters. I/O operations for queries are reduced if a logically related cluster of data is stored physically in one place. More recently, the focus has moved more to conceptual clustering where co-location is determined by semantic affiliations (although the two foci may overlap). Objects are then stored together in segments – there are several options available (e.g. Hughes, 1991, page 226). In many objectbases, dynamic clustering is used, particularly when there are more read operations than write operations. Aggregations are good targets to form the basis of a clustering algorithm.

Technique usage

In OO design for database implementation, a strategy is needed for clustering, including object migration, adding objects to clusters and reclustering. The particular deployment of this technique will depend on the specific database product in use. Many of the older OODBs described in Hughes (1991) required the user to assign objects explicitly to clusters, corresponding to page segments, when they were created. These included: Encore/Observer, GemStone and Vbase. Objects would then be swapped in and out of persistent storage by paging different segments into memory. In ODE, the strategy is simply to store all the instances of one type as a cluster. This is similar to the monolithic files created from tables in the relational approach. Some of the newer programming language environments support a different kind of object persistence strategy, in which object graphs are automatically 'serialized', that is, traversed recursively and written serially to disk as a tree in depth-first order. Memory pointers are replaced by unique IDs which may later be reconstructed as pointers when the object structure is read back into memory. It is possible to reconstruct a graph which is isomorphic with the original, although it may occupy a different set of memory locations when it is restored. This strategy was present in the Smalltalk virtual machine, offered explicitly by Eiffel's *STORABLE* class and most recently in the 'serialization' protocols of Microsoft's MFC and SunSoft's Java JDK (Cornell and Horstmann, 1998).

The clustering strategy to be adopted depends largely on how the data are to be accessed. Hughes (1991, page 226) reports four strategies:

- one object per segment – if the objects to be stored are large, expensive to transfer and are typically accessed individually
- store an object with all its sub-objects – if the group of objects are closely related and tend to be accessed together
- store all instances of a type together – if queries are posed requiring a search of all objects of the type
- cluster according to property values – if subsets of objects satisfying user selection criteria are frequently accessed.

Perhaps the most attractive general-purpose strategy for the majority of OO applications is the second of the above. Here, the storage mechanism needs to know which objects are the sub-objects of the object to be saved. Typically, programming languages do not offer enough support for this to be determined automatically. An object with embedded sub-objects (i.e. by value) may easily be written to storage, but an object that references its sub-objects through pointers is more problematic. The storage management system cannot tell whether these links are truly aggregations (part–whole compositions) or simply acquaintances (less binding relationships). Most existing serialization mechanisms will store all reachable objects from the starting object in the graph; whereas what is desired is the ability to mark out just some of these objects as the true sub-objects of the starting object. In this way, acquaintance relations would not be saved. This is useful in a majority of systems where objects are multiply related: without this discriminating ability, it is likely that serializing a collection of objects will result in some shared sub-structures being duplicated on the backing storage, leading to problems of inconsistency when they are re-read. There is ongoing research into ways of marking out different kinds of object references as aggregations or acquaintances.

Deliverables and outputs (post-condition)

Well-designed database.

Clusters – see Package construction

Cluster testing – see Package and subsystem testing

Code/document inspections – see Inspections

Cohesion measurement   Star rating **

Focus: Metrics
Typical tasks for which this is needed: Evaluate quality
Related techniques: Coupling measurement, metrics collection
Input (pre-condition): Design
Underpinning concepts: Cohesion, Coupling and Connascence

Technique description

Cohesion represents how well a CIRT 'hangs together'. One can view the cohesion from outside the class and ask questions about how well it represents the concept (semantic cohesion) or look at the structure of the code from an objective point of view and ask how much integration there is between the methods and the attributes that are used by each method (for more detail see Cohesion, Coupling and Connascence essay in CD: Appendix E). If a grouping can be perceived, then there is a lack of cohesion. In fact, the typical approach for this metric is as a 'lack of cohesion' measure (often known as LCOM after Chidamber and Kemerer (1994)[†].

Technique usage

External or semantic cohesion has no agreed metric. Page-Jones (1995) gives some guidelines on various types of external cohesion and these should be followed (see detail in CD: Appendix E).

For internal cohesion, it is necessary to ask:

- how many methods interact with each attribute
- how many attributes are affected by each method
- how many methods are invoked by other methods

plus higher qualitative judgements:

- whether the object can be partitioned into distinct parts that don't interact
- which methods are symmetric opposites like *push* and *pop*, *create* and *destroy*.

---

† But note that the Chidamber and Kemerer LCOM is incorrectly formulated – see details in Henderson-Sellers *et al.* (1996a).

These can be quantified by the modified LCOM metric, as advocated by Henderson-Sellers *et al.* (1996a) as

$$\text{LCOM}^* = \frac{\left(\frac{1}{a}\sum_{j=1}^{a} m(A_j)\right) - m}{1 - m}$$

where a class contains a set of methods, $\{M_i\}$ ($i = 1, \ldots, m$) accessing a set of attributes, $\{A_j\}$ ($j = 1, \ldots, a$).

Deliverables and outputs (post-condition)

Values of modified LCOM metric for each class in the system plus a recommendation regarding which, if any, seem to be inadequately cohesive (large value of LCOM).

Collaborations analysis   Star rating ***

Focus: System layering and modularization
Typical tasks for which this is needed: Construct the object model, identify packages, create and/or identify reusable components ('for reuse')
Related techniques: Interaction modeling
Input (pre-condition): Evolving design
Underpinning concepts: Aggregation, Membership and Containment; Collaborations; Generalization, Inheritance and Polymorphism

Technique description

Analyzing a system in terms of its collaborations is one of the more productive ways to break down and distribute processing among a society of CIRTs (Wirfs-Brock and McKean, 1996). A collaboration (q.v.) is a sub-contracting relationship between two CIRTs (Beck and Cunningham, 1989; Wirfs-Brock *et al.*, 1990), whereby the client delegates some responsibility for fulfilling its obligations to a server CIRT. Initially, thinking creatively in terms of sub-contracting helps to identify new CIRT abstractions. At a later stage, analyzing collaborations helps to identify subsystems and improve system modularity.

A collaboration may often be closely allied to a pattern (q.v.) – a smallish group of CIRTs collaborating to realize a specific, single purpose. As such, they may be equated with mechanisms (Booch, 1996; Firesmith *et al.*, 1997). A mechanism is equivalently a mid-sized chunk for pattern development *and* a description of a small scenario. Indeed, in the OML Version 1.0 metamodel it is a subtype of SCENARIO_CLASS.

Technique usage

TOP-DOWN DEVELOPMENT

Classically, a collaboration is motivated top-down by considering, at an abstract level, how a CIRT fulfils its responsibilities (q.v.) in the system (Beck and Cunningham, 1989; Wirfs-Brock and Wilkerson, 1989b; Wirfs-Brock et al., 1990). Responsibilities are broad statements of the kinds of activity that a CIRT must perform, rather than detailed service outlines.

In simple cases, which arise directly from domain modeling, it is intuitively clear that the CIRT must rely on other CIRTs, known as its collaborators, to fulfil its own responsibilities. An example from the ATM scenario in the financial domain is where a *TELLER* has responsibility for 'handling banking transactions' with a *CUSTOMER*. Clearly, the *TELLER* must collaborate with an *ACCOUNT*, which maintains the customer's balance. Later, the nature of the collaboration is elaborated further, as the 'handle banking transactions' responsibility is broken down into a specific set of services, such as *makeDeposit, makeWithdrawal, inspectBalance*. Each of these corresponds to a specific interaction, or message to be sent between a *TELLER* and an *ACCOUNT*.

In more complex cases, the developer may discover the need for a collaboration when he or she finds that a CIRT bears too great a responsibility in the system. This may become clear, for example, if refining the CIRT's responsibilities produces more than nine methods (i.e. breaking the 7 ± 2 complexity rule) in the class, or if the algorithm for performing any one of these methods is overly complex. In this case, the developer is encouraged to invent new CIRT abstractions to handle some of the responsibility of the overloaded CIRT. This can be done by partitioning the methods into related groups and inventing new CIRTs, to which the original may delegate. An example from the ATM scenario is where the *CARD_READER* is initially responsible for reading the card and checking the PIN number before handing over control to the *TELLER* to manage banking transactions. The number of different communications between the *CARD_READER*, *CUSTOMER* and the central bank *ACCOUNT* are too many, such that *CARD_READER* has too many methods. Furthermore, it is only responsible for reading the card. So, the developer invents a new abstraction, a *PIN_VERIFIER*, which handles all communication with the central *ACCOUNT*. The *CARD_READER* simply accepts the PIN data and delegates the responsibility for checking this to the *PIN_VERIFIER* (Budd, 1991). See Technique: Responsibility-driven design in CD: Appendix E; and Technique: CRC card modeling for a further elaboration of this process.

BOTTOM-UP DEVELOPMENT

An alternative method for establishing collaborations is bottom-up, by considering some set of interaction diagrams previously developed using a different technique. Here, we use 'interaction diagram' generically to refer to object interaction diagrams (Jacobson et al., 1992), sequence diagrams (OMG, 1997b), method interaction graphs (Coleman *et al.*, 1994) and other object/class diagrams (Booch, 1994) which indicate small groups of CIRTs and sequences of messages sent between them. Typically, such interaction diagrams are developed from a script (scenario, or use case), in which case they each represent a small-scale snapshot of part of the system's functionality, a sequence of interactions initiated by some top-level user operation.

By collecting together the different interaction diagrams, collaborations can be established by grouping together all the message stimuli sent between pairs of CIRTs. These stimuli may be initially recorded on different interaction diagrams. The collaboration is between the client and server CIRT. Therefore, each collaboration corresponds to a set of message stimuli sent in one direction only. If the two CIRTs in question communicate by call-back in the other direction, this is a second reciprocal collaboration. The reason for this is clear: eventually, the set of message stimuli must correspond to a set of protocols supported by the receiver; definition of these protocols (and the pre- and post-conditions) constitutes the contract (q.v.) between the two CIRTs, so call-back messaging indicates a reciprocal contract maintained by the other partner.

It is important to note that, whereas the top-down approach to establishing collaborations is quite productive in the generation of new CIRT abstractions, the bottom-up process is less so, because the CIRTs have already been fixed by the interaction modeling carried out previously (see Technique: CRC card modeling) [cf. comments made in Goldberg and Rubin, 1995, page 342]. Nonetheless, it is always useful to establish a collaboration diagram (see Collaborations in CD: Appendix E) as a precursor to investigating system coupling.

MINIMIZING SYSTEM COUPLING

The analysis of collaborations proceeds when most of the system structure is established and the communication pattern between CIRTs has been checked to ensure that all major system operations are captured somewhere. By this stage, CIRTs may have been generated directly from domain abstractions, or on the fly to handle delegated responsibilities, without much concern for the degree of connectivity being established in the system. Now, a system modeling phase (viz. system design) is entered, in which the communication patterns are analyzed and simplified. This is equivalent to the much-underrated second phase of Responsibility-Driven Design (Wirfs-Brock *et al.*, 1990).

Remember that the collaboration diagram provides a global view of system coupling, by indicating which CIRTs are functionally dependent on other CIRTs. Each collaboration is drawn as a directed arc from the client to the server, and may stand for one or more message interactions. Thinking ahead, the message sender would normally need a handle on the message receiver and this is typically implemented using an object reference (i.e. pointer). Looking at the diagram, it is likely that you will find objects which currently need pointers to rather too many others. In some cases, these handles are present purely for the sake of the required communication, not because they are naturally fields which are part of that object. Again, looking at the collaboration diagram, you may find that there are many cases of reciprocal collaborations, indicating a heavy commitment to call-back messaging. Again, you may find cycles in the diagram, indicating groups of CIRTs which are tightly coupled. These are all indications that the system should be reorganized, to reduce unwanted coupling. The approach taken involves the creation of new CIRTs which handle some of the responsibility for organizing the communications between the closely coupled parts. These new CIRTs become the managers of subsystems (packages).

AGGREGATION TECHNIQUE

Firstly, look for tightly coupled groups of CIRTs; that is, CIRTs which support many contracts with each other. For example, in the property market, a *PURCHASER* buys from a *VENDOR* in several stages, making a deposit and then paying the balance; the *VENDOR* sells to the *PURCHASER* in stages, first agreeing to the deal and later transferring the title deeds. The *PROPERTY* changes ownership, which involves the *VENDOR* removing all his/her possessions and the *PURCHASER* installing his/her own possessions and the name of the property owner has to be changed. If you model the sequence of transactions in selling a house as methods owned by these three CIRTs, you obtain a doubly linked ring of collaborations (Figure A.11). This is a bad sign, from the point of view of system modularity, since it means that each CIRT will translate into a class containing a pointer to the other two classes. Again, is it reasonable to assume that a *PROPERTY* object should contain pointers to a *PURCHASER* and *VENDOR*? Or that a *PURCHASER* should contain pointers to a *VENDOR* and a *PROPERTY*? In what order will these objects be created? How will they be linked up? The structure is prohibitively complex.

The solution to this is to create a new CIRT abstraction which encapsulates the tightly coupled subsystem. This is an entirely mechanical and systematic process – wherever you see coupling, consider encapsulation. Often, it is hard to think of a name for the new CIRT, but in this example, it is easy: a *SALE*. Now, the *SALE* CIRT is an aggregation (q.v.) of the components which participate in the sale. The *SALE* will eventually contain pointers to the *PURCHASER*, *VENDOR* and *PROPERTY* objects which participate in the exchange (Figure A.12).

This means that none of these objects need maintain pointers to each other any longer, a huge decrease in system coupling. The contracts which were supported individually by *PURCHASER*, *VENDOR* and *PROPERTY* migrate out to the *SALE* abstraction, which acquires all the methods to make the deposit, complete the purchase and transfer ownership. In turn, the *SALE* delegates smaller methods to each of the participants in the exchange. For example, the *makeDeposit* method of *SALE* will invoke *payDeposit* in *PURCHASER*, *acceptDeposit* in *VENDOR* and *markAsSold* in *PROPERTY*.

There are two options for handling communication between the aggregated components. Either, the *SALE* can manage transactions with each individually, or the *SALE* can invoke a method on one component and pass the other component as an argument. In the first case, *SALE*'s *makeDeposit* will invoke *payDeposit* in *PURCHASER*, receive the monetary amount, then in-

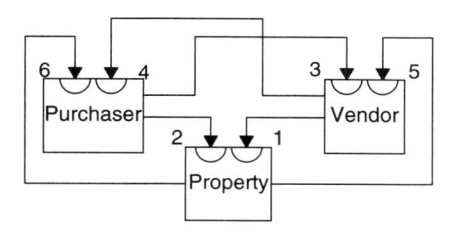

Figure A.11 Contracts for estate agent example: version 1 (using RDD's contract notation).

KEY

Purchaser contracts:
4. "receive title deed" (used by Vendor)
6. "acquire furnishings and owner" (used by Property)

Vendor contracts:
3. "receive deposit and balance" (used by Purchaser)
5. "remove furnishings and owner" (used by Property)

Property contracts:
1. "know when for sale and sold" (used by Vendor)
2. "know current offer price" (used by Purchaser)

Figure A.12 Revisions to design for estate agent example (using RDD's contract notation).

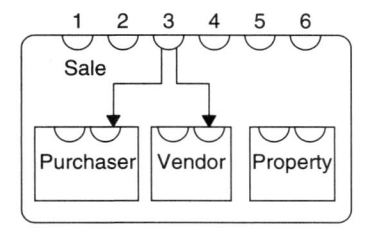

KEY

Sale contracts: (all used by clients of Sale)
1. "know current progress of sale"
2. "know and adjust current offer price"
3. "transfer deposit and balance"
4. "transfer title deed"
5. "remove furnishings and owner"
6. "acquire furnishings and owner"

voke *acceptDeposit* with this amount in *VENDOR*. In the second case, *SALE*'s *makeDeposit* will invoke *payDeposit* in *PURCHASER*, supplying the *VENDOR* as argument, such that the *PURCHASER* invokes *acceptDeposit* on the *VENDOR*-argument. In the first design option, call-back arrangements are avoided completely. In the second, limited call-backs are permitted, but managed by the outer abstraction. It is important that *PURCHASER* and *VENDOR* should never need to store pointers to each other.

This technique has many advantages. Not only does it decouple CIRTs that were previously in tightly coupled relationships, but the aggregating manager-CIRT is usually found to be a useful domain abstraction too. In this example, the *SALE* object is discovered to have useful attributes, such as the *depositDueDate*, the *completionDueDate*. Furthermore, the migration of selling-responsibilities from *PURCHASER* and *VENDOR* individually to the *SALE* allow the former objects to participate in other *SALES* – the same object may be a *PURCHASER* in one transaction and a *VENDOR* in another. All in all, this technique is thoroughly to be recommended for improving the modularity of the system.

GENERALIZATION TECHNIQUE

Secondly, look for different CIRTs which seem to use common contracts in third-party CIRTs. This is often an indication that those CIRTs behave in similar ways, up to a point. For example, in the ATM scenario, the system may have been decomposed to the extent that a *DEPOSIT_MANAGER* and a *WITHDRAWAL_MANAGER* handle separate interactions between the *CUSTOMER* and the *ACCOUNT*. Recall that in RDD (Wirfs-Brock *et al.*, 1990), contracts governing collaborations are determined on the basis that a common group of clients use the services. So, the various services offered by an *ACCOUNT* object are clustered into three contracts: *deposit* (1), *withdraw* (2) and *commit* (3) in this example, because *DEPOSIT_MANAGER* is the only CIRT to use contract 1, *WITHDRAWAL_MANAGER* is the only CIRT to use contract 2 and both of them use contract 3. Recall again that each of these contracts most probably abstracts over several message interactions, so we are not talking about individual messages here. For example, '*withdraw*' is a contract which allows *WITHDRAWAL_MANAGER* to request withdrawal and, provided the amount is agreed by the *ACCOUNT*, to proceed with the withdrawal. The '*commit*' contract used by both clients of *ACCOUNT* is the request to commit the changes in memory to some master backing store, Now, we have a situation where *ACCOUNT* offers three contracts and *DEPOSIT_MANAGER* uses contracts 1 and 2, whereas *WITHDRAWAL_MANAGER* uses contracts 2 and 3 (Figure A.13). This suggests that *DEPOSIT_MANAGER* and *WITHDRAWAL_MANAGER* behave, up to a point, in the same way, since they both perform some kind of transaction and then commit the changes on the *ACCOUNT*.

The suggested reorganization is to generalize *DEPOSIT_MANAGER* and *WITHDRAWAL_MANAGER*, inventing a new abstract CIRT called *TRANSACTION_MANAGER*. This CIRT assumes some of the responsibilities previ-

```
                    ┌─────────┐                    ┌──────────┐
                    │ Deposit │                    │ Withdrawal│
                    └─────────┘                    └──────────┘
                           │  │ │ │  │
                           ▼  ▼ ▼ ▼  ▼
                         ┌───────────┐
                         │ 1  2  3   │
                         │  Account  │
                         └───────────┘
```

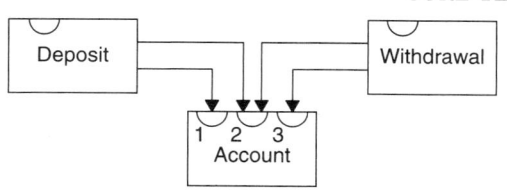

```
KEY

Account contracts:
1. "accept deposits"    (used by Deposit manager)
2. "commit changes"     (used by Deposit and Withdrawal managers)
3. "permit withdrawals" (used by Withdrawal manager)
```

Figure A.13 Contracts for ATM example: version 1 (using RDD's contract notation).

ously owned by *DEPOSIT_MANAGER* and *WITHDRAWAL_MANAGER*; in particular, it takes over the task of delegating to *ACCOUNT*. First, the collaboration to invoke the 'commit' contract is removed from *DEPOSIT_MANAGER* and *WITHDRAWAL_MANAGER* individually, and is re-established as a direct collaboration between *TRANSACTION_MANAGER* and *ACCOUNT*. Thinking ahead, this will eliminate common code in the methods of *DEPOSIT_MANAGER* and *WITHDRAWAL_MANAGER*, by factoring out the request to commit changes into a new superclass. Secondly, the remaining contracts used by *TRANSACTION_MANAGER*'s subclasses are now examined to see if they can be considered 'similar', up to a point. Here, we may choose to generalize the '*deposit*' and '*withdraw*' contracts as a single generic contract '*transact*'. This allows the *TRANSACTION_MANAGER* to handle all the collaborations with *ACCOUNT*. Thinking ahead, this will translate into a polymorphic method invocation in *TRANSACTION_MANAGER*, which is interpreted differently in *DEPOSIT_MANAGER* and *WITHDRAWAL_MANAGER* (Figure A.14).

The advantages of this technique are several. Firstly, the number of distinct contracts between server and client CIRTs is reduced, because client CIRTs are grouped together and then generalized on the basis that they use some of the same contracts. Collaborations tend to migrate higher in the inheritance hierarchy; and tend to merge as they are generalized. This reduces the degree of coupling in the system. Secondly, this technique promotes the development of frameworks, by identifying and pushing higher those patterns of communication that are common to a variety of subclasses. It is a good technique for exploiting opportunities to introduce polymorphism with dynamic binding. It reorganizes the communication structure in the system to promote extension – new kinds of *TRANSACTION_MANAGER* may easily be added into this framework, such as a *BALANCE_INSPECTOR*.

140   CORE TECHNIQUES

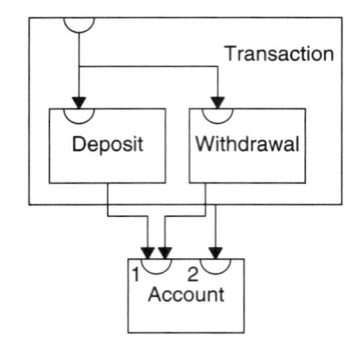

```
         ┌─────────────────────────────┐
         │        ⌒      Transaction   │
         │      ┌─┴─┐   ┌──┴───┐       │
         │      │Dep│   │Withdr│       │
         │      │osit│  │awal  │       │
         │      └─┬─┘   └──┬───┘       │
         └────────┼────────┼───────────┘
                  │        │
                ┌─▼──┬─▼───┐
                │ 1  │ 2   │
                │  Account│
                └─────────┘
```

KEY

Account contracts:
1. "permit transaction" (used by Transaction manager)
2. "commit changes" (used by Transaction manager)

Figure A.14   Revisions to design for ATM example (using RDD's contract notation).

Deliverables and outputs (post-condition)

Design fragments (which will contribute later to the full system design), each of which focuses on a particular collaboration and the CIRTs needed to effect it.

Collapsing of classes   Star rating **

Focus: DB optimization
Typical tasks for which this is needed: Design and implement physical database, optimize the design of distributed systems
Related techniques: Access analysis, clustering (DB)
Input (pre-condition): Evolving design
Underpinning concepts: Optimizing for DB by violating integrity of classes as concepts

Technique description

Determination of classes or relations which may be collapsed is dependent upon whether the database is a RDB or an OB. In the former, combined tables obviate the need for joins, but at the likely expense of loss of normalization. In other words, two normalized tables, linked by a foreign key, are merged into a single table (Figure A.15). The merged table in this figure could be said to represent a 'join class' (of *MODULE/LECTURER*). Semantic cohesion is thus lost in order to gain speed of look-up.

(a)

LECTURER

LECTURER_ID	NAME	ROOMNO
23	Jones	234
24	Smith	232

MODULE

COURSE_ID	TITLE	LECTURER_ID
CS201	Data structures	23
CS202	OT with Java	24
CS301	OOAD	24
CS303	Software eng.	23

(b)

MODULE/LECTURER

COURSE_ID	TITLE	LECTURER_ID	NAME	ROOMNO
CS201	Data structures	23	Jones	234
CS202	OT with Java	24	Smith	232
CS301	OOAD	24	Smith	232
CS303	Software eng.	23	Jones	234

Figure A.15 (a) Normalized tables for *LECTURER* and *MODULE* and (b) denormalized table (join table) for *MODULE/LECTURER*.

Translating these ideas to OT and objectbases, we can consider the join class (here *MODULE/LECTURER*) as inheriting multiply from *MODULE* and from *LECTURER* *purely* to provide a direct link between *MODULE* and *LECTURER*.

Another occasion when collapsing classes is useful is when there exists a mandatory one-to-one relationship between the classes. Merging the two classes again is effective, from a physical viewpoint; whilst, yet again, the semantic value of having one class for each distinct concept is lost.

Like denormalization in RDBs, join classes provide additional associations designed to reduce disk access for searches (Andleigh and Gretzinger, 1992). It is only recommended in cases where performance is critical and cannot be improved in any other way that does not denormalize the database.

Technique usage

In order to speed up database accesses, frequently joined objects should be identified and considered for merger. If such an identified pair is seldom used outside this context (i.e. by any other objects), then it might be worthwhile to create a merged class despite the loss of reuse potential and semantic integrity. If so, then a compound CIRT should be identified and created in the diagram/code. The creation of this compound object follows the guidelines given above and in Figure A.15. Essentially a 'join' as would be done in the DBMS software is done here manually.

Deliverables and outputs (post-condition)

Revisions to the design documentation regarding the suggested replacement of a number of a classes with a smaller number of collapsed classes.

Completion of abstractions Star rating **

Focus: Creating semantic wholeness to CIRTs
Typical tasks for which this is needed: Create and/or identify reusable components ('for reuse') and possibly undertake usability design
Related techniques: Abstract class identification, delegation analysis, generalization and inheritance identification, relationship modeling
Input (pre-condition): Set of problem-specific abstractions (CIRTs)
Underpinning concepts: Abstraction; Aggregation, Membership and Containment; Delegation; Generalization, Inheritance and Polymorphism

Technique description

To make a class more general and thus more widely useful, the class should represent a *complete* abstraction. This technique is therefore focused specifically upon creating a class which has high semantic cohesion (q.v.) but at a specific level of granularity (q.v.).

Technique usage

Completing an abstraction may involve the addition of services that are not explicitly required by the *current* package specification – in other words, domain analysis. Meyer (1988) and McGregor and Sykes (1992) recommend adding large numbers of services to the class, even if not required in the current model/system: the 'shopping list' approach. For example, a class which models a pen may have the services of writing and knowing its current level of ink. Completing the abstraction may require the addition of services for refilling the pen, or even emptying the pen.

Whilst completing an abstraction is useful, it should not be taken to extremes – after all, modeling should err on the side of simplicity. For example, a *CALCULATOR* class which has services of *add* and *subtract* is probably lacking the services of *divide*, *multiply* and *percentages*. Perhaps services such as *reciprocal* and *standard deviation* might be generally useful; but it is arguable that services of the trigonometric functions of *sinh*, *cosh* and *tanh* should be part of the standardized *CALCULATOR* class. Indeed, some recommend identifying a core/standard of wide applicability and making these sophisticated, additional services available by add-ons – modeled using aggregation. In a similar vein, Java splits strings into the fixed value-oriented `String` class and the extensible growing/shrinking `String_buffer` class, whereas in the GNU library there is a single, feature-rich `String` class.

CORE TECHNIQUES 143

Thus, completing an abstraction is relative to the understanding of the concept within the context of a specific application domain.

Another element of completing the abstractions is the possible revision of services, either by dividing them up to provide more specific functionality per service, or by amalgamating several to provide a shorthand for a frequently used combination of services (Firesmith, 1993).

Deliverables and outputs (post-condition)

Fully specified and fully complete CIRT specification.

Complexity measurement   Star rating **

Focus: Metrics
Typical tasks for which this is needed: Evaluate quality
Related techniques: Cohesion measurement, coupling measurement, metrics collection
Input (pre-condition): Completed (or partially completed) design
Underpinning concepts: Complexity Measures

Technique description

Structural complexity should be assessed by an appropriate complexity measure (metric). There are a range of possibilities (see CD: Appendix E and Henderson-Sellers, 1996). Complexity could be measured internally, for instance in terms of algorithmic complexity, or externally at the system level in terms of the architectural topology.

Technique usage

A suite of metrics should be collected at both the class and the system level in order to assess complexity. These could include, but not be limited by,

- fan-out (measure of coupling)
- average and standard deviation of number of methods per class
- average and standard deviation of the method size
- mean and maximum depths of inheritance hierarchies.

These metrics will be complemented by the collection of reuse metrics, effort metrics and so on.

It is important that a thorough and well-specified metrics program be initiated and deployed. It is also important that the focus of the metrics program is an evaluation of the quality of the product or of the process but *not* of the developers (Henderson-Sellers, 1995b).

144   CORE TECHNIQUES

Deliverables and outputs (post-condition)

Complexity metrics values, documented and analyzed for each class, package and the total system.

Composition structures – see Relationship modeling

Computer-based training   Star rating **

Focus: Learning
Typical tasks for which this is needed: Develop education and training plan, do user training
Related techniques: Customer (on-site) training, internet and web technology, lectures, PSP, train the trainer
Input (pre-condition): 'Students', training needs
Underpinning concepts: Training can be effective if undertaken at student's own pace. Computers are an effective means of presenting such training information

Technique description

Computer-based training (CBT) may be thought of as the general term for the activity in which the trainee predominantly learns via the computer through lessons, exercises and simulations, and may be directed or evaluated by the computer. As such computer-managed learning (CML) and computer-based assessment (CBA) are subactivities of computer-based training. Whilst not specifically OO, CBT is important because (1) transferring to OT requires reskilling and retraining and (2) in the late 1990s, computer-based and/or web-based education became the norm.

Technique usage

CBT is a useful and reasonably popular training technique in the IT industry. Generally, in order to arrive at a decision whether to use CBT in a given training situation, we should consider the following criteria:

- the size of the target group
- the geographical dispersion of the target audience
- the frequency with which the training is repeated
- the stability of the training material
- access to a computer of appropriate configuration.

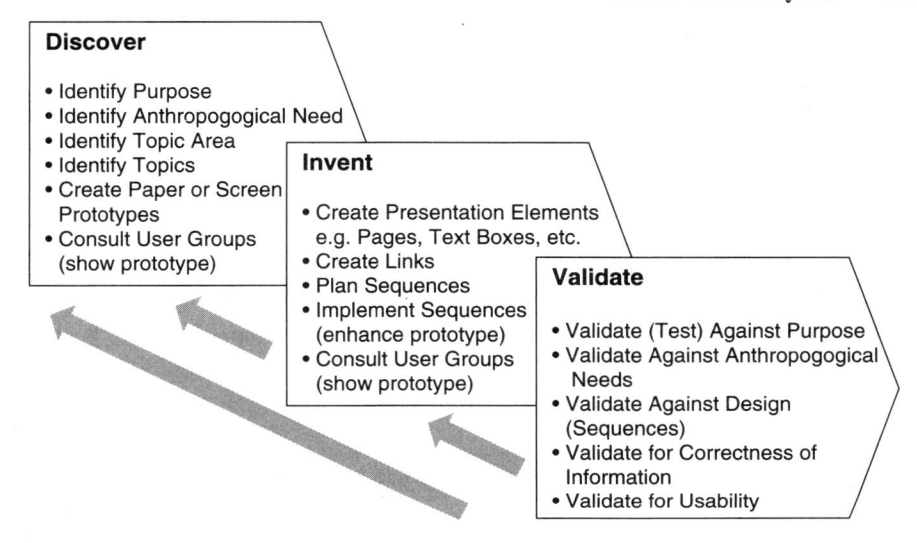

Discover
- Identify Purpose
- Identify Anthropogical Need
- Identify Topic Area
- Identify Topics
- Create Paper or Screen Prototypes
- Consult User Groups (show prototype)

Invent
- Create Presentation Elements e.g. Pages, Text Boxes, etc.
- Create Links
- Plan Sequences
- Implement Sequences (enhance prototype)
- Consult User Groups (show prototype)

Validate
- Validate (Test) Against Purpose
- Validate Against Anthropogical Needs
- Validate Against Design (Sequences)
- Validate for Correctness of Information
- Validate for Usability

Figure A.16 Stages of computer-based training.

Computer-based training is most appropriate in environments where there is a large and geographically disperse target audience who have need for frequent administration of training which itself is stable and not subject to frequent changes or updates.

To be effective, CBT, like any other software, must be designed well. The product development lifecycle of good CBT material is therefore not dissimilar to that of good software. This means that there is need for the three basic elements of discovery, invention and evaluation (Graham *et al.*, 1997b). Figure A.16 depicts the stages to follow within these three basic elements. It should be noted that in this scheme there is no implication of linearity. In fact, an iterative and incremental approach is recommended. Indeed, a comprehensive approach to training includes an iterative mix of classroom teaching, workshops, brown-bag lunches, newsletters, mentoring and on-the-job experience. CBT is only one element in this mix but can be very useful since it can be accessed at any time (providing JIT knowledge).

Deliverables and outputs (post-condition)

Well-trained workforce.

Concept maps   Star rating **

Focus: Requirements analysis
Typical tasks for which this is needed: Analyze user requirements

146   CORE TECHNIQUES

Related techniques: Brainstorming, workshops
Input (pre-condition): Requirements documentation
Underpinning concepts: Abstraction

Technique description

A concept map consists of a number of concepts (nodes) with connecting links (edges) useful in requirements analysis. Concept maps capture, at an abstract level, a variety of static and dynamic semantic relationships between concepts in the business domain; and these are all represented as static links in the concept map. The map records the current state of the developer's understanding about the domain and its organization (Duffy, 1995). Initial attempts at graphically displaying concepts and their inter-linkages may well not discover several important links or concepts or these may be invalid or ambiguous. (In many ways, this technique is an alternative to CRC card modeling.)

Technique usage

A developer skilled in both the domain and the use of concept maps will be more successful by approaching their use in two stages: concept map preparation and concept map activities.

Starting with a textual requirements statement, nouns are candidate concepts; whilst much irrelevant information (e.g. attributes, out-of-scope concepts, ambiguous concepts, superfluous concepts) should be filtered out. Verbs and verb phrases then form the links between concepts such that concept–link–concept form a well-structured natural language sentence. In summary, then, the products of this first, preparation, stage (the list of relevant concepts and the links between them) are created by

(1) making a list of words and concepts relevant to the problem domain
(2) applying the filtering process (discussed above)
(3) finding the linking words
(4) constructing sentences using words from (2) and (3).

In the second stage, concepts are ordered by building a linked concept map from the products of stage 1 (see above) in which the key concept is identified (level 0 in the hierarchy – Figure A.17). Supporting concepts, which become increasingly specific, are at lower hierarchical levels (levels 1, 2 etc.). In summary, then, a concept map is constructed by

(1) listing the key concept
(2) listing the supporting concept at lower levels of abstraction
(3) creating links between the key and supporting concepts

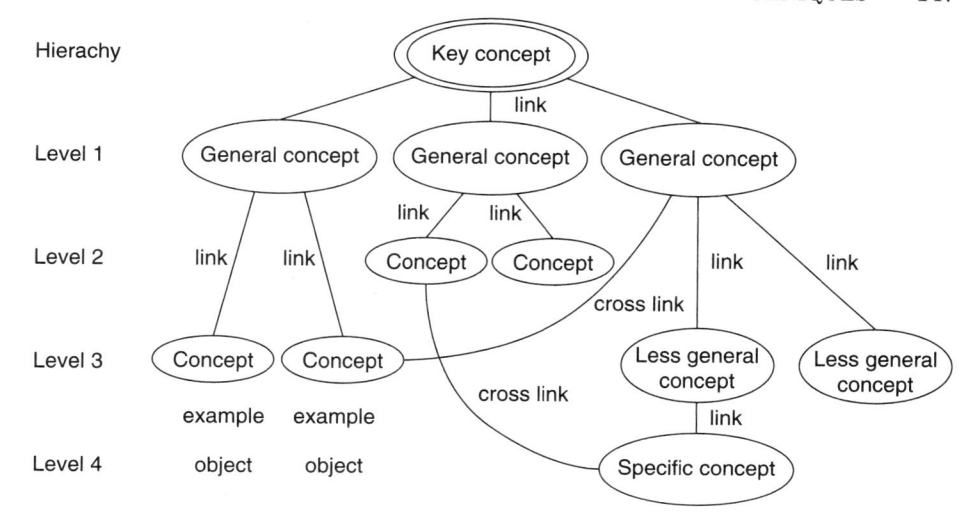

Figure A.17 Structuring concept maps (after Novak and Gowin, 1984).

(4) creating cross-links between supporting concepts
(5) iterating over steps 1–4 across each supporting concept.

Concepts are embryonic classes when translated to an OO design. Whilst links lead to relationships, in a concept map there are only three types of link: interaction, generalization and decomposition. (Duffy (1995) calls these projection, abstraction and partitioning links respectively in which projection links are action-based interactions, abstraction links relate to hierarchies and partitioning to aggregations.) The differences between concept maps and object-oriented diagrams (e.g. OML's semantic nets) are (in the latter) the existence of multiplicity information, the addition of responsibilities and services and a firmer recognition and documenting of generalization and aggregation structures.

Deliverables and outputs (post-condition)

The concept map, appropriately documented.

Configuration management   Star rating **

Focus: Detailed technical management
Typical tasks for which this is needed: Develop software development context plans and strategies
Related techniques: Audit requirements, cost–benefit analysis, inspections, PERT charts, standards compliance

Input (pre-condition): System under development
Underpinning concepts: Project management, version control

Technique description

Modern software systems are complex. As we iterate through the software development lifecycle, many different versions of various artefacts come into existence. For example, in an object-oriented development environment, we not only have a potentially large number of classes from various libraries, we might also have our local modifications of these. We usually add to these a number of classes specifically developed for the present application. These classes again may come in many versions, each representing one stage of the gradual and incremental increase towards completion. There are also many other 'non-code' artefacts such as specifications, designs, user manuals, etc. that also come in varied versions and forms. Many of these versions may be interrelated horizontally (a user manual relating to an earlier user manual) and vertically (a change in the design of a class creates a new version of that design as well as a new version of the code and the user manual). This of course creates a very complex situation. To manage this complexity, we need configuration management where a configuration specifies which version for each independent artefact is to be used. Configuration management is a technique by which system artefacts may be identified, defined, released and changed in any arrangement that constitutes a configuration, i.e. either a system baseline or a release (Buckley, 1994; Goldberg and Rubin, 1995, page 506). Tools for configuration management help to control changes in system parts, as well as to maintain the integrity and traceability of these changes throughout the development process (Goldberg and Rubin, 1995, page 319).

Configuration management may benefit from automation. Many configuration management tools exist (e.g. SCCS, RCS). Configuration management should always be addressed, even in the absence of automated tools.

Configuration management systems and procedures must be based on a set of published and available standards. These standards must include guidelines for configuration management planning, change management, version management and control and monitoring of the configuration management process itself. IEEE has a suite of standards that cover all these aspects. These are:

- IEEE 828–1990 Software Configuration Management Planning
- IEEE 1042–1987 Guide to Software Configuration Management.

PLANNING OF CONFIGURATION MANAGEMENT

This process concentrates on identifying and recording the details of the configuration management activity in an organization. These, at a minimum, are:

- the configuration management procedures, policies and records and documents

- tools utilized (automated or non-automated) and the means of recording and storing the configuration management data
- definitions of artefacts and entities under configuration management
- roles played by various staff in the management and control of the configuration management activity.

CHANGE MANAGEMENT

Change management differs from version control. Change management is the activity of identifying, analyzing, approving and effecting change to a configuration item. It starts when a change is requested. This is usually done using a Change Request Form (CRF). In an organization with well-developed configuration management systems, such requests are recorded and analyzed with respect to their viability, desirability, economy and time necessity. Should the change be approved, usually by a Change Control Board (CCB), the development team (implementation team) is advised to effect the change. Upon so doing, the configuration management system creates a new version which incorporates that change. It should be noted that in an integrated CASE environment much of this may be automated.

VERSION CONTROL

To contain the combinatorial complexity of interrelationship of software artefacts as they evolve, version control is required. Version control works on the basis of version variants or deltas. By this we mean that differences to the original and each subsequent version is recorded not as duplicate documents but as incremental differences (deltas). To build any given version, then, is a matter of applying the right deltas to the original (baseline) version. Version identification (naming), version building (building the right version of the artefact) and system building (combining the right versions of many artefacts to build the correct system) are important concerns in version control.

CONFIGURATION MANAGEMENT MONITORING

In addition to the above activities, we need to concern ourselves also with how the process of software configuration management (SCM) itself is conducted and whether it is on track. Status Accounting and Audit and Reviews will do this for us.

Status accounting is largely concerned with assessing the current state of the system:

- what happened?
- who did it?
- when did it happen?
- what else will be affected?

Wider issues concerning completeness, validation and the SCM process are handled by management reviews and audits. Audits and reviews determine to what extent:

- all changes have been properly implemented
- the actual configuration item (CI) reflects the required physical and functional characteristics.

The technical correctness of a CI that has been modified is best to be the subject of an inspection (q.v.). These should be held (as a minimum) prior to the release of a baseline and to determine whether:

- the Change Order has been implemented?
- the change has been highlighted?
- all related CI have been updated?
- SE standards have been followed?
- SCM procedures have been followed?

Technique usage

A fundamental concept of SCM is the notion of a baseline. At any given point in time, a software system is characterized by its configuration, i.e. by the arrangement of its units or components. The entities which make up a configuration are called configuration items (CI). These can include all the entities in the project that are subject to change (e.g. plans, specifications, test cases, classes, etc.).

A baseline is a milestone in development marked by the delivery and approval of a CI. It acts as a reference point and as a basis for further development. The software development process typically proceeds as the establishment of a series of baselines of increasing complexity. From this perspective the current state of a system is given by its latest baseline together with the changes made since that baseline was established.

Once configuration items have been identified and named, the problem of how they are to be physically tracked and stored needs to be addressed. We can define a number of project libraries which hold data on CI and baselines, e.g. format, location, access control procedures. These can be:

- dynamic (programmer's) library
- controlled (master) library, or
- static library (software repository).

Configuration Control (CC) activities request, evaluate and (possibly) implement changes to baselined CI. The rules of CC in essence define the interaction of the project staff with the above libraries. Changes encompass both error correction and enhancement.

CORE TECHNIQUES   151

The basic sequence of steps for CC is:

(1) identification and documentation of the need for a change
(2) analysis and evaluation of a change request
(3) approval or disapproval of a request
(4) implementation, verification and release of a change.

The configuration management team should not only keep all parties informed of important changes but should be able to restore a system to any release or version.

Deliverables and outputs (post-condition)

Multiple versions of the system, software configuration architecture.

Containment – see Relationship modeling

Context modeling   Star rating **

Focus: Business analysis
Typical tasks for which this is needed: Model and re-engineer business process(es)
Related techniques: Abstraction utilization, business process modeling
Input (pre-condition): User requirements
Underpinning concepts: The 'big picture'

Technique description

Context specification expresses the relationship between a given system and its environment (Martin and Odell, 1995, page 318). This can be shown using the context diagram of McMenamin and Palmer (1984) or the initial system diagram of Jacobson *et al.* (1992) which are essentially equivalent to that in SSADM (Ashworth and Goodland, 1990).

When using COMN, the context diagram should be used (Firesmith *et al.*, 1997, page 153). Each context diagram (e.g. Figure A.18) represents the whole system as a single unit; set in context with the external actors and agents with which the system has to interact. A context model is a very high level abstraction depicting one specific view of the situation. It is a depiction of a system that describes that particular view. As the depiction of a system, a context model has to fulfil a number of criteria. It has to

(1) be aligned with a given purpose or a set of purposes the achievement of which gives meaning to the system being modeled

152   CORE TECHNIQUES

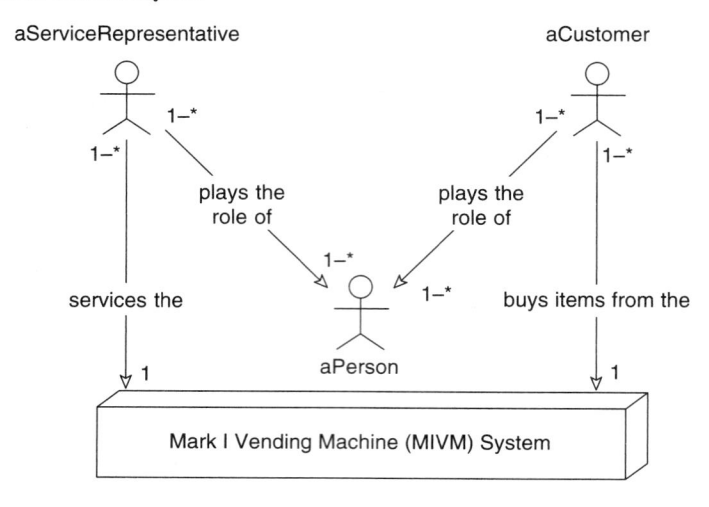

Figure A.18 COMN's context diagram (after Firesmith *et al.*, 1997).

(2) define the boundary of the system. In other words it must define what entities, activities and relationships are to be considered as belonging to the system and what fall outside this boundary. What falls outside the boundary is called the system environment

(3) provide a name (a cognitive handle) for the system (e.g. a system to do X)

(4) identify the entities, activities and systems within the system environment that interact with the system under consideration

(5) identify, broadly, the nature of the communication between the system and its environment. In other words, it has to identify what information and artefacts are exchanged between the system and the entities, activities and systems mentioned in (3) above and

(6) provide a simple notation for capture and communication of these concepts.

Technique usage

A context model may be used in requirements modeling to depict a high level abstraction of the system to be studied. In design, a context model may set out the high level abstraction of the solution proposed as it interacts with the environment in which it is proposed to be implemented.

Context models are also very useful tools in BPR. Here, they depict the business process under focus in terms of its placement, purpose and its interactions with other business systems. This allows the BPR practitioner to isolate a particular view of the business situation (of which there may be many) and study it as a given system with a specific purpose, the fulfilment of which requires the existence of a process. It is this process that is radically remodeled in the course of BPR. In OO BPR, as in traditional approaches, a model of the existing system is created. This is then converted to a logical model (of the current system) – 'reversing the business' in Jacobson *et al.*'s (1995) terms. The business is then 'envisioned', i.e. a new logical model of the *required logical system* is created; followed by documentation of the required *physical* system.

Deliverables and outputs (post-condition)

Context model, specified using an appropriate notation (e.g. COMN's context model).

Contract specification   Star rating ***

Focus: Ensuring quality by contracting
Typical tasks for which this is needed: Code, construct the object model, create and/or identify reusable components ('for reuse'), evaluate quality, optimize reuse ('with reuse'), optimize the design, specify quality goals, test
Related techniques: Formal methods
Input (pre-condition): Client–server interactions
Underpinning concepts: Assertion Language; Contracting; Encapsulation and Information Hiding; Object-Z

Technique description

Contracting relies on encapsulation and information hiding (q.v.). In requesting a service, the client needs to be sure that the service will be provided *exactly* as expected. This expectation is declared formally as the server's contract. It specifies what will be 'delivered' by means of the service and what obligations have to be met prior to acceptance of the service request. There are benefits for and obligations on *both* parties in the contract. In addition, the client wishes to remain unaware of how the supplier fulfils the request. For example, a *CUSTOMER* object requests the current balance from a *BANK_ACCOUNT* object. Perhaps this object has the information stored; perhaps it enters into its own (sub)contract with an *INTEREST_TABLE* object. Implementation is thus flexible.

Technique usage

When developing contracts, a number of guidelines are useful. Those services that occur in all states and which may occur for all values of any of the arguments require no pre-condition. Strictly the pre-condition is true. However, those services which require an object to be in a certain state before a service is called, or may require the arguments to be of a certain value before the service is valid, will require a pre-condition. Pre-conditions are used to specify the conditions under which the service is valid. Not satisfying the pre-condition indicates an error either in the model specification or in model implementation of the client. The use of pre-conditions at all stages of the development is an important approach to the development of high quality, correct software.

The effect of a service which changes some or all of the object's properties should be specified in the post-condition. An operation must not only satisfy the post-condition but also leave the object in a valid and stable state as defined by the class invariant which can be viewed as a post-condition on each service. If an operation does not satisfy both the post-condition and the invariant, there has been an error in the operation specification or implementation of the supplier/server. Once again the use of post-conditions throughout the development process is an important means of ensuring software correctness.

Contracts can be found by examining the business rules of the domain as specified in the requirements specification or embedded in scenarios. Business rules about one object will be spread among many scenarios and it is important to ensure consistency of the business rules *between* scenarios. Instead, the explicit specification of contracts often leads to the discovery of ambiguous business procedures and policies that will need to be addressed.

A complete method specification consists of pre- and post-conditions which describe the object's state before and after the operation occurs. Both are Boolean expressions. The means of expressing pre- and post-conditions varies from formal specification languages such as Object-Z (Duke *et al.*, 1991) or the BON assertion language (Waldén and Nerson, 1995) to informal English statements. Which approach is used will vary with the domain in which the model is developed and the experience of the modeler.

Contracts can be applied at various levels of abstraction making them applicable throughout the development process. Contracts are continually updated and revised during the development process as the behavior of a CIRT becomes clear from an examination of the scenario classes, user requirements, state transition diagrams etc.

Deliverables and outputs (post-condition)

Contracts for all responsibilities.

Cost–benefit analysis   (CBA) Star rating ***

Focus: Financial evaluation
Typical tasks for which this is needed: Model and re-engineer business process(es), obtain business approval
Related techniques: Approval gaining, cost estimation, risk analysis
Input (pre-condition): Cost information
Underpinning concepts: Decisions need to be made on sound data

Technique description

In a cost–benefit analysis, a comparison is made between estimated future benefits and project future costs. Benefits may be easily evaluated in terms of time saved but may also be more tenuous and thus harder to quantify, e.g. increased business generated. Costs within a CBA should include personnel costs, computer usage costs, training costs, supply and equipment costs as well as running costs. Running costs include both fixed and variable costs of usage and should be estimated as carefully as possible. Benefits cover tangible and intangible benefits; that is to say, those benefits upon which a dollar figure can be placed and those which may bring some benefit to the organization that cannot be directly counted in dollar terms, such as customer goodwill, reputation, market leadership.

A preliminary cost–benefit analysis (CBA) should be undertaken in the Project Initiation Activity in order to determine if the business benefits likely to be achieved outweigh the cost of the project. The CBA undertaken during this stage will be preliminary in the sense that it is hard to estimate likely costs when the solution has not been developed. However, it should be possible to indicate a net benefit or net loss from the project and hence permit an informed decision to be made. It is also important to balance the calculated cost of undertaking the project against the cost of *not* undertaking the project.

Technique usage

CBA or cost-effectiveness of a system can be measured by payback analysis; return-on-investment (ROI); and net present value analysis (Whitten *et al.*, 1989). Whichever method is chosen, it is important that some analysis of the economic feasibility of the project is undertaken. These are all standard techniques in financial analysis and no attempt is made to replicate them here since they are so well-known.

Deliverables and outputs (post-condition)

Cost–benefit analysis (document).

Cost estimation   Star rating *

Focus: Planning of costs
Typical tasks for which this is needed: Develop and implement resource allocation plan, obtain business approval, undertake feasibility study
Related techniques: Cost–benefit analysis, metrics collection
Input (pre-condition): Requirements documentation
Underpinning concepts: Cost Estimation Models

156   CORE TECHNIQUES

Technique description

Costing software development is notoriously difficult and using object technology doesn't make it any easier (at least not at present!). Estimation is really required before the project commences – indeed, its very commencement will need an approval to proceed which in turn will be based, at least in part, on an estimation of budget.

To date, a lot of cost estimation has been based on experience. Today, there is much effort being expended in moving from this ad hoc style to a measurement-based approach (see discussion in CD: Appendix E).

Technique usage

The basic software cost estimation process is relatively straightforward:

(1) determine how much software needs to be built (SS – Software Size)
(2) determine the rate of software production per person (DP – Developer Productivity)
(3) divide SS by DP to determine the amount of effort (Effort) required to build the software
(4) multiply Effort by an hourly rate, to obtain an estimate for the project's cost.

The difficult part, however, is the determination of how much software needs to be written, sufficiently early on in the development process, for the estimate to be useful. This needs to be done by a skilled developer or consultant who works out the number of business domain classes (BDC). Once this is complete (for a typical, medium-sized software project, a job usually taking less than a week), the cost estimation calculation is straightforward. The BDC count is multiplied by 3.6 to allow for other non-domain/non-business classes (Haynes and Henderson-Sellers, 1996) and then either divided by the known productivity level for your developers or else by an average value of around 2.5 classes per person per month:

$$\text{Project effort} = \text{BDC} \times 3.6/2.5. \tag{A.1}$$

There are other potentially influencing factors that may need to be considered. These include the application quality desired, the level of documentation specified and the size of the system. The technique has been validated on a number of commercial projects in the 3–100 person month range with accuracies of 5–15%.

Deliverables and outputs (post-condition)

An overall estimate of cost, plus error bars. The documents, if approved, should also provide the backbone for use in monitoring and managing the ensuing software development lifecycle.

Coupling measurement Star rating **

Focus: Metrics
Typical tasks for which this is needed: Evaluate quality
Related techniques: Cohesion measurement complexity measurement, metrics collection
Input (pre-condition): Design
Underpinning concepts: Cohesion, Coupling and Connascence

Technique description

Whilst coupling is necessary in an object-oriented system in order that it function, excessive coupling is regarded as highly undesirable, since it tends to prevent the development of fully reusable, independent, autonomous components. Coupling occurs whenever one object uses the services of another one. It can be measured at the architectural level in terms of potential message passing or dynamically in terms of actual invocations (the former is the more usual).

Whilst there are no absolutes, a comparison of coupling values for classes across a system can be very valuable. The aim is to distribute responsibilities fairly equably across the system (Wirfs-Brock *et al.*, 1990) so any single class with a large coupling value, particularly a large fan-out value is in reality a 'god class', i.e. a main routine controlling lots of subroutines – not OO at all!

Technique usage

Measure the CBO (coupling between objects) from the design diagrams counting one for any link (inheritance, association, aggregation etc.). The CBO count for any pair of objects is binary: yes or no. Plot histograms and investigate any anomalously large values.

If desired, look at other coupling metrics that may, for instance, count the number of connexions between objects, e.g. class A uses three services of class B leading to a coupling value of 3. A metric such as MPC (message passing coupling) may be helpful here or one of the other variants discussed in Henderson-Sellers (1996).

Deliverables and outputs (post-condition)

Coupling metrics values, documented and analyzed for each class, package and the total system.

CPM charts Star rating ***

Focus: Project management
Typical tasks for which this is needed: Develop and implement resource allocation plan

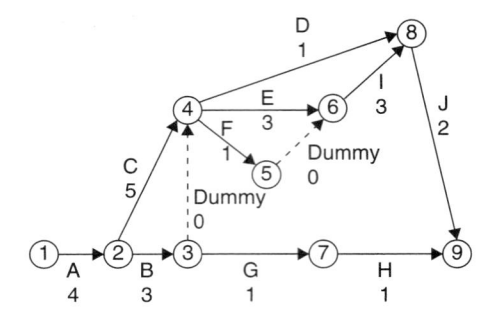

Figure A.19 Example CPM network (after Anderson and Lievano, 1986).

Related techniques: Gantt charts, PERT charts
Input (pre-condition): Information on durations of activities
Underpinning concepts: Need for objective method of formulating planning timelines

Technique description

The Critical Path Method (CPM) was developed as far back as 1957 for the management control of construction projects. It is well suited to projects that have activities of reasonably well-known duration and to processes that are applied repetitively. When these conditions are not satisfied, e.g. for cases with uncertain duration activities, the PERT technique (q.v.) is more appropriate.

Technique usage

CPM focuses on planning, scheduling and control by identification of the critical path through the network used to model the sequences of process elements. A CPM chart is a network of numbered nodes. Lines linking the nodes (Figure A.19) each represent some activity which has a duration. The duration is shown as a (numeric) label on the link (together with a label indicating the activity name). Some activities need other specific activities to have been completed before they can be actioned; others can occur in parallel (multiple lines emanating from the same node). When paths rejoin, they represent two (or more) sequences of activities, the sequences operating in parallel. The longest path, judged from all paths arriving at this node, is the critical path since any forward progression beyond that joining node depends upon completion of *all* the activities along this critical path. For example, consider Node 8 in Figure A.19. The path 1248 takes 10 days and path 12468 takes 15 days. Thus the need to do activities E and I delay any progression beyond node 8. Overall, this (upper) route takes 17 days (124689) as compared with 9 days for the lower route (12379). Thus the minimum completion time is 17 days (the 'critical path').

The use of CPM charts permits identification of earliest start times for activities and earliest finish times – similarly, latest start times and latest finish times. On some routes there may be slack time: time when there is no activity taking place. The path with zero slack time identifies the critical path.

The result of the calculations made in CPM or PERT Techniques can be depicted using a Gantt chart (q.v.).

Deliverables and outputs (post-condition)

CPM chart and assessment of critical path.

CRC card modeling   Star rating ***

Focus: Interactive discovery of CIRTs
Typical tasks for which this is needed: Construct the object model, develop business object model, identify user requirements
Related techniques: Interaction modeling, pattern recognition, roleplay, simulation
Input (pre-condition): User requirements
Underpinning concepts: CRC Cards; Idioms, Patterns and Frameworks; Responsibilities and Responsibility-Driven Design

Technique description

CRC card modeling is a conceptual tool, useful during analysis and early design, when the assignment of system operations to classes is still incomplete and the object abstractions themselves are still plastic. It is a very different matter to propose doing some CRC card modeling *after* the initial object abstractions have been fixed, say through developing an object model (Booch, 1994). Indeed, Goldberg and Rubin (1995) suggest that using CRC cards at this stage is only useful for reorganization and refinement of already-discovered objects. At its best, CRC card modeling is an active brainstorming technique, similar in intention to other prototyping techniques used to define the business problem and the users' requirements. However, CRC card modeling simultaneously identifies interaction patterns and proposes the objects responsible for carrying them out. Candidate CIRTs are selected from the vocabulary of the problem domain (Abbott, 1983; 1987).

Technique usage

The process associated with applying the CRC technique is also attractive. System responsibilities are acquired by anthropomorphically asking: 'can I suffer this operation?' or 'am I responsible for knowing this fact?' or 'am I responsible for being able to do this action?' Determination of these responsibilities can often be accomplished by roleplay (q.v.) in which each participant acts the part of the CIRT, taking an index card for documenting what they discover, and then asking: (a) what is my name? (we saw elsewhere how important a good name is; see Technique: Class naming); (b) what are my responsibilities, i.e. what system resources do I manage and what services can I offer to other CIRTs?; and (c) with whom do I have to collaborate in order to provide my services?

Cards may only acquire a few responsibilities before the space on them is used up and a redistribution is required (this forces a localized design). Cards are cheap and may be torn up and rewritten quickly during simulations. The recursive process of identifying collaborators, assigning responsibilities, identifying collaborators at the next level, and so on, may be pursued to any degree of detail. As the object model is refined, candidate CIRTs which do not seem to support any useful behavior are identified and discarded (Wirfs-Brock *et al.*, 1990), whereas useful manager concepts, which were not present in the original vocabulary analysis, may be discovered (Budd, 1991). Once classes and responsibilities have been discovered they can be linked in scenarios and tested in roleplay (q.v.) situations (Wilkinson, 1995a). Active brainstorming is encouraged by the anthropomorphizing approach during simulations, and missing behaviors are uncovered (Wilkinson, 1994).

Deliverables and outputs (post-condition)

Set of CRC cards, one for each CIRT thus identified.

Creation charts Star rating **

Focus: Detailed design and coding
Typical tasks for which this is needed: Code
Related techniques: Collaborations analysis
Input (pre-condition): Collaboration diagram(s)
Underpinning concepts: Documenting creator–created links is needed for final design and code

Technique description

In a creation chart (Figure A.20), as originally proposed in BON (Waldén and Nerson, 1995, page 97), there are two columns: 'Class' and 'Creates instances of'. The creation chart shows which classes are responsible for the initiation of instance creation by other classes and thus supplements the collaboration diagrams with specific information on creation. It is especially useful when deferred/abstract classes are being used since, not being able to be instantiated as objects, they can never appear on the collaboration or sequence diagrams and may thus inadvertently be neglected. Conversely creation charts may identify CIRTs in the design to which *no other object* ever sends a creation message. These are called fossil classes (Waldén and Nerson, 1995) and are thus extraneous to the design and can be safely removed. Having said this, in some domains,

CORE TECHNIQUES

CREATION	CONFERENCE_SUPPORT	Page: 1/1
COMMENT List of classes creating objects in the system.	**INDEXING** **created:** 1993-02-18kw	
Class	**Creates instances of**	
CONFERENCE	PROGRAM_COMMITTEE, TECHNICAL_COMMITTEE, ORGANIZATION_COMMITTEE, TIME_TABLE	
PROGRAM_COMMITTEE	PROGRAM, PAPER, PAPER_SESSION, PERSON	
TECHNICAL_COMMITTEE	TUTORIAL, TUTORIAL_SESSION, PERSON	
ORGANIZATION_COMMITTEE	MAILING, ADDRESS_LABEL, STICKY_FORM, REGISTRATION, PERSON, INVOICE, INVOICE_FORM, ATTENDEE_LIST, LIST_FORM, POSTER_SIGN, POSTER_FORM, EVALUATION_SHEET EVALUATION_FORM, STATISTICS	
PRESENTATION*	STATUS, PERSON	
PAPER	REVIEW, ACCEPTANCE_LETTER, REJECTION_LETTER, LETTER_FORM, AUTHOR_GUIDELINES	
TUTORIAL	ACCEPTANCE_LETTER, REJECTION_LETTER, LETTER_FORM	
REGISTRATION	CONFIRMATION_LETTER, LETTER_FORM, BADGE, BADGE_FORM	

Figure A.20 Example creation chart (after Waldén and Nerson, 1995).

such as artificial intelligence, these fossil classes can be essential to represent concepts that are important if uninstantiated, e.g. the class of perfect men.

Technique usage

Identify, for each class, the list of objects it is responsible for creating. Document these formally, as in Figure A.20. Identify any remaining fossil classes.

Deliverables and outputs (post-condition)

Set of creation charts.

Critical success factors (CSFs)   Star rating ***

Focus: Financial evaluation

162   CORE TECHNIQUES

```
                    ┌─────────────┐
                    │Communication│
                    │    CSF9     │
                    └─────────────┘
```

┌──────────┐ ┌──────────┐ ┌──────────┐ ┌──────────┐ ┌──────────┐ ┌──────────┐ ┌──────────┐
│ Project │ │   Top   │ │ Project │ │ Client │ │Personnel │ │Technical │ │ Client │
│ mission │ │management│ │schedule/ │ │consultat.│ │   │ │ tasks   │ │acceptance│
│   │ │ support │ │   plan   │ │   │ │   │ │   │ │   │
│ CSF1   │ │ CSF2   │ │ CSF3   │ │ CSF4   │ │ CSF5   │ │ CSF6   │ │ CSF7   │
└──────────┘ └──────────┘ └──────────┘ └──────────┘ └──────────┘ └──────────┘ └──────────┘

```
                    ┌─────────────┐
                    │ Monitoring  │
                    │and feedback │
                    │    CSF8     │
                    └─────────────┘
                    ┌─────────────┐
                    │  Trouble-   │
                    │  shooting   │
                    │    CSF10    │
                    └─────────────┘
```

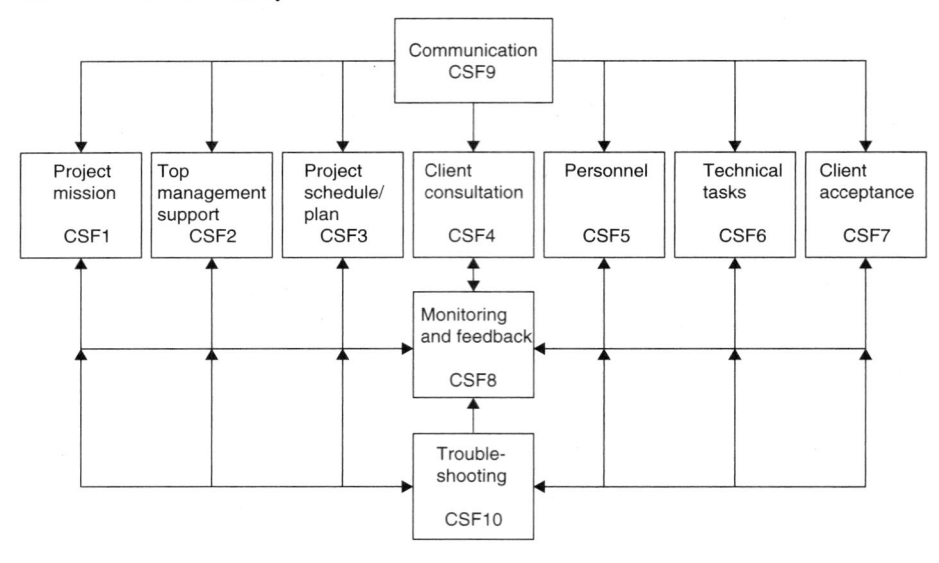

Figure A.21 The ten CSFs of Pinto and Slevin (1986) within a project implementation profile (after Thal and Docker, 1995).

Typical tasks for which this is needed: Obtain business approval, undertake feasibility study
Related techniques: Cost–benefit analysis, cost estimation
Input (pre-condition): Business aims
Underpinning concepts: Not meeting a CSF leads to business failure

Technique description

As part of the business plan evaluation, critical success factors (CSFs) for the organization should be considered. A CSF is some factor which if not realized will spell the downfall of the organizational venture (Rockart, 1979). These form the basis against which the options evaluated in the Feasibility Study can be measured. A CSF is simply a factor which, if not optimized, could be critical to the success of the company. A typical CSF may be the delivery time for a company that promises speedy deliveries (e.g. Domino's Pizza^{TM}).

Technique usage

It is important, when identifying CSFs, to elicit from the business manager those key areas of business activity in which good results are absolutely critical to achieving the manager's (or the organization's) goals. Identifying these few areas makes explicit the manager's implicit view of the organizational success factors.

CORE TECHNIQUES 163

Pinto and Slevin (1986) identified 10 critical success factor categories which they call the project implementation profile (Figure A.21):

(1) project mission
(2) top management support
(3) project schedule/plan
(4) client consultation
(5) personnel
(6) technical tasks
(7) client acceptance
(8) monitoring and feedback
(9) communication
(10) trouble shooting.

These 10 categories were augmented by Thal and Docker (1995) and were then linked to the activities of (an earlier version of) the contract lifecycle of SOMA/OPEN. The new categories, which are considered beyond the immediate control of the project manager and team, and therefore outside the project implementation profile, are identified as:

(11) organizational climate
(12) supervision of the project manager
(13) leadership
(14) power and politics
(15) environmental events
(16) urgency

and the linkages are shown in Figure A.22.

Deliverables and outputs (post-condition)

List of Critical Success Factors.

Customer (on-site) training   Star rating **

Focus: Training
Typical tasks for which this is needed: Deliver product to customer, develop software development context plans and strategies (change management)
Related techniques: Computer-based training, lectures, train the trainer
Input (pre-condition): System accepted by user
Underpinning concepts: End users need help to become adept with new system

164   CORE TECHNIQUES

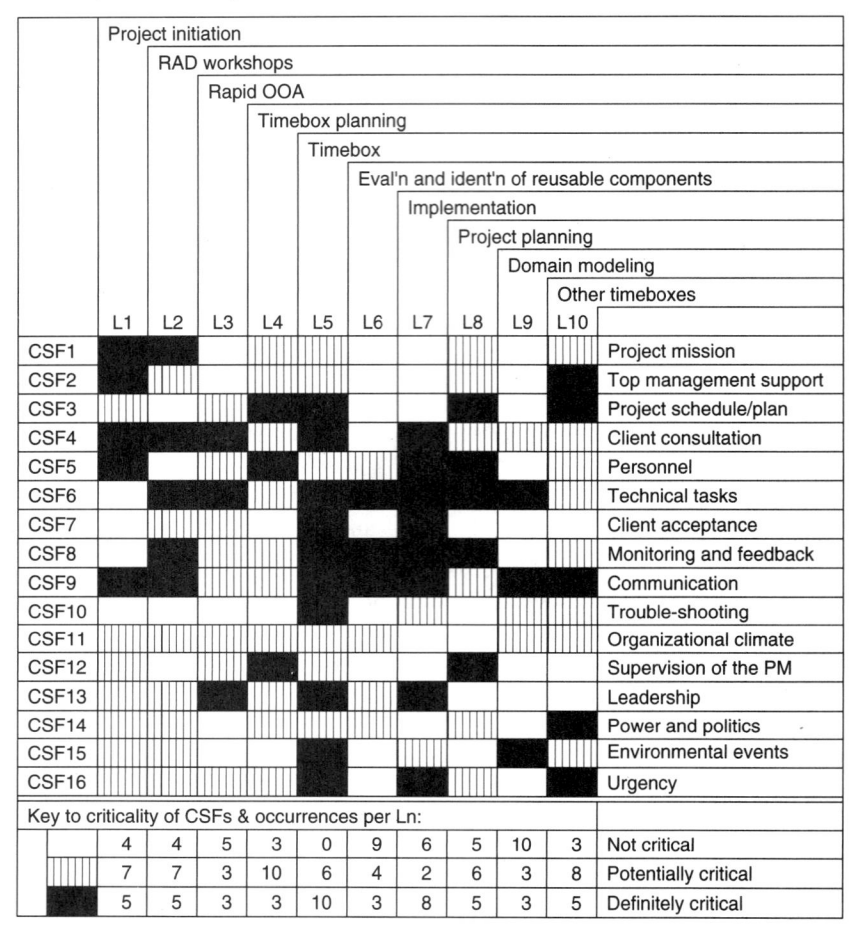

	Project initiation										
		RAD workshops									
			Rapid OOA								
				Timebox planning							
					Timebox						
						Eval'n and ident'n of reusable components					
							Implementation				
								Project planning			
									Domain modeling		
										Other timeboxes	
	L1	L2	L3	L4	L5	L6	L7	L8	L9	L10	
CSF1	■										Project mission
CSF2		▨							■		Top management support
CSF3	▨			■			■				Project schedule/plan
CSF4					■		■		▨		Client consultation
CSF5		▨			■	▨					Personnel
CSF6		■	▨		■						Technical tasks
CSF7		▨			■	■		■			Client acceptance
CSF8	■		▨				■			▨	Monitoring and feedback
CSF9				▨		■			▨		Communication
CSF10					■		▨		▨		Trouble-shooting
CSF11	▨	▨		▨						▨	Organizational climate
CSF12	▨			■				■			Supervision of the PM
CSF13		▨	■		▨			■			Leadership
CSF14	▨						▨			■	Power and politics
CSF15	▨				■		▨		■	▨	Environmental events
CSF16	▨	▨		▨		■		▨		■	Urgency
Key to criticality of CSFs & occurrences per Ln:											
	4	4	5	3	0	9	6	5	10	3	Not critical
▨	7	7	3	10	6	4	2	6	3	8	Potentially critical
■	5	5	3	3	10	3	8	5	3	5	Definitely critical

Figure A.22 CSFs criticality for OPEN timebox lifecycle activities (after Thal and Docker, 1995).

Technique description

Training of clients is frequently performed, by the consultant/trainer, at the client's own site. Training courses are usually several days. They may be lectures or workshops. They may focus on concepts or on specific products.

Technique usage

There are a number of problems with providing training at customer sites and, in principle, it should be limited to compelling cases. These include:

- There are occasions when the software can only be utilized, demonstrated or appreciated in a given context, e.g. when interacting with some specialized equipment. Whilst training for the average accounting package might be given anywhere, training for a sophisticated automated warehouse management system, or software that controls a complex manufacturing system which requires it to interface with a myriad of external equipment and systems, must be done on site.

- The developer (trainer) does not have adequate training facilities. This is particularly the case with smaller developers or training houses. The inadequacy might be in terms of physical room, computer equipment or other matters of logistics.

- The customer insists. Be careful if this happens. Find out why there is an insistence on training being provided in-house. There may be a good reason. Aside from the first point above, other reasons usually relate to some political advantage accruing to the customer. This may be at the expense of the training provider (see below), but usually is not. At any rate, find out why they wish to do so and, if it is agreeable, provide the training in-house.

- Cost and other logistics. There might be a financial or logistics reason for the training to be provided on-site. For example, if the customer wishes 200 of its staff to be trained over a two-week period and they are all in Los Angeles, whilst you (the trainer) are in New York, who should go to whom?

But why is in-house training a potential problem? The following are some of the reasons:

- The loss of 'home turf' advantage. This may sound paranoidal but is quite real. If for no other reason, when training is provided at your own organization, your trainers have access to additional material, backups, expert advice from the original developers, know the equipment and their idiosyncrasies, etc.

- Interruptions. When conducted on the customer site, there is always a much greater potential that a trainee might be called away or the training be interrupted due to some 'business emergency'. If the trainees are physically elsewhere, the likelihood of this happening is dramatically reduced. [Of course, this is changed somewhat by the advent of the ubiquitous mobile phone.]

- Hidden agendas. Sometimes, for political reasons, customers may wish to control the training process in some way. This usually does not adversely impact the process – although at times it can. In fact the hidden agenda can be at times downright sinister, aimed at destroying the value of the training and discrediting the software product or the solution provider. The author of these lines has, on one occasion, been a victim of such sinister plotting in a most dramatic way. At any rate, it is best that this impact is minimized.

166 CORE TECHNIQUES

In terms of physically providing the training, virtually all training techniques used elsewhere may be utilized on-site. However, there are two important issues to remember:

- Be prepared/come prepared. When you are on-site, 400 kilometres away from the office, it is too late to remember that you have left the training manuals behind.
- There is a reason why you are there and they are not at your organization. Keep the reason for this mode of training in mind; and make the most of it, whatever the reason.

Deliverables and outputs (post-condition)

Trained staff.

Database authorization   Star rating ** (author G.C. Low)

Focus: Establish access writes for DB users
Typical tasks for which this is needed: Develop security plan, select database/storage strategy
Related techniques: Access analysis
Input (pre-condition): Database design
Underpinning concepts: Relational Databases

Technique description

Modeling security and authorization involves assessment as to whether superclasses and subclasses should be available to agents other than their creator; in other words, consider a user who only has use for class A but, because class A is part of an hierarchy, its use necessarily brings along the baggage of all of class A's superclasses and probably subclasses. Should this user necessarily have access to all these additional classes or should their security level permit them only to see the details of the class A itself on the grounds that the other sub- and superclasses are of no concern of this specific user. Actors or groups of actors could then be granted various privileges or permissions to perform operations on objects or groups of composite objects (Figure A.23). Privilege types can include read, update, delete or create operations, or execution of an operation associated with an object (Khoshafian, 1993). These permissions are identified for all actors in the system during Task: Identify User Requirements (DB-specific).

Security is also an important consideration for any DBMS. With the networking of DBMS servers and the interconnexion of company networks to the internet, communications access to the DBMS has become much easier. All authorized users (both inside and external to the organization) should be able to access the information they need but should be prevented from obtaining unauthorized

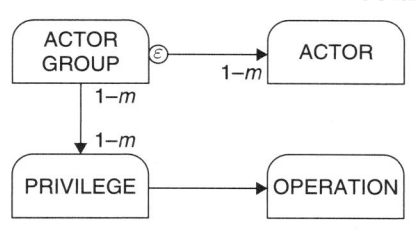

Figure A.23 An object model of security and authorization (after Case, 1993).

sensitive or confidential information. Controls should be implemented to ensure that the desired security requirements are enforced and that all attempted unauthorized access is logged. For external access additional communications-based security mechanisms, such as challenge-based password mechanisms for telnet access or hiding the DBMS behind a firewall, are implemented. In the latter case, the user connects to a WWW server in the organization's 'Demilitarized Zone' and not the DBMS. All queries to the DBMS are generated by the WWW server.

Technique usage

For each actor identified in the system, the objects on which they can perform operations and the type of operation they can perform should be identified. Group the operations that the same actors can perform to form a privilege. For example, a privilege may consist of being able to create, update and delete specific classes. In addition, actors that have similar privilege should be grouped together. Assign the privilege to the group of actors.

If a third-party product is used to support security and authorization rather than the DBMS, then security and authorization will have to be modeled into the system. Figure A.23 is one method of modeling security and authorization. The Actor Group is made up of one to many Actors and each Actor may belong to one or more Actor Groups. Each Actor Group is assigned one to many Privileges and each Privilege can perform one to many Operations.

Deliverables and outputs (post-condition)

Privilege and Actor Groups for implementation within the DBMS. In the case that the DBMS does not support security and authorization, a security model plus Privilege and Actor Groups should be documented.

Database fragmentation Star rating ** (author G.C. Low)

Focus: Fragmenting a database to improve efficiency and reliability
Typical tasks for which this is needed: Design and implement physical database
Related techniques: Optimize the design

Input (pre-condition): Database design
Underpinning concepts: Relational Databases

Technique description

To provide local access to data and reduced communications costs without redundancy, the database can be subdivided into parts or fragments which are stored at different sites (Desai, 1990). In many cases, fragmentation may improve reliability since the local site can access needed data even if other sites have failed or there is a disruption in the network. Objects may be partitioned horizontally by assigning groups of objects from the same class or associated classes to different fragments in an objectbase. In a relational DBMS, tuples are assigned to fragments. Vertical fragmentation involves assigning properties or attributes in objects or relations into separate fragments.

Technique usage

Horizontal fragmentation may improve efficiency if a class has many objects of which only a few are referenced regularly at a particular site. The frequently accessed objects are placed in a fragment which is located at the site they are accessed (Desai, 1990; Rumbaugh *et al.*, 1991). In the case of objectbases, there is the choice of placing objects that are related to each other via inheritance, aggregation or association in the same fragment.

Vertical fragmentation may improve efficiency if a class has properties with different access patterns. The system-generated object identifiers or tuple identifiers of the original object or relation must be stored in each fragment. The original object or relation can be recreated from the various fragments. However, the system would need to know which group to search. The desire to minimize the number of objects transferred between sites influences the decision as to how to allocate fragments.

Deliverables and outputs (post-condition)

Recommendations for fragmentation strategy.

DBMS product selection   Star rating **

Focus: Select specific DB product
Typical tasks for which this is needed: Select database/storage strategy
Related techniques: DBMS type selection
Input (pre-condition): DBMS type selected
Underpinning concepts: Choosing most appropriate DB product

Technique description

In this stage the particular product to be used is selected. Factors which should be taken into consideration include vendor organizational skills, vendor response time to customer enquiries, database performance, database management capabilities, database architecture, application development tools, language support, repository, integration with legacy systems and databases, and support for cooperative group work. Any benchmarking should be based on real data and include a realistically sized database, data structures that reflect the projected applications, realistic object sizes, realistic absolute and relative numbers of objects generated, and realistic applications that will be run concurrently (Rotzell and Loomis, 1991; Lai and Guzenda, 1991; Butterworth, 1991).

Technique usage

When choosing an objectbase, look for the availability of the appropriate OO language binding and whether the OB supports the same object model as your analysis and design method and your language (Goldberg and Rubin, 1995, page 371). Consider also platform availability and any existing industry standards (see e.g. Barry, 1995).

Deliverables and outputs (post-condition)

Recommendation for DB product to be used.

DBMS type selection   Star rating **

Focus: Select type of DB to be used
Typical tasks for which this is needed: Select database/storage strategy
Related techniques: DBMS product selection
Input (pre-condition): Identified need for persistence
Underpinning concepts: Choosing between RDB and OB (typically)

Technique description

The models used most frequently for databases in object-oriented systems are objectbases and relational databases. These two types of DBMS have different properties and are thus useful in different projects. Factors which determine if a relational database or an objectbase should be used are summarized in Table A.4. Generally, at present, relational databases are more suitable for on-line transaction processing, decision support systems and production systems (e.g. Loomis, 1993, page 8). Objectbases are more suitable to applications such as design databases, multimedia systems and knowledge bases (see e.g. Table A.5).

Table A.4 Summary of criteria for 'Selection of DBMS model' (after Case *et al.*, 1996).

	OODBMS	RDBMS
Data structure	Complex objects Rich data types Inheritance, aggregation and association relationships Large number of types Small number of instances	Simple objects Small number of types Large number of instances
Versioning	Different versions of data represented	Data represented at present time
Transactions	Long duration transactions Interactive and cooperative transactions Nested transactions	Short transactions Independent transactions
Queries	Navigation through logically related objects	Sequential access through all rows in a table
Distribution	Distributed databases	Non-distributed databases
Existing capital investment	Development teams experienced with object DBMSs and investment already made in tools to support object DBMS	Development teams experienced with relational DBMSs and investment already made in tools to support relational DBMS
Standards	No standard data model or database language established	Standard data model and database language established
Performance	Performance improvements for complex objects	Performance problems if many joins between relations required
Business rules	More seamless model for integrating data with business rules	Complex triggering functions required to incorporate business rules with data
Build object-oriented interface to encapsulate access to relational DBMS	Less work required	More work required

Table A.5 Advantages and disadvantages of choosing different combinations of programming language and database type for applications development (after Goldberg and Rubin, 1995).

Programming language	Database type	Advantages	Disadvantages
Object-oriented	Relational	Keeps legacy data where they already are	Conversion from tables to objects required, inconsistent language between persistent and transient information
Embedded SQL	Object-oriented	SQL is familiar to the developers	Different query and programming languages
Object-oriented	Object-oriented	Same language for persistent as well as transient information, support for objects everywhere	May have to move existing data to new database
SQL, or SQL with objects	Extended relational	Incremental change from prior practices; addition of object-like concepts and stored procedures	Hybrid language solution with object SQL, retains complexity of tuning the schema
Object-oriented	Extended relational	Retains prior data and incrementally adds the objects into the applications	Conversion from tables to objects required, inconsistent language between persistent and transient information

Technique usage

Goldberg and Rubin (1995, page 370) advise that a relational database is preferable when

- data types are simple as are the relationships between them
- transactions are short
- very little navigation is required (i.e. few joins are needed)
- there is unlikely to be significant schema evolution

whereas an objectbase is more useful when

- data types are complex and user-defined
- transactions are long lived
- multiple versions of data are required to support experimentation

```
┌─────────────────────────────────┐
│ Application object layers(s)    │
├─────────────────────────────────┤
│ Distributed Computer System     │
│ dependent objects               │
├─────────────────────────────────┤
│ Distributed Computer System (DCS)│
└─────────────────────────────────┘
```

Figure A.24 Extensions to implement features of the Distributed Computer System in layered architecture.

- navigation by reference is critical to the application.

Deliverables and outputs (post-condition)

Recommendation for DB type (objectbase, relational, object–relational) to be used.

DCS classification   Star rating *** (author G.C. Low)

Focus: Understanding distributed computer systems options
Typical tasks for which this is needed: Select database/storage strategy
Related techniques: Distributed systems partitioning and allocation
Input (pre-condition): Recognition of the possible need for a distributed system
Underpinning concepts: Distributed systems; Object Request Brokers

Technique description

Jazayeri (1992) identifies four approaches to building distributed software, all of which rely on the use of distributed computer systems. These are a distributed operating system approach, a networked operating system approach, a distributed programming language approach and a programming language toolkit approach. Distributed operating system approaches allow the application to request operating system services without concerns of being in a distributed environment. When a networked application approach is used, the application has to allow for distribution concerns itself, or utilize another application to provide distribution services for it.

The term 'distributed computer system' (DCS) is used to refer to the language, operating system or toolkit that provides support for distribution of an application across the network. Examples of these are Open Software Foundation's Distributed Computing Environment (DCE), products compliant with the Object Management Group's Common Object Request Broker Architecture (CORBA) and distributed programming languages such as Occam and Ada.

The object-based taxonomy for distributed computer systems (Martin *et al.*, 1991) can be used to determine what distributed and concurrent concepts

CORE TECHNIQUES 173

are provided by the DCS and what must be done to implement features which are not completely and transparently provided by the DCS. Extra work may be required to implement features such as persistence, restoration, replication, object partitioning, execution guarantees, object level security and migration. The work performed to implement those features should be done with modularity. The business objects should not be allowed to become dependent on the implementation environment (Jacobson *et al.*, 1992). Therefore, rather than change business objects to extend them such that they may use a specific DCS feature, a new service provider or abstract supertype should be used, so that the business objects remain independent of the implementation environment. Those CIRTs (distributed computer system dependent objects) may be treated as a layer between the business code and the DCS (Figure A.24).

Technique usage

The main areas to be considered are the support provided by the DCS for:

- threads of control
- object properties. Issues include: persistence, restoration, replication, protection and existence
- object separation. The main issues are: identification, communications, partial failures and migration.

Deliverables and outputs (post-condition)

List of distributed and concurrent concepts are provided by the DCS and what must be done to implement features which are not completely and transparently provided by the DCS but which are required by the system.

DCS optimization   Star rating * (major contribution G.C. Low)

Focus: Optimizing distribution
Typical tasks for which this is needed: Optimize the design
Related techniques: Distributed systems partitioning and allocation
Input (pre-condition): Distributed systems design
Underpinning concepts: Implementing DCS can be optimized; Relational Databases

Technique description

Optimization has a focus which is highly physical (as opposed to logical). Therefore, it should be applied in the latter iterations of the process lifecycle. A few object-based optimizations that may be used in a distributed environment are listed:

174 CORE TECHNIQUES

- partial instantiation (Bungard, 1993). Where objects are migrated from the database or another virtual node, not all instance variables need to be restored

- pre-emption (Meyer, 1988) may be used to optimize a particular scenario or service implementation

- replication of objects (in the database or in memory) may be used to reduce interprocess communication

- agents (e.g. Rieken, 1994) may be used to capture the input messages for objects that are very busy. This is a way of simulating asynchronous communications when it is not supported by the distributed computing system.

Other physical optimizations include increasing the bandwidth available on critical communications links and increasing processing power or memory on critical nodes.

Optimization may also include the reconsideration of partitioning and allocation decisions (q.v.). If testing indicates that there are problems or inefficiencies in the way software has been partitioned and/or allocated, the concurrency, fault tolerance and communications trade-offs may need reconsideration (see also Technique: DCS Architecture Specification where the Distributed Systems Approach provides the mechanism for the relevant options and decisions).

Technique usage

While partial instantiation, replication of objects and agents may be used to optimize the design, they may affect the DCS architecture specification. Consequently, the DCS specification should be briefly reviewed for any major detrimental effects. For instance, the use of agents may alter the concurrency calculations for the partitioning process while replication will affect the communication costs for the allocation process.

The bandwidth available on critical communication links and increasing processing power or memory on critical nodes should also be reviewed to ensure performance.

If testing indicates that there are problems or inefficiencies in the way software has been partitioned and/or allocated, the concurrency, fault tolerance and communications trade-offs may need reconsideration in DCS architecture specification.

Deliverables and outputs (post-condition)

Optimization document that include suggestions for partial instantiation, pre-emption, replication or objects and agents plus a revised DCS specification to ensure that no major changes are required.

Defect detection (a.k.a. defect identification)   Star rating **

Focus: Testing and quality
Typical tasks for which this is needed: Evaluate quality, test
Related techniques: Integration testing, regression testing, unit testing
Input (pre-condition): Executable system
Underpinning concepts: Defects are detrimental

Technique description

A defect is some part of a software or design artefact that is incorrect with respect to its specification. It makes no sense to talk of defects, unless a proper specification has been developed first. This could be in the form of a structured English document, or a mathematical model, the latter amenable to formal verification. Designs and implementations may then be examined with respect to the specification. They are judged correct or otherwise up to the assumptions made by the specification. No other form of judgement is possible, for example if the specification was wrongly developed, or the requirements were misunderstood. In this case, a new specification must be developed before the system can be evaluated.

The task of demonstrating that a system is free of defects is beset by a number of difficulties, which in order of importance are:

(1) Many software houses still engage in 'testing' in the absence of a proper specification (whether formal or informal). This is no more than programmers exercising parts of their code to ensure that locally there are no breakdowns.

(2) Most testing methods are non-exhaustive, and provide no guarantee that the system is correct. Conventional methods are based on path-coverage and object-oriented methods on state-transition coverage. These may ensure that all decision paths have been exercised, or that all object states have been reached, or that all state transitions have been traversed, but still cannot give any guarantee of correctness.

(3) The assumptions made by the specification may make unwarranted oversimplifications of the system.

(4) The formal techniques used to reason with the specification may be faulty.

Defect detection can only reveal defects; it cannot guarantee correctness if no defects are revealed. Once testing has finished, it is still impossible to determine, using most approaches:

- whether further defects exist in the system
- how significant these defects are
- where they are localized in the system.

Table A.6 Hours to find a defect derived from seven independent sources (adapted from Humphrey, 1994).

	Inspection	Test	Use
(1)	1	2–10	
(2)	0.26		
(3)		20	
(4)	1	2–4	
(5)	0.6	3.05	33
(6)	0.25	8	
(7)	0.7	6	

However, Ipate and Holcombe (1997) have shown that it is possible to develop a formal model and associated testing method which gives a 100 per cent guarantee of correctness for system integration. This means that, although the components may be taken on trust, the system in which they are incorporated is proven to integrate them correctly. Once testing has finished, any remaining defects are guaranteed to reside in the components themselves and not in the system integration. A refinement strategy may then be followed to demonstrate that a system is correct down to trivial components whose correctness is assumed.

Technique usage

It is important to identify defects early in the development process. Defects tend to become more expensive to identify and fix as the process unfolds (Table A.6). This is one reason why direct defect identification techniques such as inspections are gaining in popularity, since there is no need for the executable to be available before defect identification can commence.

Another important issue in defect identification relates to the recording of defects and failures. Firstly, there is a confusion between what is a defect (something that needs rectification) and what is a failure (a behavior inconsistent with expectation). These are not the same. In fact, failures are usually consequences of defects. However, in many 'defect classification lists', no distinction is made between defects and failures. Secondly, there is no standardization in the recording of defects and failures (even if distinguished from each other).

These two issues result in wide discrepancies with respect to inter-project comparisons (e.g. Grady and Caswell, 1987). In OPEN, we provide two templates, Tables A.7 and A.8 (after Goldberg and Rubin, 1995), the former for the recording of failures and the latter for the recording of defects. As it is logical to assume that the intention will exist to rectify at least most defects detected, an example Change Report Template is also given in Table A.9. This is particularly relevant for reuse as changes may be observed in (a) interface, (b) implementation, (c) base class (superclass) or (d) derived class (subclass).

Table A.7 Template for recording an incident (after Goldberg and Rubin, 1995).

Aspect	Description
Identification	A unique number or other unique identifier
Description	Description of what happened, when and how it happened
Originator	Name of person or organization reporting the incident
Product descriptor	Specific aspect of the project referenced by the incident
Configuration	Hardware and software configuration in which the incident took place
Attachments	Additional information that may help reproduce the incident, including software that recreates the problem
Record date	Date the incident was recorded
Severity	Severity from the originator's perspective
Priority	Urgency from the originator's perspective
Responder	Persons assigned to handle the incident
Status	Current status of the incident
Cause	Why the incident occurred (known after the incident is closed)
Resolution	How the incident was handled if incident is closed
Resolution date	Date that the incident was resolved and communicated to Originator
Comments	General comments that capture the discussions of possible causes and solutions
Incident references	References to other incidents that are similar to this incident

Deliverables and outputs (post-condition)

List of defects together with suggested remedies.

Delegation analysis Star rating **

Focus: Modeling
Typical tasks for which this is needed: Construct the object model, create and/or identify reusable components ('for reuse')
Related techniques: Contract specification, Law of Demeter, pattern recognition, responsibility identification
Input (pre-condition): Design
Underpinning concepts: Delegation

Table A.8 Template for recording a defect (after Goldberg and Rubin, 1995).

Aspect	Description
Identification	A unique number or other unique identifier
Reference	Reference to the incident report(s) that uncovered the defect
Originator	Developer who created the defect report
Product descriptor	Which part of the product is affected
Development activity	Development activity during which the defect was introduced into the product
Cause	Why the defect occurred
Priority	Urgency for fixing the defect from the perspective of the development organization
Responder	Persons assigned to handle the defect
Status	Current status of the defect
Changes	References to change reports that describe how the defect was repaired
Attachments	Additional information provided by the Originator that may help describe the defect (may be useful for regression testing)
Comment	General comments reporting the handling of the defect

Technique description

Delegations can occur whenever an object decides it cannot fulfil the responsibility itself but has to call in a collaborator. Analyzing possible delegation tends to force a good, decentralized design as advocated in RDD (q.v.). Further examples are provided in CD: Appendix E.

Technique usage

Identify where a collaboration may be needed where a particular service request makes sense to be delegated to another object. In doing so, evaluate concurrently the coupling metrics for the system.

Deliverables and outputs (post-condition)

An improved design, under version control.

Dependency – see Relationship modeling

Table A.9 Template for recording a change in a deliverable (after Goldberg and Rubin, 1995).

Aspect	Description
Identification	A unique number or other unique identifier
Description	Description of the required change
Product descriptor	Which aspect of software development product has been changed
Reuse implication	Comment on whether and how a reused asset was modified
Type of change	Classification of the change that was applied to a system artefact
Change date	Date when the change was introduced into the product
Responder	Persons responsible for making the change
Cost	Cost to implement the change (in staff hours)
Status	Status of the change, such as tested, reviewed, done, rejected
Reference to fix	Reference to system components, versions or files that create the changes
Dependencies	Reference to other needed changes or installation requirements when integrating the change
Comment	General comments reporting the handling of the change
References	Reference to the defects repaired by the change
Disposition	What was done and why

Dependency-based testing   Star rating **

Focus: Testing
Typical tasks for which this is needed: Test
Related techniques: Integration testing, unit testing
Input (pre-condition): System under test
Underpinning concepts: Testing can help find errors/problems

Technique description

In dependency-based testing, a dependency diagram is constructed which shows all inter-class dependencies, i.e. client–server relationships. This gives an ordering in which all server classes are tested before those dependent upon them.

Technique usage

Develop a dependency diagram that documents the various dependency relationships from client to server among the classes including inheritance, aggregation, collaboration/delegation, attribution and parameterization. To test new classes on a foundation of previously tested classes, unit/integration test all classes on the dependency diagram so that a class is tested before its dependents are tested.

180   CORE TECHNIQUES

If two classes depend on each other, stub out the more complex class and test the simpler first. Also, test the methods in a class in dependency order; typically (1) constructors before read accessors before write accessors before queries before services and (2) private operations before public operations (Firesmith, 1996; McGregor, 1997).

Deliverables and outputs (post-condition)

Results of testing with defects highlighted.

Design by contract – see Contract specification

Design patterns – see Pattern recognition

Design templates   Star rating *

Focus: Translation to code
Typical tasks for which this is needed: Code
Related techniques: Implementation of services, implementation of structure
Input (pre-condition): Design
Underpinning concepts: There may be options in late design and coding for a single model

Technique description

Many of the relationships in OPEN (association, aggregation, generalization etc.) have a direct parallel in most OOPLs[†]. Translating from analysis to design to code is then straightforward. However, in other situations, there may be other options. In a non-OOPL, inheritance needs to be faked; aggregations may be implemented by pointer or by reference. To assist in these choices, a set of design templates has been proposed (Odell and Fowler, 1995a, b, c), several of which are valuable to OPEN.

---

† Here we include detailed design considerations. In OPEN, we support a seamless transition yet recognize some disjoint nature as we move into language-influenced (or detailed) design together with coding (see detailed discussion in Graham et al., 1997b).

Technique usage

Associations

In OPEN, associations are uni-directional mappings. In general, these require two operations: an accessor and a modifier (Odell and Fowler, 1995a). Accessors need no arguments and return an object; modifiers may have an argument and will change the object in some way or reassign the point to another object. These are often referred to as *get* and *set* methods – although these should only access data indirectly; data should never be *externally* reset (Wirfs-Brock and Wilkerson, 1989a). Since multi-valued accessors return a set of objects, they need two modifier operations which permit addition and subtraction of elements to/from this set. Pre-conditions must of course always be met, by appropriate checking in the client CIRT.

The normal implementation of OPEN's associations (which are mappings) (q.v.) is using pointers (or references) in one direction only. If queries are required in both directions, the second option of buried pointers in both CIRTs may suffice. Queries (e.g. in a database sense) will be faster at the expense of a severe loss of potential reusability of each CIRT independently of the other. Referential integrity should be considered since this approach is really an implementation of a mapping and its adjoint between the power sets (Graham *et al.*, 1997a).

A third option, valid if the association has sufficiently strong semantics so as to be a candidate CIRT itself, is to turn the association into an object linked by pointers to the two original objects.

Aggregations

Since aggregation is generally regarded as a kind of association, appropriate design templates are also similar. For most associations, pointers/references will be one-way: from aggregate to component. Propagation is not always well supported in languages (Odell and Fowler, 1995c) so that appropriate code may well need to be written.

Generalization/inheritance

Finally, design templates for the generalization relationship also give the designer a choice. Whilst the most obvious is through the inheritance mechanism, flags may sometimes be used, even in OOPLs since it supports both multiple and dynamic classification (Odell and Fowler, 1995b). A similar situation where there are multiple subtype partitions may be implemented using multiple inheritance (which can be problematic) or using a design template in which combination subclasses are used, perhaps as mixins. Generalization (subtyping) can also be handled by the use of delegation. Object slicing (Odell, 1992a) is another useful metaphor which currently has no direct support in OOPLs.

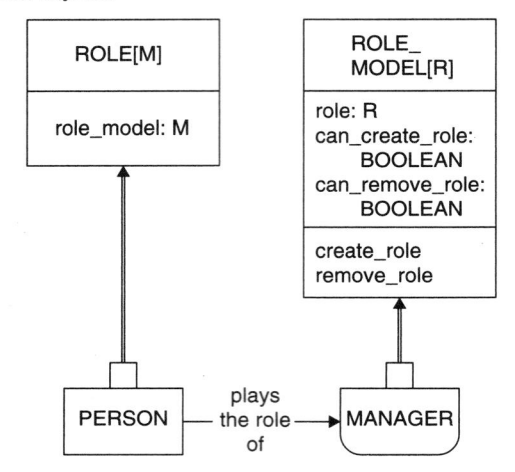

Figure A.25 Implementation of a *PERSON_MANAGER* role relationship by means of two generic classes: *ROLE[M]* and *ROLE_MODEL[R]* (after Renouf and Henderson-Sellers, 1995).

Roles

It is also important to note that examples used in these design templates may in fact be better discussing using role models (q.v.). Role models (e.g. Reenskaug *et al.*, 1992, 1996), although primarily analytical, can be implemented by use of the pattern described in Renouf and Henderson-Sellers (1995) – see Figure A.25.

Deliverables and outputs (post-condition)

Design improvements in which ad hoc design structures have been replaced by design templates.

Dialog design in UI   Star rating **

Focus: User interface design
Typical tasks for which this is needed: Design user interface
Related techniques: Usability measurement, usability testing
Input (pre-condition): Systems requirements
Underpinning concepts: Color in UIs; Usability; human psychology

Technique description

Dialog design is important for all user interfaces, graphical or otherwise. Dialogs depend on shared understanding and knowledge of a common domain (Graham,

1995a, page 95). They represent the ongoing conversation between user and machine.

A dialog between machine and user may be needed predominantly to give commands, or to convey information or data; although there may be other contexts. Commands may be cryptic (as in Unix) or visual (as in a good GUI in which the point-and-click metaphor is common). It is reasonable to expect that any command given by the user will result in some action by the computer. It is therefore important that all interactions initiated by the user should give an observable result, either confirming that the task is complete and giving the expected results, reporting an exception or, when the task takes more than a second or two, indicating visually that computation is proceeding correctly – as opposed to the occasions, unfortunately all too frequent, when an error occurs, the machine is halted in mid-command execution and yet the user has no clue with which to decide whether the machine is slow or 'dead'.

Although there is no single universally accepted technique for dialog design, there are a number of guidelines and rules that if followed would present a good starting point at least. Much of the work that is presented in these guidelines goes back to the work at Xerox Parc in the 1970s. Bailey (1989), Galitz (1989), and Marcus (1992) are all good sources of such guidelines for user interface design. Cox and Walker (1993) state that in general these guidelines require the dialog to be designed according to the following principles:

- be concrete rather than abstract and where possible give examples rather than just rules
- continue to make the information visible whilst it is still required for the completion of the task or dialog
- do not force the user to generate new solutions or ways of interaction with the machine; use modified versions of those already mastered or at least previously encountered
- do not force the user to remember what to type. For example, as much as possible give them options to choose from a pick list, let them to recognize an existing artefact rather than have to generate it, and allow editing of existing texts or figures rather than entering them
- as much as possible provide interaction and feedback to the user. For example, some 'ticking clock' icon that indicates that the system is still 'working on it' is of particular use, especially on slow systems
- keep things simple and uncluttered.

Technique usage

Graham (1995a, page 95) identifies some commonly used heuristics for dialog design (Table A.10). In a multi-depth menu system, frequent users need to be able to take shortcuts, perhaps using 'hot key' combinations. Shortened forms of commands (e.g. CD for CHDIR in DOS) can be useful for the expert but

Table A.10 Heuristics for dialog design (after Graham, 1995a, page 95).

Minimize input movements

Maximize input bandwidth/channels

Use words and language carefully

Ensure that the interface has a pleasing 'look and feel'

Be consistent (keys, positioning, etc.)

Keep the system modeless or provide a high level of context-sensitive feedback

A natural response time is desirable

Process continuity should be sought

Ease of use should be paramount

Make the system customizable

Make the system non-pre-emptive

Follow standards

---

confusing to the novice who sees two more alternative commands to do the same thing. Undo/redo facilities are often useful but can be problematic in cases where some actions cannot be consistently undone or re-done. Graham (1995a, page 96) reports that some designers emphasize careful choice of wording (Table A.11) – noting, for example, that some female users can be disturbed by words like 'abort'. Consistency is important. For example, in some PC applications, the application is exited through selecting the word 'close' and in others via 'exit' or 'quit'.

Other guidelines for good dialog/interface design are

- 2–7 options per menu (avoid overloading the user)
- partition menus by logical subsection (cf. Smalltalk, MS-Windows)
- max depth 5 in menu tree (avoid hunting – minor problem in Windows 95)
- feedback on actions in progress (mouse icon change, dialog box)
- expert shortcuts vs beginner's long menus
- consistency of appearance (e.g. Motif, OpenLook)
- consistency of interactions (quit/exit, close/shrink conflicts).

Command-line driven software should also observe similar principles of consistency. Unix commands are a case in point: they have short names, a number of command-line options introduced by '–' and often source and destination files. However, they are often inconsistently designed:

Table A.11 Use of language in error messages (after Graham, 1995a, page 96).

Error message	Evaluation
ABORT: error 451	Bad
I'm tremendously sorry but I have discovered that a file you want to use is already open (error number 451)	Better but verbose
Error number 451. File already open. This error normally occurs when you forgot to close the file at the end of a previous subroutine	Better but tedious
Error number 451: File already open. Explain? <Y/N>:	Good-ish
Left as an exercise for the reader!	PERFECT

- Unix programs are most flexible if they use redirection and pipes to specify source and destination; programs should read and write from standard input/output and rely on > and < to redirect files; instead, some Unix programs do this and others expect you to supply filenames as parameters. Consider the following common commands:

    ```
    unix2dos fname.unx fname.dos
    ls workdir > outfile
    uuencode text.doc text.doc > text.uue
    ```

    which handle source/destination files quite inconsistently!

- Command-line flags are '-' followed by a code-letter. Some programs allow you to specify several codes at once: -augx; others require parameter values after the flag: -n2; others require spaces between the flag and the parameter value: -o outfile; and finally, still others allow long-name flags as options: -nup 2 which is inconsistent with the usage with short flags, because additional spacing required to separate parameter values from the flag names. All of this is highly inconsistent.

In terms of actual dialog design approach Table A.12 depicts a general set of steps advocated by Cox and Walker (1993) which reflects a fully iterative process and deliverables.

Abstraction, detailing, prototyping and construction stages of the framework above are essentially the same concepts described elsewhere in this book in relation to non UI object-oriented development. What remains, therefore, is a need for a technique for dialog visualization. What follows is a description of one such technique called Logical Dialog Design (LDD) which develops artifacts

Table A.12 Dialog design steps (after Cox and Walker, 1993).

Design stage	Design outcomes	Tests
Visualization	Sketches of possible solutions	Do these solutions 'look right?' Do they solve the right problem?
Abstraction	A set of objects (with attributes) and actions on those objects	Is the set of objects complete? Are all the attributes included? Can the actions be used to perform the functions of the system?
Detailing	Detailed representation of the objects and actions	Do these representations look right? Do they contain enough information? Are they usable to perform the functions of the system? Do they conform to guidelines and standards?
Prototyping	Detailed design and implementation of screens	User interaction with system screen layout, usability of actions and dialog structure
Construction	Program design and implementation	Correctness of results Reliability, performance, reusability Modifiability, maintainability

called Logical Dialog Outlines (LDO) and Logical Dialog Controls (LDC).

The basic objectives of Logical Dialog Design has been reported by Downes *et al.* (1991) as:

- to communicate screen handling and HCI concepts to the users
- to represent dialog sequences
- to provide a basis for physical program design.

The technique is based on a number of design symbols (Figure A.26(a)) somewhat compatible with those used in control flow charts, and a dialog design chart which forms a background on which the symbols are placed.

Dialog design procedures follow six steps:

(1) identify on-line events

(2) identify I/O items

(3) create an LDO, one per event

(4) review LDOs against design (design of the rest of the system)

(5) create logical dialog controls

(6) validate the diagrams.

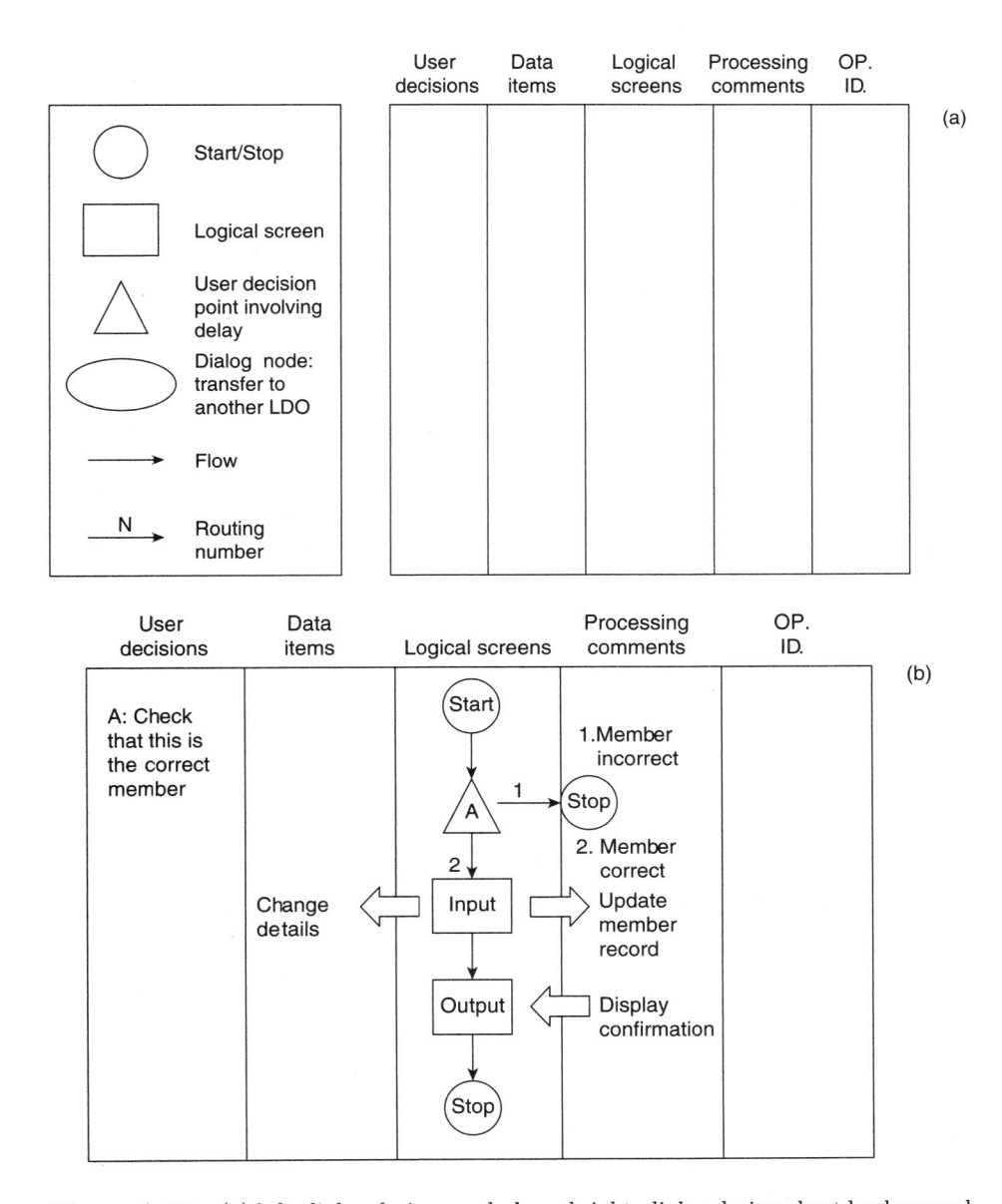

Figure A.26 (a) left: dialog design symbols and right: dialog design chart background and (b) logical dialog design for 'Amend Member' (after Downes *et al.*, 1991).

Logical dialog controls (LDCs) are charts that represent a higher level grouping of screen objects and eventually of screens themselves. Figure A.26(b) depicts a simple example of the Logical Dialog Outline (LDO) for 'amend member details'. Logical Dialog Design is an integral part of the SSADM methodology and a detailed description of it may be found in Downes *et al.* (1991). Alternatively, Parnas (1969) advocates the use of state transition diagrams as a means of dialog visualization.

Deliverables and outputs (post-condition)

Recommendations for an improved design for the user interface.

Distributed systems partitioning and allocation Star rating *
(Major author G.C. Low)

Focus: Partitioning and allocation
Typical tasks for which this is needed: Establish distributed systems strategy
Related techniques: DCS optimization
Input (pre-condition): System architecture with no DCS concerns addressed
Underpinning concepts: Distributed system as most appropriate approach

Technique description

In a distributed system, components need to be identified and often partitioned (broken down) before allocation to a cpu. In a distributed system, there are multiple cpus available, so the allocation decision is non-trivial. There are many influencing factors as discussed in CD: Appendix E (Distributed Systems). Also in this appendix the four main approaches to partitioning and allocation are described in full:

(1) *A client–server topology approach* which divides the application into several layers of presentation logic, business logic and data management logic. Standard templates are then used for the partitioning and allocation decisions where different templates simply place the layers on the client or server. For an organization that is inexperienced with distributed systems development, this approach reduces complexity and therefore risk.

(2) *A packaging approach* where the original object model is decomposed into packages or subsystems. These packages should have high internal cohesion and low external coupling with other packages. Each package may be further decomposed into other packages and/or partitioned by any other of the techniques described here. The resultant packages and/or object models are then allocated to physical nodes (Low *et al.*, 1996).

CORE TECHNIQUES 189

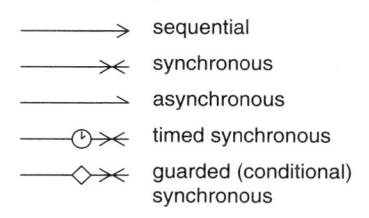

```
———————→      sequential
———————⇥⇤      synchronous
———————⇀      asynchronous
————⊕⇥⇤        timed synchronous
————◇⇥⇤        guarded (conditional)
               synchronous
```

Figure A.27 Arrow styles in OML Version 1.1 for sequential, synchronous and asynchronous referential relationships together with annotations for timed and guarded relationships.

Label with distribution unit

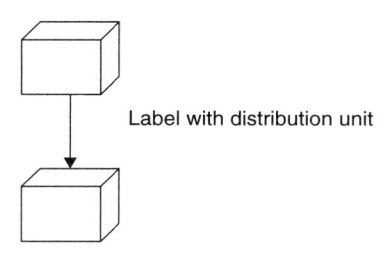

Figure A.28 OML Version 1.1 notation for deployment diagram for DCS.

(3) *A distributed systems approach* where the object model is partitioned into cohesive and independent components based on requirements for concurrency and communications (Shatz and Wang, 1989). These are then allocated to one or more processors with the actual allocation being dependent on issues such as interprocess communication cost, execution cost, load balancing, reliability and scalability (Shatz and Wang, 1989).

(4) *A layered approach* (Low *et al.*, 1996) where objects from the logical design are assigned to the generated, configured and relation layers. Objects in the configured layer are active or passive and are allocated to their own virtual nodes. Objects in the relation layer are active and allocated to their own virtual nodes. The generated objects reside in one or more database server virtual nodes, or migrate between the configured objects. These virtual nodes are then allocated to one or more processors with the actual allocation being dependent on issues such as interprocess communications cost, execution cost, load balancing, reliability and scalability.

Technique usage

Decide on the appropriate partitioning and allocation strategy (see CD: Appendix E for full details). Identify and document (see Figure A.27) concurrency; synchronous versus asynchronous versus sequential communications and any

190   CORE TECHNIQUES

guards. Allocate to hardware components using deployment and/or migration diagrams (e.g. Figure A.28). Evaluate comparative costs for migration versus replication.

Deliverables and outputs (post-condition)

The output is a recommended distributed systems application topology.

Domain analysis   Star rating **

Focus: Analysis of problem *beyond* current problem
Typical tasks for which this is needed: Create and/or identify reusable components ('for reuse'), undertake architectural design
Related techniques: Analysis patterns
Input (pre-condition): System requirements plus wider understanding of business domain
Underpinning concepts: Systems are more flexible if they address broader domain issues

Technique description

Domain analysis is concerned with an understanding of the broader problem domain and business context *beyond* the constraints of the immediate project[†]. Ideally, domain analysis should be undertaken as an integral part of each project since this will create a product that is readily extensible in the future. However, in most cases, domain analysis is not undertaken *until* that expansion is required and is thus 'only practical in an environment that exploits the information for reuse in expanding the current system or in building future systems' (McGregor and Sykes, 1992, page 60). The results of domain analysis include a set of high level abstractions representing the knowledge domain.

Good domain analysis should lead to an unique and consistent model of the abstractions in the domain. These would then be encoded as a set of library classes. Unfortunately, study of library classes reveals that commercial libraries purporting to model the same domain are, in fact, based on very different configurations of the abstractions (Yap and Henderson-Sellers, 1997). For example, the various positionings of classes Collection, Container, Bag and Set in four libraries are shown in Figure A.29.

[†] This strict interpretation of domain analysis is used in OPEN. Others use the term to mean extracting the obvious business object model.

Booch Components

Bag   **Set**

Borland Version 3.0

```
                    Object
                      ↑
                  Container
                      ↑
                  Collection
                      ↑
        ┌─────────────┼─────────────┐
   AbstractArray     Bag        HashTable
        ↑             ↑
      Array          Set
                      ↑
                  Dictionary
```

C++/Views

```
                    Object
                      ↑
          ┌───────────┴───────────┐
      Collection              Container
          ↑
    ┌─────┴──────────┐
   Set         OrderedCollection
    ↑
Dictionary
```

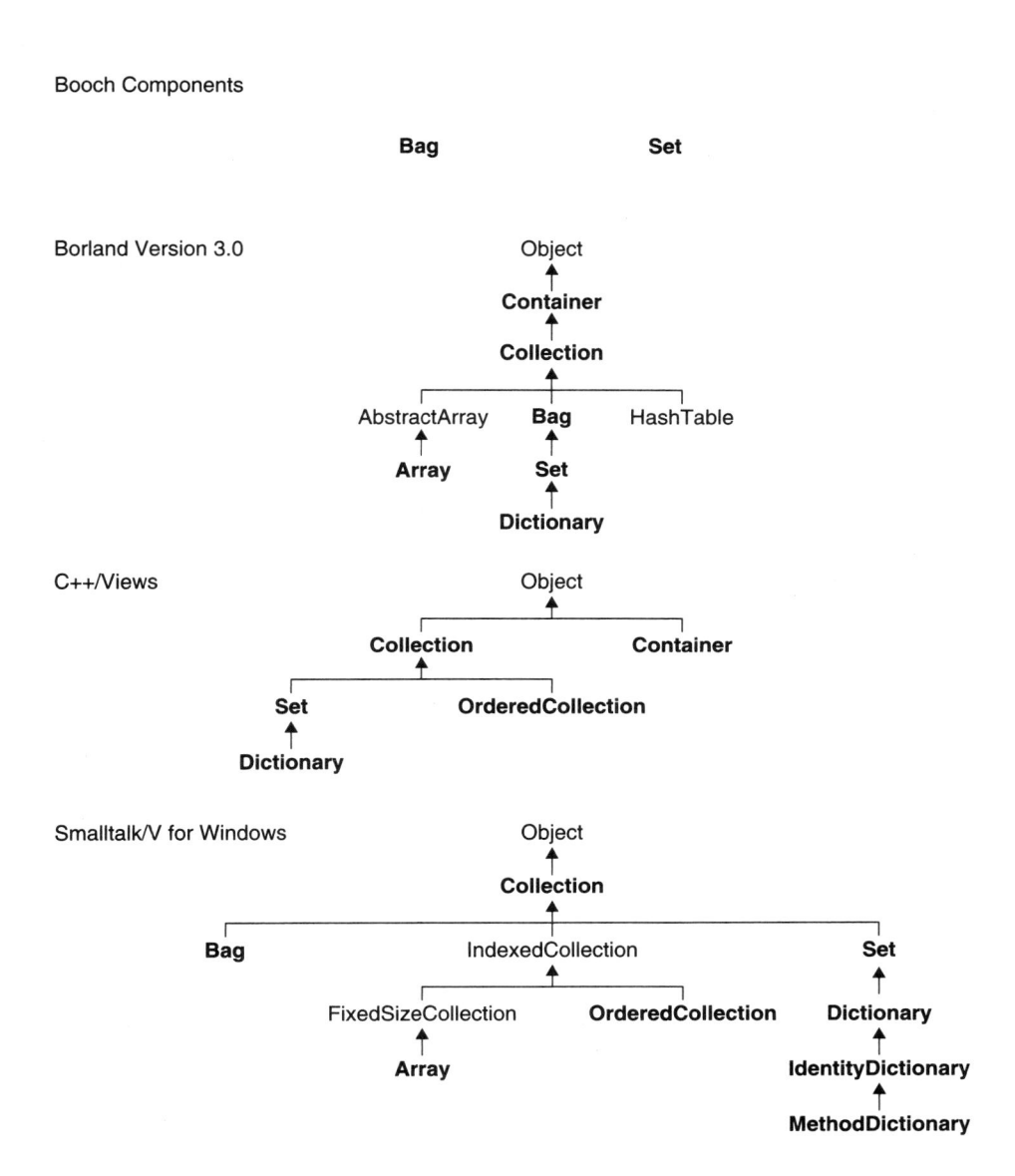

Smalltalk/V for Windows

```
                         Object
                           ↑
                       Collection
                           ↑
        ┌──────────────────┼──────────────────┐
       Bag           IndexedCollection        Set
                           ↑                   ↑
              ┌────────────┴──────────┐    Dictionary
         FixedSizeCollection   OrderedCollection  ↑
                ↑                            IdentityDictionary
              Array                                ↑
                                            MethodDictionary
```

Figure A.29 The positioning of Collection and Container classes in four class libraries (after Yap and Henderson-Sellers, 1997).

Technique usage

In essence, domain analysis is little different from project-focused analysis — except that the domain is broader. For example, in undertaking analysis prior to building a software version of tic-tac-toe (noughts and crosses), a domain analyst would consider the broader spectrum of board games such as chess, checkers (draughts), go etc. (McGregor and Sykes, 1992, page 264). Domain analysis is thus more of a reuse-focused, strategic investment which supports future flexibility and modifiability.

Domain analysis is thus a good basis for building application frameworks and many class libraries and is therefore highly relevant to an object-oriented approach.

Deliverables and outputs (post-condition)

Documented domain understanding, plus recommendations for building current system to take advantage of this domain analysis, particularly with respect to reuse opportunities.

Envisioning   Star rating **

Focus: BPR
Typical tasks for which this is needed: Model and re-engineer business process(es)
Related techniques: BPR, business process modeling
Input (pre-condition): Understanding of existing business processes
Underpinning concepts: Lateral thinking can create better business processes

Technique description

Envisioning creates a new vision for a company or a project. It often requires lateral thinking to ensure the company's strategic goals match the goals of the envisioned company/project. In addition, envisioning needs, as a prerequisite, to create an understanding of existing processes in order to create a new vision; to seek required improvements by interviewing the existing client base; and to benchmark the envisioned company with other companies in the same line of business (Davenport, 1993, pages 117–135).

Technique usage

Envisioning is often undertaken by members of a re-engineering team or a strategic 'think tank' including representatives of customers. Strategic rethinking needs to be aligned with the company's core business(es). Specific support by envisioning for BPR in the context of OT is given in Jacobson *et al.* (1995).

The necessary steps are:

- imagine the kind of business goals for the future
- determine what business practices are required to achieve these goals
- discard and/or adapt the old (current) business processes in the logical model of the current business.

Deliverables and outputs (post-condition)

List of suggested goals and ways to meet these goals.

Event modeling Star rating ** (author D. Fowler)

Focus: Describing the dynamics of the model
Typical tasks for which this is needed: Construct the object model, identify CIRTs
Related techniques: Interaction modeling, state modeling
Input (pre-condition): Functionality requirements
Underpinning concepts: State Machines

Technique description

An event is a noteworthy change of state (Martin and Odell, 1995, page 126).

Event modeling is a dynamic modeling technique used to model the behavioral effect of some kind of stimulus on a system. Events can be external, triggered by something in the external world and over which the system has no control, or they may be triggered from within the system. Event models are most useful in those systems which have recognizable states.

It is useful to make a distinction between whole-system event modeling and within-object event modeling. Techniques such as Finite State Machines and Harel statecharts may be used to model system level state changes (see Technique: State modeling).

The control structure of systems is usually either menu-driven (hierarchical) or event-driven (heterarchical). Choosing an appropriate match for this structure is sensible: for instance, JSP-like structures would be useful for the first and statecharts for the second.

While modeling whole-system state machines for event-driven systems is often most meaningful for presenting behavior, modeling individual objects is useful from the point of view of verification and testing. The states of an object here correspond to logical modes in which some of its methods behave differently, or are disabled (e.g. *pop* on an empty stack). Events are simply messages which cause an object to change mode.

An aspect of most state-based diagramming techniques is that the relationship between corresponding static and dynamic models is poor, because they describe the system as a finite state machine and let events correspond to transitions between (interesting) states (Waldén and Nerson 1995), with no indication of the object structures involved. BON takes a different approach, viewing internal events as operations applied to objects. Messages passed can therefore be tied to corresponding classes and operations in the static model; these are represented in the dynamic model. A similar approach is taken by Fowler and Swatman (1996), who use event chain models to show the collaborative behavior of objects in response to a system stimulus. Each event chain is made of a set link diagrams, showing the classes and operations associated with one state change in the chain. The diagrams are used to show association between use case like behavioral models and Object-Z.

OML uses Embley *et al.* (1992) state modeling as extended by Firesmith (Firesmith *et al.*, 1997). The approach is based on OO concepts: in OML each obejct has a state machine, defined for a class, which is an aggregate of a number of states and transitions. A transition is a change of state caused by an event. As the values of state properties are changed by an event, triggers are messages or associated operations, or exceptions.

Technique usage

Event modeling is useful where the domain in question is amenable to being modeled in terms of states, whether at the object or system level. Event models are designed to show the effects of an event, or trigger, on a system: consequently they are widely used in the modeling of real time systems, but they are are also useful for a wider variety of systems.

State models typically show the behavior of object instances or classes, by describing the lifecycle of the object: the states it can be in, from creation to destruction, and the ways in which these states are interrelated. Preparing a state model of an object can help in the discovery of attributes or operations for the object or class, and is particularly useful when the lifecycle for the class is in some way interesting or complex, or dependent on other classes.

Deliverables and outputs (post-condition)

State transition diagrams (STDs).

Exception handling   Star rating **

Focus: Code for handling exceptions
Typical tasks for which this is needed: Code
Related techniques: Defect detection
Input (pre-condition): Existing/developing system
Underpinning concepts: Errors need to be trapped and handled correctly

Technique description

An exception is an abnormal condition which is triggered, or 'raised', during the execution of a piece of software which fails to satisfy its intended purpose. Software failures may occur for various reasons: incorrect coding (errors) leading to semantic inconsistencies which are later detected; resource allocation problems, such as running out of heap memory, unavailable files, timeouts, deadlocks and livelocks; or hardware-related problems, such as overflows, underflows, disk failures or network crashes and power cuts. When such failures occur, an exception is raised, meaning that the system enters an abnormal state in which the normal flow of control is suspended. The system may shut down; or some special purpose procedures may be invoked to attempt to rectify the problem: this is known as exception handling.

Once an exception has been raised, the system may respond in one of two ways:

(1) repair and retry (the 'fix it' solution)
(2) clean up and retire (the 'organized panic' solution).

The system should never be allowed to ignore the exception and carry on regardless (Meyer, 1988). If the failed software operation can be fixed by some work-around, the exception is cancelled and the routine is considered to have succeeded. If the operation merely cleans up and retires, then it is judged still to have failed; in this case the exception is passed to the next outermost calling routine, which may choose to handle it. If eventually no routine handles the exception, the program must terminate.

Exception-handling models can be simple, as in Eiffel: here, control is transferred to a single point (the 'rescue' clause). In C++ v4.0 and Java, the model is more complex: control is transferred to one of several exception handlers, which are selected by discriminating on the type of datum that is passed when the exception is thrown. Other mechanisms are based on state-machine models, such as Cook and Daniels' (1994) guarded transitions: here, if an exception is raised, but the guard fails, the exception is passed up the sender stack as if the transition to the handler were not there. In this model, the transitions may have actions and post-conditions, in particular, a post-condition defining the resulting value of an update (Cook and Daniels, 1994, page 189).

Technique usage

It is important to distinguish normal from abnormal operating conditions when designing a system. Normal control flow is handled with conditional and branching constructs, such as the 'if, while (loop)' and 'switch (case, select)' statements provided in the language. Exceptional conditions should be handled using the exception mechanisms provided. Ada, Eiffel, ATT C++ version 4.0 and Java all provide exception-handling facilities. What constitutes an abnormal operating condition may vary, depending on the specification of the system. For example, it is usual for a *STACK* to assert that it is not *empty* before a *pop* or *top* method is invoked – usually, these operations are undefined for empty *STACK*s. However, a fault-tolerant system specification may request that a *STACK* always return some object, even when empty. In this case, the recovery from the *empty* state should not be coded as a caught exception, but rather as a normal branching condition, since it is something which is regularly expected. Since what is considered normal depends on the context of use, this sometimes presents a problem to object-oriented reuse: an exception in one context may be a normal operating condition in another. Fortunately, fault-tolerant wrappers may be written for library classes (which normally throw exceptions) to overcome this problem.

OPEN recommends the 'programming by contract' metaphor for determining when to throw exceptions, and for deciding which classes should be responsible for handling exceptions (see Technique: Contract specification). In this metaphor (Meyer, 1988; 1992c), classes and objects enter into contracts with each other, each guaranteeing one half of the bargain between the client and the supplier of services. If the client calls the supplier's method with its pre-conditions satisfied (i.e. the client called the routine legally), the supplier must return a result to the client with its post-conditions satisfied (i.e. the result is correct). If either of these conditions is broken, then the offending party is identified and is responsible for rectifying the problem. This viewpoint helps the programmer to determine where failure-trapping tests should be placed in the code. In particular, it prevents under-detection (which leads to crashes) and over-detection (duplicate testing, which leads to inefficiency).

Not all exceptions are caused by local failures; and not all are raised by the software itself – an exception may be raised (cf. Waldén and Nerson, 1995, page 212):

(1) in a supplier class method which fails to satisfy its own post-conditions when it terminates (the supplier is responsible for the failure in this context)

(2) in a client class method which invokes another method in a supplier, but fails to satisfy the required pre-conditions (the client is responsible for the failure in this context)

(3) in any method, if a signal is received from the hardware environment indicating some major hardware failure, such as a disk crash

(4) in a client class method, if one of the supplier methods which it invokes raises an exception which is not handled by the supplier.

These cases show how exceptions may result in non-local transfers of control.

In Eiffel, tests for semantic failure are called 'assertions'. These are simple Boolean tests, listed under the **require** clause (pre-conditions), or **ensure** clause (post-conditions) or the class **invariant** clause (data type invariants) – post-conditions that are true after every operation. In addition, Eiffel supports various other types of assertion not discussed here, such as loop variants, loop invariants and general check assertions. If an assertion is violated, then normal control flow is suspended and exceptional control is passed to the **rescue** clause of either the supplier or client method, in accordance with the contracting rules above. The pattern for an Eiffel routine is therefore:

methodName(arguments : ARG_TYPES) : RESULT_TYPE **is**
require
        - - pre-conditions
do
        - - main method body
ensure
        - - post-conditions
rescue
        - - exception handling:
        - - cleanup, possible retry statement
end

In C++ and Java, less explicit support is given to the contracting metaphor. However, the programmer may achieve the same effect through careful use of `try` blocks with `throw` statements and corresponding `catch` handlers. The general pattern for this is:

```
ResultType ClassName::methodName(ArgTypes args)
{       if (! pre1)
                                throw pre1Violated;
        else if (! pre2)
                                throw pre2Violated;
        try
        {               // main body of method, which invokes a
                        // server object which throws a further
                        // exception post2Violated
                        if (! post1)
                                throw post1Violated;
                        return normalReturnValue;
        }
        catch post1Violated
        {               // repair code for post1
        }
        catch post2Violated
        {               // repair code for post2
        }
                        // possible final instructions
}
```

In this pattern, `pre1`...`post2` are testable Boolean conditions; `pre1Violated`...`post2Violated` are the values that are passed when an exception is thrown. In the C++ 4.0 and Java exception-handling model, `catch` handlers may handle exceptions which occur in the immediately preceding **try** block. This means that `pre1Violated` and `pre2Violated` will not be caught locally, since they are thrown outside the **try** block. Control will pass to the caller of `methodName` when these exceptions are thrown, and may be handled there, or else passed up the execution stack. In this way, the client-side of the contract is enforced: repairing failure is the responsibility of the client. Exceptions which are thrown inside the **try** block may be handled by the immediately-following **catch** handlers. This enforces the supplier-side of the contract, in which the supplier is responsible for repairing any abnormal condition encountered, whether caused by local or non-local failure. In the pattern above, `post1Violated` is thrown by a post-condition test placed at the end of the block, but `post2Violated` is thrown non-locally by some supplier routine which `methodName` calls. In this way, both sides of Meyer's 'programming by contract' are represented.

In Eiffel, control is transferred to a single **rescue** clause when exceptions are raised within the main body of a routine. Inside the **rescue** clause, branching tests may be used to discriminate among the exceptions thrown and appropriate action taken. A class may inherit from the parent class *EXCEPTION* if finer-grained handling of exceptions is required. This class supplies exception codes as predefined constants. In C++ and Java, control is transferred to one of several handlers. The programmer may determine which handler to use for different exceptions by selecting a different type of value to throw. For example, expanding on the pattern above, in C++:

```
catch (int num)
{    cerr << 'Argument too small, resetting/n';
     num = 1;
     return supplierMethod(num, arg2);    // try again
}
catch (char* errmsg)
{ cerr << errmsg << endl;
     exit(1);       // halt system
}
```

we see that the two exceptions are distinguished on their types `char*` and `int`. In Java, thrown exception values must be instances of the class `Throwable` (or one of its descendants). In this way, it is possible to wrap up information about an exception in an instance of a class. The exception-object exists for the duration of the **catch** block and may be interrogated by the code there. The programmer may define arbitrary exception-classes.

In Eiffel, the **rescue** clause may simply perform clean-up: if so, the exception still exists and is passed onto the caller. If the **rescue** clause terminates with the **retry** statement, control flow passes to the beginning of the routine. It must always either succeed or fail. This simple binary choice must be enforced explicitly in C++ and Java. The first clean-up above tries to fix the problem; the second clean-up simply prints an error message and terminates the program. As an alternative to specifying what next action to take at the end of a **catch** block, the C++/Java programmer may include final instructions after the last `catch` block to decide where control should pass next. In Java, this block is introduced with `finally`. The final block is always executed, regardless of whether exceptions were thrown or, in Java, even if the main `try` block returned early. This illustrates how a programmer must take care to ensure that a program resumes its execution at the proper point after a `catch` block is executed. It is possible, in C++ and Java, to think that you have handled an exception by catching it and printing a message. If nothing else is done, control simply resumes after the end of the last `catch` block – equivalent to carrying on regardless!

Deliverables and outputs (post-condition)

Additions to evolving OOAD documents showing how exceptions are to be treated.

Expected value analysis Star rating **

Focus: User requirements
Typical tasks for which this is needed: Analyze user requirements, identify user requirements
Related techniques: Impact estimation table
Input (pre-condition): Objectives requiring prioritization
Underpinning concepts: Need for objective way to determine priorities

Technique description

Expected value analysis is a technique which assists software developers to prioritize their objectives (see, e.g. Graham, 1995a). For each entry in a list of objectives, an approximation of the likely benefit is derived. This also often tends to reveal groupings between objectives. Such a prioritization supports the identification by the project manager of critical modules.

Technique usage

For each critical module, a list of objectives is derived. Of course, the objectives belong to more than one CIRT, so a matrix of CIRTs and objectives can be constructed (Figure A.30). Scores are entered into the matrix for each specific CIRT/objective link. The CIRT(s) with the highest total(s) are the most critical and, incidentally, the column totals will confirm (or negate) the original rankings for the business priorities as expressed by these several objectives.

Deliverables and outputs (post-condition)

Completed CIRT/objectives matrix.

	Objective 1	Objective 1	Objective 1	Total
CIRT1	76	30	80	186
CIRT2	88	30	50	168
CIRT3	15	40	5	60
Total	179	100	135	

Figure A.30 CIRT/objective matrix (after Graham, 1995a).

Fagan's inspections – see Inspections

Finite state machines – see State modeling

Framework creation   Star rating **

Focus: Reuse
Typical tasks for which this is needed: Construct the object model, create and/or identify reusable components
Related techniques: Application scavenging, pattern recognition
Input (pre-condition): Existing components
Underpinning concepts: Frameworks

Technique description

A framework is a large-scale skeleton system for a particular family of applications. The framework captures, at a very general level, the control structure and pattern of communication between the components of all applications of this type. The purpose of developing a framework is so that new applications of the same type may be developed more rapidly, using the foundation supplied by the framework. A framework is open-ended, containing 'hot spots' which may be extended or instantiated by the developer to suit the needs of the current application. A framework is the dual of a component – whereas a component is a reusable part, a framework is a reusable whole.

Frameworks are language-specific and usually problem-domain specific. It is common for a software house to develop 'niche markets' in some particular business field, and so they may well develop a framework for this kind of business application. Such frameworks are usually called 'vertical frameworks' because they handle a particular business application within a narrow field of concern, from start to finish. Certain general-purpose frameworks are valid for a variety of (or all) business domains, but typically deal with only one layer of a system, such as the GUI or presentation layer. Such frameworks are usually called 'horizontal frameworks' for this reason. Examples include Microsoft's MFC library for interfacing with the Windows desktop, or SunSoft's Java AWT (Cornell and Horstmann, 1998), which is customizable to different windowing systems.

Framework creation is an expensive task, both in terms of developer effort and in the time spent fine-tuning it. According to the OPEN technique: Application Scavenging (q.v.), it is not usually worth investing the effort in creating a framework until at least three applications of the same general kind have been developed. Although some companies set out to build frameworks, more usually frameworks are something that emerge as being of proven value in the particular business domain. Naturally, software houses are eager for the productivity gains promised by frameworks, but are equally wary of the costs involved in their development. To do the job properly, personnel must be assigned specifically to this task (see Technique: Application scavenging); and these personnel are removed from revenue-earning project development. So it is in the interest of the software house not to develop frameworks until the general structure of the vertical business domain is well understood. Frameworks are costly to develop, in proportion to the developers' early mistakes. A comparison may be made with complexity of algorithms: whereas reuse of a component through composition has constant cost, and extension of a class through inheritance has linear cost in the functionality of the new class, reworking the communication-pattern of messages sent between framework foundation classes has polynomial and even exponential cost.

Frameworks may be characterized as either whitebox, or blackbox (Pree, 1997). A whitebox framework is a system of abstract or deferred classes which the developer is expected to specialize. It is so called because the developer must appreciate the communication pattern among the abstract classes in the framework and know which methods to redefine in descendant classes. Therefore the developer must appreciate in detail how the framework implements its functionality. A blackbox framework is based around a cluster of parameterized classes, which the developer is expected to instantiate with appropriate components. It is so called because the developer need only be concerned about the component interfaces expected at the plug-in points of the framework and need not appreciate how the flow of control is handled internally within the framework. Whitebox frameworks are completed using inheritance, whereas blackbox frameworks are completed using composition. A blackbox framework may come supplied with a library of ready-made plug-in components, in which case it is sometimes called a toolkit. A framework that reaches this level of maturity has realized the decade-old notion of real pluggable component-based software.

Technique usage

The development of a framework usually takes the following course. A group of similar business classes is generalized into a local inheritance hierarchy, such that each application-specific class inherits (ultimately) from a single abstract root class, describing the most general component of its kind. Those methods that depend directly on the physical representation of each leaf class are coded for each, and the same methods are declared deferred in the root class (see Technique: Abstract class identification). Now, other methods owned by the leaf classes may be rewritten in terms of the small set of deferred methods and migrate upwards to the root class. The root class becomes the abstract node declaring all those services which every variant of the business component must eventually provide.

An example of this strategy is given in the Smalltalk Collection classes. Each specific kind of Collection (Set, Array, Bag) is responsible for implementing the add: and do: methods, but a large number of methods manipulating collections may be written in terms of just these two, for example, including all the elements of one Collection into another:

addAll: aCollection

"include all the elements of aCollection in self"

aCollection do: [:anElement | self add: anElement].
^ self

The meaning of adding a single element may be different in Set and Bag (Set allows no duplicates); however, including all the elements of one collection in another may be predicated upon this more basic method in a truly general way.

The next stage depends on whether a whitebox or blackbox framework is being developed. So far, we have generalized a number of groups of business classes into local hierarchies. The abstract classes at the roots of these describe the principal roles played by generic components in the business application. In the original applications, the specialized versions of these components communicated with each other to fulfil their task. Using the working applications as a guideline, the communication pattern between the abstract roles is re-established, taking care only to use methods declared in the interface of each abstract role. In many cases, this is accomplished anyway during the earlier generalization activity. The result is a whitebox framework in which the abstract role classes bear the responsibility for controlling the system. They initiate and respond to top-level system operations; control is distributed among them, according to whichever class is the focus for initiating a particular business operation.

In this model, the abstract role classes play the parts both of a business component and a controller object. In a blackbox framework, the abstract role classes only play the first part. Slightly more imaginative effort is needed to separate out the control abstractions from the simple domain abstractions. A separate layer of classes is designed to handle the flow of control, where each controller object has a plug-in point expecting to receive an abstract business component. At the same time, all control methods are removed from the business classes. In this way, the interfaces between controllers and business components are fixed. Clearly, this requires greater confidence that the business components have stabilized. However, the advantages are that control-related functions no longer reside in the simple business classes, a separation of concerns which, in the long run, will help with the maintenance of the framework. The controller objects in a blackbox framework are bound to their business components by composition. It is possible to use genericity (see Technique: Genericity specification) to parameterize the controllers by the type of component expected, and thereby obtain static binding with the business components. Alternatively, the controller objects may expect to interact with an abstract (deferred) class component, whose methods are necessarily bound dynamically.

It is now easier to see why whitebox frameworks are often developed before blackbox: during the early generalization activity, methods are migrating up the class hierarchy. It is only when the abstract business role objects are identified that it becomes clear which methods constitute the control loop. The whitebox framework may even evolve in this state. For example, if a further application is developed and it is decided to adapt the library framework to accommodate new insights into controlling this kind of application (see Technique: Application scavenging), then further intermediate nodes in the local business generalization hierarchies may be established which support control methods or there may be found an even more general root class than previously. During this stage of framework development, the methods constituting the overall control structure may migrate up the hierarchy and at the same time may be broken down into more subroutine-like calls which are intercepted lower in the hierarchy. This pattern of high level generalization with low level interceptions is known as the yo-yo effect (Taenzer *et al.*, 1989), because tracing the complete call graph for a given system operation requires hunting up and down the class hierarchy to find the methods which implement it. Eventually, such a framework will collapse under its own complexity. So there usually comes a time, when the abstract business components are relatively stable, when it makes sense to remove the control loop from the abstract business classes and create a separate control layer. This is a later evolution of the framework.

Deliverables and outputs (post-condition)

The final deliverable is the framework and its full documentation; an interim deliverable is the next version of the framework, under version control.

Games Star rating **

Focus: Developers, end users
Typical tasks for which this is needed: Develop education and training plan, do customer training, system investigation
Related techniques: Group problem solving, PS–PPS, roleplay
Input (pre-condition): Problem needing solving and experiences needing creating
Underpinning concepts: Synthetic experience provides safe and sound preparation for the 'real thing'

Technique description

Games provide a workshop-focused, experiential learning environment. This may concentrate on software developers and their managers in their skills upgrading as their organization migrates to object technology; it may be to 'train the trainers'; or to educate the end-users. Anthropomorphizing is found to be a useful technique in learning to 'think like an object'.

Games are simulations of real life situations. As with other simulation techniques, their primary advantage is that we can learn from enacting a situation without exposing ourselves to risks existing in the real life situation. Games also symbolize our interactions, conflicts, abilities, shortcomings and aggressive tendencies, without the high prices we tend to pay when indulging in these tendencies in real life. If designed and played correctly, games are therefore an extremely productive and efficient means of learning.

Technique usage

To be effective, games have to be 'good games'. This means they have to:

- Be good metaphors. This means that they have to represent the situation they are simulating to an adequate degree.

- Be reasonably easy to play. This means that the gains in playing the game rather than experiencing the real thing must be substantial.

- Be memorable, preferably enjoyable. However, contrary to common belief, not all games must *necessarily* be enjoyable. In fact, what *is* necessary is for them to be memorable. That is their true value. Some people tend to forget enjoyment more quickly than suffering, others the reverse. However, if the game is to entail some 'suffering' (e.g. loss of money, physical exertion, worry, etc.) all participants should be pre-warned and aware of the possibility of such conditions and be prepared to participate. Sometimes you need to have this in writing! Even with games incurring suffering, this may still be less in the game than the equivalent 'suffering' in the real world the game tries to simulate.

- Have clear rules. The effectiveness of games and game playing relates to the fact that they are abstraction devices. A well-designed game should highlight the rules that are important in the simulation and de-emphasize the conditions that are not. Everyone must know the rules necessary for them to play the game before they need to apply the rule for the first time. An exception to this is, of course, when the objective of the game is to 'discover' a rule.

- Have clear objectives and outcome(s). All participants must be told clearly why the game is played and how it is to be won.

There are, however, some common mistakes made when designing games, generally as a consequence of not observing one or more of the following guidelines:

- A game need not be fair. Life is not. The point of playing a game is to simulate a situation and to learn from it. This simulation has to be true to the nature of the situation; if unfair, so be it!
- There needs to be a real, obvious and personal gain for the winners or loss (for the losers) even though small, otherwise the game will not be taken seriously.
- A binary outcome (winner/loser) is best. An ordinal ranking (first, second, third, etc.) is acceptable but not as good.
- The scope of the game must be specific. Games that try to teach you about life, pursuit of happiness, motherhood, apple pie and system tuning, won't work.
- Games need not be original and creative, although original and creative ones work best since they pique the interest of the participants.
- There must always be a debriefing or post-mortem.

Games tend to be created by specific consulting and training companies for their clients and seldom made public – although there have been some examples given at OOPSLA Educators' Workshops.

CRC cards are often used as the basis for roleplay (q.v.) games in which workshop participants take on the roles of individual objects in the system. This type of game can enhance learning of many concepts including responsibilities, collaborations, encapsulation and message passing.

The PS–PSS framework (q.v.) created by Class Technology is supported by a boardgame (Figure A.31) which 'brings to life' the concepts of use cases, model building, patterns and responsibilities (more in terms of behavior modeling).

Deliverables and outputs (post-condition)

Various – at least improved understanding.

206 CORE TECHNIQUES

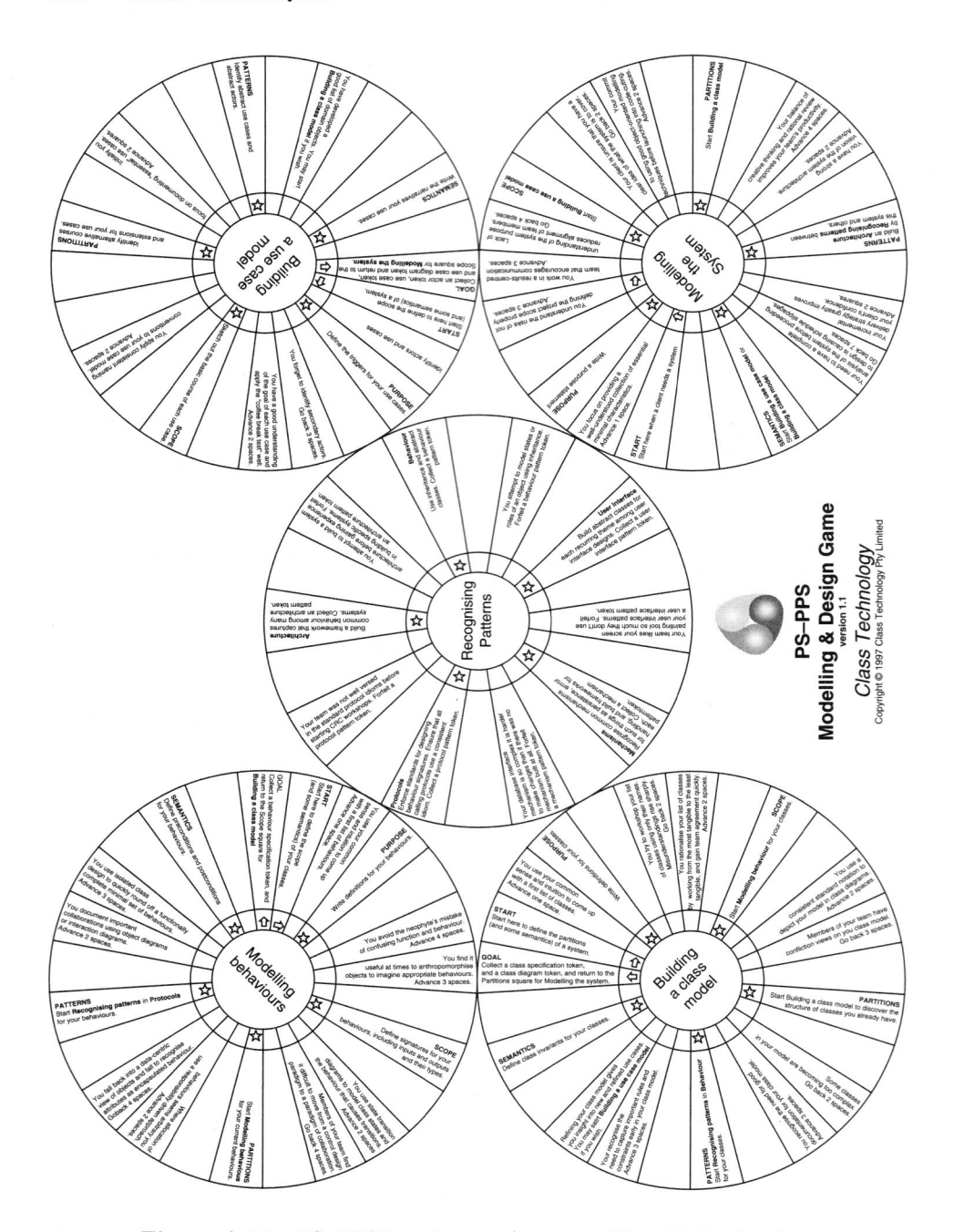

Figure A.31 PS–PPS board game (courtesy, Class Technology).

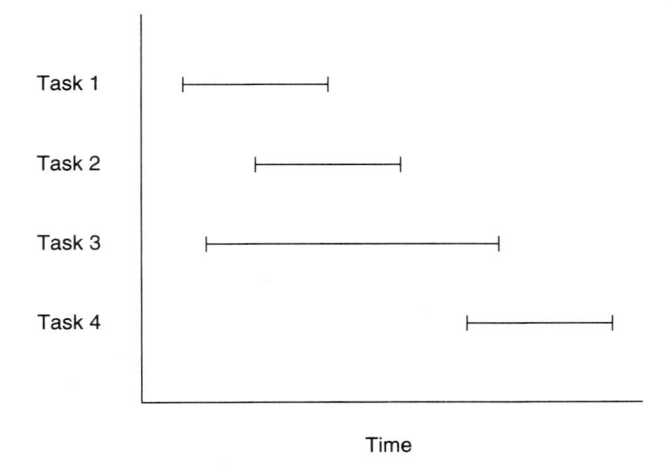

Figure A.32 Gantt chart.

Gantt charts   Star rating **

Focus: Project management (timelines)
Typical tasks for which this is needed: Develop and implement resource allocation plan
Related techniques: CPM charts, PERT charts
Input (pre-condition): Information on durations of activities
Underpinning concepts: Need for objective method of formulating planning timelines

Technique description

A Gantt chart (Figure A.32) shows the duration, sequencing and overlap of tasks in time.

Technique usage

To construct a Gantt chart, list the activities/tasks vertically on the left hand side and, along the top, construct a timeline. Mark the planned beginning and end of each activity on this timeline thus showing planned start and end times and, by inference, which tasks have as a pre-condition the termination of another task (if this is critical then a different scheduling technique such as CPM should be used instead). A Gantt chart represents planning decisions and is useful in reviewing progress against planned schedules.

An interesting modification of the standard Gantt chart, which, as noted above, does not indicate anything about critical paths, is given by Baudoin and Hollowell (1996). Merging in ideas from PERT charts, these authors suggest adding a vertical line to the Gantt chart to indicate task dependencies

208   CORE TECHNIQUES

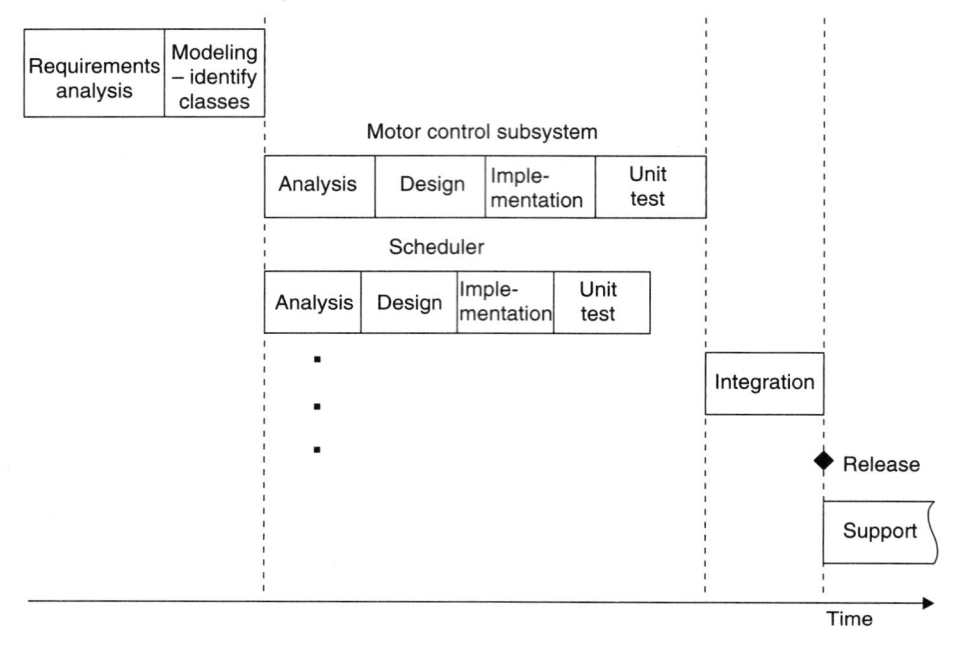

Figure A.33 A first version of an object-oriented project schedule (after Baudoin and Hollowell, 1996).

(Figure A.33). Here, if the right edge of a box is aligned with the left edge of another box, as indicated by the dotted vertical line, than the second task requires the completion of the first task as a prerequisite to its commencement.

Deliverables and outputs (post-condition)

Gantt chart as part of project plan.

Generalization and inheritance identification   Star rating **

Focus: Semantic relationship (is-a-kind-of) and its implementation using inheritance in an OOPL
Typical tasks for which this is needed: construct the object model, create and/or identify reusable components ('for reuse'), test
Related techniques: Relationship modeling
Input (pre-condition): Draft design
Underpinning concepts: Abstraction; Classification and Partitions; Generalization, Inheritance and Polymorphism

Technique description

Generalization and inheritance can be identified in terms of semantic or structural (actually definitional) relationships. Both refer to a hierarchy or a network which contains CIRTs connected in the roles of 'parents' and 'children'.

Generalization is an abstraction process which creates a generalization hierarchy representing knowledge (the is-a-kind-of relationship dominates). Inheritance, on the other hand, is a computer science support tool which has several flavors (specialization, specification and implementation – LaLonde and Pugh, 1991; Yap and Henderson-Sellers, 1993). Specialization inheritance is the inheritance equivalent of generalization – indeed in most OO approaches, including OPEN, no real distinction is made between the two, other than focus. Specification inheritance is also known as subtyping or blackbox inheritance. Here CIRTs are related to each other in such a way that the subtype can always be substituted for the supertype. This is the Liskov substitution principle.

Whilst dynamic substitutability is the essence of polymorphism and hence of OT, the final style of inheritance may be used (but is not recommended) for code reuse at the expense of semantics. This is known as implementation inheritance or whitebox inheritance. Whilst everyone is in agreement that this is a dangerous practice, both from a semantic and reusability viewpoint, OML offers a notation specific to implementation inheritance in order to draw the developer's attention to the danger of the practice. On the other hand, UML does not offer any notation on the grounds that it should never be done and therefore it should never need notating.

For each flavor of generalization/inheritance (discussed in detail in CD: Appendix E), it is also possible to inherit either from a sole parent (single inheritance/generalization) or from two or more parents (multiple inheritance/generalization). Multiple inheritance/generalization is powerful yet dangerous and is not supported by some OO programming languages. Indeed, good examples are hard to find.

Technique usage

Definitional relationships should be identified which reflect either is-a-kind-of (or knowledge representation) connexion or a subtyping relationship. (In practice these can be confounded although strictly they represent different relationships in theory). Do not be misled by mere factoring of characteristics into a superclass. Ask yourself if the question 'Can I say the subclass is a particular kind of the parent?' can be answered positively. This means that the subclass is both an extension and a restriction of the parent (Meyer, 1988). It is an extension because instances of the subtype have more extended characteristics (than the parent). It is a restriction because the number of specific individuals that can belong to the set of objects represented by the subtype is less than those which could legitimately lay claim to being members of the supertype.

210 CORE TECHNIQUES

Deliverables and outputs (post-condition)

Documentation on inheritance hierarchies/networks. Using a notation such as UML, these relationships will be an integral part of the class diagrams. Using a notation such as OML or Fusion, separate inheritance diagrams are recommended, particularly for describing large systems.

Generalization for reuse – see Revision of inheritance hierarchies

Genericity specification Star rating **

Focus: Low level design of container classes
Typical tasks for which this is needed: Construct the object model, create and/or identify reusable components ('for reuse')
Related techniques: Library class incorporation
Input (pre-condition): Partial design, user requirements
Underpinning concepts: Containment, Genericity

Technique description

Genericity (q.v.) is the term used in OPEN to describe parametric polymorphism. A generic CIRT is one whose type structure is not completely fixed and therefore it may be adapted to work with different types. Common candidates for generic implementation are the container datatypes, such as *STACK*s, *QUEUE*s, *LINKED_LIST*s and so on, because these are structures which can be used with almost any element type. The type flexibility is represented by a type parameter where the type of the element would normally be given. The generic CIRT offers a type interface, which allows a programmer to substitute the desired element type in place of the parameter at the point of use.

Genericity should always be used (in languages that support it):

- when there are many possible variants of the same type, but these all behave in the same way
- polymorphic adaptability is desired, but strong static typing and static binding is required.

The object-oriented languages Eiffel, C++ 3.0 and Ada 95 all support genericity.

Technique usage

Many C++ class libraries developed since version 3.0 was released have made extensive use of genericity. The Booch components (Rational, 1993) and the

C++ Standard Template Library (Stepanov and Lee, 1994) are good examples. In these, the container classes typically have two type parameters, one for the element type and one for the implementation type. To explain this, consider that a `Stack` may be implemented either using an `Array` with a fill counter, or as a `List` of `Cells`. To give client programmers maximum flexibility regarding `Stack` performance (in terms of the time versus space tradeoff), abstract data types like `Stack` are not bound to a particular implementation. Instead, the client programmer chooses this when the `Stack` is instantiated. In C++, the above `Stack` class might look like:

```
template<class ELT, class IMP>
class Stack
{ public:
        // constructors omitted
        void push(const ELT
        void pop();
        ELT& top(); // element type is ELT
  private:
        IMP _implementation; // implementation type is IMP
};
template <class ELT, class IMP>
void Stack<ELT,IMP>::push(const ELT& e)
{       _implementation.insertFirst(e);
}
...
template <class ELT, class IMP>
ELT     Stack<ELT,IMP>::top()
{       _implementation.firstElement();
}
```

Here, the abstract data type `Stack` provides public `push()`, `pop()` and `top()` operations, but relies on its implementation to do the work of these functions, using `insertFirst()`, `removeFirst()`, `firstElement()` and so on. Provided the implementation type, represented by the parameter `IMP`, supports these operations, any such `IMP` may be used. If we assume that both the classes `List<ELT>` and `Array<ELT>` support such operations, we may declare Stack instances with different implementations:

```
Stack<int, Array<int> >  fixedIntStack;
Stack<int, List<int> >   linkedIntStack;
```

Here, the instance `fixedIntStack` is a `Stack` of `Integers`, with an `Array`-based implementation. The `linkedIntStack` has a linked `List`-based implementation, which is economical on space and slightly slower in time, due to the need to create list `Cells`. However, the `Array`-based implementation may fill up and overflow, whereas the `List`-based implementation may grow indefinitely (to the limit of heap memory).

Note how this model requires no dynamic binding of the basic `Stack` operations. When `IMP` is replaced by the actual type `Array<int>`, for example, the compiler detects that the routine to call for `insertFirst()` is, in fact, `Array<int>::insertFirst(const int&)` and links this statically. The `Stack` operations could even be declared inline, delegating all calls to the implementation type. This is both maximally flexible and maximally efficient. Although the same design technique may be applied in Eiffel, the efficiency gains are not the same, because, as noted above, the Eiffel compiler cannot guarantee to bind functions statically.

There is a down-side to templates in C++, which is that their usage tends to slow down compilation times. Object-code cannot be generated early for template classes – the compiler would need to know full type information before it could do this. This means that every instantiation of a template class is compiled from source. It is possible, however, to pre-instantiate template classes in code modules where complete type information is known, and then pre-generate object-code for such modules.

Deliverables and outputs (post-condition)

Design documents describing classes with a higher potential for reuse – largely 'container' classes.

GQM   Star rating ***

Focus: Goal, then question, then metric
Typical tasks for which this is needed: Evaluate quality
Related techniques: Metrics collection
Input (pre-condition): Identified need for metrics collection
Underpinning concepts: Formal approach to metrics identification

Technique description

A widely used and highly recommended framework for a metrics program is the 'Goal/Question/Metric' paradigm (Figure A.34) of Basili and Rombach (1988).

Technique usage

As its name suggests, the first step of selecting metrics is to identify the goal, 'G'. This leads to questions, 'Q', such as how to increase code quality, decrease enhancement schedules. In turn, these questions help to elucidate the appropriate metrics, 'M', which need to be be collected. An additional, vital component is the interrelationship with theories and modeling (Figure A.34(b)). Models permit explicit description of relationships between components and properties of interest within the realm of the stated goal.

Typical *clear* objectives and goals could be:

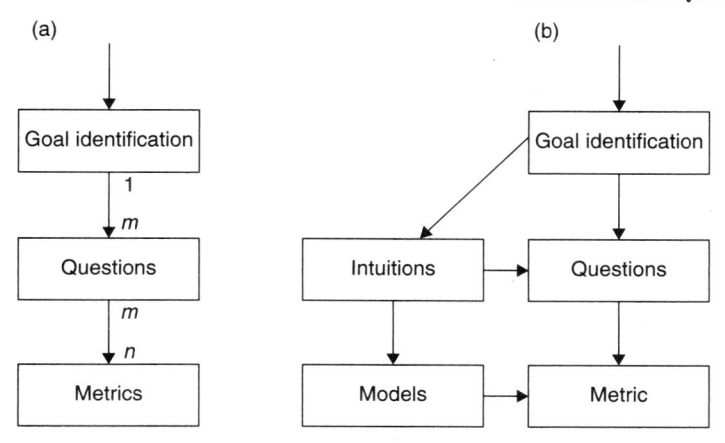

Figure A.34 The GQM paradigm: (a) original version of Basili and Rombach (1988) and (b) modifications suggested by Shepperd (1990) (after Henderson-Sellers, 1996).

- an objective concerned with a single product: improve the reliability of a product such as the company's own accounting system which undergoes continual change and maintenance

- an objective concerned with a single person: improve the software manager's ability to estimate project costs

- an objective concerned with a specific group of people: improve the productivity of all software designers or

- a company-wide objective: improve quality of all software products which are developed.

The statement of these goals leads to appropriate questions such as 'How do we increase code quality?' or 'How do we decrease enhancement schedules?'. Once established, the questions should lead naturally, within the GQM framework, to selection of the most appropriate metrics. The problem with the application of this approach to OO metrics is that the set of metrics available may be empty. Thus a complementary activity is that of simply identifying a large number of 'potentially useful' metrics, i.e. the 'M' component of 'GQM' *independently* of specific goals and questions.

Offen and Jeffery (1997) have provided an extension to GQM called the Model, Measure, Manage Paradigm (M^3P) (Table A.13) which adds well-defined links between the quantitative data and both the software development and business contexts. These ensure that the technical reports directly answer the concerns of the senior executives. To date, application of M^3P has been limited and outside of the OO development environment, e.g. in one case to evaluate function points.

Table A.13 The eight stages of the M^{3}P of Offen and Jeffery (1997).

---

(1) Understand the business strategy

(2) Identify business goals, substrategies, risks and tactics that depend on successful software development, use and support

(3) Determine the critical success factors

(4) Define specific software development goals, based on steps 1–3

(5) Pose questions

(6) Identify and define measures

(7) Set up the program: generate detailed procedures and define reports (for all stakeholders)

(8) Regularly review the program by iterating over steps 1–7

Deliverables and outputs (post-condition)

Well-documented goals and questions together with a list of recommended metrics.

Granularity   Star rating *

Focus: Level of abstraction needed
Typical tasks for which this is needed: Construct the object model, create and/or identify reusable components, develop business object model, undertake architectural design
Related techniques: Abstraction utilization
Input (pre-condition): Draft design
Underpinning concepts: Abstraction

Technique description

The granularity of a system may be imposed by the abstraction level of the problem domain. However, for many software systems, a choice of relatively coarse or relatively fine granularity can be made (Unhelkar, 1997). A fine granular system takes more effort but creates classes which are more reusable; whereas a coarse granular system can often provide faster time to market at the expense of future increased reuse and maintenance costs.

The granularity of a system is also strongly related to the notion of the abstraction level. The more granular a system is, the more detail is shown and the lower the abstraction level.

Technique usage

Choice of granularity level depends upon a number of considerations. Typically, reuse will be of main concern balanced against the time and effort required to create highly reusable classes. More finely granular classes are generally more reusable both in future projects and across domains. However, creating high quality fine granular classes can be extremely expensive. If, therefore, there is no foreseen reuse for any particular class, then it is probably unwise to design it as anything other than a coarse granular class. This, of course, can frequently lead to the confounding of two concepts within the one class and bears some relationship (from a physical viewpoint but with a different focus) to the notions embodied in OPEN Technique: Collapsing of classes, which has a database focus.

Deliverables and outputs (post-condition)

The choice of the granularity level dictates the appropriate documentation abstraction level. It also links closely with the reuse planning documents produced as part of the project planning process.

Group problem solving Star rating **

Focus: Problem identification and analysis
Typical tasks for which this is needed: Develop education and training plan, do user training, identify user requirements
Related techniques: Brainstorming, workshops
Input (pre-condition): A problem
Underpinning concepts: Groups can often solve problems more effectively and faster than individuals

Technique description

Also known as Joint Sessions, Group problem solving (GPS) goes beyond what its name suggests. It is not held merely for the purpose of problem solving but, in addition, is actually quite an effective approach to data acquisition and requirements elicitation. The key principle behind GPS is the involvement of a wide array of stakeholders, particularly the users, in key decision-making about the project.

Technique usage

GPS has four basic phases, each with their own sub-phases:

(1) Planning

- Plan the objectives and scope of the workshop
- Arrange facilities and organize logistics
- Select appropriate stakeholder participants and inform them of the venue, time and purpose of the workshop
- Prepare and distribute workshop agenda and background material.

(2) Conduct of workshop

- Introduce the session and the participants
- Describe the objectives of the session
- Highlight the ground rules
- Manage the agenda and the flow of the session
- Ensure and maintain participants' focus
- Document important facts and issues. These may be:
    - issues
    - agreed facts
    - disputed facts
    - requirements
    - further clarifications to be sought
    - ideas
    - solutions (be careful with this one as it may predispose the rest of the development)
- Review
- Conclude the session.

(3) Results documentation

- Document and order all information gathered during the workshop
- Send the document to all participants for their verification.

(4) Follow up

- Assess workshop output and determine unresolved issues
- Determine if follow-up is needed. This could be in the form of follow-up action points or conduct of another workshop
- Follow up all action points
- Plan a future workshop if necessary.

There are a number of specific roles played in a GPS. These are:

(1) Session facilitator

The session facilitator is responsible for ensuring that the workshop runs smoothly. The facilitator

- Moderates the session and ensures that the objectives are met and the agenda is kept
- Remains neutral and also acts as arbiter if necessary
- Introduces and concludes sessions and
- Encourages user participation.

(2) Participants
These are the stakeholders that provide business expertise, opinion, or guidance. They usually include but must not be restricted to representatives of users only.

(3) Project sponsor
The sponsor is usually a senior manager from the business who is funding the project. The sponsor confirms the project and the objectives of the session and states the business need and commitment from management for the project.

(4) Scribe
The scribe visibly documents the findings during the workshop and is also in charge of physical logistics.

(5) Observer
Optionally, an interested party or domain expert might be present at the workshop. They must remain silent unless specific issues are directed to them for clarification.

Deliverables and outputs (post-condition)

Documentation of the problem solving experience highlighting questions, choices made and solutions discovered.

Hierarchical task analysis   Star rating **

Focus: Requirements capture, modeling of business tasks
Typical tasks for which this is needed: Design user interface, develop business object model, identify user requirements
Related techniques: Brainstorming, Kelly grids, protocol analysis, questionnaires
Input (pre-condition): User requirements
Underpinning concepts: Scenarios, Task Scripts and Use Cases

Technique description

'A task is an activity or set of actions undertaken by an agent assuming a role to change a system's current state to some goal state. Goals may have subgoals and be achieved by executing procedures (sets of actions)' (Graham, 1995a, page 99). Each task fulfils a goal and provides the method by which this fulfilment occurs. For instance, my goal is to be in Sydney later today; my task is therefore to book

Table A.14 The objectives of task analysis (from Graham, 1995a, page 294).

The objectives, or goal, of the task

The procedures used

Any actions and objects involved

Time taken to accomplish the task

Frequency of operations

Occurrence of errors and exceptions

Involvement of subordinate and superordinate tasks

---

an appropriate flight; which in itself may involve other subtasks such as finding the telephone number of a travel agent, ringing that travel agent etc.

The broad objectives of hierarchical task analysis are given in Table A.14. The task descriptions captured in this way are then formalized, perhaps as SVDPI sentences (see below) or logic trees (Graham, 1995a, page 294). Hierarchical task analysis thus identifies and documents tasks, typically at the level of the user interaction. This is usually (in OPEN) in terms of requirements engineering but can also be valuable for user interface design (Graham, 1995a, page 99). Indeed, much of the theory and practice of task analysis comes from the HCI community. There are also links to Schank and Abelson's (1977) script theory and to expert systems/knowledge engineering.

Tasks are then broken down into smaller tasks until all tasks can be considered as being *atomic*, i.e. they can be broken down no further without departing from the declared scope or domain or interest (e.g. as determined by the context diagram).

Technique usage

Task analysis can be facilitated by a number of other techniques such as Kelly grids, brainstorming, questionnaires, protocol analysis and so on. Tasks themselves are documented by task scripts (see CD: Appendix E for further discussion) in the form of an SVDPI sentence expressed as

Subject – Verb – Direct.Object – [Preposition – Indirect.Object]

The sentence's subject corresponds to an actor – an external user of the system. The overall objectives of task analysis are tabulated in Table A.15. The task object model thus derived describes knowledge (see Graham, 1997a).

Tasks are then decomposed recursively to the level of an atomic task which is defined as the granularity beyond which further decomposition exits the contextual domain (or Universe of Discourse). The resulting Task Object Model (TOM), where the objects are the tasks, is then transformed to the Business

Table A.15 General objectives of task analysis (after Graham, 1995a, page 294).

Task analysis focuses on the definition of:

- the objectives, or goal, of the task
- the procedures used
- any actions and objects involved
- the time taken to accomplish the task
- the frequency of operations
- the occurrence of errors and exceptions
- the involvement of subordinate and superordinate tasks.

Object Model (BOM) (Graham, 1996b). Thus, for instance, in the task 'book flight', the grammatical object in the sentence is likely to become a business object in the BOM (and subsequently the SOM and IOM – for OPEN process details see Graham *et al.*, 1997b).

Deliverables and outputs (post-condition)

Task decomposition tree.

Hotspot identification – see Pattern recognition

Impact analysis Star rating **

Focus: Project management
Typical tasks for which this is needed: Develop software development context plans and strategies
Related techniques: Configuration management
Input (pre-condition): Required change
Underpinning concepts: Alterations can cause unforeseen, and possibly major, problems if not handled carefully

Technique description

Change is an inherent component of software development – changes in user requirements, design modifications, recoding and corrective actions in maintenance. Of importance here is the appreciation of the potentially major impact

220   CORE TECHNIQUES

of an apparently minor change. This is evaluated using impact analysis (Pfleeger, 1991, page 433) which focuses on the many risks involved, such as effects on resources, effort and the schedule. These may best be illustrated in inadequate or outdated documentation, poorly patched software, poor designs, bad coding idioms, non-conformance to standards etc. Comprehension, especially in maintenance, can be costly.

Technique usage

Measurement of the impacts of changes are analyzed by Pfleeger and Bohner (1990). They identify a number of stages, each of which provides a measurement for managing the impact of the change. For each work product, vertical traceability describes interdependencies whereas horizontal traceability addresses interrelationships of components across collections of work products. Both are represented using directed graphs wherein the nodes represent information in documents and other work products and the edges represent the relationship within a work product or between work products. A complexity metric can then be used to predict the likely cost and error rate (Card and Glass, 1990).

Deliverables and outputs (post-condition)

Documented risks, impacts and recommended responses to minimize impacts.

Impact estimation table   Star rating *

Focus: Project management
Typical tasks for which this is needed: Develop and implement resource allocation plan, develop software development context plans and strategies
Related techniques: Kelly grids
Input (pre-condition): Various options
Underpinning concepts: Objective analysis of various impacts of various options

Technique description

An impact estimation table (Gilb, 1988) is a quantitative technique for facilitating decision making. It describes, in tabular fashion, a number of objectives and values related to a number of tactics to meet these objectives. In a two-dimensional spreadsheet fashion, these can be summed to give an overall guestimate of the impact of that particular strategy to reach the objectives.

Technique usage

When a number of options is available (in Table A.16 for training), the requirements are all listed against the design ideas. The impact of each design on

Table A.16 Impact estimation table for training example (after Gilb, 1997a).

	Design idea			
	Training course	Peer training	On-line tutorial	*Total achievement*
Requirements				
S1 *Staff skills* – ability to use the core system functionality – PAST [Jan 1997] to PLAN [Jan 1998]				
S1.1 *Training* Availability of advanced training Six months to within two weeks	10%	90%	98%	198%
S1.2 *System input issues* Input error rates 5% to 1%	10%	10%	5%	25%
% Input problems 10% to 5%	10%	40%	5%	55%
Turnaround of an input problem 15 min to 5 min	25%	75%	40%	140%
Total benefit	55%	215%	148%	
Development cost	$20k	$20k	$25k	
Operational cost [1998]	$30k	$5k	$2k	
Benefit–cost ratio	1.1	8.6	5.5	

each requirement is then estimated, expressed as a percentage of the achieved requirement from the use of that specific design idea (Gilb, 1997a). In addition, other supplementary data are required: for evidence of the estimate, the estimate's source, the margin of uncertainty associated with each estimate and its credibility rating. Summing all entries gives a likelihood of achievement. Summing the percentage impact estimates of a design factor gives an idea of that design idea's effectiveness in meeting the requirements. Finally the cost of each design idea can be quantified as a benefit–cost ratio. Decisions can then be based on these benefit–cost ratios. In the example in Table A.16, the highest benefit is for peer training which also has the highest benefit–cost ratio.

It should also be noted that the task/objective and object/objectives matrices in SOMA (Graham, 1995a) are impact estimation matrices.

Deliverables and outputs (post-condition)

Set of impact estimation tables together with recommended responses.

Implementation inheritance – see Generalization and inheritance identification

Implementation of distributed aspects of system Star rating **
(major contributor G.C. Low)

Focus: Distributed systems coding
Typical tasks for which this is needed: Code
Related techniques: DCS classification, distributed systems partitioning and allocation
Input (pre-condition): Final design
Underpinning concepts: Client–server/DCS topologies and concepts; distributed systems

Technique description

Once the partitioning and allocation process has been completed, it is possible to determine the code distribution of executable images. Decisions must be made on what code is included in each executable image based on partitioning and allocation decisions and migration possibilities.

Technique usage

Each class's services should initially be implemented independently of distribution. This increases the portability of code and ensures that the complexities of distribution do not affect the task of producing good quality, correct code to satisfy the business's functional requirements.

Different compilers (and even programming languages) may be required for the software modules to be compiled on to their physical node. Copies of class code that are slightly changed to allow for a different compiler should be well documented to ensure they are maintained along with the primary copy.

The procedures for updating software once it has been installed on the physical nodes around the network should be planned.

Deliverables and outputs (post-condition)

Code for distributed aspects of system.

Implementation of rules Star rating *

Focus: Coding rules within classes
Typical tasks for which this is needed: Code

Related techniques: Rule modeling
Input (pre-condition): Final design
Underpinning concepts: Rules

Technique description

Business rules are 'declarations of policy or conditions that must be satisfied' (OMG, 1988). They represent IF-THEN-type business decisions that need to be represented in the software system. They may be constraint rules (which specify policies or conditions) or derivation rules (for inferring or computing facts from other facts).

Fung *et al.* (1997) note that the business policies and rules should form an integral part in the analysis of the behavioral aspect of an object (Graham, 1995a). Rules formalize the assumptions, guidelines and obligations of an object in providing services in a system. Fung *et al.* (1997) also note that it is unfortunate that in most information systems, these rules are not properly declared or as well documented as they should be. Instead, they are transformed into programming code for execution. As a result, these sets of business rules are scattered around in various program modules and hidden from the users who originally defined them and who will be the ones most likely to request changes in the future.

Technique usage

One of the ways to incorporate business rules in an object model is by way of conditions under which a service could be utilized by others. Meyer (1988, 1992b) introduced the contracting theory to object-oriented construction of software. A contract (q.v.) represents the obligations and the benefits resulting from an interaction (i.e. use of a service) between the client class and the supplier class. It applies to each service within a class by the use of pre- and post-conditions and to the class as a whole by the use of class invariants. The contract thus stipulates a number of conditions for which a service will perform its function and returns the results of that service (see also Henderson-Sellers and McKim, 1994). These conditions (pre- and post-) are used, therefore, to implement the business rule. The concern of the developer is how this contracting concept can be incorporated into the building of an object model.

Graham (1995a) suggests that the conversion from rules to assertions may be conducted quite mechanically. He suggests a classification of rules (Table A.17) as being of use here.

Deliverables and outputs (post-condition)

Addition of rules to coded classes.

Table A.17 Rule categories (adapted from Graham, 1995a, pages 447/8).

Type A rules:	Rules that relate attributes to themselves. These are not rules but constraints on attributes and can be expressed as assertions about the standard *get* and *put* methods for each attribute. Usually they are pre-conditions on *put*.
Type M rules:	Rules that relate operations to themselves. These are not rules but assertions concerning operations/methods.
Type AA rules:	Rules that relate attributes to other attributes. These are expressed as pre- or post-conditions on the *put* and *get* methods associated with one of the attributes.
Type MM rules:	Rules that relate methods to methods. These are usually to do with sequencing and would be normally expressed as pre- or post-conditions in any case.
Type AM rules:	Rules that relate attributes to methods or vice versa. Rules which relate attributes to methods are triggers or pre-conditions and could be implemented directly as database triggers or pre-conditions or indirectly as special code. Rules which relate methods to attributes are invariants or post-conditions.
Type CA rules:	Rules that describe behavior of attributes under global control strategies. These require specific code descriptions in many cases.
Type CM rules:	Rules that describe behavior of methods under global control strategies. These too may require specific code descriptions.
Type EA rules:	Rules that describe exception handling for attribute values. If the language supports exception handling, these map directly to such language constructs. Otherwise, purpose-written code is required.
Type EM rules:	Rules that describe exception handling for methods. If the language supports exception handling, these too map directly to such language constructs. Otherwise, purpose written code is required.

Implementation of services Star rating **

Focus: Coding services/responsibilities within classes
Typical tasks for which this is needed: Code
Related techniques: Class internal design, implementation of structure, service identification
Input (pre-condition): Class internal designs are complete
Underpinning concepts: Idioms, Patterns and Frameworks; Implementation using an OOPL

Technique description

Implementation of services refers to applying the particular coding standards for the target programming language to the detailed method designs resulting from Class Internal Design (q.v.). A companion Technique: Implementation of structure discusses how data attribute information should be coded in particular programming languages.

After the class internal design stage is complete, the developer will have available a detailed outline of the class and its required methods. The detailed design stage will have taken into account such issues as the cohesion between the candidate methods and attributes of the class; and the intended calling patterns whereby methods invoke each other. The public methods of the class should typically make use of a small set of underlying principles, and may call common supporting private methods (see the example of the *locate* method discussed as a supporting method for hash tables under the Technique: Class internal design).

To aid him/her in writing method code correctly, a programmer may have up to four different kinds of specification documents:

- method protocols (type signatures, class interface) describing the expected inputs and outputs to each method
- call graphs (method interaction graphs) describing the expected calling pattern of methods and whether they create new objects
- state diagrams (Harel statecharts) describing the different abstract states that an instance of the class passes through as various message stimuli are received
- formal pre- and post-conditions, describing conditions that must hold before and after method invocations.

The code that is written must conform to any such specification; and the programmer should make it possible for the testers to verify that his/her code conforms to the specification documents. Various techniques for achieving this are discussed in CD: Appendix E.

Technique usage

Classes need to contain constructors which may be explicitly defined, as in C++, or implicit as a class method, as in Smalltalk. In OOPLs without automatic garbage collection, such as C++, a destructor method must also be written.

Access methods need to be supplied for all data resulting in services which *get* and *set* internally stored data values.

To enhance quality 'programming by contract' is highly encouraged in OPEN whereby all coded methods have pre- and post-conditions. Exception handling must be considered seriously and provides a second route to higher quality software.

In the context of a *distributed system*, each class's services should initially be implemented independently of distribution. This increases the portability of code and ensures that the complexities of distribution do not affect the task of producing good quality, correct code to satisfy the business's functional requirements.

Deliverables and outputs (post-condition)

Code for each service.

Implementation of structure   Star rating **

Focus: Coding of relationships between CIRTs
Typical tasks for which this is needed: Code
Related techniques: Class internal design, design templates, implementation of services, relationship modeling
Input (pre-condition): Detailed class designs, design templates
Underpinning concepts: Idioms, Patterns and Frameworks; Implementation using an OOPL

Technique description

Translation from the final design to code can often be accomplished in one of several ways. If the steps advocated in OPEN Techniques: Collaborations Analysis, Visibility Analysis and Class Internal Design are followed, then implementing the internal structure of a class follows automatically, since these techniques yield optimal minimum coupling between classes. Alternatively, or in addition, boilerplate coding styles may be derived more directly from analysis models, by using Odell and Fowler's (1995a, b, c) design templates (q.v.), which are also recommended by OPEN. The implementation of structure in a distributed computing system should initially be performed independently of distribution concerns for the same reasons as the implementation of services (q.v.); existing guidelines on loose coupling (e.g. McGregor and Sykes, 1992) are also ideal for distributed systems.

The structure of a class is represented by its attributes and relationships to other classes. Particular language idioms (q.v.) must be followed to encode such information, either as value-based data members, pointers or reference-based data members. Certain cosmetic styles may be observed for linking data structure members with corresponding access functions. Finally, the inter-module dependencies between different classes may have to be considered and represented in the programming language concerned.

Technique usage

To reiterate the process so far, the system layering techniques described in Technique: Collaborations analysis will have determined which inter-object connexions are quasi-permanent. Examining the semantics of these connexions (see

Underpinning concept: Visibility) will determine whether the association may be implemented as a pointer/reference, or by embedding the server object in the client. Although many bi-directional connexions (represented in OPEN as two associations) may arise during early analysis, many of these will have been transformed, e.g. through the use of Mediator Design Patterns, by way of the Aggregation component of collaborations analysis, into uni-directional connexions from the Mediator to the component objects. These techniques ensure loose coupling between CIRTs and help to minimize interactions, cf. the recommendations made in McGregor and Sykes (1992). Loose coupling between classes is extremely important for reuse; the degree of coupling may be tracked using coupling metrics (Henderson-Sellers, 1996). During class internal design, the attributes are extracted from the data models and the relationships are extracted from the collaboration models, and are given a `private` or `protected` export status.

An alternative path, using design templates (q.v.), examines the semantics of relationships and interactions in the analysis models, proposing different boilerplate designs to handle particular cases. To give some simple examples, a client CIRT which communicates with a server CIRT translates into a reference to the server in the client, whereas an association with multiple CIRTs translates into a reference to a container object (such as a *SET*), containing multiple instances. Choosing between different design templates depends on trade-offs in efficiency and reusability in the context of maintaining seamlessness across the lifecycle. Some of the templates described correspond to Observer and Mediator-style Design Patterns (q.v.).

Coding structure depends on the OOPL in use – since each language has its own idioms (q.v.). For example, Smalltalk, Java and Eiffel use reference semantics for assignments such as `a:=b;`. In C++, on the other hand, the programmer is expected to distinguish explicitly between value, reference and pointer-based semantics. (A more detailed discussion of coding approaches is to be found in Technique: Implementation using an OOPL in CD: Appendix E.)

Deliverables and outputs (post-condition)

Code for internal structure and inter-module dependencies for each class.

Indexing   Star rating ** (major contribution from G.C. Low)

Focus: Adding index to optimize DB usage
Typical tasks for which this is needed: Optimize the design
Related techniques: Access analysis
Input (pre-condition): Design for database schema
Underpinning concepts: DB accesses can be optimized

Technique description

An index is a qualified association that does not add any new information. Rather it speeds up access (Andleigh and Gretzinger, 1992). Indexes are maintained on a property or a combination of properties of a class. Indexing decisions are made differently for relational databases and objectbases. In a RDB, objects (tuples) are often accessed through a key rather than by a navigation path, so indexes are appropriate. This, thus, converts value-based (state-based) primary keys into identifiers. Use of indexes when using an objectbase are more limited since objects are usually accessed through traversal between objects and not directly through a key (Thurston, 1993); although Kim (1990) identifies two types of indexing that may indeed by appropriate for objectbases: class hierarchy indexing and nested property indexing.

Technique usage

For each event, the access paths, object classes, relationships, properties and operations, whether sequential, association, aggregation or inheritance paths are used as the basis of the navigation, should be identified. The type of access, whether it is create, retrieval or update is noted. Note the times of day that access may occur and the average access rate. Also note the peak load times for the system and the access rate at this time.

Those operations that offer the highest returns from creating index associations should be selected for indexing. However, the use of indexes should be limited since objects in objectbases are usually accessed through traversals between objects and not directly through a key. Indexes should only be used on large collections (Thurston, 1993). Index parameters such as placement, free space, lock size, total initial size and extension size must be determined.

Identify bottlenecks which could be eliminated by use of an index. Also identify whether an index might be useful to cache results or commonly accessed joins (in an RDB). This gives direct, rather than indirect, access to a collection of instances.

Deliverables and outputs (post-condition)

Recommended indexes for addition to the design and implementation.

Inspections   Star rating **

Focus: Objective evaluation of success of programming
Typical tasks for which this is needed: Evaluate quality, test
Related techniques: Defect detection
Input (pre-condition): Existing artefact ready to be inspected
Underpinning concepts: Identification of defects/problems is best when done early

Technique description

Direct defect identification techniques are based on the direct, static and detailed study of the work-product (e.g. source code) to identify work-product defects as opposed to the study of the performance of the software simulation in the hope of identifying failures (e.g. testing). As a collection, these techniques are called by a variety of other names such as:

- static verification (Sommerville, 1995)
- peer review (IEEE 1028)
- software analysis (Ghezzi *et al.*, 1992).

It should be noted that, unlike testing, the final code product does not need to be available when performing direct defect identification (unless it is the code product itself that is being verified) and that it can therefore be applied to all software process work-products. Indeed, early detection and removal of defects becomes possible.

We can identify defects in work-products by looking for them. Specific techniques exist that allow this work to be done in an orderly and rigorous fashion. We call these techniques 'Inspection'.

Most of these techniques are variants or expansions on the process developed by an IBM software engineer, Michael Fagan, in the mid-1970s (Fagan, 1976). The technique was initially devised in relation to the determination of defect content of code, yet subsequent development saw it applied to other software process artefacts such as requirement and design documents. Inspection techniques of Gilb and Graham (1993) and Strauss and Ebenau (1995) are two such developments that expand the scope of the original Fagan inspection to include other work-products.

Technique usage

A typical contemporary (1990s) software inspection process generally consists of six distinct stages. These are:

(1) inspection planning

(2) inspection overview

(3) inspection preparation

(4) inspection meeting

(5) rework

(6) follow-up.

We will discuss each of these stages briefly.

INSPECTION PLANNING

The author or the author's proxy works with the coordinator to collect the necessary inspection material (the input) and ensures that they meet all the entry criteria. They then select a moderator for the inspection team. The moderator and the author or proxy then select the remaining team members and schedule a meeting time at least a week in advance, ensuring that all selected team members are available and can attend the inspection meeting scheduled. The moderator then duplicates and distributes the necessary input material to all inspection team members.

INSPECTION OVERVIEW

Optionally, and when it is deemed necessary or useful to educate the inspection team members in some aspect of the process or the material to be inspected, an overview session is held. This usually takes the form of the author, or his/her proxy, making a half-hour to one-hour presentation on the aspect that requires special attention. The moderator arranges and schedules an overview which is attended by all team members.

INSPECTION PREPARATION

Upon receipt of the inspection material and before the inspection meeting, each inspection team member studies the inspection input material and thoroughly familiarizes himself/herself with what is provided, so that they can better find defects during the inspection. Guided by appropriate checklists and guidelines, each inspector is responsible for his or her own adequate preparation and is required to record the time spent in preparation. During such preparation, an inspector may come across what is deemed to be a defect. At this stage, the inspector notes down the details of the defect on the Inspection Preparation Notes Form (e.g. Figure A.35) the contents of which may then be discussed during the inspection meeting.

INSPECTION MEETING

This meeting is scheduled by the moderator and is attended by all inspection team members. At the start of the meeting, the moderator who is in charge of the conduct of the meeting reviews the agenda and highlights the purpose of the meeting and ensures that all team members have completed their preparation. During this meeting, the purpose of which is to locate defects, the reader presents and paraphrases the work in small segments. As the material is presented, each inspector looks for defects and notes them down on their form. As defects are recognized and accepted, they are recorded and classified on the Inspection Defects List (Figure A.36). At the end of the meeting, the moderator ensures that all inspectors are unanimous on the number and the nature of all defects identified and arrives at a 'Disposition' for the output work-product.

CODE INSPECTION PREPARATION LIST

Program Identifier: [   ]   Meeting Date: [   ]

Your Name: [   ]   Moderator: [   ]

Total Preparation Time: [   ]   Other Members:

Name	Role

LIKELY DEFECTS

LOC.	TYPE	DESCRIPTION	TIME

LEGEND:
LOC: Location of the defect given as code line in which the defect appears (e.g. 31).
TYPE: Defect type according the Defect Classification List (form I-7). Include the defect type code (e.g. C1) and the number of defect from sample defect numbers (e.g.C1–1 is devision by zero or other impossible computation).
DESCRIPTION: A short description of the defect as found, not as classified in the defect classification scheme (e.g. X=M/Y, Y assumes value of zero when Z=3).
TIME: The number of minutes into the preparation time when the defect was first identified and recorded (e.g. 35).

Please supply comments (if any) on the back of this form.   Page [   ] of [   ]

Figure A.35 Inspection Preparation Notes Form.

CODE INSPECTION DEFECT LIST

| Program Identifier: | | Meeting Date: | |

Disposition:
- A: Accept
- C: Conditional
- R: Re-Inspect

Total Preparation Time:

Moderator:

Other Members:

Name	Role

DEFECTS

LOC.	TYPE	DESCRIPTION	TIME

LEGEND:
LOC: Location of the defect given as code line in which the defect appears (e.g. 31).
TYPE: Defect type according the Defect Classification List (form I-7). Include the defect type code (e.g. C1) and the number of defect from sample defect numbers (e.g.C1–1 is devision by zero or other impossible computation).
DESCRIPTION: A short description of the defects as found not as classified in the defect classification scheme (e.g. X=M/Y, Y assumes value of zero when Z=3).
TIME: The number of minutes into the Code Inspection Meeting when the defect was accepted and registered (e.g. 35).

Please supply comments (if any) on the back of this form.   Page ___ of ___

Figure A.36 Inspection Defect List.

Rework

The Inspection Defects List will be presented to the author or the person responsible for making the changes necessary to remove the defects who carries out this task or organizes for it to be carried out to the satisfaction of the exit criteria.

Follow-up

Once the defects have been removed, the moderator follows up the revisions and may or may not call another inspection meeting to ensure adequate proximity of the work product to the requirements of the exit criteria. Once satisfied, the moderator submits an Inspection Summary Report to the coordinator.

Participants in the inspection process may play various roles. The following roles are present during inspections:

- author/author's proxy
- moderator
- reader
- scribe.

Below is a brief discussion of each of these roles.

Author/author's proxy

This is the individual who has produced the work product (e.g. a programmer), is responsible for its production (e.g. a team leader), is responsible for effecting any changes or someone sufficiently familiar with the work to act as a proxy. The role of the author/proxy is to work as part of the inspection team to identify defects based on his/her special understanding of the material being examined. This role may not be combined with that of moderator, scribe or reader.

Moderator

The moderator organizes and conducts the inspection meeting. This is a central role and the success or failure of any inspection exercise is very sensitive to the quality of the moderator. In general the role of the moderator is to plan the inspection, ensure that all other team members have completed their preparatory tasks and that all input material meets their respective input criteria. The moderator also must ensure that during the meeting:

- attention is focused on effective defect identification and no other task such as discussions on style or approach, trivialities, solution provision, etc.
- bias is avoided and all participants are treated equally and their contributions received and considered equitably

- focus is kept on inspecting the work product and not finding faults with the author, and comments are directed to the scribe and not the author or the proxy, particularly critical ones and
- resources, particularly time, are used effectively and defect finding effort is maximized.

The moderator is also the liaison person with all other stages of the process and other stakeholders and at the conclusion of the meeting it is he or she who collects, collates and reports on the inspection. Following up on defect resolution is also a moderator's task.

READER

The reader, a person other than the moderator, the author/proxy or the scribe, is responsible for presenting and paraphrasing the work product to the rest of the team during the inspection meeting. The reader must be thoroughly familiar with the work-product and have organized a logical order for its presentation. The reader should also work with the moderator to determine a pace for presentation in concert with the inspection rate intended. The reader is also responsible for answering all questions made with regard to the work-product but may refer to the material or the author or the proxy if need be.

SCRIBE

The scribe is responsible for recording all the necessary data generated during an inspection.

Virtually all experience with inspection has been very positive. Fagan in his original article reports a 23 per cent increase in code productivity (Fagan, 1976) compared to the then existing IBM practices. Gilb and Graham (1993) assert that inspections are effective as they contribute directly to:

- development productivity improvement
- reduction of the development time scale
- reduction in testing time and costs and
- reduction in cost of maintenance.

Deliverables and outputs (post-condition)

Inspection report (defect list), duly signed off.

Integration testing   Star rating **

Focus: Testing the integration of packages and classes

Typical tasks for which this is needed: Test
Related techniques: Acceptance testing, regression testing, unit testing
Input (pre-condition): Tested classes prior to amalgamation as a full system
Underpinning concepts: Large-scale testing identifies problems with interactions which transcend problems in individual classes

Technique description

Integration testing takes classes which are internally checked, both semantically and syntactically, and evaluates their 'correctness' when part of the whole system. In other words, it evaluates the ability of methods or objects to work together; for example, to create a chain of command or to process a use case. Jorgensen and Erickson (1994) suggest that integration testing is the least well understood of the different testing granularities. Essentially, integration testing involves seeing whether the classes have been developed in a coordinated manner to fulfil the systems requirements. Testing is thus focused on the incremental integration of the system. Jorgensen and Erickson (1994) describe these test paths, called a Method/Message (MM) Path, in terms of the sequence of method executions linked by messages whereby the full path (a sequence of atomic system functions, or ASFs, each of which contains a set of MM-Paths) effectively represents the execution of each behavior, i.e. the use cases. The success of a use case is indicated by the ability of the class model to support the required functionality and fulfil the contracts of the classes. Task scripts, use cases and scenarios, by their very nature, involve many classes and hence form the basis of the largest-scale integration testing procedure.

Integration testing is generally less traumatic than a system test would be for a structured system – system or acceptance testing (q.v.) is the final validation of the system before delivery and testing is really an external test of the system and should be performed by a separate testing team.

For a *distributed system*, changes to integration testing include testing for fault-handling, stress/load effects, extensibility and portability.

Technique usage

Use cases can be used to initially identify behavioral sequences in which (usually) more than one CIRT is involved. MM-Paths begin with an initiating event and end when no further messages are issued – termed 'message quiescence'. This gives an atomic system function (ASF) which underpins the integration testing. Once the ASFs in each thread/use case have been determined they should be tested.

Deliverables and outputs (post-condition)

Test results from all ASFs in the system.

Intelligent agent identification   Star rating *

Focus: Active objects
Typical tasks for which this is needed: Construct the object model, identify CIRTs
Related techniques: BPR, collaborations analysis
Input (pre-condition): Embryonic design
Underpinning concepts: Collaborations; Complex Adaptive Systems Theory; Intelligent Agents

Technique description

Intelligent agents, also known as intelligent objects, smart agents or active agents, are active, goal-seeking objects that collaborate with other agents and may operate in a client–server or a peer-to-peer protocol (Fingar *et al.*, 1997). The term 'agent' has many interpretations in the literature, which can be divided into (Kendall *et al.*, 1997):

- weak agents – autonomous (leading to ideas of migration and transferability), social, reactive and proactive
- strong agents – a weak agent plus veracity, rationality and adaptability as well as notions of beliefs, goals, plans and intention.

Agents contain two sorts of knowledge (Graham, 1997c):

- persistent – often in the form of attributes and methods in an OO environment representing its object-like skills, although the methods may, in fact, end up being coded non-procedurally, e.g. in Prolog
- transient – including plans which vary during execution; current assumptions, beliefs, acquaintances; short-term goals.

Agents can be used to personalize systems for users' individual needs and skills, acting autonomously on behalf of the users. This has the effect of reducing the cognitive and learning burden on these users. Agents that can learn, adapt and exchange goals and data can then be used to speed up information searches, especially across networks or the internet. Agents are also likely to play a major role in effecting complex adaptive systems (q.v.) (Odell, 1998).

Technique usage

Since agents are objects that can reason and collaborate via structured messages; and are active objects with their own thread of control, they can be modeled, using appropriate modeling language concepts. For example, in OML Version 1.1 (Henderson-Sellers and Firesmith (1998a), a thread-safe active object is denoted by the shield symbol (Figure A.37). Migration diagrams then show migrational aspects of these active objects across the network. Kendall *et al.* (1997) recommend the storage of the capabilities of strong agents in a plan library where a

Figure A.37 Thread-safe concurrency shown in model of agent.

plan is instantiated following the triggering of an event leading to the execution of a particular thread in the agent. Of course, supporting concurrency as they do, agents may contain several, simultaneously executing threads.

Deliverables and outputs (post-condition)

Identification of intelligent agents within the evolving design.

Interaction modeling Star rating **

Focus: Dynamic modeling
Typical tasks for which this is needed: Construct the object model
Related techniques: Collaborations analysis
Input (pre-condition): Collaborations graph, use case information
Underpinning concepts: Interaction Diagrams

Technique description

An object-oriented system works because of interactions between objects. Interactions is a wide-ranging term in OT which encompasses

- static relationships
- message-passing dynamics
- higher level user interactions as expressed by use cases or task scripts.

Each of these is discussed in detail elsewhere. Here, we focus primarily on the dynamics as expressed by interaction diagrams (see CD: Appendix E). While, strictly speaking, only collaboration diagrams show true interactions, in UML the name (interaction diagram) has been elevated one metalevel to include both collaboration diagrams and sequence diagrams. In this technique, we focus on interaction/collaboration diagram building – or rather on understanding the model which happens to be documented using a collaboration diagram.

Collaboration diagrams depict the coupling between CIRTs in a dynamic way by focusing on specific message traces that need to be supported, i.e. how objects interact to fulfil each specific service. This is in contrast to relationship modeling in which, typically, there is a single (or no) connexion of any relationship type between two CIRTs.

Technique usage

Modeling of interactions can be done in several ways. Interactions reflect the enactments of collaborations. Thus a collaboration approach can be useful although strictly a collaboration is a static description and an interaction its corresponding dynamic embodiment.

Typically interactions occur on message paths defined by relationships such as associations and aggregations (see OPEN Technique: Relationship modeling). However, interactions tend to be at a more granular (q.v.) level because they show individual message paths and, in the dynamic form represented by interaction diagrams, as described in CD: Appendix E, have sequencing information.

To identify interactions, ask what CIRTs need to be involved in the delivery of one specific service. Trace that service and any delegation/subcontracting. These message paths are all part of the interaction currently being modeled. Describe these interaction paths in terms of a collaboration diagram or a sequence diagram, both types of interaction diagram (see CD: Appendix E on Interaction Diagrams).

Deliverables and outputs (post-condition)

Elaborations of the semantic nets/class diagrams describing the system. Interactions in the form of various relationships/connexions are now shown.

Interfacing to relational DBMS and legacy code Star rating **
(contribution by G.C. Low)

Focus: Clarify connect from OO system to non-OO DB
Typical tasks for which this is needed: Design and implement physical database
Related techniques: DBMS type selection
Input (pre-condition): Existing (new) system plus legacy code and RDB
Underpinning concepts: Relational Databases; Wrappers

Technique description

This is an optional step to cater for situations in which an object-oriented project utilizes a relational database, rather than an objectbase, for object persistence. Typically, this is performed after a DBMS model is selected and after an initial CIRT model has been constructed in which persistent object classes have been identified.

An intermediate 'factory' system may be given responsibility for object retrieval and storage. Two strategies may be used for mapping between application objects and DBMS schema (Waldén and Nerson, 1995, page 294):

- data-driven where a dictionary contains information on object composition and DBMS mapping and
- object-driven where the application objects are programmed to be self-describing in terms of their instance variables and to carry information about DBMS schema mapping.

The data-driven approach provides database transparency from the factory system allowing for database reorganization for performance reasons or the inclusion of more data items without requiring changes to the application software. This transparency, which is fundamental to the RDBMS, is not provided by the application-driven approach. However, the application-driven approach is faster since the data models are memory resident and fast to navigate. For a detailed discussion of the pros and cons of both approaches see Waldén and Nerson (1995).

The data-driven approach is generally preferred due to its low coupling between application objects and application schema. The application-driven approach may be applicable for very stable data models where performance is an important issue.

Technique usage

Access objects should be built to define the interface transition for a relational DBMS (Booch, 1994). These access objects hide the details of the RDBMS and any arbitrary restrictions of the RDBMS may be removed (Premerlani *et al.*, 1990). The class interface object classes translate object operations to SQL and map SQL results back to objects.

This or other forms of wrapper technology (q.v. in CD: Appendix E) provide a route from a non-OO to an OO environment, albeit less satisfactory than a 'clean sweep' – a luxury affordable only to the lucky few!

Deliverables and outputs (post-condition)

Interfaces to legacy systems.

Internet and web technology Star rating ** (author M. Lin)

Focus: Users
Typical tasks for which this is needed: Develop education and training plan, do user training
Related techniques: Computer-based training, train the trainers
Input (pre-condition): The need for distributed facilities via the web or the internet
Underpinning concepts: Technology aids dissemination of information and learning

240   CORE TECHNIQUES

Technique description

The web and the internet relate to networks using higher level protocols such as HTTP, FTP, SMTP, as well as various other technologies all based on underlying TCP/IP and physical hardware layers. These terms thus apply equally to both the public internet, as well as internal corporate intranets.

Some of the benefits of using web development (even in its current early state) include:

- an organizational structure able to allow widely dispersed, disparate and transient teams to work on large, complex projects
- the common and encouraged use of open standards
- production of high quality software with little or no formal QA process
- large amounts of documentation written by developers notorious for their resistance to producing it.

Technique usage

Booch (1996) discussed three aspects of web usage in OO:

(1) 'Development of the web' is the most prominent. However, it soon becomes clear that there is little in the way of software development in this area, with most of the work being carried out by either skilled graphic artists to create visually effective web sites.

(2) 'Development for the web' – in fact there is little difference between developing applications for the web and other types of software development. The features of web development such as distributed computing, client–server architecture, database interfacing, hypertext user-interfaces, use of scripting and OO programming languages are all present and well known in other areas of software development (and discussed elsewhere in this book).

(3) 'Development by the web'. Booch (1996) notes 'the tremendous value to be gained by using an intranet to manage the products of development'. This use of the web as an *environment* for software development holds the most promising future use of this technology for the software development world.

Deliverables and outputs (post-condition)

Recommendations for web/distributed nature of application.

Interviewing   Star rating ***

Focus: Elicit users' requirements by direct interview
Typical tasks for which this is needed: Define problem and establish mission and objectives, design user interface, identify CIRTs, identify user requirements

CORE TECHNIQUES 241

Related techniques: Brainstorming, group problem solving, questionnaires, workshops
Input (pre-condition): Interviewee and interviewer(s) available
Underpinning concepts: Human communication

Technique description

Interviewing is one of the most important and most powerful techniques available for the elicitation and confirmation of requirements. It is very flexible and useful but must be used carefully as conducting interviews well requires much training and skill.

Interviews are conducted mainly for the following reasons:

- Requirements elicitation – a well-conducted interview can uncover a large volume of facts, requirements as well as needs, wants and hidden agendas.

- Data collection – related to requirements elicitation, one can use an interview to collect the data or type of data that are to be used in the system.

- Ambiguity resolution – during the course of an interview, a skilled interviewer can concentrate on existing points of ambiguity and points of misunderstanding on the part of the interviewer and resolve these with the help of the interviewee.

- Influencing opinions – views and opinions of the interviewee, particularly those that may be contrary to or conflicting with the overall aims of the project may be identified and influenced. Misunderstandings on the part of the interviewee may also be identified and resolved.

- Provide participation and create a sense of ownership – interviews make interviewees feel as if they are participating in the development of the new system and will therefore contribute to the sense of ownership of the resultant system which in turn will assist in the system being better accepted.

Technique usage

There are essentially three main stages, each composed of several steps, in the interview process.

PREPARATION

Preparing for an interview is a very crucial step in the eventual success or failure of the interview process. Adequate time and attention must be expended to prepare adequately for an interview.

Prepare yourself Learn about the:

- organization and the people involved
- project and the system
- domains involved and technologies used.

Identify interviewees Identifying who to interview is also important. Generally the decision as to who to interview first is taken for you, either by your boss or by the customer. This is usually a high level technical person (IT manager) or a high level executive (Chief Operating Officer). Who to interview next usually becomes evident after the first interview and a bit more detailed involvement in the project.

Adequate coverage of viewpoints and requirements of all stakeholders becomes important here. Techniques such as Viewpoints (q.v.) are recommended.

Arrange interviews Arrange interviews well in advance allowing for inevitabilities such as illnesses, business trips, holidays, etc. Do not arrange too many interviews at once. Usually the information obtained at one interview will determine whether a subsequent interview with this person or someone else is needed. Canceling interviews that have been arranged but are now deemed unnecessary can therefore be avoided (at least minimized) if only a few interviews are scheduled at any one time. Of course, a balance must be reached as scheduling too few has its own obvious problems.

If you intend to record the interview on video or audio tape, make sure that you secure the interviewee's consent at this stage. It is always a good thing to follow this with a written note confirming the above details.

Prepare your questions When you prepare questions for an interview, you must pay attention not only to what you need to ask, but also how and why. Each and every question has to have a purpose, and must be included for a clear reason aimed to elicit a requirement or clarify an ambiguity. You must also make certain that the question, as posed and if answered adequately, has the capability to get you the answer that you need. In other words, remember that it is getting useful answers that you are there for, not merely to ask questions. How you ask these questions is therefore important.

Remind the interviewee and re-confirm appointment A few days before the interview, call and remind the interviewee of the impending interview. Re-confirm with him or her the time and the place, and determine whether he/she has had time to prepare for the interview (if such preparation is necessary). If not, give the interviewee the option to postpone, but do make a firm new appointment. Otherwise give a gentle and professional 'push', securing the interviewee's commitment that he or she will be ready by the time you arrive.

CONDUCT

How you conduct an interview is obviously going to have an impact on the outcome of the process. The following are some points to observe.

Conduct the interview professionally

- be on time!
- do spend some time (a minute or two) on pleasantries, but do not overdo it
- if the interviewee is ready, then move naturally to state the purpose of your visit and review or restate the context of the interview
- assure the interviewee of confidentiality and/or anonymity if such assurance is required or a condition of the interview
- if you are to tape the proceedings, confirm you have permission to record the interview.

The interview itself

- start by asking top level, general questions and navigate through to the more specific
- be flexible and be prepared to change your mode and approach
- stay at the same level of granularity with the interviewee
- stay on the same context as the interviewee
- do not shift context or granularity abruptly.

An interview is as much about listening to what is being said (and often not said) as it is about asking questions. Active listening (q.v.) is the technique recommended here. Remember the aim is to elicit requirements that are correct and unambiguous.

Remain in control of the process

- be assertive but not confrontational
- control the number of questions the interviewee asks you. You are there to get information not to provide it. Be careful, however, since questions can potentially shed light on the thinking and approach of the person who asks them
- do not interrupt. When people are volunteering information, let them. Just lead them back with your next question
- do interrupt, e.g., if the conversation digresses to the interviewee's favorite football team, or his/her golf handicap. Something must be done. Politely but assertively lead the conversation back to the topic of the interview
- be aware of body language; theirs and yours.

244   CORE TECHNIQUES

And at any time, if you feel the interview is off track, take corrective action.

Ending the interview   End the interview appropriately. An interview is over when any one of these conditions occurs:

- all answers are obtained
- time draws to a close (five minutes before the time allowed is up)
- parties are drained, have lost interest, or the interviewee ceases to cooperate further
- the interview is out of control.

Ask the interviewee if there are any vital matters that have not been explored. If so, determine if they can be dealt with in the available time (maximum of two minutes), or whether an extension to the present meeting or a subsequent meeting is required. Otherwise, take the final five minutes of the allotted time to recap and check for correct understanding.

Try to resolve any misunderstandings, difficulties in interpretation, ambiguities, and contradictions.

- thank the interviewee once more
- re-confirm your next appointment, if any
- mention what will happen next with the process and particularly how the information obtained at this interview will be used and bring the meeting to an end.

Follow-up

Prepare a written transcript of the interview.

- research the facts that you have been given (i.e. whether the interviewee's assertions that there will never be more than 300 transactions a minute is indeed correct)
- use the transcript and your research results to analyze and re-arrange facts in order to identify any ambiguities, conflicts or missing information.

Send a copy of the interview transcript to the interviewee and ask him or her to review and sign it as confirmation that the information in it is correct. Of course this might be done unofficially in cases where anonymity is promised.

Graham (1991, section 8.2.2) gives useful guidelines on conducting interviews in an object-oriented development environment. He advocates the use of a trained interviewer, if possible two: one to talk and listen and one to take notes. If feasible, interviews should be taped for later analysis. Interviewers should be trained both in interview techniques as well as in object technology (Graham,

Table A.18 Types of probe questions (after Graham, 1995a).

Definitional	What is a ...?
Additive	Go on ...
Reflective	What you're saying is ...
Mode change	How would your colleagues view that?
	Can you give a more concrete example?
Directive	Why is that?
	How?
	Could you be more specific?

1991, page 299). Interviews should be arranged with the end-users regarding business requirements. These should be well scoped in advance and revolve around an agreed agenda (Graham, 1995a, page 292). In such a structured interview, probe questions, as exemplified in Table A.18, are particularly useful types of open-ended questions. In a focused interview, a smaller range of topics is explored in greater depth. Here, repertory or Kelly grids (q.v.) and task analysis (q.v.) are commonly used (Graham, 1995a, page 293).

However, it is important to note that the user/customer is not interested in the use/non-use of object technology in providing them with their demanded quality product. The final product will be independent of its method of production. Quality and maintainability will be the only manifestations of OT which the end-user will ever perceive. Commitment of top executives is particularly needed for the successful adoption of new technologies – and object technology (OT) is no exception. Hence interviews with senior management may also be useful.

Deliverables and outputs (post-condition)

Interview notes.

JAD   Star rating ***

Focus: Rapid application development approach
Typical tasks for which this is needed: Identify user requirements
Related techniques: RAD, workshops
Input (pre-condition): Users
Underpinning concepts: User involvement is crucial

Technique description

JAD (Joint Application Development) has a longer history than RAD yet has similar characteristics of an emphasis on user involvement. Its focus is on user involvement *throughout*.

Technique usage

In OPEN, we support a merged form of JAD/RAD (see also Graham, 1997b). Consequently, we refer you from here to the Technique: RAD and the Technique: Workshops.

Kelly grids Star rating **
(author I. Graham, © Addison Wesley, 1995)

Focus: Finding objects
Typical tasks for which this is needed: Identify CIRTs
Related techniques: Brainstorming, interviewing
Input (pre-condition): Requirements
Underpinning concepts: Evaluation of opposites can create a new focus

Technique description

One of the most useful knowledge engineering techniques for eliciting objects and their structures is that of Kelly, or repertory, grids. These grids were originally introduced in the context of clinical psychiatry (Kelly, 1955). They are devices for helping analysts elicit 'personal constructs'; concepts which people use in dealing with and constructing their world.

Technique usage

Constructs are pairs of opposites, such as slow/fast, and usually correspond to either classes or attribute values in OOA. The second dimension of a Kelly grid is its *elements*. These usually correspond to objects. Elements are rated on a scale from 1 to 5, say, according to which extreme value of the construct they correspond most closely. These values can then be used to 'focus' the grid; a mathematical procedure which clarifies relationships among elements and constructs. In particular, focusing ranks the elements in order of the clarity with which they are perceived and the constructs in order of their importance as classifiers of elements. The details can be found in any decent book on knowledge acquisition – for example, Graham and Jones (1988) or Hart (1989).

To illustrate the usefulness of Kelly grids, suppose we need to interview a user. The technique involves first identifying some 'elements' in the application. These might be real things or concepts, but should be organized into coherent sets. For example, the set {Porsche, Jaguar, Rolls Royce, Mini, Driver} has an obvious odd man out: Driver.

The use of the Kelly grid technique in its full form is not recommended. However, questioning techniques based on Kelly grids are immensely powerful in eliciting new classes and attributes and extending and refining classification structures. There are three principal techniques:

Concept	Rolls Royce	Porsche	Jaguar	Mini	Trabant	Opposite
Economical	5	4	4	2	2	Costly
Comfortable	1	4	2	4	5	Basic
Sporty	5	1	3	5	5	Family
Cheap	5	4	4	2	1	Expensive
Fast	3	4	2	4	5	Slow

Figure A.38 A Kelly grid. Scores are between 1 and 5. The left-hand pole of the concept corresponds to a low score for the element and the right (its opposite) to a high one. The grid is not focused (after Graham, 1995a).

- asking for the opposites of all elements and concepts

- laddering to extract generalization

- elicitation by triads to extract specializations.

Considering Figure A.38, we might have discovered that *SPORTY_CAR*s was a key class. Asking for the opposite produced not *UNSPORTY_CAR*s but *FAMILY_CAR*s; not the logical opposite but a totally new class. Thus, asking for the opposite of a class can reveal new classes.

In laddering, users are asked to give names for higher level concepts: 'Can you think of a word that describes all the concepts {speed, luxury, economy}?' might produce a concept of *ValueForMoney*. This technique elicits both composition and classification structures. It generally produces more general concepts. Asking for term that sums up both Fast and Sporty we might discover the class EgoMassaging cars, for example.

Elicitation by triads is a technique whereby, given a coherent set of elements, the user is asked to take any three and specify a concept that applies to two of them but not to the third. For example, with {Porsche, Jaguar, Mini}, top speed might emerge as an important concept. Similarly, the triad {Mini, Jaguar, Trabant} might reveal the attribute *CountryOfManufacture*; or the classes *BRITISH_CAR* and *GERMAN_CAR*. As a variant on this technique, users may be asked to divide the elements into two or more groups and then name the groups. This is known as card sorting.

All of these techniques are first-rate ways of getting at the conceptual structure of the problem, if used with care and sensitivity. Exhaustive listing of all triads, for example, can be extremely tedious and can easily alienate users.

Deliverables and outputs (post-condition)

Completed Kelly grids together with recommendations.

Layering (using aggregations) – see Collaborations analysis (minimizing system coupling; aggregation technique)

Lectures   Star rating ***

Focus: Users
Typical tasks for which this is needed: Develop education and training plan, do user training
Related techniques: Computer-based training, train the trainers
Input (pre-condition): Students, topic to be learned
Underpinning concepts: Information dissemination

Technique description

We have all attended lectures, have been stimulated by them, have been bored by them, have learned from them a great deal, or have considered them a total waste of time. In recent years, there has been a great deal of publicity against lectures and lecturing as an effective medium of learning. Yet surprisingly, high quality research comparing lecturing with other teaching and learning methods provides insufficient evidence to clearly favor one method over another. The one exception appears to be the superiority of a form of lecturing called the discussion method or the 'Socratic' approach (Cannon, 1992). This result can only mean one thing: the decrying of lecturing on an absolute basis is unjustified. However, it should also be noted that high quality in lecturing can do much to enhance the efficacy and effectiveness of the experience. In the words of Mager (1968): 'If telling was the same as teaching, we would all be so smart we could hardly stand it!' Lecturing is, in fact, a very flexible and economical vehicle for teaching. A skilled trainer can prepare a course very quickly and can cope with many different student types. Lectures also benefit from economies of scale. Once developed, they may be delivered many times and to virtually any number of people in the audience. An interactive lecture can be an excellent forum for exchange of ideas and for learning from each other.

Lectures can, however, vary in quality, this being almost totally dependent on the skill of the trainer and the amount of time and resources that he or she has put into preparing the material. Lectures also often suffer from the disadvantage that they are usually run at the pace of the trainer and not of the trainees. If used as the sole means of training, it may in fact develop a teacher/student dependency which is a very undesirable thing particularly in professional training situations.

CORE TECHNIQUES

Technique usage

To be most effective, a lecture has to be (1) well planned, (2) well delivered, (3) well supported and (4) evaluated. We will briefly discuss these points below.

PLANNING

Course planning, preparation of lecture series, planning and organization of individual lectures. Trainees look for clarity and visibility. The following are some points to consider.

Prepare the physical environment Ensure that there is comfortable seating for all trainees, that there is sufficient light and a comfortable ambience. Also ensure that everyone has a clear view of the lecturer and the presentation material.

Prepare the subject matter Knowledge of the world is not acquired in a linear fashion, but eventually a lecturer has to deliver the material as a linear narrative. An approach that has worked is to limit the extent of the material to be presented to only a few major topics and deliver these using the following structure:

- Introduction and overview. Here we introduce the purpose and the context of the lecture, overview of the main points and we revise earlier material if any.
- First main point. Develop and explain the main ideas, provide examples and then restate the point for emphasis.
- Other main points. These also follow a structure similar to the first main point.
- Summary and conclusion. Restate and review the main points, conclude or state any implications, and provide a quick overview of future lectures.

Prepare the delivery Plan an attention grabbing beginning, provide links between concepts, maintain visual interest by use of slides, drawings, film, models, demonstration of the utility of some software, etc. The use of color, sound and motion must be carefully considered as these can be effective but also distracting.

DELIVERY

Starting the lecture This can be daunting – even for seasoned speakers. Begin with your carefully rehearsed attention-grabbing introduction, along with its link into the rest of the material. A quotation, a tasteful joke, a cartoon or something similar, provided that it carries a centrally relevant point to the lecture material, can be invaluable.

Pace and speech   Speak about 10 to 25 per cent more slowly than normal speech. Actively seek cues from the audience about your pace and the level of detail in your treatment of the material and make appropriate adjustments. Ask questions frequently and pause for the audience to compose and volunteer an answer. Give them a visual cue that you wish them to answer the question posed. Open arms whilst pausing after asking the question has proved useful. Allow students who are taking notes to do so, but do not moderate your pace to cater for slow note takers. Whatever you do, never talk for more than 50 minutes (an absolute maximum) without giving the audience a break. Breaks should not be shorter than 5 minutes and not longer than 15.

Support

Subject material support   Support the material of your lectures with examples, references and, most importantly, 'personal war stories'. One reason many people attend lectures is to benefit from the experience of the lecturer. Do not deny them this.

Delivery support   The auditory sense is important, but it is one of the five we have been blessed with. In fact, the visual channel has been studied to be much more efficient in absorption of information (Eysenck and Keane, 1990). Use of appropriate visual aids such as chalk-boards or whiteboards, overhead projectors, slides, film or video footage, and demonstration of software when done carefully and appropriately can enhance the effectiveness of a lecture. Always remember, however, that these materials are aids to your lecture not the other way around. Do not use them as crutches.

Evaluation

Feedback is important in improving any process. Lecturing is no exception. Seek feedback on your lectures and their effectiveness and act to improve the process. The following are effective ways of seeking feedback on lectures:

- video recording your lectures
- use of participant questionnaires, and
- attendance and evaluation by a peer.

Deliverables and outputs (post-condition)

(Hopefully) a more knowledgeable audience.

Library class incorporation   Star rating ***

Focus: Identifying and using existing assets in library

Typical tasks for which this is needed: Optimize reuse ('with reuse')
Related techniques: Application scavenging, framework creation, library management
Input (pre-condition): Evolving design
Underpinning concepts: Software libraries should be used effectively

Technique description

Integrating and reusing the corporate class library in a new development is of importance. The developer should continually examine existing software libraries to maximize reuse of already existing classes (the 'reuse mindset'), thus encouraging elements of a bottom-up approach. This is particularly useful during coding, whereas in OOAD there is initially an emphasis on top-down refinement process. This mixture of approaches appears 'fuzzy' and undisciplined but, in fact, more closely reflects the way many designers operate (Turner, 1987).

Software libraries encapsulate somebody's chosen architecture and their logic of abstraction(s). The current software development may reflect a different philosophy. Thus there may well be incompatibilities in the two architectures: new project and existing library. This can lead to some tension. Another problem of the same type is that of varying granularity (q.v.) – when the abstraction level in the library is clearly different to the one the current team members are likely to find most useful.

Whilst reuse is not new, object technology has resurrected interest in the subject. Years of computer programmers have been educated to believe 'they can do it better' leading to the so-called NIH syndrome. If it's 'not invented here', then it can't be good value. Thankfully, we are seeing signs of change. In informal polls of present and future software engineers, the majority now believe that if it already exists and is of proven quality, then not-invented-here is preferable.

Technique usage

McGregor and Sykes (1992) categorize five types of software library: (a) team specific components (classes developed by a team for their own later use); (b) project-specific components (classes developed as part of a team's project for their own use); (c) problem domain-specific components available from a third party vendor – such vendors are likely to develop classes for resale in specialized domains such as banking, finance, insurance etc.; (d) general components from a components vendor; (e) language-specific primitives obtainable from a compiler vendor, possibly bundled with the language (as in Smalltalk and some versions of Eiffel) or available separately.

When considering any of these later categorized libraries (c–e) for possible purchase, McGregor and Sykes (1992) introduce some guidelines, derived from Korson and McGregor (1992). They provide a useful checklist (Table A.19). These guidelines are also useful for classes you build yourself (Ratjens, p.c., 1993). Other useful library documentation includes patterns to describe the kind of domain modeling and knowledge representation and examples of usage together with appropriate indexing.

Reusing classes from in-house-developed and purchased software libraries should also be monitored using reuse metrics (q.v.). In the future, library class incorporation will focus increasingly on components as a better granularity for reuse success.

Deliverables and outputs (post-condition)

Recommended list of classes 'with reuse' and their incorporation into the design.

Library management   Star rating **

Focus: Management of existing library artefacts
Typical tasks for which this is needed: Create and/or identify reusable components ('for reuse'), manage library of reusable components
Related techniques: Application scavenging, framework creation, library class incorporation
Input (pre-condition): Existing library
Underpinning concepts: Libraries without a management strategy are useless

Technique description

Libraries have to be managed. Developers have to be encouraged to contribute and also use existing components. The manager must know how to rapidly archive and retrieve files; to have a high quality endorsement program in place; and possibly (although this may be higher management/strategic) some remuneration scheme in place for (re)users of the library contents.

Technique usage

Library management is to do with quality control, elicitation from developers of reusable components, creating an archiving strategy and an advertising campaign to publicize what goodies the library already contains. Strategies include the use of a good cataloguing and retrieval tool (see e.g. discussions in Freeman and Henderson-Sellers, 1991; Henderson-Sellers and Freeman, 1992).

The library manager needs to instigate a newsheet advertising library contents and 'this week's new addition'. HP even went as far as making a specific appointment as the 'Reuse Rabbi' – here called reuse manager. This is one of four major roles in this reuse area, the others being librarian, application developer and application scavenger.

Deliverables and outputs (post-condition)

A consistent and well-managed software library.

Table A.19 Checklist for software libraries (adapted by Henderson-Sellers and Edwards (1994a) from McGregor and Sykes (1992) and Korson and McGregor (1992)).

- give a complete general model (logic to classes and their interrelationships)
- be designed around a few key abstractions
- model standard knowledge in the domain
- use inheritance
- be designed as networks of classes without free-standing data or procedural items (avoid hybrid styles)
- be designed with low level of coupling between classes
- provide a consistent and easily understood approach to error handling
- provide 'inspector' functions to check pre-conditions
- make it impossible for users to violate abstractions represented
- conform to minimal set of standards
- have maximum efficiency
- provide consistent naming scheme
- provide generic classes
- provide full documentation as specified below
- provide commercial-strength support (from vendor)

In addition, a good library should include good examples of class usage (Nerson, 1993).

Documentation required for library classes (after Korson and McGregor, 1992).

- documentation on state of completeness of each class implementation
- documentation reflecting structure of library
- documentation containing overview of library, including contents and structure
- different documentation for different levels of user
- documentation accessible by a minimum of three methods:
    - alphabetic by class name
    - hierarchical via inheritance structure
    - keyword facility

254   CORE TECHNIQUES

Mapping to RDB   Star rating **

Focus: Translation from OO design to relational DB
Typical tasks for which this is needed: Code
Related techniques: DBMS type selection, normalization
Input (pre-condition): Database schema
Underpinning concepts: Relational Databases

Technique description

A relational database stores data in the form of tables. It does not store functionality. An object-oriented system encapsulates both data and functionality together. Thus if the functionality is stripped out of the objects, then they map readily to a relational table, although objects are typically not normalized in any sense. Mapping to a relational database (RDB) therefore requires objects to be normalized and then translated into tables (see full details in CD: Appendix E). The main difficulty comes in translating back from an RDB to objects since the functional information has been thrown away or at best decoupled from the data aspect of the objects.

Technique usage

Map each class into a relational table. Map each OO relationship into a relation in the RDB using keys as appropriate (e.g. Premerlani *et al.*, 1990; Case *et al.*, 1995, 1996). Evaluate the inheritance structure. There are several possible mappings to relational tables (see CD: Appendix E for details). Finally, integrity constraints should also be considered. These may be present in the object model in the form of rules (q.v.).

Deliverables and outputs (post-condition)

A set of tables representing the object model.

Mechanisms – see Collaborations analysis; Scenario development

Membership – see Relationship modeling

Mentoring   Star rating **

Focus: Project management, migration

Typical tasks for which this is needed: Develop and implement resource allocation plan
Related techniques: Computer-based training, lectures, train the trainers
Input (pre-condition): Team requiring assistance in migrating to OT or advancing their knowledge and skills
Underpinning concepts: An apprenticeship can be a good way to learn

Technique description

In moving to any new technology, an organization will often seek outside help. This is often in the form of one or more consultants: experts in their field who are contracted for a short period to work in the organization and impart their knowledge. What has often happened in the past is that consultants have joined an organization temporarily, done the job well, but left having not interacted sufficiently with the permanent staff; the result being that no knowledge has been transferred 'from the expert to the novice'. This has led to a shift from consulting in the traditional mode to mentoring.

Technique usage

It has often been said that a consultant is paid to do a job and a mentor is paid *not* to do a job. A mentor works closely with members of a team but in an advisory capacity, adding ideas to the project, critiquing aspects of design, encouraging the team members to think. In this way, the team members increase their own skills because it is they, not the mentor, that are really doing the work. They thus have full ownership and at the same time are learning from the expert who is fully part of the team.

A mentor may be a full-time or a part-time member of the team. Whilst the former is preferable, it may be overly expensive. A good mentor is someone who is not only highly knowledgeable in the area (here OT) but has the teaching skills to impart that knowledge to the team. In other words, the relationship is very much akin to that of an apprentice learning from the expert. The choice of mentor is most important in order to identify someone who is skilled, who will get on with the team members *as a team member* and is willing to take a facilitating and not a dominating (some might say bombastic[†]) role.

Deliverables and outputs (post-condition)

Skills transferred from mentor to developer.

[†] Unfortunately, some experts are so full of their own importance that they seem unwilling to share that knowledge with others since they seem to think it degrades their marketability in the future.

Mixins (take care)   Star rating **

Focus: Non-pure-OO use of multiple inheritance
Typical tasks for which this is needed: Code
Related techniques; Generalization and inheritance identification
Input (pre-condition): Design
Underpinning concepts: Generalization, Inheritance and Polymorphism

Technique description

A mixin has been regarded as a type of abstract class (e.g., Bobrow, 1989; Booch and Vilot, 1990) or as an 'abstract subclass' (Bracha and Cook, 1990) – for example, a subclass that might add a border to a wide variety of window classes. Perhaps a better description would be that of a 'free-standing extension' class (Simons, 1995). In practice, a mixin looks like any other class, except that it rarely embodies a full conceptual 'entity' and with the distinction that it is 'not intended to be instantiated separately'.

A mixin is a class that is probably not one logical concept, but rather an encapsulation of several closely associated features bundled together as a class available to be 'mixed in', via multiple inheritance, to add capabilities to a wide variety of classes, possibly not related. The behavior of the mixin is often (but not necessarily) seen as orthogonal to the behavior of the classes with which it is to be combined, insofar as it adds extra characteristics in 'sideways'.

Technique usage

Mixins are of interest in OOP because they describe the notion of a component extension, in much the same way that languages with encapsulation support the notion of component sub-parts. The difference is that mixins are combined using the inheritance rules of the language, rather than using ordinary composition. Whereas composition respects the client interface of the component, preserving the abstraction barrier between the parts and the whole, mixin combination involves a subtle linking of inherited methods and mixin methods. Figure A.39 illustrates a mixin class designed to add a two-dimensional coordinate system on to any class with which it is combined. In any resulting combination, the methods x, y and *move* do not interact with inherited methods, since they provide orthogonal functionality. However, the method *equal* extends the functionality of some basic *equal* method in order to compare object coordinates as part of the equality test. The basic method, which is assumed to compare the states of two objects, is accessed through *super.equal(...)*, where *super* is a self-referential variable denoting the inherited part of the combination. At the time the mixin is defined, the exact binding of *super* and its type are not known. However, *super* must eventually refer to some object possessing at least an *equal* method for the combination to be well defined.

```
mixin class XYCOORDINATE
private attributes
    xcoordinate, ycoordinate: INTEGER;
public methods
    x: INTEGER;
            { return xcoordinate }
    y: INTEGER;
            { return ycoordinate }
    equal (other: SELF): BOOLEAN
            { return (super.equal(other) and xcoordinate=other.x
                     and ycoordinate=other.y) }
    move (newx, newy: INTEGER): SELF
            { xcoordinate:=newx; ycoordinate:=newy; return self }
end
```

Figure A.39 Mixin supplying a two-dimensional coordinate system (after Simons, 1995).

A mixin therefore has a *client interface*, describing the methods that it exports, and a *superclass interface*, expressing a minimum requirement on the methods owned by any class with which it is to be combined. This is because the services offered by a mixin depend in general on services inherited from the class with which it is eventually combined. The superclass interface is analogous to a socket, expecting to receive a plug-in parent class *possessing* at least a certain set of methods.

Deliverables and outputs (post-condition)

Addition or identification of mixin classes to static architectural diagrams (i.e. the object model).

Multiple inheritance – see Generalization and inheritance identification

Object lifecycle histories   Star rating **

Focus: CIRT dynamics
Typical tasks for which this is needed: Code, construct the object model
Related techniques: State modeling
Input (pre-condition): Partial design
Underpinning concepts: State Machines

258   CORE TECHNIQUES

Technique description

Individual objects in an OO system each have their own individual lifecycle. They are created, they live and interact within the system and then they are deleted from the dynamic system. Creation and deletion events must be monitored carefully, particularly deletions since failure to do so or to do so incorrectly can lead to memory leaks, particularly if implemented in a language like C++ with no automatic garbage collector. This type of lifecycle is called a 'born-and-die' lifecycle (Shlaer and Mellor, 1992, page 55).

At a finer granularity, individual objects pass through several states during their lifetime, some more than once. There are many examples, however, where the states form a true cycle. For example, an aircraft might be said to go through the states

- parked at gate
- taxiing
- taking off (wheels on ground)
- flying
- landing (touching down on runway)
- taxiing
- parked at gate

in a repetitive cycle. Transitions between states are, of course, associated with events. Thus lifecycle histories are generally formally documented using Technique: State modeling (q.v.).

Deliverables and outputs (post-condition)

Descriptions of states through which an object may/will pass.

Object replication   Star rating ** (author G.C. Low)

Focus: Optimizing database for RDB usage
Typical tasks for which this is needed: Optimize the design
Related techniques: DCS architecture specification
Input (pre-condition): Database schema and implementation
Underpinning concepts: Duplication of objects may assist in optimization; Relational Databases

Technique description

The trade-offs between update-synchronization costs and the cost of having replicated local copies of objects needs to be considered. The patterns of stages that change objects need to be understood to achieve performance, autonomy and integrity. The objects that need to be replicated for performance and autonomy considerations need to be determined. Integrity procedures must be developed to ensure that replicated data are consistent and in the same state; that is, when an object is updated, all copies of the object must be updated in a timely manner.

Technique usage

Determine if the application can tolerate the delayed synchronization of data. For instance, Loomis (1993) cites a telephone directory. The data are replicated in area telephone books, directory assistance and personal telephone books. Here it is also acceptable if the updates only happen periodically. These updates could be timed to occur during low transaction volume times.

If the system requires updates in real time, the updates cannot be delayed. For instance, the customer's account balance must reflect the most recent activity on the account. Here, the decision as to whether to replicate is largely impacted by the relative frequency of updates versus read operations on the data. In the unlikely event that the number of enquiries is high compared to the number of deposits and withdrawals in the banking system, then replication may still be beneficial. In this case, it will also reduce communication costs since the data are local rather than stored on a remote database server.

Data replication is only generally recommended where the DBMS supports replication. In this case, the DBMS should ensure that replicated data are consistent and all in the same state.

Deliverables and outputs (post-condition)

Physical data model showing all replicated data. An impact assessment for each replication decision should be included.

Object retention requirements Star rating **
(contributor G.C. Low)

Focus: Database constraints
Typical tasks for which this is needed: Identify user DB requirements
Related techniques: Configuration management
Input (pre-condition): Evolving storage system requiring 'cleaning up'
Underpinning concepts: Persistence is valuable, but unaccessed persistent objects are a liability; Relational Databases

Technique description

Information about how long objects must be retained for backup and retrieval purposes should be determined as part of the determination of user database requirements.

Technique usage

The object retention information which must be ascertained from the users includes backup or archival data that should be kept for recovery purposes; the length of time objects need to be retained; the procedures required to archive or to scrap objects that are no longer required; the locations at which backup and archival must be performed; the storage medium to be used for archives; and the objects to be versioned, the type of versioning and how these versions are to be reconciled.

Deliverables and outputs (post-condition)

Report detailing the requirements for object retention.

Package construction   Star rating **

Focus: Architecture, division of system into smaller chunks for easier management
Typical tasks for which this is needed: Construct the object model, undertake architectural design
Related techniques: Package coordination
Input (pre-condition): Partial design
Underpinning concepts: Packages

Technique description

The objective of the identification of packages is to manage complexity, particularly relevant to large projects. Packages abstract out the major characteristics, or responsibilities, of a group of related classes so as to hide detail, yet retain a coherent overall view of the system design. They may be created in either a top-down or a bottom-up fashion. Packages are not formally part of the object-model and they are not supported by any major OOPLs except Java, although similar concepts may be managed by the software environment[†]. It should be noted that a number of other methodologies have also found the need to include a unit of decomposition greater than that of a class (e.g. Wirfs-Brock *et al.*, 1990; Booch, 1991; Rumbaugh *et al.*, 1991; Firesmith, 1993; de Champeaux, 1991; Coad and Yourdon, 1991; Nerson, 1992).

---

† For example, Rational's CASE tool, ROSE^{TM}, supported categories and subsystems and now packages and subsystems.

Technique usage

If constructing packages top-down, the division should be done on the basis of high-level responsibilities or overall services which should be documented on the package (a.k.a. a cluster) CRC cards of COMN (Firesmith *et al.*, 1997). Top-down identification of responsibilities involves the project manager or analyst decomposing the responsibilities into groups that act upon similar abstractions. As an example, Henderson-Sellers and Edwards (1994a) discuss a set of high-level requirements which included the ability to browse models and data, manage models and data, and print data files and documentation relating to models. These requirements should be decomposed around the abstractions they act upon resulting in two sets of services: one to manage models involving printing, editing, creating and browsing models, and one to manage data involving printing, editing, creating and browsing data. In contrast, functional decomposition would have been to group the services around similar functionality.

If constructing packages bottom-up, sets of collaborating classes are identified as having high intra-coupling and low coupling to other classes, thus forming a logically (and hopefully semantically) cohesive grouping – the package. Bottom-up identification of package services thus involves abstracting the overall objectives of a collection of collaborating CIRTs. This approach is useful in managing the complexity of a large system. Using the same example as Henderson-Sellers and Edwards (1994a), we might identify CIRTs for the database and model-base packages that provide services to edit, print, create and browse. These services can be abstracted as a package responsible for managing data and models respectively.

Packages are documented using a dashed roundangle (rounded rectangle) in OML (or a tabbed rectangle in UML). Packages may have internally nested packages and/or packages on the boundary – see OOUI package in Figure A.40. Of the five internal clusters in this example, as an illustration, one of them (domain package) is shown with a drop-down box which indicates that the contents of the Domain cluster are five classes: *CUSTOMER*, *EMPLOYEE*, *ITEM*, *RENTAL* and *PERSON*.

Deliverables and outputs (post-condition)

Well-defined packages, well documented.

Package coordination   Star rating ***

Focus: Coordinating the parallel development of packages
Typical tasks for which this is needed: Manage packages
Related techniques: Package construction
Input (pre-condition): Existing packages
Underpinning concepts: Packages

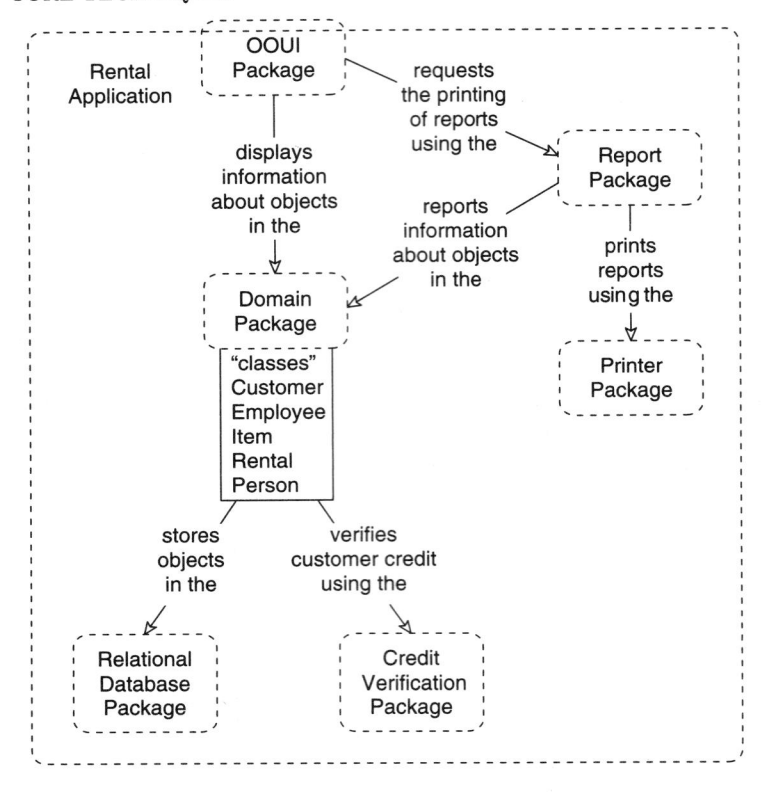

Figure A.40 Packages on an OML configuration diagram for a rental application (after Firesmith *et al.*, 1997).

Technique description

Package coordination is essentially a project management technique to ensure the coordination of teams of developers who are working on separate packages.

Technique usage

The objective of this technique is to ensure that redundancy is not occurring in the development effort by virtue of different teams developing similar abstractions in isolation. Potential redundancy is thus identified and responsibility for a class allocated to one team. Other teams that require services from this class will therefore subcontract the work to the team responsible for that class.

Deliverables and outputs (post-condition)

Contribution to project plan on package management and coordination.

Package and subsystem testing   Star rating **

Focus: Evaluation at package level
Typical tasks for which this is needed: Test
Related techniques: Integration testing, walkthroughs
Input (pre-condition): Completed packages ready for testing. Classes in the package have been fully unit-tested
Underpinning concepts: Packages

Technique description

Package level testing focuses on the interactions of groups of collaborating classes (Smith and Robson, 1992) as encapsulated in packages/subsystems. Scenarios form the basis of the testing strategy. Essentially it involves 'driving' a scenario through the CIRT model. The results of the execution are recorded in a testing table. Basic and alternative courses should all be tested.

Technique usage

Testing at the level of the package/subsystem/cluster has three stages (Murphy et al., 1994):

(1) *Package test plan* – test cases are designed and documented in the plan. This needs to include defined execution sequences with appropriate input values and expected results

(2) *Review* – the package test plan is crticially evaluated for completeness

(3) *Test plan execution* – following package implementation, the test plan is executed and the results recorded.

In the context of a *distributed system*, when nondeterminism exists, test cases may not simply aim to exercise the application code fully, by providing cases that traverse all code branches. Even if this works in one test, it may fail in another, due to the concurrent activities elsewhere in the application, i.e. there are interactions between the local module and the other concurrent modules which cannot be exhaustively tested.

Several techniques are discussed in the distributed system literature to cope with nondeterminism. Some of these are event recording (Gait, 1986), event control (Curtis and Wittie, 1982) and event monitoring (Shatz, 1993). The first of these is mostly applicable to debugging, while the last two are applicable to testing and debugging. Petri nets (see CD: Appendix D) may also be useful.

Deliverables and outputs (post-condition)

Test report at package level.

Partitioning and allocation – see DCS architecture specification

Path navigation   Star rating *** (author G.C. Low)

Focus: Database
Typical tasks for which this is needed: Design and implement physical database
Related techniques: Access analysis, query optimization
Input (pre-condition): Database schema
Underpinning concepts: Access paths can increase speed of database use

Technique description

Access paths (q.v.) to objects are in the form of direct pointers, which is maximally efficient in memory, but may require some reconstruction for OIDs. A query is performed by 'navigating' from one object to another. A *STUDENT* object might contain all the student and inherited person details locally, together with a pointer to a *SET* object containing the *COURSES* that the *STUDENT* studies. Each *COURSE* may also point to a *SET* of *LECTURE* objects, giving the time and place for each lecture for that *COURSE*. In this way, executing the query 'find all the students over 25 who study C++ on Mondays' would involve traversing pointers to *SET*s and eventually returning a *SET* of the requested *STUDENTS*. The first query will reconstruct, in memory, the required *SET* of *STUDENTS*. Depending on the OID indexing policy, this may not be as efficient as random access. If similar queries are subsequently executed on the same, or even an overlapping, group of *STUDENT*s, then it is likely that many of them will still be in memory.

It should be clear that the network structure of such a database is pre-designed to operate most efficiently for certain forms of query, such as: 'what courses are studied by a particular student?', which chase direct pointers to their result. If the database stores pointers from *STUDENTS* to *SET[COURSE]*, then an 'inverse' request to return all the *STUDENTS* enrolled on a particular C++ course will execute no more efficiently than in the relational approach: all the *STUDENTS* have to be traversed to find all their *SET[COURSE]*s, which are tested for the membership of the course C++. To improve this, 'access path optimization' would try to ensure that each *COURSE* object also contains a corresponding pointer to a *SET[STUDENT]* – the inverse relationship. This allows queries to execute equally efficiently in either direction. However, there is a cost: every time a *STUDENT* is enrolled on a *COURSE*, the *STUDENT*'s *SET[COURSE]* must be updated and also the *COURSE*'s *SET[STUDENT]*. It is hard to keep track of these referential dependencies; and inefficient to have to maintain them, especially if memory paging ('thrashing') results.

Some OBs maintain hierarchical relationships in one direction only, such that, when an inefficient query is executed, the resulting *SET* may be cached in memory. Alternatively, simple inspection-queries may be defined as methods

```
        Access
         Path
┌────────┐  ┌────────┐  ┌────────┐  ┌────────┐
│ CLIENT │→ │        │→ │        │→ │SUPPLIER│
└────────┘  └────────┘  └────────┘  └────────┘
     └──────────────────────────────────↑
```

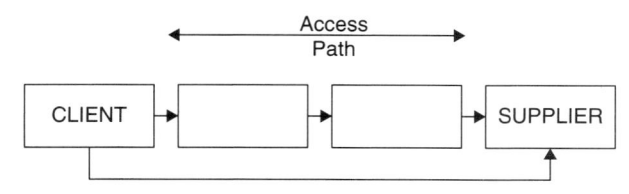

Figure A.41 Maintenance of local reference to supplier can create a redundant path (figure supplied by P. Horan).

on the classes. Such a method could cache the requested result in an instance variable of the object executing the query. A subsequent invocation would simply return the cached result. Naturally, caches have to be flushed if the objects on the other side of the relationship are updated in any way.

Technique usage

By examining the predicted response times against the required response times for each kind of query, it is possible to identify those query operations for which some kind of optimization would be suitable.

In the relational model, this is usually achieved using an index file. A redundant link is created, in the form of an access support relation, a table which contains only the foreign keys of the source data type and destination data type. Instead of having to traverse all the joins between the source and destination data files, the index file provides a shortcut to the keys of the related items in the destination file. Certain DBMSs offer a facility for pre-computing such index files.

In the object-oriented model, this is usually achieved using set-valued object attributes. A redundant link is created, in the form of a cache attribute, pointing to a set of related object instances. Instead of having to traverse all the intermediate objects on the access path, the related instances may be reached directly through the set of OIDs. Note that this solution presupposes the ability to store variable-length object records, in which set-valued attributes may take up an unpredetermined amount of space for each object.

Both of these approaches only work where the pre-computed access paths have to be traversed frequently, but are only modified infrequently. If just one object on an indirect access path is deleted from the database, this would force the flushing of all caches/indices that were computed using it. Different DBMSs and ODBMSs offer different levels of support for caching and flushing.

The examples cited above are all equivalent to introducing a redundant link into the entity-relationship diagram, or alternatively, the static CIRT diagram (see Figure A.41). That is, for each source object, the set of destination objects reachable by the new shortcut link is identical to the set reachable via the indirect link, through joined queries. This shortcut is simply a way of removing join-like operations (and the OO equivalent), where these would be too costly.

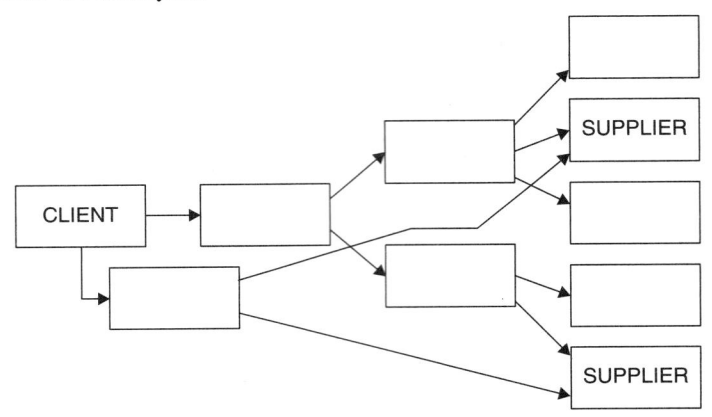

Figure A.42 Redundant paths may obviate the need for searching (figure supplied by P. Horan).

However, a more complex case for optimization is offered in Rumbaugh *et al.* (1991) in which supplier objects with certain characteristics are sought from a set. Unfortunately, if the number of objects is large, but the number with the required characteristics small, such a search is inefficient. In this case, a list of the suitable supplier objects can be maintained by the client, avoiding the need for searching, except to build the list for the first time (Figure A.42).

Object-oriented data modeling also introduces two further cases that might benefit from access path optimization. Inheritance is typically handled, in the relational model, by splitting objects into a common base part and incremental derived part, which are stored in separate files (described above). The benefit of this is that it allows the modeling of overlapping specializations – the same base instance may relate, in the database, to several incremental derived instances, belonging to separate subclasses of the base class. For example, a *TEACHING_ASSISTANT* might be held in the database as a base *PERSON* instance, an incremental *STUDENT* instance and an incremental *LECTURER* instance, where *STUDENT* and *LECTURER* are specializations of *PERSON*. However, the cost of this flexibility is that all inheriting objects must be reconstructed using join operations when they are to be treated as a whole. A less flexible alternative strategy is possible where all specializations are mutually exclusive, i.e. it is impossible to be both a *STUDENT* and a *LECTURER* at the same time. If this condition holds, then the inheritance joins may be precomputed – the database would store only *STUDENT* and *LECTURER* instances and not care that these files share some common attributes.

A further optimization is possible in object-oriented databases in which certain queries execute as methods belonging to objects. Where the cost of executing the method is high, it is possible to make this method cache the value it computes in an attribute, such that further invocations of the method simply access the attribute. Naturally, the cached value must be flushed if any of the object state-values, on which the cached result depends, are changed. This is a hard consistency-maintenance problem.

Deliverables and outputs (post-condition)

Access paths documented prior to coding.

Pattern recognition   Star rating *

Focus: Largescale patterns in design
Typical tasks for which this is needed: Construct frameworks, construct the object model, optimize reuse ('with reuse'), undertake architectural design
Related techniques: Framework creation
Input (pre-condition): Evolving design
Underpinning concepts: Idioms, Patterns and Frameworks

Technique description

Patterns were originally introduced into OT to describe a design-level solution to a problem in a context; although the concept is also being applied increasingly to other domains of object technology such as analysis artefacts. Practically, a pattern is an oft-repeated set of collaborating classes which can be named and used as a single entity in design thus obviating the need to keep 're-inventing the wheel'.

Technique usage

Patterns have been identified and documented from wide usage. It is thus hard for a novice to recognize the need for a pattern. Increasingly, as a developer works with objects, pattern recognition becomes another 'tool in the armory' of the good developer. Patterns can then be recognized because of prior experience, prior study of the various patterns books/manuals. Buschmann (1995) relates the identification of patterns to a number of known characteristics (see Idioms, Patterns and Frameworks essay in CD: Appendix E).

Patterns (and also frameworks) often have frozen spots and hotspots which it is important to identify. Frozen spots are points of defined and fixed behavior and hotspots are points where variation is introduced by the definition, redefinition or adjustment of default behavior of the superclasses (Wirfs-Brock and McKean, 1996; Buschmann *et al.*, 1996, page 396). Indeed, two patterns in, e.g., Gamma *et al.* (1995) often differ only by the meaning of the hotspot. Hot spot cards are recommended by Wirfs-Brock and McKean (1996) for documentation.

Patterns are still a relatively new tool in OO. They have obvious value but their recognition is, at present, more of an art based on experience, than a fully repeatable technique. However, in OPEN, we recognize their value and thus include pattern recognition as a most useful technique.

Deliverables and outputs (post-condition)

Recommendation for where and when to use patterns in development

Peer review – see Reviews

PERT charts Star rating ***

Focus: Project management (timelines)
Typical tasks for which this is needed: Develop and implement resource allocation plan
Related techniques: CPM charts, Gantt charts
Input (pre-condition): Information on durations of activities
Underpinning concepts: Need for objective method of formulating planning timelines

Technique description

Whilst CPM is useful for project planning when activity durations are well understood and forecastable, PERT (Program Evaluation and Review Technique) is more applicable when activity duration times can better be regarded as being random variables.

Technique usage

PERT assumes activity durations are random variables following the beta distribution. Three estimates of activity times are required: the optimistic time, the pessimistic time at the other extreme and, in between, the most likely time. Roughly, the optimistic and pessimistic times should represent a one per cent probability of exceedance.

From these three times, the mean activity duration is calculated together with its standard deviation. The mean is the sum of the pessimistic time, the optimistic time and four times the most likely time, all divided by six. The standard deviation is given by the difference between the pessimistic and optimistic times, again divided by six.

Using the mean and standard deviation, a network is built along similar lines to that used in the CPM technique (q.v.). This gives the earliest and latest start and finish times and a critical path. The time for this critical path is also a random variable and leads to the calculation of probabilities associated with the project completion time. Worked examples are to be found in standard texts on operations research (e.g. Anderson and Lievano, 1986).

The result of the calculations made in CPM or PERT techniques can be depicted using a Gantt chart (q.v.).

CORE TECHNIQUES 269

Deliverables and outputs (post-condition)

Contribution to planning documents on activity durations and critical paths and timelines.

Pistols at dawn   Star rating ***

Focus: Decision making
Typical tasks for which this is needed: Construct the object model, design user interface, develop and implement resource allocation plan, identify user requirements, model and re-engineer business process(es), optimize the design, undertake architectural design, undertake usability design
Related techniques: Political systems analysis, knobble the committee, publish ahead of the others, reveal the irrelevant weakness ...
Input (pre-condition): A disagreement
Underpinning concepts: None

Technique description

A technique for resolving differences of opinion. It may be used at any stage during the development process – from requirements engineering to final coding.

Technique usage

To resolve difficult decisions, it is customary for the two opposing factions to be represented by two people. The two leaders, accompanied by their seconds, meet at a prearranged location at dawn (the actual time will depend on geographical location and time of year). The second will supply their leaders with one of a pair of perfectly matched and loaded pistols. The two 'opponents', each representing one view of the difficult decision to be made, stand back to back and on the cry 'Walk', take 10 paces forward, turn and fire. [A more up-to-date version is given by Constantine, 1997b: frisbees at 30 paces.] The person remaining then has the right to take the (difficult) decision. This is a rapid and reasonably certain way to resolve decisions in a variety of software development contexts.

Deliverables and outputs (post-condition)

A decision – that is no longer challenged.

Power analysis (a.k.a. political systems analysis)   Star rating **

Focus: Management, decision making
Typical tasks for which this is needed: Obtain business approval
Related techniques: Pistols at dawn, social systems analysis

Input (pre-condition): Information on organizational politics; some understanding of the stakeholders and their viewpoints

Underpinning concepts: Organizational politics should not be ignored; human psychology

Technique description

Politics is defined by many as the activity concerned with managing relations between different stakeholders (Plato, 1974; Lasswell and Kaplan, 1950; Dahl, 1970).

Political systems analysis is the investigation of the mechanisms by which various stakeholders in the problem who might have differing interests reach accommodation. Accommodations are generated, modified or dissolved by politics which ultimately rests on disposition of power. Political systems analysis can therefore be seen as the investigation of how power is

- acquired
- utilized
- protected
- preserved
- transferred, and
- relinquished.

Such analysis is critical in adding to our understanding of the problem and our ability to propose implementable solutions. This is particularly the case in situations where there is no general consensus in terms of the problem(s) and the solution(s) to it (them). Such situations arise very frequently with respect to situations in which more than one stakeholder is involved. Solving business problems is one such situation.

Technique usage

Despite the large number of works written in 'political analysis' (e.g. Dahl, 1970), there is no universally agreed methodology for analysis of politics and power. The following is, however, a list of areas to which the analyst might wish to pay attention in investigating the mechanisms of power within organizations:

- Who are the key players?
- What is their power base? How did they acquire it?
- What are the mechanisms of relinquishing power?
- What are the mechanisms of being stripped of power?
- Who are the role models? Why?
- Are all the role models also the key players?

- How did they become role models?
- What are some of the rites and rituals to be observed?
- What is the nature of the language and symbolism dominating the situation?
- What historical factors/ personages or events are of significance? Why?
- Are there any 'sacred cows'? What are they? And why?
- What are the current economic and legal factors impacting the situation?
- How do these economic and legal factors compare with past situations?
- How are these economic and legal factors changing?

Deliverables and outputs (post-condition)

An understanding of stakeholder power systems.

Priority setting Star rating **

Focus: Planning
Typical tasks for which this is needed: Develop and implement resource allocation plan
Related techniques: Approval gaining, PSP, SMART goals
Input (pre-condition): Range of tasks
Underpinning concepts: Prioritization focuses on most important tasks

Technique description

There are many cases when simple priority setting is a valid management tool. As an example, consider the developer in a monthly meeting with the end user acceding to all modification and extension requests. Editorials in *Object Magazine* have repeatedly, implicitly or explicitly, suggested the need for prioritization. Certain amendments are either trivial, and thus acceptable, or of high priority. Leaving high priority tasks to last perhaps because they seem less 'exciting' should not be tolerated.

Technique usage

Prioritized user requests should be linked to a work schedule and to a timeline for deliverables, possibly using timebox techniques. Similarly, in requirements engineering, priority lists need to be constructed by the users. In both cases, OT provides support, through modularization, of component/package delivery by ensuring autonomy, information hiding, high semantic cohesion and loose coupling between components.

Deliverables and outputs (post-condition)

Priority list.

Process modeling – see Business process modeling

Protocol analysis Star rating ** (author S. Howard)

Focus: User requirements
Typical tasks for which this is needed: analyze user requirements, identify user requirements
Related techniques: Inspections, interviewing, Kelly grids, record and playback, videotaping, walkthroughs
Input (pre-condition): Domain expert and interviewer
Underpinning concepts: Human communication

Technique description

Verbal protocol analysis is a collection of techniques that are useful in gaining insight into how a person performs a task.

Verbal protocol analysis has been used during requirements elicitation, prototype testing and user interface evaluation. It has been applied successfully in the development of human computer interfaces and knowledge-based systems and in domains as varied as graphical user interface design, process control, accident analysis and military strategic decision making. It can help developers understand the tasks carried out by system users and identify difficulties and particular bottlenecks in the human–computer interaction. For example, the causal reasoning behind a subject matter expert's actions could be collected and then represented using decision trees. This information could then be used both for building the correct decision logic into systems and in designing appropriate user interfaces tailored to the expert's way of working.

The major problems with these techniques relate both to their practicality and validity. It may be difficult or impossible to observe the relevant behavior – it may be expensive to analyze the data in detail and specialist skills may be required for both data analysis and setting up the recording sessions when decisions about who and how to record are make. The validity of the data collected can be challenged on a number of grounds, including its completeness and accuracy and the fact that the act of verbalizing itself may change the performance of the task.

Other techniques that might be considered along with verbal protocol analysis include walkthroughs and inspection techniques, card sorting and various statistical techniques including repertory (Kelly) grid analysis.

Technique usage

STEP 1: TASK ANALYSIS

Before verbal protocol analysis can start, questions concerning who will be recorded and what they will be doing need to be answered. Typically, attempts are made to record data from a representative set of subjects performing key or critical tasks, though the selection of the number and types of subjects used is often determined by practical issues like who is available and how long the process can take.

STEP 2: ELICITATION

The selected subjects are asked to 'think aloud' whilst they perform the task of interest.

What they say is recorded, either manually by a notetaker or, ideally, via audio or videotapes (q.v.) which are later transcribed for detailed analysis.

Often an observer is present when the subject performs the task, ensuring that the recording equipment is operating and encouraging the task performer to 'talk aloud' when they fall silent. Attempts are, however, made to limit the intrusions and consequent effects on the data.

Many variations on this basic form have been used, including:

- retrospectively asking the task performer to comment on their videotaped behavior
- getting task performers to work in pairs, possibly expert/novice diads. This cuts down on the amount of prompting the observer will have to do, and often encourages the performers to be clearer in what they say
- incorporating question/answer sessions during data collection to probe specific issues.

The detailed nature of the data elicitation process followed will vary according to the technique used.

STEP 3: TRANSCRIPTION

Often the data recorded is then fully transcribed into narrative form. This greatly eases detailed analysis.

STEP 4: ANALYSIS

Many forms of data analysis are available depending on need, ranging from low cost, 'quick and dirty' data skimming to detailed statistical analysis. Data analysis is usually concerned with identifying the decision-making processes followed and the information that is heeded during task execution, and identifying any difficulties the subjects are having in executing the task.

Deliverables and outputs (post-condition)

A structured set of documents describing how an expert performs his/her job.

Prototyping Star rating ***

Focus: Building a mockup to gain rapid client feedback
Typical tasks for which this is needed: Construct object model, code
Related techniques: Simulation
Input (pre-condition): User requirements
Underpinning concepts: Prototypes

Technique description

Prototyping is when a 'quick and dirty' or mockup of the system is created. This may be done for one of several reasons, e.g. to show the customer; to use to answer questions regarding customer preferences; to test out some technique in the design or code and see if it is a realistic solution; or to uncover design or analysis flaws. Prototyping may be regarded as a very rapid application of a lifecycle model; but one only done for such specific means as listed above and not merely to shorten the lifecycle of development.

Prototyping is best used when the project has some unusual characteristics. Conversely if the development is very similar to previous ones, then prototyping is not appropriate. Its use permits more rapid feedback of queries from the developers to the users and can therefore be readily linked to an iterative delivery in OT. More frequent interactions with the user can help clarify ambiguous or muddy user requirements or, later in the lifecycle, can be used to test out different architectures. However, there is a great danger that the user will either come to believe the prototype is reality and expect delivery of the finished product months earlier than is humanly possible or else the developers will get engrossed in a rapid 'design–code' cycle to the extent that the coding parts consume the design element.

A prototype will often focus on specific areas with stubs for the remainder of the system. It is not uncommon to use prototyping to present the user with mock screens. Beneath the screens there is nothing but a class stub; no functionality capability is coded and any numbers (often very convincing) are hard-wired into the demo.

Technique usage

Build a prototype to answer a specific question (see discussion on Prototypes in CD: Appendix E). Focus on answering one specific question and go through a rapid iteration to build a mockup in code which can be shown to the customer or else used by the development team to answer that specific query.

Deliverables and outputs (post-condition)

A working prototype.

Quality templates Star rating **

Focus: Quality and quality management
Typical tasks for which this is needed: Evaluate quality, specify quality goals
Related techniques: Metrics collection
Input (pre-condition): Quality levels desirable
Underpinning concepts: Need to undertake quality assessment

Technique description

Quality templates, as proposed by Gilb (1988) and described by Goldberg and Rubin (1995) are one element in quality assessment.

Technique usage

An example of the type of information that should be captured in a quality template is given in Table A.20. The entries for Worst, Plan, Best, Current refer to numbers on a scale. Worst describes the worst acceptable test result – anything worse is assessed as a failure. Plan is the value you are trying to achieve by Date.
  Quality templates encourage interworking of developers and users in order to define measurable quality for the product. They also provide essential input to the development process.

Deliverables and outputs (post-condition)

Completed quality templates plus recommendations.

Query optimization Star rating *** (author S. Brown)

Focus: Database access
Typical tasks for which this is needed: Design and implement physical database
Related techniques: Access analysis
Input (pre-condition): A database schema, data partitioning and population information, a set of typical query examples
Underpinning concepts: Relational Database

Table A.20 Example quality template for average response time (after Goldberg and Rubin, 1995, page 453).

Name and Description	Unambiguous and meaningful to the end-user	Average response time – average time needed for system to perform common queries
Prerequisites	Conditions that must be met before measurements are meaningful	Test data exist in the database, test framework exists
Date	Date by which the test should be run	Alpha testing (actual date obtained from project schedule)
Test	Precise test or measure used to determine the value on the provided scale	Perform the five most frequent forms of queries 20 times each. Compute the average elapsed time for all queries
Scale	Scale along which measurements will be made	Number of elapsed seconds
Worst	Worst acceptable limit on the scale; worse that this is defined as failure	30 seconds
Plan	Level on the scale that must be met by Date	20 seconds
Best	Engineering limit, state-of-the-art, best ever	10 seconds
Current	Some existing system for comparison with Plan and Worst cases	40 seconds
Reference	Reference to more detail	See query document for a description of the five test queries and the information content of the database
Source	Authority for the objective	Marketing

Technique description

Given a particular query over a database schema, there are usually a number of ways it can be processed. Each possibility is known as a 'processing plan'. Different plans will require differing amounts of resources, such as processor time, network bandwidth and secondary storage access. Optimization involves predicting which plan will involve the minimum usage of a particular combination of resources. Queries are usually optimized for 'turn-around time' which is the time between the submission of the query to the time the last result is received, assuming that results are delivered incrementally to the source of the query. Kinds of optimization strategy include semantic optimization, which requires knowledge about the likely values populating the database, and syntactic optimization, which transforms the query expression to execute faster. Where a database is distributed, it is worthwhile partitioning the data according to the most common classes of query, so that these may execute concurrently in different locations on the appropriate data sets.

Technique usage

Optimization involves a number of different stages. Semantic optimization involves removing redundancies from the query, based on known or approximated features of the particular data in the database. Statistical sampling techniques may be used to decide which parts of a predicate may filter out the largest amount of data and so these can be executed first. For example, if it is known that the average age of employees in a company is 28, then a predicate that requires all the employees under the age of 20 is likely to reduce significantly the number of objects to be processed and hence should be processed earlier, before other 'less selective' predicates. The predicate part of the query may be written as a series of conjuncts (conjunctive normal form, i.e. independent logical conditions joined by 'AND'). If it is known that one conjunct is more likely to be false given the kind of data in the database, then that conjunct may be evaluated first so as to reduce the chance that the rest of the predicate needs to be evaluated.

Query plan generation requires the query to be represented in an algebraic form. The algebra can then be manipulated with rewrite rules to produce alternative processing plans that will produce the same result. The plans are then costed according to their desirability against what is being optimized. A complete query plan optimization system will involve a variety of different mechanisms to achieve its goals. There are usually too many possible plans to be costed exhaustively, so heuristics are used to provide a sub-optimal best. A simple rule might be to execute selections before joins, so as to reduce the input size of the data to join.

Deliverables and outputs (post-condition)

A query plan (giving execution order) for each common kind of query expected by the database.

Questionnaires Star rating ***

Focus: Eliciting users' views
Typical tasks for which this is needed: Identify user requirements
Related techniques: Brainstorming, interviews, workshops
Input (pre-condition): List of potential contacts and their addresses
Underpinning concepts: Surveys can provide useful information

Technique description

There are a number of techniques useful for requirements elicitation – questionnaires offer just one. Questionnaires are most useful in eliciting priorities for known options, not for eliciting new requirements. They may be used for requirements elicitation or for assessment of reaction of users to the systems or some aspect of it. Questionnaire design is an art in itself (De Vaus, 1996).

Questionnaires can be very effective as they can:

- cover a large audience particularly when many of them are at a distance
- gather a lot of data quickly and inexpensively
- be precisely targeted
- be time effective in that it does not take very long to fill out a properly designed questionnaire
- be anonymously filled out, which is of particular use in politically sensitive environments.

Of course designing effective questionnaires is a difficult task as they can be often misunderstood, or respondents may ignore them or not take sufficient time or care to respond to them. Another common criticism of questionnaires is that there is no direct contact between the parties involved, so that clarification of ambiguities is not possible.

Technique usage

It is important to target questions at the right level – for instance, individual users find it difficult or impossible to answer questions at the corporate level which are better answered by the CEO or President. Questions should be non-intrusive, non-personal. Since many people do not take questionnaires seriously or give their answers sufficient thought, it is good practice to ask questions twice – once phrased positively and once negatively. Anyone who just answers 'Yes' to everything will be trapped and their data can be safely discarded.

In designing questionnaires there should be a balance between open-ended and close-ended questions. Open-ended questions are advantageous as they allow the response to be made in such a way that carries a lot of information (much more than a yes/no answer). A closed question, however, has the advantages of being quicker to answer and quicker for the answers to be analyzed. Also the responses are very precise and not open to interpretation.

The overall length of questionnaires should be evaluated in the context of the importance of the information being sought. If the relevance to the respondent is clear and potentially advantageous to them, they are likely to retain an interest as they answer.

Designing questionnaires is an art in itself. Below are some guidelines to serve as a starting point:

- At the top and before the respondents can start with the questions, clearly explain the purpose of the questionnaire.

- Phrase the questions so that they are unambiguous, concise and unbiased. Remember that one person's unambiguous question may be ambiguous to another. Therefore, test the questionnaire using a small pilot group.

- Questions need to be bounded, i.e. no blue-sky answers.

- Questions should reveal no bias or be phrased in such a way that the respondent feels compelled to answer in a certain way to avoid embarrassment, e.g. a question such as 'OO is good and only fools use anything else: agree/disagree?' only elicits one answer!

- Questions should not have overlapping answers. If only a single answer is required, then it must only be possible to tick one box and not to regard oneself as falling between two boxes (e.g. one author recently answered a question that asked something along the lines of 'Was this recent experience we gave you (a) highly satisfactory or (b) unbearable?').

- In the necessary pilot, also evaluate whether responses fall in required ranges. For example, if, in a Likert 5 point scale, all answers fall into one extreme value, then the question has been phrased wrongly.

- Keep the questions short.

- Decide, *a priori*, how the results are to be analyzed.

- Impose a deadline for the respondents to observe.

- Allow the questionnaire to be completed anonymously when possible and appropriate.

- Make it easy for the respondents to return their answers, make them available on the net or supply a self-addressed, stamped return envelope.

Finally, the questionnaire designer needs to address the difficult question: 'How am I going to analyze the data and with what (potentially statistical) analytic techniques?' Too many open-ended questions may give interesting reading individually but cannot be summarized. Data input on an ordinal scale cannot be averaged. And so on.

Deliverables and outputs (post-condition)

Raw data from questionnaires ready for quality assurance and data analysis.

RAD   Star rating ***

Focus: Rapid application development approach
Typical tasks for which this is needed: Identify user requirements
Related techniques: JAD, workshops
Input (pre-condition): Users
Underpinning concepts: User involvement is crucial

Technique description

The technique of RAD (Rapid Application Development) aims to enhance requirements engineering and requirements analysis. It usually uses a workshop (q.v.) session consisting of both business domain experts and systems architects/analysts together with representatives of the user community (for further details see Graham, 1995a, 1996d).

Perhaps the most important characteristic of RAD is extensive user involvement in the process. RAD is *not* an excuse for 'rabid application development advocated by the salesman for some 4GL or other' (Graham, 1996d).

Technique usage

In a RAD workshop, the aim is to facilitate, in a relatively short period of time, the development of the software system. RAD sessions need to be set up to involve developers and users. The brainstorming session of a RAD workshop produces a prototype as part of the requirements elicitation process. Detailed suggestions on the workshop setting for RAD are found in Technique: Workshops (see also Graham, 1995a, 1996d).

Deliverables and outputs (post-condition)

The output is a statement of the business user's requirements and, if possible, their expectations. This document will probably be written in a language concomitant with task scripts or possibly use cases.

RAD workshops – see Workshops

Record and playback   Star rating **

Focus: Requirements elicitation
Typical tasks for which this is needed: Analyze user requirements
Related techniques: Interviews, videotaping
Input (pre-condition): A subject, recording and playback equipment, a set of questions for the interview
Underpinning concepts: Human communication

Technique description

Recording the verbal communication between individuals engaged in a conversation where considerable information is exchanged creates a potentially permanent record of such proceedings. Such recordings can be an important and useful part of the repertoire of the requirements engineering, particularly during the requirements elicitation phase and later during requirements analysis.

Such simple techniques of recording and analyzing the recorded text have also been extended to further utilize the power and availability of the recorded word. A specific technique called 'Record and Playback Game', during which verbal communication recorded earlier is played back in order to elicit further information, clarification or expansions on ideas, is one such development. Record and Playback Game (which incidentally is not a game at all) particularly assists in managing multiple levels of granularity in information. From the initial, complete recording, specific sentences can then be played back and further information at a finer level requested.

Technique usage

All you need is a good small tape recorder, plenty of tape and the ability to operate the tape recorder. Recording of verbal communication as input into protocol analysis (q.v.) is one obvious use of this technology. It is also possible for conversations recorded with one person or group of people to be played back for a different person or group, thus effectively running a 'virtual brainstorming session'.

These are the three fundamental uses of this technique. Although the basic concepts are simple, there are two specific conditions that must be present for the technique to succeed. These are:

- Trust should be built amongst all participants. Saying something is one thing, going on record (literally) with it is another. Many professionals are apprehensive about providing recorded interviews. This need not necessarily imply a sinister motive, a hidden agenda or 'skeletons in the closet'. It is just that a lot of people get nervous about being recorded or filmed.

- The information must not be used for any reason other than that for which it is intended: to assist in elicitation and analysis of requirements. Particularly tapes of this nature must not be used (at least directly) as a means of 'gotcha', i.e. as a 'proof' of the customer 'having changed their mind'. You will only do this once! However, do not forget that the reason why you are using this technique at all is to elicit and analyze information so that the true requirements of the user are made known. Within this context, anything 'professional' goes.

It is therefore important to explain, to all parties concerned, the process of what *exactly* will happen during the exercise and also exactly what will happen to the recordings once obtained. You need also to obtain (preferably written) permission to record these sessions. This will give you the opportunity to identify those who might be reluctant or resistive. Do not 'push' these people; just use another approach, even if it means using a technique that you might feel is not quite as suitable.

Usually returning the tapes to the customer when you are finished is considered a good positive gesture. Of course, as there is likely to be only one set of tapes you can only return these to one person. Choose this person correctly for maximum kudos.

Deliverables and outputs (post-condition)

A set of tapes, some requirements, textual (verbal) input for protocol analysis.

Redundant associations – see Access analysis

Refactoring   Star rating *

Focus: Evolution and revisions to existing object model
Typical tasks for which this is needed: Construct the object model, identify CIRTs, undertake architectural design
Related techniques: Revision of inheritance hierarchies
Input (pre-condition): Existing system
Underpinning concepts: Small changes are often more effective than large changes

Technique description

Refactoring is a rapidly emerging technique to increase the quality of evolving systems orthogonally to its ongoing evolution, i.e. in terms of enhancements. Refactoring is a set of small changes made to a program, each of which makes the program easier to understand and easier to work with but which do not affect any aspect of its functionality (Fowler and Scott, 1997, page 31). It is also critical that appropriate tests are in place to ensure that nothing is broken during refactoring. Steps should be small and deliberate.

In the Smalltalk community there is a refactoring tool available on the website: http://st-www.cs.uicu.edu/users/droberts/Refactory.html.

O'Callaghan (1997b) also recommends the technique for converting non-OO systems to objects. He suggests, as one would if starting from scratch, identifying key abstractions in the problem domain and modeling these with a single CIRT. Some of these, when derived from a legacy system, will be large objects. Using abstraction techniques we can identify such large objects as packages and then look inside at a lower level of granularity and reapply the refactoring and object design principles. The use of the façade pattern (Gamma *et al.*, 1995) is also encouraged in this context.

Technique usage

Some refactoring steps:

- fuse two similar methods together by creating a new superclass
- add or improve the comments to a method to make it more understandable
- restructure an algorithmic detail without changing the pre- and post-conditions
- find patterns and utilize those rather than ad hoc coding
- identify tightly coupled groups of classes and re-evaluate them
- identify any classes which are becoming less cohesive (use appropriate metrics) and consider splitting them into two or more classes linking them via delegation. Ensure all necessary contracts are in place if the design is split in this way
- use measures broadly to try to evaluate alternatives since there is a dearth of good advice available (Whitmire, 1997, page 49).

Deliverables and outputs (post-condition)

Recommended improvements to design documentation.

Refinement Star rating *

Focus: Modeling
Typical tasks for which this is needed: Construct the object model
Related techniques: Collaborations analysis, implementation of services
Input (pre-condition): Existing design
Underpinning concepts: Collaborations

Technique description

Refinement is a term describing the process of converting from an abstract specification into a concrete design, i.e. conversion of formal specification into an actual algorithm. A specification for $\sqrt{y} = x$ might be non-computable, defined in terms of its inverse: $x^2 = y$. On the other hand, an algorithm must be computable – for example, use the Newton–Raphson technique to find the root. Refinement is a key technique of the OO method, Catalysis (D'Souza and Wills, 1995, 1997) which can be annotated in UML (see below). It is also a technique in OPEN. Initially, refinement in Catalysis was focused on Collaborations (q.v.) and is a technique of clarifying a collaboration by moving to a finer level of detail (finer granularity q.v.). This is done in an orderly and controlled fashion by monitoring the current abstraction level, maintaining traceability and compatibility of pre- and post-conditions.

In Catalysis and UML, refinement is shown as a relationship between an *abstraction* which contains less information than its *realization*, i.e. a move from abstract to concrete, which is in accordance with the classical use of the term. An example is the realization of a (more abstract) type into a fully-fledged class. In the UML metamodel, refinement is a kind of dependency.

Technique usage

Refinement is a very general technique in that it can be applied in a wide variety of situations. It is used in turning an abstract class into a concrete class, probably via subclasses; to add interface details to an architectural sketch with only names present; to design a specific algorithm to implement one specific operation; to add implementation aspects to existing interfaces; and so on.

OML sees no need to support this notationally since the 'before' and 'after' refinement artefacts are well supported, refinement really being the translation process. However, if you are using UML, the official notation is a dotted line with open arrowhead (a dependency relationship: Figure 2.23) with a stereotype label of ≪refine≫.

Deliverables and outputs (post-condition)

Improvements to OOAD documents.

Regression testing   Star rating ***

Focus: Testing
Typical tasks for which this is needed: Test
Related techniques: Integration testing, unit testing
Input (pre-condition): Modified system ready for testing
Underpinning concepts: Modifications should not change quality of pre-modified system

Technique description

When a fault is corrected, or when a new feature is introduced, the system must be re-inspected and re-executed to ensure that no new faults have been introduced by this addition. This is called regression testing. It is beneficial to construct an automatic test harness for regression tests. The simplest and most powerful way to do this is to record all input events (for example, keystrokes) during tests and the corresponding output. These events are then replayed to the modified system and the output from the two runs compared. Any differences must then be examined to see if they are due to failure or not. There are many software tools on the market nowadays to help with this kind of testing. It is advantageous if these testing products run on separate hardware to avoid the possibility of them interfering with the test results themselves.

Technique usage

In OT, regression testing is useful in giving confidence about the reusability of components; in checking that the iterative nature of the lifecycle has not itself introduced any defects; and that inheritance has been used appropriately and correctly (Firesmith, 1995a).

Three main techniques have been found useful for object-oriented regression (and other forms of) testing:

(1) Duplicate inheritance structure in the test drivers – the test harness has an inheritance hierarchy which is isomorphic to that of the system under test. An advantage is that it keeps the class hierarchy separate from the test harness. The disadvantage of this option is that it is restricted to blackbox testing; however, this may be overcome if the classes under test grant privileged access to the tester classes, through `friend` declarations in C++, or the use of the basic method `instVarAt` in Smalltalk.

(2) Embed test operations – operations are added to the classes under test themselves in this whitebox testing option. (The 13 steps of this technique are given in Table A.21.) One major disadvantage is the need to manually remove test code from the classes themselves prior to delivery.

(3) Duplicate inheritance structure in test mixins – a combination of options 1 and 2 using the concept of mixins (q.v.). Rather than embedded test code, it is inherited from the mixin classes – which of course has the same effect.

Deliverables and outputs (post-condition)

Test report with any problems highlighted for further action.

Table A.21 Thirteen steps in regression testing using embedded test code (from Firesmith, 1995a).

(1) Testing begins when the *tester interface* object sends the *test class* message to the class under test. The test class message will eventually return the number of errors found to the *tester interface* object.

(2) The associated *test class* operation calls the constructor.

(3) The constructor constructs one or more instances (e.g. the object under test) that will be used to indirectly test the class under test.

(4) The *test class* operation then sends the *test instance* message to the newly constructed object under test. After testing is complete, this message will return the total number of errors found to the *test class* operation.

(5) The *test instance* operation then calls the hidden *test initial property values* operation that determines whether the object under test was properly initialized.

(6) Any errors found are then documented in the *error log* object, and the number of errors is returned to the *test instance* operation.

(7) The *test instance* operation then calls the hidden *test operations based on states* operation, which tests each operation in each state by placing the object in the proper pre-test state, executing the operation, and checking for the proper result including the proper post-test state.

(8) Any errors found are then documented in the *error log* object and the number of errors returned to the *test instance* operation.

(9) The *test instance* operation then calls the hidden *test exception handling based on states* operation, which determines if the object under test raises and handles exceptions properly.

(10) Any errors found are then documented in the *error log* object, and the number of errors is returned to the *test instance* operation.

(11) The *test instance* operation then calls the hidden *test scenarios* operation, which tests each usage scenario of the object. This test operation may not be necessary due to the previous test operations.

(12) Any errors found are then documented in the *error log* object, and the number of errors is returned to the *test instance* operation.

(13) If the number of errors returned is greater than zero, the *tester interface* object will display the number of errors on the screen and print an error report based on the *error log* object.

Relationship modeling

Focus: Relationships between CIRTs
Typical tasks for which this is needed: Code, construct the object model, design and implement physical database, optimize the design
Related techniques: Collaborations analysis, coupling measurement, delegation analysis, generalization and inheritance identification, granularity
Input (pre-condition): CIRTs
Underpinning concepts: Aggregation, Membership and Containment; Delegation; Generalization, Inheritance and Polymorphism; Responsibilities and RDD

Technique description

Figure E.10 in CD: Appendix E describes the metamodel for referential relationships. These include:

- associations
- aggregation
- membership
- containment
- usage; dependency
- subclassing; subtyping
- powertype relationships.

Whilst each of these are described in detail elsewhere (see, in particular, essays in CD: Appendix E), it is worthwhile evaluating them all together under the technique of relationship modeling.

ASSOCIATIONS

An association in OPEN is a uni-directional mapping. It is a named relationship between one CIRT and another (e.g. a *CUSTOMER* uses the services of a *BANK*). Cardinalities are likely to be associated with these connexions although details of the constraints is a concern of late OOAD. Directionality often requires a statement of the semantics of the relationship; in other words, such directed relationships need to be labeled with a descriptive name. An association gives the static architecture and can be equivalently interpreted from a dynamic viewpoint as a potential message passing path, i.e. a using relationship. Association and using are purposefully confounded in OPEN (Henderson-Sellers, 1997b) and have the same representation in OML (but differently notated if using UML's notation) although a used/not-used stereotype might be usefully applied in some cases (Firesmith and Henderson-Sellers, 1998b). The full metamodel for associations (and other referential relationships) is given in Figure E.10 in CD: Appendix E.

Aggregation and membership

'Aggregation' structures represent the 'is-part-of' relationship or 'whole–part' (meronymic). It is important to note that, for the relationship to be valid, the whole (a.k.a. composite or aggregate) *must* have at least one emergent property (a property of the aggregate that cannot be deduced from the evaluation of the properties of the individual components) (Kilov and Ross, 1994). In addition, at least one property of the composite/aggregate should be dependent upon the value of one or more properties of one or more of its components/parts. Furthermore, aggregations are generally considered to be anti-symmetric and transitive (e.g. Rumbaugh *et al.*, 1991). Also some operations to the whole are propagated to the parts (e.g. Kilov and Ross, 1994). There are a number of subtypes for the whole–part relationship. Henderson-Sellers (1997a), following Odell (1994a), lists seven and groups these as:

- aggregation – the four configurational relationships
- membership – the remaining three, non-configurational relationships.

An important use of aggregation is in support of abstraction leading to layered diagrams at different granularities (Edwards and Henderson-Sellers, 1991).

Membership is still meronymic (whole–part) but is no longer configurational. In a configurational relationship, the parts bear some structural or functional relationship to each other or to the whole (for example, the configuration of an engine, the transmission shaft and the axles in a car are highly constrained to one specific configuration). In membership, this constraint does not apply. So, for example, we have a forest (the whole) with very many members (trees). The parts of a forest are its trees but any pair of individual trees has no particular connexion to each other and changes in that configuration do not affect the viability of the forest as an entity.

Containment

Containment is not a meronymic relationship – although many methods confuse it in this way. Containment, called by Odell (1994a) topological inclusion, refers to a temporary relationship in that the entries in the container bear no semantic (structural or functional) relationship to the container itself. Examples would be *INTEGER*s in a *STACK*, suitcases in an automobile trunk.

Dependency and usage

Whilst associations/mappings are strictly static and architectural, the superposition of a message-passing topology turns each association into a usage relationship. Using relationships mirror the visibility (q.v.) of each object – if objects are visible to each other, then a connecting usage relationship must exist.

In OPEN, usage and mapping are purposefully confounded such that an 'association' arrow can be interpreted either in a static sense as a mapping or in a dynamic sense as a message path (using relationship). In all cases, the connexion is uni-directional, thus supporting seamlessness.

SUBCLASSING AND SUBTYPING

Subclassing and subtyping are examples of relationships currently implemented using inheritance. In these relationships, one CIRT is at a lower or 'child' level to a second at the 'parent' level. In subtyping, the child is a kind of (or a subtype of) the parent. There is a strong semantic connexion in that the child is a member of the set of objects represented by the parent CIRT as well as a member of its own (sub)type. In subclassing, the similarity is at the code rather than the semantic level. Reuse is thus compromised as is any semantic relationship.

An adjunct in subtyping is the use of the discriminant (described in CD: Appendix E).

POWERTYPE RELATIONSHIPS

A power type is an object type the instances of which are subtypes of another object type (Odell, 1994b). It is an advanced concept with limited applicability and has not been incorporated into the current (1997) version of the OMG OADF (UML Version 1.1). It is described in detail in CD: Appendix E.

Technique usage

In modeling relationships, associations/mappings (static view) and using relationships (dynamic view) are the most common and should generally be identified first. In many instance, using the notion of a whole–part relationship comes naturally and, if so, should be used. At the same frequency of usage are membership and containment. Generalization and inheritance structures are generally best left until late in OOAD since they provide a highly constrained connexion (which in fact breaks encapsulation). Freezing in such subtyping structures too early can lead to brittle designs.

The identification of problem domain associations will primarily occur from the scenarios and the requirements specification. Any interaction or relationship between classes thus specified should at first be modeled as an association – initially undirected (TBD). Only upon refinement will directionality (usually uni-directionality) be added; or possibly a modification to an aggregation, membership or containment connexion – which are subtypes of association.

Useful guidelines for modeling associations are given in Rumbaugh (1992) and Kilian (1991) including:

- ensuring associations are structural properties, not simply transient events or actions
- checking that ternary associations are really necessary to describe the problem domain. Quite often they can be decomposed into binary associations

without loss of information. Note that in OPEN, we advocate the total avoidance of ternary relationships

- removing redundant associations, especially at the detailed design stage. However, note that earlier in this phase, redundant information may actually be useful to optimizing the solution.

The identification of associations may also arise from the dynamic model, which tends to lead to using relationships whereby the need for information by one CIRT requires a connexion to another. Unless the relationship fits the semantics of aggregation, it is likely that this will require the identification of a further association/using relationship.

Aggregations occur naturally in some domains and not in others. The major question here is 'Is one thing a part of another?'. Aggregation is a modeling construct – in code it is represented no differently than an association. Its use is therefore in representing our understanding of the business problem, it is not an end in itself. Use it if it helps you to understand or analyze the problem; do not feel obliged to use it. COMN supports both analysis and implementation aspects of aggregation (see Chapter 2 of Firesmith and Henderson-Sellers, 1998a).

Membership and containment should be regarded similarly to aggregation in the sense that they provide support for many developers in analysis; whilst others will be as happy to use a single association-style relationship, expressing the additional information merely by cardinalities. In notations, like COMN, which support these additional relationship modeling constructs, their availability can help create a more understandable diagrammatic representation of the business issues.

All these relationships, as with all other features of a CIRT, should be moved as far up the inheritance hierarchy as possible. The inheritance structure itself should be used for is-a-kind-of relationships and only in highly extreme circumstances for implementation inheritance.

CIRT hierarchies can be developed in two ways, firstly by generalizing from several common classes to a more general class, and secondly by specializing a class to several descendants. The latter approach extends the model while the former consolidates the model. The two approaches may occur throughout the evolutionary development activity (Graham *et al.*, 1997b) and are achieved by an examination of the services and relationships of classes and the identification of commonality. Remember that there is no unique hierarchy to be sought (Lakoff, 1987, page 121) – several may be equally acceptable depending on viewpoint and the current context.

Refinement of generalization hierarchies, in terms of specializing and generalizing classes, is once again an iterative process that will start later than the other activities but then occur concurrently with them. The decomposition of roles into subclasses may be a useful technique in understanding the abstractions and developing more reusable concepts.

Deliverables and outputs (post-condition)

Addition of relationships to the semantic nets and interaction diagrams (which must be kept in synch of course).

Reliability requirements   Star rating ** (author G.C. Low)

Focus: DB user requirements
Typical tasks for which this is needed: Identify user DB requirements
Related techniques: Database fragmentation, object replication, object retention requirements
Input (pre-condition): Evolving user requirements for database
Underpinning concepts: Database systems typically have a critical need to be fully operational

Technique description

Business can be severely hit by the unavailability of objects. Reliability requirements should include the average and maximum time periods that objects can be unavailable.

Technique usage

Determine the average and maximum time that objects can be unavailable together with the DBMS method of restart after hardware, transmission and software failure; controls to prevent objects being invalidated during a failure and subsequent restart; methods to back-out of partially processed transactions; support for roll-forward of completed transactions using the archival database and transaction log following a DBMS failure; and methods to reconstruct objects and their properties, operations and relationships if accidentally damaged.

Deliverables and outputs (post-condition)

Documented detailed reliability requirements.

Repertory grids – see Kelly grids

Responsibility identification   Star rating **

Focus: Anthropogenic modeling via responsibilities of CIRTs
Typical tasks for which this is needed: Construct the object model, design user interface, evaluate quality, identify CIRTs, test

292   CORE TECHNIQUES

Related techniques: CRC card modeling
Input (pre-condition): CIRTs
Underpinning concepts: Responsibilities and Responsibility-Driven Design

Technique description

Responsibilities are high level abstractions representing responsibilities for (a) knowing, (b) doing and (c) enforcing. Each responsibility will be implemented by one or more operations in the interface. A responsibility is thus defined as any high level purpose, obligation, or required capability of a CIRT, typically provided by one or more characteristics (see CD: Appendix E for further details).

Technique usage

Identification of responsibilities requires a higher focus/mindset than merely looking at the individual services (in the sense of the set of messages to which an object will respond) of a CIRT. Good ways of identifying responsibilities are embodied in a responsibility-driven design (q.v.) – OPEN is one example of such an OOAD method. Typically, CRC card modeling can provide some of the responsibilities; and possibly task scripts/use cases – although in this case, these tend to focus on individual tasks and effecting those tasks rather than the higher level responsibilities of a CIRT.

Deliverables and outputs (post-condition)

A high level semantic net focusing on what responsibilities are attached to which CIRTs. These can be documented directly in OML using the trait 'responsibility'. In UML a stereotype can be used. In either case, it is important that seamlessness is maintained so that higher level responsibilities are linked smoothly to visible operations and thence into methods inside the classes.

Reuse measurement   Star rating *

Focus: Metrics, reuse
Typical tasks for which this is needed: Evaluate quality, specify quality goals
Related techniques: Metrics collection
Input (pre-condition): Existing system
Underpinning concepts: Reuse Metrics

Technique description

Measurement of reuse is not easy, particularly since the granularity level can vary very much across organizations. Indeed, one can readily appreciate that reuse still requires a good definition when one hears of various figures such as 'an excellent level of 20 per cent reuse was obtained' to others claiming 70–80 per cent reuse. One must ask what is the 'yardstick' here?

Although such global reuse statements are of dubious validity, at the more technical level there are a (small) number of reuse measures proposed in the literature. These are discussed in full detail in CD: Appendix E.

Technique usage

There is no standard way to measure global reuse across a system. One could count the number of classes in the current system which were *not* built for this system specifically as a percentage of the total number of classes in the system. However, many classes may be reused with minor modifications so that there are a number of classes which could be counted as having been reused even though they were not done so in the sense of a 'plug and play' construction. However, the number of classes says nothing about the granularity of those classes. Indeed, it is the case that more granular classes are more likely to be reused more frequently. Whilst not wishing to advocate the use of LOC as a measure of reuse, it is clear that care must be taken. In any single organization, we suggest you devise your own standard until an industry standard reuse metric is developed.

At the technical level, it is possible to use the metrics suggested in CD: Appendix E to assess the extent to which reuse by derivation and by polymorphism is used. The two ratios, reuse ratio (U) and specialization ratio (S), indicate some of the qualities of reuse within a hierarchy. More detailed discussion is given in Henderson-Sellers (1996) and in Yap and Henderson-Sellers (1997).

We suggest, as with other metrics, that the best use of reuse metrics is as thresholds (q.v.).

Deliverables and outputs (post-condition)

Counts of specialization ratio and reuse ratio for the various inheritance hierarchies in the system. Counts of number of reused classes. Comparison of these values with benchmarking historical data *from the same organization.*

Reverse engineering   Star rating *

Focus: Legacy systems
Typical tasks for which this is needed: Develop software development plans and strategies, maintain trace between requirements and design, write manual(s) and prepare other documentation
Related techniques: Application scavenging
Input (pre-condition): Code
Underpinning concepts: 'Seamlessness' and 'reversibility'

Technique description

It is generally considered the norm to progress, albeit iteratively and incrementally, from analysis to design to code. Whilst OPEN's contract-driven lifecycle simply requires any sequencing of activity objects (within the constraint of ensuring that preconditions are met), many projects will turn an OO design into OO code. Unfortunately, there are also many organizations to whom processes and project management seem to be anathema. They produce code with no apparent (or at least no documented) design. This can also be the result of over-exuberant application of the notion of OO $\equiv$ prototyping. Finally, systems (code) exist for which the documentation has been lost. In all such situations, a need can arise to reverse engineer the design *from* the code. Reverse engineering may be regarded as the representation of a system at a higher level of abstraction (O'Callaghan, 1997a).

Technique usage

In reverse engineering, many constructs in the code are easily translated, e.g. the overall class definitions and structures; but should a pointer or reference be reverse engineered to a mapping/association, an aggregation, ...? Consequently, whilst users increasingly demand tools to support reverse engineering into one of a number of OOAD concept sets (metamodel) and design notation, such a translation is likely to be ambiguous and effective tool support difficult to provide.

Reverse engineering is usually undertaken using a tool rather than manually. Good reverse engineering tools should also support design re-creation from code if/when the originally used OOAD method has stagnated or is no longer supported. Similarly, imported code, from say a subsidiary company using an alternative OOAD method, could be reverse engineered into the OPEN OOAD framework and notated accordingly.

Deliverables and outputs (post-condition)

Design created to document existing (but undocumented) code.

Reviews Star rating **

Focus: V&V
Typical tasks for which this is needed: V&V
Related techniques: Acceptance testing, inspections
Input (pre-condition): High level project management documents (not specific work products)
Underpinning concepts: Visibility assists in keeping project on track

Technique description

A number of techniques fall under the title of 'static defect management'. IEEE standard 1028 categorizes these according to their primary objective such as evaluation of project progress, resource allocation and technical adequacy. We refer to these techniques as 'Reviews'. These are distinct from inspections or walkthroughs (which are themselves distinct from each other) (Wheeler *et al.*, 1996). Techniques described in IEEE1028 – Management review, MIL–STD 1521B and IEEE1028 – Technical reviews, we place in the category of reviews.

Technique usage

IEEE 1028 – MANAGEMENT REVIEW

The management review technique described as part of IEEE 1028 does not have as its primary objective the detection and removal of defects. Management reviews are conducted to ascertain project progress, to recommend corrective action at project level and to ensure proper allocation of resources. As the name suggests, 'management' and technical leadership of the project are involved in this management-led process in which a potentially high volume of material may be reviewed in a short period of time. This is in contrast to inspection techniques (q.v.) in which a low volume of material is inspected by a peer group, for the purpose of defect identification at the work product level.

MIL–STD 1521B

This process is very similar to the IEEE 1028 – Management review process in many respects including its nature, objectives, volume of material reviewed, and the responsibilities and positions of stakeholders present. Where the two processes differ is in the team leadership. In a MIL–STD 1521B review this is shared by the representative of the contractor (customer) and that of the contracting agent. The number of people in a review team of this type could be as high as several tens of individuals. There is usually no formally specified process or specification for the type of data to be collected.

IEEE 1028 – TECHNICAL REVIEW

IEEE–1028 states the objective of technical reviews to be evaluation of conformance to specifications and project plans and ensurance of the integrity of the change process. Similarly to the IEEE 1028 – Management review, technical reviews have no predefined number of participants and a high volume of material is usually studied during one session. Data collection is not a mandatory or specified process. Unlike management reviews, however, the composition and leadership of the technical review team is of a technical nature as are the process outputs and issues investigated. Management is usually absent.

   The respective standards cited describe how these techniques should be applied in some detail.

Deliverables and outputs (post-condition)

Project progress report.

Revision of inheritance hierarchies Star rating **

Focus: Improving design for reusability
Typical tasks for which this is needed: Create and/or identify reusable components ('for reuse'), optimize the design
Related techniques: Abstract class identification, abstraction utilization, application scavenging
Input (pre-condition): Inheritance hierarchies/networks
Underpinning concepts: Generalization, Inheritance and Polymorphism

Technique description

Revision of hierarchies should be ongoing during the development process, and its inclusion as a separate technique is a reminder that in developing inheritance hierarchies the developer should be thinking of other situations in which such a hierarchy might be applied. This leads to a more robust and reusable hierarchy.

Inheritance hierarchies should be continually reassessed as to whether they are general enough to support the insertion of new concepts, perhaps as sub-branches to the tree/network – or does the current structure preclude this by making a one level transition actually cover several abstraction levels? This can easily happen when no domain analysis has been used and only the classes of immediate interest have been included in the inheritance model.

Conversely, inheritance hierarchies sometimes grow following the exhortation to practice 'programming by difference'. Incorrectly used, this can lead to (a) implementation inheritance or (b) deep hierarchies with no side-branches. Such a structure suggests that a single abstraction has, in fact, been spread over several levels of the hierarchy.

On the other hand, indiscriminate growth of inheritance hierarchies should be avoided. Inheritance is not necessarily the best solution. Several studies (e.g. Lorenz and Kidd, 1994; Yap and Henderson-Sellers, 1997) have shown that the majority of hierarchies in both in-house developments and in commercially available class libraries have depths of less than about 5–7 levels. In fact, DIT (depth of inheritance tree) is often suggested as an appropriate OO metric (q.v.).

Technique usage

Evaluate the inheritance model in terms of whether it encapsulates a single, consistent semantic model of the domain of interest. Check that all relationships are correctly is-a-kind-of.

For all abstract classes, check that these are nodes and not leaves. It is generally agreed that all nodes should be abstract classes, although this assumes

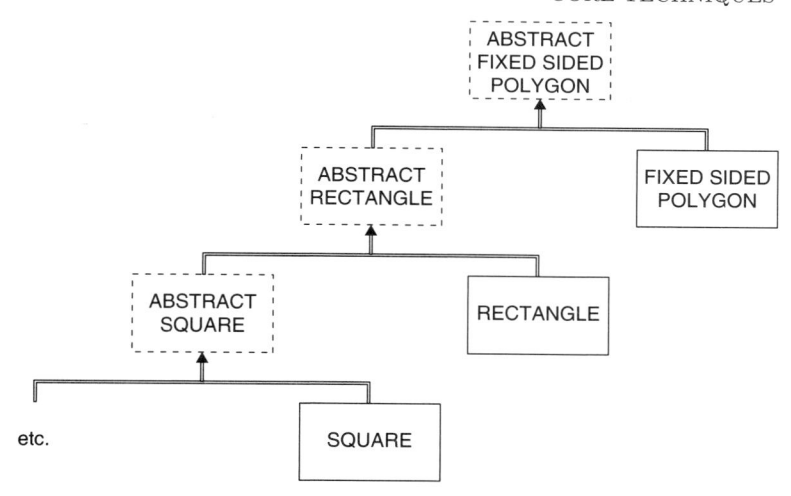

Figure A.43 Rather than an inheritance hierarchy in which *SQUARE* inherits from *RECTANGLE*, a more complex structure can be created which is more reusable and is satisfying to both mathematicians and code implementors.

that all subclassing is exhaustive. De Paula and Nelson (1991) and Taivalsaari (1996) also recommend that in general abstract classes should not inherit from concrete classes.

As an extension to the above rule, Grosberg (1993) suggests that no concrete classes should have subclasses. This leads again to all nodes being abstract classes and all leaves concrete classes and can be used to alleviate some of the problems of the well-known rectangle and square problem (Figure A.43). *SQUARE* can now inherit from *ABSTRACT_RECTANGLE* (thus satisfying the geometrician's claim that a square is a special sort of rectangle) and those services of rectangles, such as alter the aspect ratio, which must not be inherited by square, can be allocated as services to the concrete class, *RECTANGLE*.

Evaluate whether abstract classes contain sufficient information to support polymorphism as much as possible by ensuring that features likely to be called on subclasses are available in the superclass as deferred services.

Deliverables and outputs (post-condition)

Revised and improved inheritance hierarchies.

Rich pictures Star rating **

Focus: User requirements
Typical tasks for which this is needed: Analyze user requirements, identify user requirements

298   CORE TECHNIQUES

Related techniques: Action research, brainstorming, interviewing, soft systems analysis, workshops
Input (pre-condition): Requirements
Underpinning concepts: 'A picture is worth a thousand words'

Technique description

During the facts gathering stage of any process, the insights gained must be recorded in such a way that the capture, retention and communication of these insights is deemed understandable, natural and effective. The world, however, is not understood as a linear sequence of objects or events. Consequently, systems practitioners have identified that drawing pictures is often a much more effective way of capturing the complexities of the problem situation, particularly the cultural issues. A stylistic depiction of the situation, termed a rich picture, is usually employed.

Technique usage

Whilst there are no formally specified notations for composing rich pictures, some standard styles are informally emerging. Shown in Figure A.44(a and b) are illustrative examples of typical rich pictures drawn in two different emerging styles.

Irrespective of style, what is important in a rich picture is that it conveys the preoccupations of its compilers, expressing issues and value judgements. A rich picture should also convey the present variety of relevant views and relationships which might require deeper study.

It is noteworthy that, although a graphic depiction is usually used, many other forms of capturing and communicating perceptions may be utilized, including:

- video and/or audio recordings
- short narratives and notes
- diagrams and charts and
- photographs.

Deliverables and outputs (post-condition)

Set of rich pictures documenting requirements.

Risk analysis   Star rating **

Focus: Evaluate project risks
Typical tasks for which this is needed: Develop and implement resource allocation plan, obtain business approval

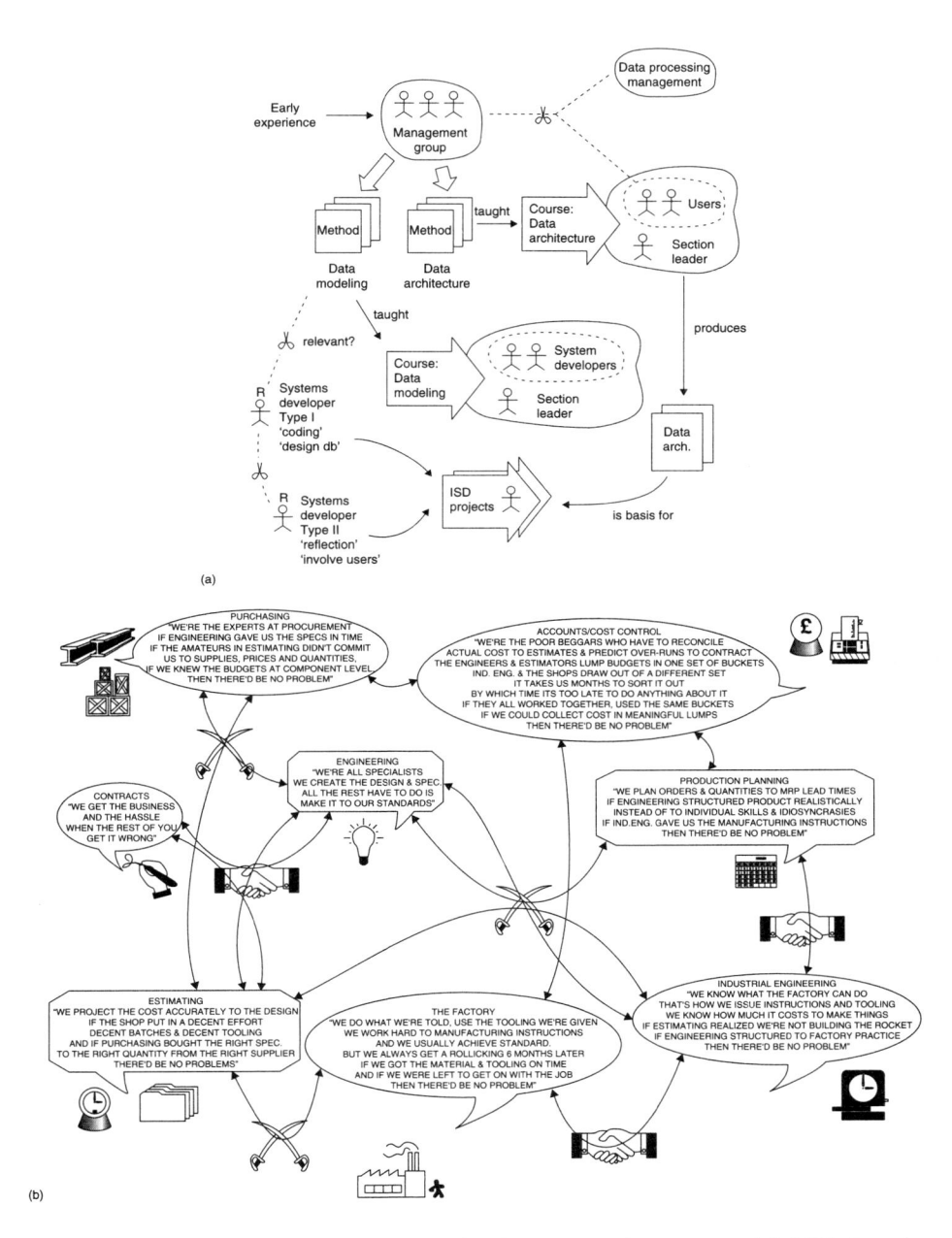

Figure A.44 Examples of two styles for depicting rich pictures: (a) MIS domain (insurance company) (after Mathiassen and Nielsen, 1989) and (b) engineering domain (after Checkland and Scholes, 1990).

300   CORE TECHNIQUES

Related techniques: Cost–benefit analysis
Input (pre-condition): Project has been viewed as generally feasible
Underpinning concepts: Resources are limited and chance of failure must be minimized

Technique description

There are many risks associated with software development. Leffingwell (1997) quotes numbers indicating that 31 per cent of all software projects are canceled before completion (with an associated dollar wastage of $81 billion) and a further 62 per cent will either be late or over budget.

Transitioning to OT brings an inevitable risk. Understanding the risks is tantamount to being able to minimize them. Risks also increase as the investment in the new technology increases (Baudoin and Hollowell, 1996, page 410).

RISK IDENTIFICATION

Management of risk begins with identification of sources and potential of risks, perhaps classified as either requirements risks, technological risks, skills risks or political risks (Fowler and Scott, 1997). This is called risk identification which includes approaches such as use of checklists, decision analysis, examination of assumptions and project tasks dependency analysis.

Checklists One popular approach to identification of project risks is to use a checklist of typical risk areas to the project and asking whether these risks are likely to be significant with respect to the project or not. The checklist is likely, at a minimum, to contain items relating to staff, schedules, budget, technology utilized and the degree of difficulty and complexity of the project. Checklists are dynamic documents and, as new risks are identified, they should be added to the existing ones.

Decision analysis Another popular approach to identification of project risks is to identify and analyze how decisions that impact the project have been taken. A wrong decision, or one taken for the wrong reason, is likely to contribute to an exposure to the risk.

Examination of assumptions This approach requires the identification and analysis of the assumptions underpinning the project and the degree of optimism or simplicity by which they have been made. Each over-optimistic or simplistic assumption defines a potential risk area. Some examples in the object-oriented development environment include:

- software to be reused will not require rework
- development cost per class is a constant
- associated classes (or packages) will be available when needed.

Project tasks dependency analysis This approach requires the analysis of the project CPM chart and to identify high fan-in and high fan-out nodes. These nodes are potential sources of project schedule risk. The problem with a high fan-in node is that if any one of its input activities slips, the output activity slips. With a high fan-out node, a slip of the input activity(ies) causes a large number of subsequent activities to slip. The effects of such slippage may be even more serious if these nodes are on the critical path.

ANALYSIS OF RISK

Having identified project risks, it becomes important to analyze their impact on the project as, due to the fact that resources are often limited, it is only the sufficiently critical risks that should be mitigated against. The concept of risk exposure (RE) is a fundamental concept that assists in doing so.

Risk exposure is closely related to the two concepts of probability of unsatisfactory outcome: $P(u)$, and the value of the loss the project will sustain should the outcome be unsatisfactory: $L(u)$. Thus:

$$\text{RE} = P(u) * L(u). \tag{A.2}$$

Note that it is always possible to reduce the risk exposure but this will be at a cost. Facing the 'law of diminishing returns', we must stop somewhere. Calculating the risk reduction leverage (RRL) will assist in determining when to stop spending resources on risk exposure (RE) reduction. Risk reduction leverage is defined as:

$$\text{RRL} = (\text{RE}_{\text{before}} - \text{RE}_{\text{after}})/\text{Risk reduction costs} \tag{A.3}$$

where $\text{RE}_{\text{before}}$ and RE_{after} refer to the risk exposure before and risk exposure after the employment of the risk reduction activity concerned, respectively.

Technique usage

One useful approach to risk management is the one developed by the Software Engineering Institute (SEI). As reported by Williams *et al.* (1997), this approach is based on the 'plan-do-check-act' paradigm, the spirit of which is captured in their Risk Management Cycle shown in Figure A.45. A more specific model of the SEI risk management approach highlights a program that involves customers, suppliers and the risk management team. This model places the major risk management element of 'sponsorship' and the various critical risk management activities of:

- risk evaluation
- continuous risk management
- conduct of risk clinics and
- team risk management

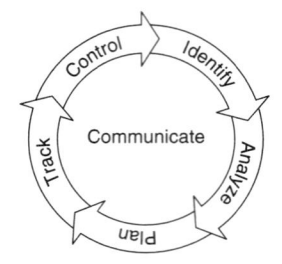

Figure A.45 The SEI risk management paradigm (after Williams *et al.*, 1997).

into a logical sequence that may be instantiated by development organizations. A typical instantiation requires

- identification
- evaluation
- classification and
- prioritization

of new risks and the

- planning
- tracking and
- review and adjustment

of risks and their associated mitigation plans. A central risk and mitigation database forms the backbone of such instantiation.

As mentioned above, risk identification may be achieved by various means including use of checklists. One such checklist can be found as an integral part of RAMP. Developed by Mitre Corporation (Garvey *et al.*, 1997), RAMP is a risk management information system that provides automated support for identification, analysis and sharing of risk mitigation experience. 'RiskCheck!' is the component that allows identification of risks within a project.

A risk spreadsheet (Figure A.46) can help to summarize and prioritize risks through the utilization of a simple ordinal scale of probability and impact. A risk information sheet (Figure A.47) will help with documentation and monitoring risk mitigation effort. The mitigation status report uses information in the database to indicate the current status of the mitigation action taken. It uses color to indicate the degree of effectiveness of the project personnel action in the management of the risk.

Deliverables and outputs (post-condition)

Risk management plan, risk management database.

CORE TECHNIQUES 303

Risk ID	Risk statement	Priority	Probability	Impact	Assigned to	Status	Red flag
9	Potenial slip in module translation schedule; will impact rest of system coding.	1	H	H	Smith	Mitigate	Red
99	Allocation of development hardware to sites doesn't match needs; delivery of modules from sites will be delayed.	2	H	H	Smith	Mitigate	Red
91	Display performance requirements not quantified; won't know if we'll pass acceptance testing.	3	H	H	Jones	Mitigate	
10	Integration Lab Time may not be sufficient, integration and test will be delayed or cut short.	4	H	M	Brown	Mitigate	
89	Contract authorities from different countries have different program objectives; may cause conflicts in priorities.	5	M	H	Jones	Mitigate	
1	Potential slip in module translation schedule; will impact rest of system coding.	6	H	H	Smith	Mitigate	
94	System impact of YYY display/timing/interface problems is not known; planned fix schedule may not have taken all issues into accout.	7	H	M	Brown	Mitigate	
88	Government furnished equipment does not work; test schedule may be in jeopardy if GFE not repaired or replaced by the time testing begins.	8	H	M	Smith	Mitigate	
96	Potential slip in module translation schedule; will impact rest of system coding.		M	M			
13	Compiler bugs require vendor fixes (which may not come quickly enough); could delay coding.		L	M			
...							
87	New coders don't all have tool documentation; impacts their schedules to go looking for answers.		L	L			

(Top n (=8) risks indicated on left side of table, spanning rows 9 through 88.)

Figure A.46 A risk spreadsheet can help work groups summarize risk information for a number of risks. It shows the probability and impact of individual risks using a simple high (H), medium (M), low (L) rating system to establish the top n list. The 'red flag' category indicates that the mitigation plan is not working and that action is required (after Williams et al., 1997).

Role assignment Star rating ***

Focus: Team building
Typical tasks for which this is needed: Choose project team
Related techniques: Team building
Input (pre-condition): Team members
Underpinning concepts: Team structures

304 CORE TECHNIQUES

ID	ABC 23	**Risk Information Sheet**	**Identified** 3/2/98
Priority	6	**Statement**	
Probability	High	With our lack of experience in X Windows software, we may not be able to complete the GUI code on time and it may not be the quality of code we need.	
Impact	High		
Timeframe	Near	**Origin** G. Smith	**Class** Personnel Experience	**Assigned to:** S. Jones

Context
The graphical user interface is an important part of the system and we do not have anyone trained in the X Window system. We all have been studying it, but it is complex and only one person in the group has any graphic/user interface experience and that was with a completely different type of system and interface requirements. There are other personnel within the company who have relevant experience and training, but they may not be available in time to support this project.

Mitigation Strategy
1. Update coding estimates and schedules to reflect the need for increased training and for hiring an expert in X Windows (changes due 5/1/98).
2. Coordinate with customer and get approval for changing schedule (approve by 6/15/98).
3. Identify an available expert from other projects in this division (hired by 6/15/98).
4. Bring in outside training source for current programmers (training complete by (7/30/98).

Contingency Plan and Trigger
Plan: Subcontract GUI development to LMN Corp. and accept the increase in our cost, $25,000. LMN has a level of effort contract with ABC Headquarters and can support with 1 week notice.
Trigger: If internal expert is not on board and training not completed by 7/30/98.

Status	**Status Date**
GUI code delivered on time, required quality.	1/30/99
GUI code has been delivered for testing on shedule.	11/13/98
Code 50% complete and 1 week ahead of schedule.	9/15/98
Personnel completed 2 week training; will monitor progress and quality of work.	7/15/98
Brown from project XYZ will be available on 6/5/98 to provide quality assurance, mentoring, and critical path programs.	6/1/98
Customer approved revised schedule milestones.	5/3/98
	4/23/98

Approval	**Closing Date**	**Closing Rationale**
J. Q. Jones, ABC Project Manager	2/15/99	Code delivered on time, Acceptance test excellent. Risk is gone.

Figure A.47 A risk information sheet can help you document and monitor risk mitigation plans (after Williams *et al.*, 1997).

Technique description

People playing different roles require different skills and different ongoing training (see Subtask: Develop education and training plan in Graham *et al.*, 1997b). Locating those team members requires identification of role responsibilities, educational background and basis for performance evaluation.

Technique usage

Roles within an object-oriented development team overlap and extend traditional team roles (Figure A.48) – nineteen are identified by Goldberg and Rubin (1995, page 493). The ten most significant roles are:

- analysis prototyper – who develops executable prototypes during analysis, which are then used to evaluate the requirements
- design prototyper – who develops executable prototypes during design. The design prototyper is seen as 'the designer's pragmatic conscience'
- object coach – who is a general resource. This person probably has the skills and experience to become the reuse engineer and is clearly an object champion
- object technology expert – who provides expertise at various levels, has a strategic role and can recommend on both technological and management implications of object technology
- framework designer – who is responsible for reuse at the framework level
- reuse administrator – who is responsible for identifying and acquiring reusable assets for the corporate or project library
- reuse evaluator – who is the quality control administrator for the reuse process lifecycle
- reuse engineer – who is responsible for creating and maintaining reusable assets. He/she must be able to locate, retrieve, understand and use these assets if required to do so
- reuse librarian – who is responsible for the classification and storage of new reusable assets
- reuse manager – who is responsible overall for reuse in terms of policies, certification approaches and liaison with other managers on reuse issues.

Other useful roles, identified by, for example, McGibbon (1995, page 132) are:

- mentor – a guide and counselor, often external
- methodologist – like the object coach but focused on method issues
- tool builder – developing productivity enhancing tools for internal use
- tester – an equivalent to a traditional tester but with OO skills in testing
- user interface controller – similar to the framework builder but focused on the usability of the interface, and
- documentor – focusing not only on written/printed documentation (OPEN places great emphasis on production and provision of documentation), but also on developing on-line help systems.

306   CORE TECHNIQUES

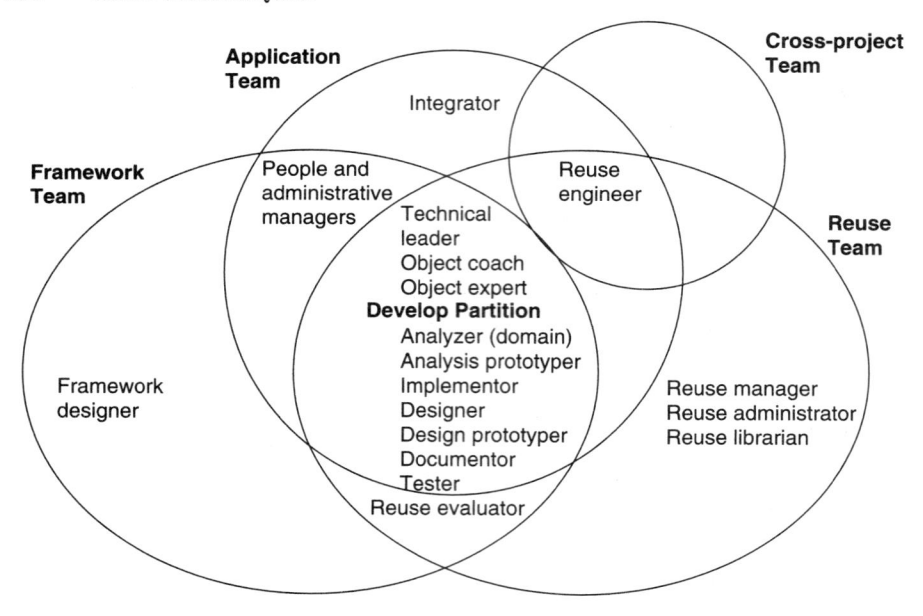

Figure A.48   Teams and overlapping roles (after Goldberg and Rubin, 1995).

Diagram labels:
- **Application Team**: Integrator
- **Cross-project Team**
- **Framework Team**: Framework designer
- **Reuse Team**: Reuse manager, Reuse administrator, Reuse librarian
- People and administrative managers
- Reuse engineer
- Technical leader, Object coach, Object expert
- **Develop Partition**: Analyzer (domain), Analysis prototyper, Implementor, Designer, Design prototyper, Documentor, Tester
- Reuse evaluator

An important role identified by both Unhelkar (1995a) and Williams (1995) is that of the technical writer whose full-time responsibility is the preparation and maintenance of all (paper) documentation.

Goldberg and Rubin (1995, page 296) suggest three principal characteristics should be evaluated: talent, motivation and interpersonal skills. Generally team players should be preferred, although they note that exceptions can be made for *outstanding* talent.

Organizations who simply select team members without due selection procedures are taking a high risk approach. Invitations for applications to join an OO team at least reveals the level of motivation – but not talent. A team of highly motivated but unqualified people is more likely to fail than to succeed. Rather, Goldberg and Rubin (1995) urge, the team should be built up by proactively seeking people who either have or can learn the skills needed to fulfil the team roles. Evaluation of skills (or potential skills) can be accomplished by teaching a simple OO course and evaluating who 'gets it'. Or get them to perform a job-related task to assess their performance in a small-scale version of the real thing.

Other organizations use personality or communication-ability evaluation; although a team can, and should, contain many personalities that sometimes conflict whilst overall contributing significantly to the successful outcome of the team effort.

Hiring external team members, such as expert consultants, requires some careful groundwork. Many give public presentations which you could attend; many previous employers will give honest references; but evaluate each on his/her own merits, not on the merits of the organization for which they work (Goldberg and Rubin, 1995, page 298).

Deliverables and outputs (post-condition)

Recommendations for roles and assignment of these roles to individuals in the team.

Role modeling   Star rating *

Focus: Modeling with (temporary) roles that objects play
Typical tasks for which this is needed: Construct the object model, create and/or identify reusable components ('for reuse')
Related techniques: Abstraction utilization, collaborations analysis, relationship modeling
Input (pre-condition): Partial design, user requirements
Underpinning concepts: Abstraction; Classification; Roles

Technique description

A role is a classification subordinate to the main classification of the object which is not permanent. For example, a *PERSON* object plays the role of CHAUFFEUR object in taking his son to school. In fact, a role can be regarded as a partial object encapsulating a specific set of cohesive responsibilities. Including role modeling as part of the toolbox of object modeling techniques offers a slightly different perspective from purely class modeling and object modeling. In OML, there is an icon to represent the ROLE and ROLE is seen as a peer to CLASS, INSTANCE (object) and TYPE in the metamodel (together they are the CIRT (= class, instance, role or type) much discussed in this book). Indeed, OPEN uses the term CIRT because it is sometimes just not clear at an early stage whether the concept we are describing is, in fact, a whole class; or simply a role played by some instances, some of the time; or even just a single instance (a one-off object or singleton – see Gamma *et al.*, 1995). The role icon (the Greek tragedy actor's role mask) represents the very frequently required model of a role in a software design diagram.

Technique usage

Wherever you might use a class icon, or more particularly whenever you might be tempted to invent a subclass or subtype, think carefully if it is a real (and permanent) subtype. If the concept is a true subtype, then use inheritance; but

308   CORE TECHNIQUES

it is really the more temporary role, then use role modeling (and appropriate graphical icons) to represent the concept. In UML, you can use a stereotype. [For further guidelines and advice on roles, see the entry in CD: Appendix E.]

Note that in implementation, commercial languages do not support roles directly (although it can be fudged: Renouf and Henderson-Sellers, 1995) – only experimental languages such as Cecil and Kea have this much-needed support.

Deliverables and outputs (post-condition)

The addition to the semantic nets/class diagrams of role icons.

Roleplay   Star rating **

Focus: Interactive discovery of CIRTs
Typical tasks for which this is needed: Identify CIRTs
Related techniques: CRC card modeling, games
Input (pre-condition): Team members
Underpinning concepts: Anthropomorphizing

Technique description

A technique that can be efficacious in both requirements engineering and object identification (and possibly elsewhere) is roleplay. In roleplay, participants take on the mantle of an actor in attempting to replicate the behavior of another entity – another person, a software object.

Technique usage

In using roleplay for requirements engineering, 'getting into the skin' of an end-user may give the systems analyst new insights. Emulating the role of a customer coupled with the knowledge of the analyst can provide for effective and efficient problem solving.

Roleplay is also seen as a component of object identification in one use of CRC cards (q.v.). Here, each team participant 'becomes' an object, animating that object in such a way that questions such as 'What services do I offer to other objects?' can be answered. Roleplay here is equivalent to the frequent exhortation (e.g. Wirfs-Brock *et al.*, 1990) to 'anthropomorphize'. In using CRC cards (q.v.) as a modeling technique, the participants are asked to be that object and act as if the object, if it were brought to life, would act in terms of what the object knows and can do.

Deliverables and outputs (post-condition)

Increased understanding of the problem.

Rule modeling   Star rating *

Focus: Business rules, quality
Typical tasks for which this is needed: Construct the object model, evaluate quality, identify CIRTs
Related techniques: Contract specification
Input (pre-condition): Business requirements (rules, policies and procedures)
Underpinning concepts: Rules

Technique description

A significant part of the processing in a business information system is necessarily dictated by business needs. All business processes are guided and supported by a core set of business policies and rules. In other words, the definition of an information system depends on a set of business policies. Without business policies or rules being identified and documented in the object model, the conceptual modeling task could not be said to have been completed (Henderson-Sellers *et al.*, 1995b). There are thus two foci for rule modeling:

(1) rules as a natural means of expressing business activities and hence the need to capture these and write them down; and
(2) the incorporation of business rules into the object model.

From the developer's perspective, it is important that a modeling methodology should have the facility to document explicitly the business policies and rules (as is done in OPEN) so that they can be reviewed by the users. This documentation should be at a high level and be encapsulated in the classes to which the policy statements apply.

Technique usage

Business rules can be defined as 'declarations of policy of conditions that must be satisfied' (OMG, 1988). They are expressed in natural language often as IF THEN constructs. However, it should be noted (Rubin *et al.*, 1994) that not all IF THEN structures represent rules. For example,

> IF proof of identity is a bank card or a credit card
> THEN it is acceptable

is not a rule, since a rule must have two (or more) alternative outcomes.
    Odell (1993) notes that 'rules do not just reflect the business, they *are* the business'. He categorizes business rules as constraint rules (which specify policies or conditions) and derivation rules (for inferring or computing facts from other facts). For example, in the latter category we might have

> *The profit is calculated as follows*
> $profit = cash\ received - expenses$ (see also Graham, 1995a, page 252).

310   CORE TECHNIQUES

The business policies and rules form an integral part in the analysis of the behavioral aspect of an object (Graham, 1995a). They lay down the assumptions, guidelines and contractual obligations of an object in providing services in a system (Waldén and Nerson, 1995). These rules determine the scheduling of an event and/or the triggering of a state transition.

Business policy statements should be defined by the users in their own language within their own context. They should be declarative and at a high level, as close to the users' own language as possible. However, it is unfortunate that, in most information systems, these rules are not properly declared or as well documented as they should be. Instead, they are transformed into programming code for execution. As a result, these sets of business rules are scattered around in various program modules and hidden from the users who originally defined them and who will be the ones most likely to request changes in the future.

One of the ways to incorporate business rules in an object model is by way of conditions under which a service could be utilized by others. Meyer (1992c) introduced the contracting metaphor to object-oriented construction of software. A contract represents the obligations and the benefits resulting from an interaction (i.e. use of a service) between the client class and the supplier class. It applies to each service within a class by the use of pre- and post-conditions and to the class as a whole by the use of class invariants. The contract thus stipulates a number of conditions for which a service will perform its function and returns the results of that service (see also Henderson-Sellers and McKim, 1994). The concern of the developer is how this contracting concept can be incorporated into the building of an object model (a focus of MOSES and also of BON).

Deliverables and outputs (post-condition)

Documentation on OOAD for business rules.

Scenario classes – see Scenario development

Scenario development   Star rating **

Focus: Dynamic modeling
Typical tasks for which this is needed: Construct the object model
Related techniques: Collaborations analysis
Input (pre-condition): User requirements
Underpinning concepts: Scenarios, Task scripts and Use cases

Technique description

In OO scenario development, a model is created to represent the system functionality as depicted by the interactions the user has with the system. Each interaction is described by a use case or task script (see CD: Appendix E for full details). A scenario describes an individual's interaction with the system whilst a use case describes the same interaction but at the 'class' level. Task scripts describe user interactions at a higher, business-focused level of abstraction. The user, represented by an actor (it is the user's role that is important not the user *per se*), interacts with the system in one or more ways. Each scenario (use case or task script) is described by free text which can later be represented by a sequence diagram.

A scenario represents a goal of the user. Each goal is depicted as a single scenario so that for functionality with two possible end points (success or failure), two scenarios are needed, i.e. a single scenario is a single, individual thread of control through the system (Cockburn, 1997a) – a point disputed by Rumbaugh (1994) who permits 'choices, iterations and parameters'. Indeed, another, more useful, view on a use case is as a system level responsibility (q.v.), particularly a responsibility for doing.

Technique usage

The process of developing scenarios (here using scenario as a generification of, primarily, task scripts and use cases, i.e. short for scenario class) is essentially one of interviewing the business user to identify possible interactions. Initially scenarios (as task scripts or use cases) should be developed for a 'typical' interaction and only later extended to cover abnormal or error conditions. All scenarios should be significantly different; minor differences may be recorded within the same scenario.

Identify the required functionality of the system by constructing a use case diagram (Figure A.49). For each scenario, the details are described in text first. From these sentences, grammatical objects become CIRTs and the verbs are actions on them, viz. services offered by them. The subjects of the sentences are likely to represent collaborators.

Based on experience of applying use cases in an industrial setting, Jaaksi (1998) suggests 'ten commandments' for more effective scenarios:

(1) the most important functional requirements must be specified
(2) a use case describes something of which the designer can be proud and for which the customer is willing to pay
(3) a use case depicts a typical system usage – but nothing more
(4) a use case is a play
(5) a use case is structured to have a beginning, a middle and an end
(6) a use case is like an essay written by an elementary school student
(7) a use case fits on one page

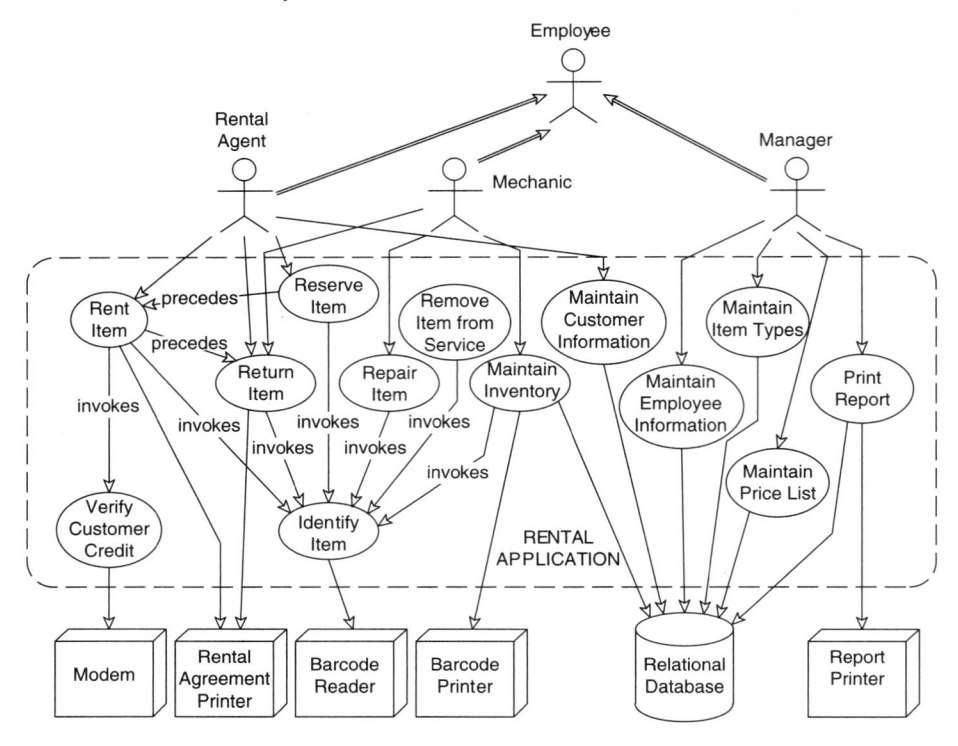

Figure A.49 Example use case diagram in COMN for a rental management application (after Firesmith *et al.*, 1997).

(8) a use case is loud and clear

(9) customers and software designers can both sign off the use case

(10) a use case can be used in system development and system testing.

In truth, using scenarios to identify CIRTs is naïve and simplistic – certainly useful but not sufficient (see Technique: CIRT identification for further details). However, scenarios are also *very* useful in usability (and other types of) testing (see also Bilow, 1995).

Deliverables and outputs (post-condition)

Use case or task script diagram(s). Text for each individual scenario (task script or use case). Possible depiction as sequence diagram(s).

Screen painting Star rating ** (author W. Harridge)

Focus: User interface
Typical tasks for which this is needed: Design user interface
Related techniques: Dialog design in UI, RAD
Input (pre-condition): Need for improved UI
Underpinning concepts: Usability

Technique description

The screen painting technique has been in use from the earliest days of computer screens, originally developed for the implementation of 'forms' for character cell terminals, now almost exclusively used for the development of graphical user interfaces (GUIs) in which the user 'paints a screen' in terms of graphically laying out the elements of the interface. Screen painting tools are often known by the following aliases: form managers, UI builders, UI toolkits, window builders, and various other names based around the themes of user interface, windows and construction. Screen painting is generally made available as an integrated component of most rapid application development (RAD) and 'visual programming' environments.

Typically a screen painter will offer the following features:

- a comprehensive pallette of 'widgets' (menus, text boxes, radio buttons, etc.) from which the screen layout can be developed relatively quickly
- editing functions (e.g. cut, paste, drag and drop) to assist the developer in development of the layout
- facilities to create a composition hierarchy of widgets to implement a screen design
- widget classes with a multitude of attributes and operations to manipulate the appearance and behavior of widgets at run time
- generation of skeletal code for handling the events generated by the widgets in response to user actions.

In addition some screen painters will also provide:

- cross platform (hardware and operating system) development facilities
- plotting and graphing features
- prototyping support, allowing the developed screen to be tested within the tool environment.

Technique usage

In an OO system, the icons painted on to the screen represent library objects with their queries and commands. This means that the GUI builder must be well-linked to the class libraries – a situation not that frequently encountered

(Baudoin and Hollowell, 1996, page 173) which leads to some restriction on the usefulness of existing GUI builders in an OO development environment. Notwithstanding, screen painters are increasingly being implemented in an OO language and their components described by comprehensive inheritance and composition structures, although the UI 'widgets' do not often map logically to the classes of the application domain.

Valaer and Babb (1997) detail the criteria for selection of an appropriate UI development tool and also list a range of products available.

Deliverables and outputs (post-condition)

Screens for UI.

Screen scraping Star rating ** (author W. Harridge)

Focus: Interfacing to legacy applications
Typical tasks for which this is needed: Code, integrate with existing non-OO systems
Related techniques: Application scavenging, interfacing to relational DBMS and legacy code
Input (pre-condition): Existing, non-OO application
Underpinning concepts: Wrappers

Technique description

Often when a new application is being developed there is an essential requirement to utilize facilities already provided by an existing ('legacy') application. A screen scraper can fulfil this need by providing both 'screen' data capture facilities and keystroke input to emulate the interaction a human operator would normally have with the legacy application and also provide an interface to the new application (typically via an API). Essentially a screen scraper is a 'smart' terminal emulator, minimally consisting of a terminal emulation part where a representation of the 'screen' is held in memory and a scripting part to control input to the legacy application and return of data from the 'screen' representation ('scraping') back to the controlling application.

Technique usage

While screen scraping is not an intrinsically OO technique it can be used to enable legacy applications to present an OO like interface to the new application components.

Screen scraping is not generally considered to be an ideal technique for 'wrapping' legacy applications, but is often used as an interim measure until a legacy application can be replaced.

The screen scraping technique has the following advantages:

- enables access to legacy data where the underlying data structures are inaccessible directly or are indecipherable except through the legacy application
- preserves the security, validation and business rules inherent in the legacy application
- requires no changes to legacy application code (often the source code is unavailable for various reasons)
- can provide integration of multiple legacy applications and present a uniform interface to the end user
- through scripting, can enable sophisticated workflow management for multiple applications.

The inherent disadvantages of a screen scraping implementation are:

- for a legacy application which is still undergoing evolution, both the legacy application and the screen scraping software will need to be maintained and kept in synchronization
- inefficiency when compared with an application programming interface (API) implementation (if this was available)
- may not allow evolution of business rules and processes, compared to an implementation which has direct access to the legacy data
- can be complex to program. Often legacy applications may behave in a 'bizarre' manner with which a human operator can readily cope, although dealing with this behavior within a scripting language may be difficult.

Commercial screen scraping products can provide the following features:

- pattern matching of any data which would normally appear on the 'screen' to enable event generation or conditional control of the screen scraper
- scripting to provide screen navigation, error trapping and data entry to the legacy application
- event generation based on data presented on the 'screen', cursor position or video attributes (e.g. reverse video, blinking, etc.)
- Support for emulation of multiple character cell terminal types, e.g. IBM 3270, 5250, Digital VTxxx, TTY, etc.
- support for emulation of multiple GUI environments (Motif, Microsoft Windows)
- support for multiple communication protocols for connexion of the screen scraper to the legacy application, e.g. Telnet, SNA, DEC LAT, etc.
- implemented either in a desktop environment or in a server environment acting as 'middleware' between the legacy application and the desktop application

316   CORE TECHNIQUES

- application programming interface (API) allowing access to the screen scraper component from the new application directly or via object request brokers (ORBs) (q.v.) or other middleware.

Deliverables and outputs (post-condition)

Interface between new system and legacy system.

Scripting – see Scenario development

Security requirements (DBMS) – see Database authorization

Service identification   Star rating ***

Focus: Delineating responsibilities/services offered
Typical tasks for which this is needed: Construct the object model, create and/or identify reusable components ('for reuse')
Related techniques: Collaborations analysis, CRC card modeling, responsibility identification
Input (pre-condition): CIRTS, with their responsibilities identified
Underpinning concepts: Collaborations; Responsibilities and Responsibility-Driven Design; Services

Technique description

Services implement responsibilities (q.v.). Once responsibilities have been identified, these should be translated to services. Services may describe behavior (a.k.a. operations or commands) or properties (a.k.a. query or as an attribute[†] in UML), i.e. may have a signature which returns no object or one which returns an object of a stated type. Services are thus visible characteristics and each service then crosses the boundary of an object to be implemented by a method or attribute internal to the object. The invocation of an operation effects an action, the invocation of a property results in the return of an object to the client (the parallel to a responsibility for doing and a responsibility for knowing). Full background details on services are to be found in CD: Appendix E.

---

† In UML, attribute must be interpreted either as logical attribute when viewed as a property service or, at the implementation stage, as a physical attribute. Visibility (q.v.) annotations in UML are thus important in the necessary differentiation.

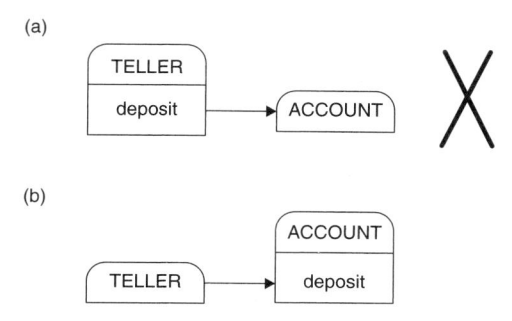

```
                    (a)
                          ┌─────────┐
                          │ TELLER  │
                          ├─────────┤         ╲  ╱
                          │ deposit │──→┌─────────┐  ╲╱
                          └─────────┘   │ ACCOUNT │  ╱╲
                                        └─────────┘ ╱  ╲

                    (b)
                                              ┌─────────┐
                                              │ ACCOUNT │
                          ┌─────────┐         ├─────────┤
                          │ TELLER  │────────→│ deposit │
                          └─────────┘         └─────────┘
```

Figure A.50 Location of individual services can be difficult. They should be identified with the CIRT to which they have the closest affinity on the basis of a semantic analysis (based on Henderson-Sellers and Edwards, 1994a).

Technique usage

When responsibilities have been identified first, translation to services is relatively easy. In other instances, it may be desirable (or the standard project approach may be) to identify services directly as visible characteristics of the CIRT. In this case, we ask what the CIRT can do in terms of behavior or functionality. The CIRT can also be described as possessing properties, which reflect the logical data stored within the CIRT (the physical data, as attributes or associations to other objects should *not* be visible in the interface).

Placing of properties and re-evaluation of properties is part of the iterative development process of OO development, although the model should begin to stabilize after a small number of iterations. As CIRTs become evident, the object modeler will label them with obvious services (properties and operations). This is the beginning of the class specification which will be slowly 'fleshed out', finally to form a complete description of the class interface.

Initial operations may also be derived from the general subsystems' responsibilities. These do not have to be implemented by a single class; they can be divided up between a number of classes if necessary. It is important to try to take on the role of a class and continually ask oneself 'can I do this operation?'. This anthropomorphic view allows the designer to visualize what does and does not belong to a particular class of objects (Wirfs-Brock *et al.*, 1990 – see Technique: CRC card modeling).

Operations may also be found by examining other classes and seeing what operations they may need to request. If, for example, a class A requires class B to be in some state before it can execute an operation, then there should be some way for that class A to request class B to change its state; in other words, class B should provide that operation in its interface.

It is important that services are *services offered* and never services demanded. This is the essence of OT. In other words, if class A sends a message to class B, it is class B that offers a service compatible (in name and character) to the message. Whilst it is tempting to model *TELLER* deposits $100 into my account as in Figure A.50(a), in a correct object model, the verb in the above sentence (deposits) is a service of the grammatically direct object (my account) – as in Figure A.50(b).

Deliverables and outputs (post-condition)

Static architectures in which the properties and operations (services) are increasingly being 'fleshed out'. At each (planned) iteration, the diagrams representing the CIRTs will have more detail in terms of the interfacial elements identified by this technique.

Simulation Star rating ***

Focus: Simulation experimentation for many purposes
Typical tasks for which this is needed: Define problem and establish mission and objectives, evaluate quality, identify CIRTs, identify user requirements, test, undertake usability design
Related techniques: CRC card modeling, games, roleplay
Input (pre-condition): Requirements
Underpinning concepts: Modeling assists understanding

Technique description

Simulation is modeling in motion. It is useful in evaluating what-if scenarios by showing the *dynamic* response of the system (over time) to some pre-determined response.

Technique usage

Simulation may be used to show message passing sequences in static (architecture) diagrams or to evaluate the dynamics of a business in a BPR exercise.

Simulation is also at the very root of OO since the very first manifestation of OO resides in the 30-year-old simulation modeling language, Simula. It is also important to recognize that in creating a simulation model/environment, as in any modeling exercise, abstraction and granularity (q.v.) will be very important techniques. Simulations use models *at a stated and pre-determined* level of abstraction. Simplifications have to be made. Which simplifications are appropriate are determined by the context, resolution and skill of the simulation modeler. The major question in interpreting the results from simulation models is whether their output is relevant to the problem under investigation, at an appropriate scale/resolution/granularity and whether the removal of specific elements, perhaps in simplifying a more complex model, are justified or whether some important element or interaction has been unjustly eliminated or ignored.

Deliverables and outputs (post-condition)

Increasing understanding.

SMART goals Star rating **

Focus: Personal goal setting
Typical tasks for which this is needed: Specify individual goals
Related techniques: PSP
Input (pre-condition): Individuals aiming for self-improvement
Underpinning concepts: Goal setting can provide motivation

Technique description

SMART goals are (Blanchard and Johnson, 1983; McGibbon, 1995, pages 229–230):

- **S**pecific: is it clearly understandable?
- **M**easurable: what would a good (and a bad) job look like?
- **A**ttainable: is it realistic for the individual?
- **R**elevant: will it make any impact?
- **T**rackable: how will anyone know?

In addition, setting of SMART goals requires a statement on the associated timeframe. In other words, setting goals must be done over a realistic and attainable timescale.

Technique usage

Setting SMART goals requires three stages (McGibbon, 1995, page 146):

(1) identifying the objective and areas of responsibility
(2) specification of priorities
(3) detailing of at least three ways in which success can be measured.

Stage 1 not only identifies what is to be done and by whom, but also the deadline. In Stage 3, at least three measurements must be identified. Examples might include percentage of classes deemed reusable (on the basis of your organizational reuse guidelines); classes of a stated defect level; and prototype delivery deadlines met. For each measurable characteristic selected, some thresholds must be identified as to what value of the measured characteristic can be called acceptable and what outstanding.

SMART goal setting, augmented by PSP (q.v.), helps to improve both individual and, subsequently, team performance perhaps evaluated by the ability

320   CORE TECHNIQUES

to meet timebox deadlines, to deliver with small defect rates, to react flexibly to change/enhancement requests from the user/client.

Deliverables and outputs (post-condition)

Set of SMART goals.

Social systems analysis   Star rating *

Focus: Management, Decision making
Typical tasks for which this is needed: Obtain business approval
Related techniques: Pistols at dawn, political systems analysis, viewpoints
Input (pre-condition): Some understanding of the stakeholders and their viewpoints
Underpinning concepts: Sociological aspects of software development should not be ignored

Technique description

We define a social system as the pattern of interactions between the stakeholders in a society. For present purposes, this society is the client organization and its employees and customers, for whom the object-oriented software system is being developed. Social systems analysis is a core term describing a variety of approaches used to elicit the pattern of interactions between the business stakeholders, such as observing the behavior of clients, or discerning the roles they play or positions they seek to attain during debate. The analyst is advised to record and model any such social behavior observed using Vickers' (1965) and Checkland and Scholes' (1990) three-part model:

- roles: social position recognized as significant by people in the problem situation
- norms: expected behavior which characterizes roles, and
- values: local standards used to judge the performance of a particular individual or individuals performing a role (Vickers, 1965; Checkland and Scholes, 1990).

Technique usage

It is extremely unlikely that an analyst could elicit the necessary information from clients directly by interviewing them because clients may be unaware of their social agendas, or they may deliberately conceal them when questioned directly. Instead, this information should be captured as a side-task during other activities. The analyst should be aware of the effect of social and political (q.v.) status on the successful integration of a software system into a business. The following list represents some helpful areas of concern to the analyst as he or she tries to compose a social picture of the situation:

- What structures exist? And why?
- How firm are these structures? And why?
- What policies exist?
- How firm are these policies? And why?
- Who has instituted these policies? When? And why?
- What rewards and reward systems are instituted? When? And why?
- What penalties exist? When? And why?
- What are the formal and informal norms of behavior?
- What levels of conformity are expected?
- Does this change with respect to the levels of the hierarchy? How?

Understanding the social interaction climate, including that of political interaction, is critical for identification of 'real' requirements, resolution of conflict and development of models of the system that accommodates various viewpoints. Political systems, politics and power plays are one related and very important aspect of such interaction and as such are worthy of separate study and attention (see Technique: Power analysis). However, not all social interaction should be viewed from a power struggle viewpoint. An understanding of norms, organizational culture and values, particularly the last two, will assist the requirements engineer to potentially gain a better understanding of what issues are important, why and for whom, and similarly what potential solutions have a greater likelihood of being accepted.

Deliverables and outputs (post-conditions)

Understanding of stakeholder social systems and interactions.

Specialization inheritance – see Generalization and inheritance identification

Specification inheritance (subtyping) – see Generalization and inheritance identification

Standards compliance Star rating ** (author B. Unhelkar)

Focus: How to meet national and international standards
Typical tasks for which this is needed: Evaluate quality
Related techniques: Metrics collection
Input (pre-condition): Embryonic project and quality plans
Underpinning concepts: Need for quality

Technique description

This technique is aimed at ensuring that the project complies with accepted standards. A non-exclusive list of standards that the project needs to comply with includes:

- project management standards (project plans, meeting guidelines, tracking and reporting progress, organizational structures)
- documentation standards (user guides, technical documentation, help files)
- modeling (inclusive of design) standards (system architecture, component designs, notations for designs)
- coding standards (C++/Smalltalk/Eiffel standards within the project, indentation, coloring, naming of attributes, functions)
- testing standards (test structures, test harness layouts, usage of automated tools, regression testing).

Technique usage

Each area of the project needs to be considered in the light of these identified standards, in order that the project complies with them. In order to do that, the manager has to ensure that the standards are available and are sufficiently understood by the people concerned. For example, it is essential that a programmer has the coding standards available to him/her all the time and understands how they are being used within the project. Similarly, a technical writer must be fully cognizant of the documentation standards for the project and should be able to produce documents that comply with the standard. Once the participants are aware of the standards, and start using them knowledgeably, it is essential to cross-check the compliance at the end of every iteration of the project lifecycle. If the project is complex and has been divided into subsystems, then the compliance checkpoint will be at the end of an iteration of a subsystem development. This compliance, at the very beginning, can be performed visually by checking the project plan, or the code written against the standard specified. For large and complex projects, the review sessions (including inspections and walkthroughs, q.v.) at appropriate times in the development process can provide valuable checkpoints for standards compliance.

Deliverables and outputs (post-condition)

All deliverables produced at the end of each phase of the development process are affected by the standards compliance technique; for example, project plans, designs and test reports at the end of their respective phases in development.

A standards compliance report may also be produced, essentially specifying the areas of lack of compliance and which need further work before they are fully compliant. This report may be in numbered point form to facilitate ease of work and cross-checking towards attaining a final compliance.

State modeling Star rating ***

Focus: Dynamic modeling
Typical tasks for which this is needed: Construct the object model
Related techniques: Relationship modeling
Input (pre-condition): Requirements, class/package diagrams
Underpinning concepts: State machines

Technique description

Objects have state. State is represented by the current values of all attributes, associations and aggregations. Changes of state occur when a message, acting as a trigger, is received which alters one of these values. Any change of state thus engendered is a *transition*. A transition is regarded as instantaneous, whereas an object remains in a specific state for some duration.

Modeling state is thus focused at the granularity of a single object or, since all objects in a given class are represented by the same state machine, at the class level. Each state machine (q.v.) is thus affixed to one and only one class, whereas the converse is not necessarily true. It is arguable whether it is better to permit a class to have several state machines (conceptually permissible) or whether to model these as a single 'and-ed' state machine. In either case, multiple or concurrent states can be successfully modeled. On the other hand, classes with very simplistic state changes (e.g. ON → OFF → ON) are seldom documented by the use of state modeling – which is basically overkill in such situations.

Technique usage

For each class with 'interesting' states, construct a state machine (q.v.) using a selected notation, e.g. UML, COMN, Embley *et al.* (1992). Identify triggers from other diagrammatic views of the system which show message passing – messages in these diagrams are the triggers causing the transitions in the state model. Ensure all states in the state model can be represented as attributes or relationships (particularly associations) in the static architecture model.

The process of developing a state model begins by identifying states applicable to an object. Transitions between these states are then identified based on services that are offered by the object. States should be 'interesting' from the point of view of having some effect on the object behavior.

Deliverables and outputs (post-condition)
State transition diagram for each class with 'interesting' state changes.

State transition diagrams (STDs) – see State modeling

Statistical analysis of data Star rating ***
Focus: Quantitative tools for metrics collected
Typical tasks for which this is needed: Analyze metrics data
Related techniques: Metrics collection
Input (pre-condition): Data for analysis
Underpinning concepts: Statistical theory

Technique description

Statistical techniques are found in a whole range of texts. They are standard and only the most relevant are summarized here.

Statistics may be subdivided into descriptive statistics and inferential statistics. In OPEN, we mostly use descriptive statistics, predominantly in the analysis of metrics data.

The most appropriate descriptive statistics depend significantly on the type of data being collected and analyzed. Whilst most developers tend to think of summary statistics in terms of means and standard deviations, it is critical to note that these measures are only valid for interval or ratio metrics. Most software measures are, on the other hand, on an ordinal scale (see e.g. Zuse, 1990). A regular histogram can be valuable to depict these data and many other discrete (as opposed to continuous) data sets.

Correspondingly, in inferential statistics, only data on interval, ratio and absolute scales can be investigated with classical statistical methods; other data types need robust or nonparametric techniques (e.g. Whitmire, 1997, page 129).

Technique usage

From a data set, simple calculations should be made of central tendency and spread. For interval, ratio or absolute data, means or averages can be calculated together with standard deviations (or its square, the variance). For ordinal data, modes (most commonly occurring value) and medians (mid-point values) are most appropriate.

CORE TECHNIQUES

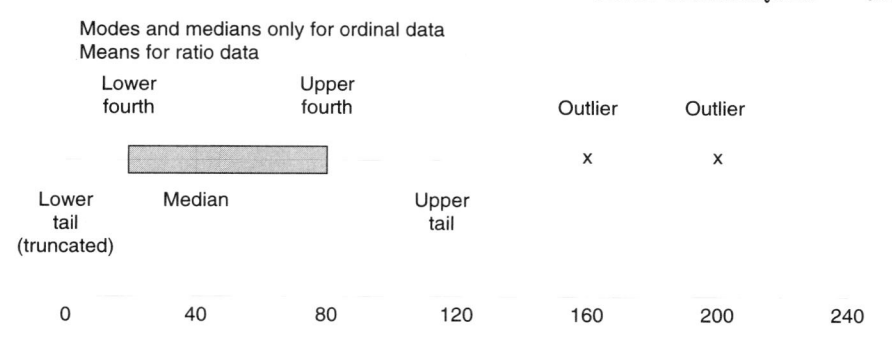

```
Modes and medians only for ordinal data
Means for ratio data
      Lower              Upper
      fourth             fourth                  Outlier    Outlier

                  ┌──────────────┐                  x          x
                  │░░░░░░░░░░░░░░│
                  └──────────────┘
      Lower       Median          Upper
      tail                        tail
      (truncated)


      0       40      80      120     160     200     240
```

Figure A.51 Box–whisker diagram for the display of data, particularly those collected on ordinal scales.

Summary statistics may be displayed as frequencies or histograms. Box–whisker plots (Figure A.51) are also a very useful way of depicting medians and quartiles (when means are inappropriate). They show the ranges, often with obvious outliers shown separately, and the quartiles. The length of the box compared to the whiskers indicates the degree of central tendency, and the centrality of the mode with respect to the range indicates the degree of skew.

It is also important that the precision of the data collected is well known to all those handling the statistics. As well as the errors implicit in any measurement technique, it is also important to keep the same degree of precision throughout the process: the precision of data collection should match the precision of the conclusions that you wish to draw. You cannot measure staff time in months and declare results to the nearest day; conversely, measuring staff time in seconds with the planning intention of reporting on person-months of effort is a waste of time if the acceptable error bars on the final result are several days (Goldberg and Rubin, 1995, page 463).

If you correlate together two data sets *do* remember that a positive correlation (at *whatever* significance level) is only indicative. It needs an underlying *model* before any causation can be implied.

Deliverables and outputs (post-condition)

Statistical analysis of data set currently under investigation.

Stereotyping   Star rating *

Focus: Typical object behavior
Typical tasks for which this is needed: Construct the object model
Related techniques: Abstraction utilization, revision of inheritance hierarchies
Input (pre-condition): Class diagrams, evolving design
Underpinning concepts: Classification and Partitions; Discriminant; Stereotypes

Technique description

A stereotype is a metasubtype which creates a partition of all objects in the extension of the parent type. It thus provides a named grouping. For instance, a *pen* object may be stereotyped by the label {*entity object*}. Whilst each group in the partition can be given an additional name (its stereotype), there is no real difference in responsibilities between the members of this stereotyped group and the 'parent' CIRT. The stereotypes thus represent partitions and not a true subtyping relationship (since a subtype would be expected to be just like its parent but with additional responsibilities). Stereotypes are thus used as an additional label to facilitate understanding throughout the OOAD process. (Further details are to be found in CD: Appendix E).

The idea of a stereotype is stated to be a user-defined partitioning. However, in both UML and COMN a number of suggestions are made for particular predefined stereotypes. The predefined stereotypes for each of the traits help the developer by providing suggestions of useful partitions.

Technique usage

When a CIRT or indeed a relationship needs further clarification, the use of a stereotype should be considered. A stereotype partitions the CIRT or relationship and is indicated by the name of the stereotype in braces in OML or in guillemets in UML.

Having identified the need for a stereotype, consider the pre-determined list of stereotypes in your chosen notation. Consider whether you wish to create a new icon for a stereotype which you find common and useful in your own development. This is permitted in the evolving OMG standard notation.

There is, however, one particular danger of which you need to be aware. Since stereotyping represents partitioning, it is important to be aware that certain stereotypes might overlap each other. Whilst this might be easy to police in your own development, it is likely that in borrowing suggestions from other developers (e.g. by reading the user groups on the net), you might inadvertently create a situation akin to the problem described in the entry on multiple generalization which leads to the need for a discriminant (q.v.) which is essentially a mark of a bad design. In other words, multiple overlapping partitions are not implementable without encountering a combinatorial explosion created around a multiple inheritance (conceptual) hierarchy.

Deliverables and outputs (post-condition)

Added stereotype labels and names to selected CIRTs and/or relationships in the OOAD diagrams, model and documentation.

Storage of derived properties Star rating ***
(major contributor G.C. Low)

Focus: DB strategies for storage
Typical tasks for which this is needed: Design and implement physical database, select database/storage strategy
Related techniques: Access analysis
Input (pre-condition): Database schema
Underpinning concepts: Relational database and objectbase theory

Technique description

In some situations when an operation provides a value that is not stored, the data value may be stored as a property if it is accessed frequently and the time taken for the operation to calculate the value impedes performance (Hawryszkiewycz, 1991). As another option for operations that involve many calculations and intermediate processing, intermediate results may be stored in special libraries for the duration that an object is in memory.

Technique usage

Determine those properties that must be calculated frequently and the time taken for the operation. Where this time may significantly impede performance, consider storing the derived value. Ensure that mechanisms are in place to automatically recalculate the derived value if any of the parameters from which it is derived are changed.

Deliverables and outputs (post-condition)

Addition of stored properties to design.

Storyboarding Star rating ***

Focus: User requirements
Typical tasks for which this is needed: Identify user requirements
Related techniques: Brainstorming, CRC card modeling, interviews, scenario development, workshops
Input (pre-condition): Availability of users
Underpinning concepts: Scenarios, Task Scripts and Use Cases

Technique description

Storyboarding is derived from the motion picture industry whereby a scene is depicted using a sequence of still shots or sketches. It thus provides a thread through the software and is useful for picturing task scripts. As well as the temporal thread, it of course identifies key actors (in both the movie and software sense!). It thus provides a communication vehicle between developers and users and is a fast way to outline high level functionality of a software system. It is often used to develop screen layouts in the context of a use case (IBM, 1997).

Technique usage

A set of storyboards is created to depict stages in each scenario. A drawing (a 'thumbnail sketch') is made of the screen illustrating the state of the screen before the associated scenario commences. Additional sketches are made for subsequent screens that the user would view as the scenario progressed. The suite of drawings thus created depicts the topology and partial content of the user's (external) view of the whole software system (IBM, 1997).

Deliverables and outputs (post-condition)

Identification of actors and scenarios.

Subclassing – see Relationship modeling

Subsystems – see Package construction

Subsystem coordination – see Package coordination

Subsystem identification – see Package construction

Subsystem testing – see Package and subsystem testing

Subtyping – see Relationship modeling

System event modeling – see Event modeling

Systems audit   Star rating ***

Focus: Quality check on system development
Typical tasks for which this is needed: Evaluate quality, undertake in-process review
Related techniques: Inspections, reviews
Input (pre-condition): Completed system
Underpinning concepts: External validation

Technique description

Auditors may be internal or external. An internal auditor reports to an organizational group such as the board of directors. On the other hand, an external auditor serves an external group such as the stockholder or the major creditors.

An internal audit aims to verify the adequacy of the organization's internal controls by checking on the existence and effective operation of the processing controls, i.e. with overall good management practices as opposed to day-by-day operational control. Specific audit areas include (Jackson, 1986) administrative controls, hardware controls, software controls, standards, policies and procedures, error tracking, security/privacy and contingency planning.

An external audit may use similar techniques (see below) but with a different focus, aiming as it does to report on the fairness of the information in the annual financial statements of the organization as reported externally. These audits are more financially focused than the more technology/management focus of the internal audit and may also evaluate the internal auditor's report as part of their duties.

Technique usage

Auditing techniques usually follow a set and agreed methodology; for instance (Institute of Internal Auditors, 1977 as quoted in Jackson, 1986):

(1) define objectives

(2) gather basic information, e.g. using interviews and questionnaires

(3) gather detailed information

(4) evaluate controls

(5) design audit procedures relevant to the organization

(6) perform the audit testing

(7) evaluate the findings and make a report.

Deliverables and outputs (post-condition)

Report detailing inconsistencies between stated plans, processes, controls and quality levels.

Task analysis – see Hierarchical task analysis

Task decomposition – see Hierarchical task analysis

Task modeling – see Scenario development

Team building   Star rating **

Focus: Creating team and maintaining morale
Typical tasks for which this is needed: Choose project team
Related techniques: Role assignment
Input (pre-condition): People (individuals)
Underpinning concepts: Team structures

Technique description

Teams are crucial to developing software. In an OO-focused team, the numbers are smaller than in a traditional team so the team tends to become well-knit and hence it is crucial that the synergy between team members be facilitated and optimized.

Teams may be built for different purposes (see CD: Appendix E on Team Structures) and must be created *within the context of* the specific organizational culture (see, for example, Constantine and Lockwood, 1994).

Technique usage

Team members should be selected for their wide-ranging competencies and skills in object technology, project management and software delivery. Team members should work well together, providing skills across the whole lifecycle – it is no longer adequate for each team member to possess only a single skill since OT is integrative and collaborative requiring *all* team members to have at least some knowledge of the full development process.

As well as specific selection criteria, many organizations find value in organizing retreats at an off-site (often exotic) location in order to facilitate and accelerate the normal processes of on-site team building. Removing people from their normal surroundings when pressures are high, yet within their normal working schedule, is seen by many as an excellent way of building up camaraderie, friendships and loyalties, all necessary for a successfully functioning team.

Deliverables and outputs (post-condition)

A smoothly functioning development team.

Textual analysis Star rating ***

Focus: Identifying CIRTs
Typical tasks for which this is needed: Identify CIRTs
Related techniques: Analysis of judgements
Input (pre-condition): Text (requirements specification)
Underpinning concepts: Abstraction; Classification and Partitions

Technique description

One technique for identifying CIRTs is textual analysis: nouns in the requirements document may indicate potentially useful concepts (Abbott, 1983). Such a list should be regarded as identifying *candidate* CIRTs and can represent intangible as well as tangible nouns. Candidate classes in the model will be those entities that the modeler deems primary within the model boundaries. Those outside the scope should be rejected.

Technique usage

Create a first pass list of potential or candidate CIRTs from the requirements documentation. In particular, look for events, roles played, locations and organizations (Coad and Yourdon, 1991) as well as tangible objects. Mass nouns (e.g. water, air) make poor CIRTs – if you can answer the question 'how many', the candidate CIRT may be useful. Jacobson *et al.* (1992) suggest categorization of CIRTs as (1) interface classes, (2) controller classes and (3) entity classes; whereas Iivari (1991) recommends also (4) user classes, (5) information-type classes (e.g. I/O documents, databases) and (6) classes of abstract technology (i.e. those required solely on technical reasons demanded by implementation decisions).

Having identified *potential* classes, it is often the case that this list contains significant redundancy. It is thus necessary to re-evaluate the list of classes continuously as the analysis is refined. Wirfs-Brock *et al.* (1990) recommend looking for two CIRTs with names which are essentially synonyms (discarding the less descriptive or more abstract CIRT), and to be wary of the use of adjectives as qualifiers (see Technique: Analysis of judgements) which may or may not identify different CIRTs – for example, *paid invoice* and *pending invoice* may be two states of a single CIRT: here *INVOICE*. Sentences involving 'or' in describing a concept should probably be conceptualized as two more candidate CIRTs.

Deliverables and outputs (post-condition)

List of candidate classes, revised to eliminate redundancies etc.

Thresholds   Star rating **

Focus: Decision making based on metrics
Typical tasks for which this is needed: Evaluate quality
Related techniques: Metrics collection, statistical analysis
Input (pre-condition): Metrics data
Underpinning concepts: Metrics are not absolute but are best used as indicators of possible problem areas

Technique description

In collecting metrics data, analyzing and visualizing them, perhaps in histograms, tables or box–whisker diagrams, there is no knowledge of whether the calculated values predict problem areas, e.g. parts of the system which are overly complex, have high coupling, are likely to be less maintainable. In other words, there is seldom any link made between the internal characteristic (typically a variable that is measurable) and the external characteristic (Fenton, 1994; Henderson-Sellers, 1996) – see Figure A.52. Without that model, the best we can do is to use the threshold technique.

Technique usage

For any specific metric, assuming it is formulated in such a way that increasing values of it are regarded as decreasing quality, we can deduce that larger values are more probably indicative of a problem than smaller ones. We thus need to derive a threshold or cutoff value such that higher values are investigated further. This is analogous to the arguments of inferential statistics in which confidence levels and Type I/Type II errors have much the same impact on decision making.

Experience suggests that typical values, as shown in the right-hand column of Table A.22, are:

- for class size, 60 LOC
- for method size, 2.5 LOC

CORE TECHNIQUES

```
                INTERNAL                      EXTERNAL
                OBJECTIVE MEASURE             CHARACTERISTIC
                e.g. size,                    e.g. quality, effort, cost
                structural complexity
```

Figure A.52 A model linking measurement and estimation for internal and external characteristics of software. Measurements of internal measures can be used to estimate external characteristics either by use of correlation (route A) or by use of an underlying model (route B). If internal characteristics cannot be measured directly, they may perhaps be estimated (route C) which in turn can then be used to estimate the external characteristic using correlation techniques (route labeled AC: A following C) (after Henderson-Sellers *et al.*, 1995a).

Table A.22 Recommended thresholds.

Metric	Suspect point	Maximum	Expected value
Class size (LOC)	160	200	55–65
Method size (LOC)	15	15	2.5–3.5
Class coupling	18	24	10–14
Instance variables	8	12	1.8–2.5
Methods per class	40	60	20–28

etc. If values are a small multiple of these expected values, then the developer's attention is drawn to these possibly problematic classes. A 'watch' is placed on the classes. In some cases, exceeding a suspect point may effect action – reaching those maxima (as shown in Table A.22) certainly should. It should also be noted that there is still a (low) probability that a class which exceeds these threshold values may be perfectly OK – but there is a higher probability that it won't! Conversely, we will always fail to notice a low quality class in which, for some reason, these thresholds are not exceeded – again there is a low probability of such occurrences.

In the context of rigorous statistical optimization, thresholds can be notoriously arbitrary. Extensive work undertaken in speech recognition has shown that it is far better to build a statistical model for each speech unit to be recognized (e.g. a phoneme or word) than to rely on yes/no threshold tests on raw measurements taken from input speech. The model parameters are estimated by 'training' with respect to a large set of examples (of spoken speech) for which the correct recognition results are already known. This enables each parameter to 'find its natural level'. When novel speech is presented, the recognizer matches the most likely statistical model with the input.

Thresholds are usually ill-behaved with respect to proper statistics viz. they only contribute in one direction (when 'exceeded'), whereas both negative and positive information may be extracted from statistics (evidence for and evidence against a particular decision).

Deliverables and outputs (post-condition)

Lists of classes being 'watched' and those which should be the target of immediate investigation and quality evaluation.

Throwaway prototyping Star rating ***

Focus: Understanding problem and/or domain
Typical tasks for which this is needed: Define problem and establish mission and objectives, design user interface, obtain business approval, undertake architectural design
Related techniques: Prototyping
Input (pre-condition): User requirements
Underpinning concepts: Prototypes

Technique description

A prototype is generally a hand-crafted, one-off experimental mock-up of the 'real thing' constructed to undergo tests of feasibility, stability etc. In engineering prototypes (e.g. cars, ships, planes), this one-off construction is a proof of concept never intended to be sold. It is thus a throwaway prototype. Thus the terms prototype and throwaway prototype are synonymous in these engineering domains.

It is only in software circles that the word prototype is no longer, *de facto*, a *throwaway* prototype. Indeed, prototyping a software product all too frequently leads to that prototype being later refined to become the final product – hence the need to introduce the term throwaway prototype.

Technique usage

A throwaway prototype should be used to test out hypotheses, to evaluate possibilities and to achieve a rapid, high-level approximate solution to the problem which can be shown to the customer. Often the prototype will be coded in a different language than intended for the final product. Use of Visual Basic for prototyping can be a very effective precursor to a full system written in Smalltalk or C++, for instance.

It is also likely that a throwaway prototype will not be constructed within the constraints of the rigorous application of the methodology but will be more of a 'hacking' environment – quick and dirty, yet fast. Indeed, many authorities recommend using throwaway prototyping in OT rather than regular (evolutionary) prototyping since a throwaway prototype is *clearly* non-commercial – there is no other option than to throw it away.

Deliverables and outputs (post-condition)

Prototype system, together with its evaluation by the users.

Timeboxing   Star rating ***

Focus: Delivery schedules
Typical tasks for which this is needed: Develop timebox plan
Related techniques: Gantt charts
Input (pre-condition): Draft schedule of tasks to be done
Underpinning concepts: On-time delivery is more important than complete (but late) delivery

Technique description

Timeboxing is the application of an absolutely rigid delivery deadline to any part of the software development process. Creating a timebox states that an activity will start at a given time and will have an absolute maximum to its duration. The due deliverables *must* be delivered on the stated data even if full functionality has not been completed.

The advantage of timeboxing is that clients know reliably when the next version of the software will be shipped; and suppliers will receive intermediate-stage feedback on the product from the user. The disadvantage is that the shipped product may not yet completely satisfy *all* user requirements.

Technique usage

As part of the planning process, agree timelines and immutable delivery dates. Inform customers of these dates. Deliver the current, working version on the stated data even if it does not yet meet 100 per cent of the user's requirements.

Deliverables and outputs (post-condition)

Current working version of system and its documentation.

Time-threads Star rating **

Focus: Concurrency
Typical tasks for which this is needed: Code, construct the object model
Related techniques: Intelligent agent identification
Input (pre-condition): Partial design
Underpinning concepts: Concurrency and time-threading

Technique description

A time-thread is a theoretically possible sequence of operation calls and/or exception flows between or within objects and classes. It describes a sequential set of events but in a concurrent environment there will be main threads co-existing. Concerns include interference and cooperation. In Java, there is a *synchronized* construct to prevent interference and a *wait* and *notify* method to engender synchrony of multiple threads as they re-join (D'Souza, 1997b).

Technique usage

Threads of control represent sequential operations. In a concurrent environment, there may be at any one time multiple threads of control co-existing within the one (active) object. These need to be identified as well as whether they are threadsafe, i.e. they cannot be interrupted between commencement and completion (see DCS aspects of Interaction Diagrams in CD: Appendix E for further details).

Interaction between threads often causes the most difficulties within concurrent systems (Selic *et al.*, 1994, page 25). Consequently, synchronization and communication interactions need to be clearly identified and documented and potential conflict areas highlighted and evaluated.

Deliverables and outputs (post-condition)

Additions to documentation, especially interaction diagrams, of multiple threads with potential problem areas highlighted.

Train the trainers Star rating ***

Focus: Education
Typical tasks for which this is needed: Develop education and training plan, do user training
Related techniques: Computer-based training, customer (on-site) training, lectures, mentoring
Input (pre-condition): People to be trained as trainers; training subject identified
Underpinning concepts: Educational and skills transfer techniques

Technique description

Training can be a lucrative profit earner for many development organizations. However, situations do exist in which the product developer cannot or does not see fit to provide training or at least all of the training required. The causes might be:

- that the development organization is short of staff and there are higher business priorities for which staff are required
- that the customer-installed base is geographically dispersed and it is not economical for the development organization to provide training for a small number of individuals over a wide geographical area
- that the frequency with which training courses are required is very high and disruptive to the developer organization's business, and
- that the customer organization prefers to control the training or restrict the exposure of staff to the developers.

Under these conditions it may be prudent for the developer organization to simply provide a 'Train the Trainer(s)' service. In this, local personnel from within the customer organization are trained to handle the training required.

Technique usage

There are a number of considerations to be had when training the trainer:

- the trainer must be knowledgeable and competent in the use of the technology in which he or she is to provide training
- the trainer must be sufficiently senior or have enough 'clout' with respect to the staff he or she is to train so that the training dynamics commence on an appropriate footing
- the trainer must have a personality appropriate to a training task. Skills in human interaction, particularly empathy, are the most important factors here, and
- the trainer should be given enough time, and support to do an effective job. Preferably the job should be a dedicated role for a person or a group of individuals.

In training a trainer, we should keep in mind that the person is a technologist primarily and a teacher secondarily. This is important since the trainer should be able to do what he or she teaches not just teach it, otherwise people will see through the veil and the training experience will collapse.

An appropriately trained trainer should know how:

- people learn
- to analyze the situation and diagnose training needs

- to plan for a training program
- to organize material and design a training session
- to manage the training time
- to present effectively, including the use of instructional media
- to evaluate the effectiveness of the training.

Deliverables and outputs (post-condition)

Well-trained personnel capable of running a training course themselves.

Transformations of the object model Star rating *

Focus: Revising the object model
Typical tasks for which this is needed: Construct the object model
Related techniques: Collaborations analysis
Input (pre-condition): Design
Underpinning concepts: Aggregation, Membership and Containment; Associations, Dependency and Usage; Generalization, Inheritance and Polymorphism

Technique description

The system object model is built using the techniques described in OPEN. However, some solutions may be expressed using more than one (equivalent) construct. For example, over the years, there has been much discussion on whether to use aggregation or inheritance for certain problems; there is a growing realization that in some cases an 'attribute' may be equally represented as an association or aggregation. Transformations may be useful in maintaining traceability, reverse engineering and schema evolution and integration (Premerlani, 1994).

In the initial construction of the model, a choice will be made. However, later some reconsideration may be appropriate and the object model transform into a semantically equivalent but cleaner design. Premerlani (1994) describes a number of these transformations which we can also use in OPEN. He defines a transformation as 'a language independent function that maps a source object model into a target object model'. The effect is localized and the semantics should be unchanged.

Technique usage

Figure A.53 shows one such model in which the original model (upper) shows that an **Address** is either a **PersonalAddress** or a **DistributionList**. In turn, a **DistributionList** is composed of both **PersonalAddress**es and other **DistributionLists**. This is shown by the two many-to-many associations in

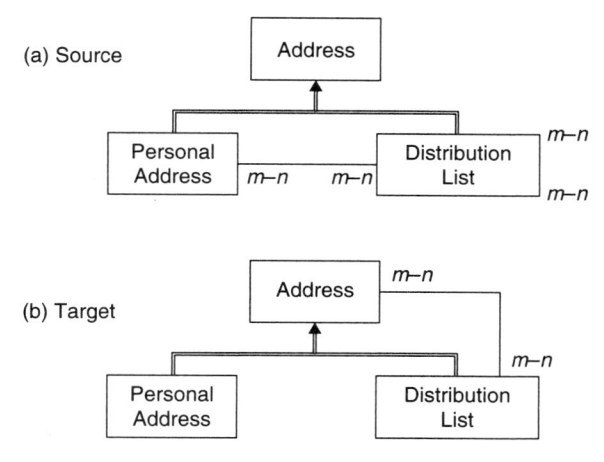

Figure A.53 An example transformation (redrawn from Premerlani, 1994).

this diagram. However, when we note that (as above) 'a distribution list can contain personal addresses and/or other distribution lists', then an equivalent diagram (and one which is arguably simpler) is that shown in Figure A.53(b) in which a `DistributionList` is composed of several `Address`es (which via the inheritance structure may be either `PersonalAddress`es or `DistributionList`s). The choice between this pair of designs (and others similarly) may also be influenced by items such as optimizing database designs, optimizing the use of particular constructs in a nominated programming language or on the ease of communication with the developers and users.

Premerlani (1994) suggests that transformations may be

- equivalence (a.k.a. reversible)
- integrity-losing
- integrity-gaining
- renaming.

In an equivalence transformation, both source and target object models can be applied to the same set of instances. For example, a *FLIGHT* class may have a characteristic of '*airline name*' which is equivalently shown as either an attribute or as an association to an (instance of) the *AIRLINE* type. The reversible nature of this transformation means that the two alternatives are both equally valid and, for different purposes, useful.

Integrity-losing and integrity-gaining transformations, on the other hand, are one-way: the integrity-losing transformation resulting in a target model which is less constrained than the source model and the integrity-gaining transformation giving a more constrained target model.

Premerlani (1994) also notes that the rules for when/how a transformation

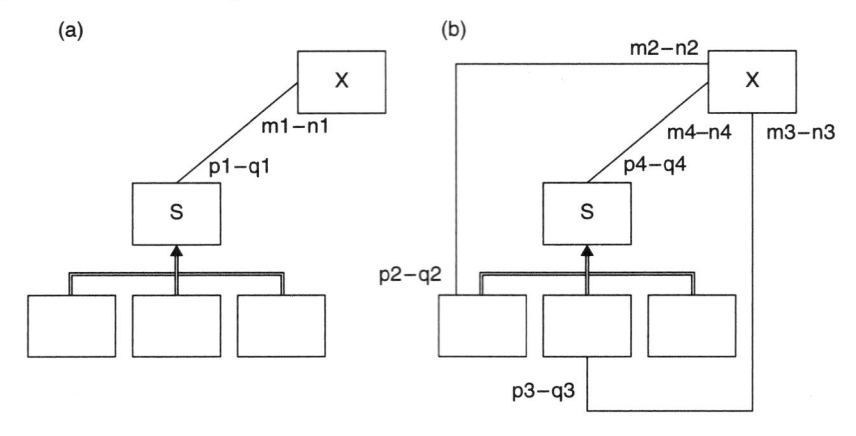

Require:
p1 ≤ p2+p3+p4
q1 > q2+q3+q4
m1 ≤ m2; m1 ≤ m3; m1 ≤ m4
n1 ≥ n2; n1 ≥ n3; n1 ≥ n4

Figure A.54 An example showing how a transformation is defined by pre-conditions and post-conditions (redrawn from Premerlani, 1994).

can occur is governed by appropriate pre- and post-conditions in which the preconditions are applied to the source object model and the post-conditions to the target object model. In Figure A.54, an association is transferred from the superclass to the subclass in the generalization hierarchy.

The areas in which localized transformations have been found to be useful, *inter alia*, are (Premerlani, 1994):

- moving an association, class or attribute up or down in an inheritance hierarchy
- adding or removing a class from an inheritance hierarchy
- converting to or from an exhaustive or overlapping generalization relationship
- converting a generalization relationship to or from association relationships
- working around multiple inheritance
- converting an attribute to or from a class
- partitioning or merging of classes
- adding or removing a class, attribute or association.

Deliverables and outputs (post-condition)

Revisions to object model.

Tuning of database   Star rating * (author G.C. Low)

Focus: Optimizing database usage
Typical tasks for which this is needed: Database performance evaluation
Related techniques: Access analysis
Input (pre-condition): Database design
Underpinning concepts: Optimization

Technique description

Performance is impacted by operational considerations, distribution design and issues such as indexing, clustering, object replication, storage of derived properties, and classes that can be collapsed (Case *et al.*, 1996). Operational considerations include recovery, concurrency control, security control and versioning.

Technique usage

Decisions on how to fragment the database and where to store each fragment must be made. The distribution of the data is based on the access paths and costs (Desai, 1990, page 669) and on reliability requirements. The fragmentation design is determined using the Database Specification component of the Object Storage Requirements Document created as a deliverable in subtask: identify user database requirements (Case *et al.*, 1995).

Objects may be partitioned horizontally by assigning groups of objects from the same class or associated classes to different fragments in an objectbase or by making groups of tuples of a relation into fragments in an RDB. On the other hand, objects may be partitioned vertically by assigning properties or attributes in objects or relations to separate fragments. Horizontal fragmentation may improve efficiency if a class has many objects of which only a few are referenced regularly at a given site. Vertical fragmentation may improve efficiency if a class has properties with different access patterns.

Indexes (q.v.) speed up access while not adding new information (Andleigh and Gretzinger, 1992). Indexes are maintained on a property or a combination of properties of a class. In a RDBMS, tuples (objects) are accessed through a key rather than a navigation path so indexes are appropriate. In the case of an ODBMS, objects are usually accessed through a traversal between objects and not directly via a key (Thurston, 1993); although Kim (1990) identifies two types of indexing that may be appropriate for an ODBMS: class hierarchy indexing and nested property indexing.

Clustering (q.v.) is used in both objectbases and relational databases (Kim, 1990). It refers to the practice of storing objects that are logically related or commonly retrieved at the same time physically near to each other on the secondary storage medium. This minimizes costs of retrievals.

The trade-offs between update-synchronization costs and the cost of having replicated local copies of objects needs to be considered. The patterns of stages that change objects need to be understood to achieve performance, autonomy and integrity. The objects that need to be replicated for performance and autonomy considerations need to be determined. Integrity procedures must be developed to ensure that replicated data are consistent and in the same state; that is, when an object is updated, all copies of the object must be updated in a timely manner.

In some situations when an operation provides a value that is not stored, the data value may be stored as a property if it is accessed frequently and the time taken for the operation to calculate the value impedes performance (Hawryszkiewycz, 1991). As another option for operations that involve many calculations and intermediate processing, intermediate results may be stored in special class libraries for the duration that an object is in memory.

Determination of classes or relations which may be collapsed is dependent upon whether the database is a RDB or an OB. In the former, combined tables obviate the need for joins, but at the likely expense of loss of normalization. In objectbases, combinations may be engendered by use of special join classes which are classes with two or more superclasses created to relate two other classes (the superclasses). Like denormalization in RDBs, join classes provide additional associations designed to reduce disk access for searches (Andleigh and Gretzinger, 1992). This is only recommended in cases where performance is critical and cannot be improved in any other way which does not denormalize the database.

Deliverables and outputs (post-condition)

Improved database design.

Unit testing Star rating **

Focus: Testing at CIRT level (coded class usually)
Typical tasks for which this is needed: Test
Related techniques: Integration testing
Input (pre-condition): Classes ready to be tested
Underpinning concepts: Testing at lowest modularity enhances quality

Technique description

Unit testing for OO systems relates to classes. It is important to test the ability of a CIRT to retain state information between accesses and to check that data are fully encapsulated within objects and not passed around the system in a non-OU manner. Repeatability in testing is thus less guaranteed than in a traditional testing program.

Validation of new classes and revalidation of modified classes is considered explicitly in the testing methodology of Harrold and McGregor (1992) who aim to minimize testing based on the existence of well-tested classes in the higher levels of the hierarchy. On the other hand, Perry and Kaiser (1990) warn that reliance on the 'well-testedness' of superclasses does not necessarily obviate the need for retesting the same services in subclasses.

Unit testing is usually performed by the developers themselves. Unit testing involves developing a test bed for the class which sets up a simulated environment around the class to be tested (Jacobson *et al.*, 1992). The class is then sent messages and the results analyzed according to a set of expected criteria based on the service contract (q.v.).

Technique usage

Testing of classes with zero fan-out is recommended first (Turner and Robson, 1992), then the CIRTs which use their services etc. Operations must be tested individually and also with respect to their interactions with (1) other services within the same class and (2) other classes (McGregor and Sykes, 1992, page 207).

Unit testing strategies for OO remain immature at this stage, although many of the traditional testing procedures can readily be applied. Testing can also be used directly to uncover defects (Goldberg and Rubin, 1995, page 126).

Deliverables and outputs (post-condition)

Test results at the unit (class) level.

Usability measurement   Star rating *

Focus: Measuring how usable the software is
Typical tasks for which this is needed: Design user interface, evaluate quality
Related techniques: Metrics collection, usability testing
Input (pre-condition): System to be measured
Underpinning concepts: Usability is crucial for high quality software

Technique description

Constantine and Lockwood (1998) divide usability metrics into preference metrics, performance metrics and predictive metrics. Preference metrics reflect the subject's first choice and are by nature highly subjective. Questionnaires used to elicit these preferences include questions, *inter alia*, on how much the user likes the design (effect), how well the software supports productivity (efficiency), how supportive the software is (helpfulness), how consistent the response is (control), how easy the software is to master (learnability), the degree of attractiveness (aesthetics), graphical layout (organization), understandability (interpretation) and overall ease of use (facility).

Performance metrics can only be obtained from a working software system (in contrast to predictive and preference metrics which can be gathered at all stages in the development cycle). They quantify how users perform when using the software – measurements taken in the field or in a specially controlled usability laboratory. Predictive metrics are measures of artefacts such as visual layouts which, it is anticipated, may be useful in the prediction of some performance characteristic of the software.

Constantine (1997b) discusses three usability metrics which are based on evaluations focused on use case narratives and, in particular, on essential use cases (Constantine, 1997a). The number of steps in the essential use case (when enacted) is compared to the number of steps in the interface design which realizes this essential use case. The ratio of interface steps to essential use case steps is called the *essential efficiency* of the design.

The second usability metric, *task consolidation* or *task visibility*, evaluates the extent to which users can see *all* they need in order to complete a given task. Task consolidation is measured by the percentage of non-optional steps undertaken before a context switch is mandated. High values express that all elements of the use case have been well consolidated, a low value indicates too much context switching.

Whilst essential efficiency and task consolidation are scoped at a single use case (although they can be grossed up over several essential use cases), the third proposed usability metric evaluates how well the entire suite of use cases matches the overall interface design. Good interfaces facilitate commonly undertaken tasks (as exemplified in a single essential use case) whilst less used use cases can be tolerated as requiring more complex user interaction. Use cases are ranked by frequency of occurrence and a concordance sought between this ranking and the actual implemented values. Such a correlation is highest when frequent tasks are supported by short task paths in the interface design.

A measure not underpinned by use cases is that of visual coherence, VC (Constantine, 1996a), which is a measure of the semantic cohesion based on visual groupings of interface components. When these components are substantially related, the VC value is 100 per cent and when essentially unrelated, the value is 0 per cent (Constantine, 1997c).

A final metric, layout uniformity, relates to the structural characteristics of the system and extends the earlier work of Comber and Maltby (1994, 1995). Constantine (1996b) defines a new measure which is neither task-sensitive nor context-sensitive, later extended by Noble and Constantine (1997).

Technique usage

Essential efficiency

Sum the steps needed in the design of each essential use case and the number of steps whereby each use case is implemented. Calculate the essential efficiency as the ratio of the former to the latter, i.e.:

$$\text{Essential efficiency} = \frac{\text{Essential length}}{\text{Operational length}} \qquad (\mathbf{A.4})$$

(Constantine, 1996a). In a good design, all ratios should be very near one; in a bad design small values might be anticipated. Essential efficiency can be computed for a given task or as a weighted average based on a mix of tasks (Constantine, 1996b).

Task consolidation/task visibility

Task consolidation/task visibility measures the fraction of a series of required steps needed to perform the task that can be completed *without* switching contexts, e.g. to another window or screen. This relates to a single use case and is given by (Constantine and Lockwood, 1998):

$$\text{Task visibility} = \frac{1}{S_{total}} \sum_{\forall i} V_i \tag{A.5}$$

where S_{total} is the total number of enacted steps to complete the use case and V_i is the feature visibility (0 to 1) of each enacted step (for full details see Constantine and Lockwood, 1998, chapter 17).

Task concordance

For all use cases, estimate the rank order of their frequency of occurrence in the user environment. Calculate the number of steps needed in the implementation of each case and rank these. Calculate a rank order correlation (Kendall's tau) between these two sets of rankings (Constantine, 1997a). Values for the task concordance metric range from -1 (completely wrong for the tasks) through 0 (completely unrelated to the tasks) to 1 (perfectly suited to the tasks) (Constantine, 1996b).

Visual coherence

The measure needs to be sensitive to both the grouping and the meaning of those grouped components. Constantine (1996a) gives, for N_l components in group l:

$$VC = \frac{\sum_{\forall l} G_l}{\sum_{\forall l} N_l(N_l - 1)/2} \tag{A.6}$$

where

$$G_l = \sum_{\forall i,j, i \neq j} R_{ij} \tag{A.7}$$

and R_{ij} is the measure of relatedness between components with a value between 0 and 1. Constantine (1996a) gives measured values of $VC = 0.62$ for a highly structured version of a Windows 3.x-based system and a value of $VC = 0.29$ for a semantically disordered yet visually organized variant.

LAYOUT UNIFORMITY

Constantine (1996b) defines layout uniformity as:

$$\text{Layout uniformity} = 1 - \frac{(N_{size} + N_t + N_l) - A}{3C - A} \qquad (\textbf{A.8})$$

where C is the number of components under consideration (on screen, in dialog box etc.), N_{size}, N_t and N_l are the number of different sizes, top edge alignments and left edge alignments respectively and A is an adjustment (for minimum possible alignments and sizes) given by:

$$A = 2\sqrt{C} + 1. \qquad (\textbf{A.9})$$

An extension to Equation (A.8) by Noble and Constantine (1997) also includes the effects of height, width and all-edge alignments:

$$\text{Layout uniformity} = 1 - \frac{(N_h + N_w + N_t + N_l + N_b + N_r) - A}{6C - A} \qquad (\textbf{A.10})$$

where Equation (A.9) is rewritten as:

$$A = 2 + 2 \times \lceil 2 \times \sqrt{C} \rceil \qquad (\textbf{A.11})$$

where $\lceil\,\rceil$ is the ceiling function which gives the smallest integer greater than the enclosed value.

Deliverables and outputs (post-condition)

Values of usability metrics.

Usability testing   Star rating **

Focus: Testing how usable the software is
Typical tasks for which this is needed: Design user interface, evaluate quality, test
Related techniques: Acceptance testing, usability measurement
Input (pre-condition): Final system for user testing
Underpinning concepts: Color in UIs; Usability

Technique description

OPEN endorses the urgent need for improved usability of software systems. Usability tests therefore need to focus on frequency of use, organizational cultures and personal skills levels. Graham (1995a, page 98) recommends the categorization of a person's skills as:

Table A.23 Checklist for usability evaluations (after Graham, 1995a, pages 417–418).

- Is the interface consistent?
- Are tasks grouped in a logical manner?
- Is the user's memory overloaded or is too much information presented at once?
- Are all actions reversible?
- Can the user curtail a session and safely resume it later?
- Is the user comfortable with the terminology?
- Is adequate feedback provided? Is there a sense of completion?
- Are there unnecessary modes? Are all modes indicated clearly by color changes, and so on?
- Does use of the system either lead to the user acquiring a model of the underlying model or make such a model unnecessary?
- Is the help system usable at all levels of skill?
- Are all task scripts supported as described and without backtracking?
- Does the system ask for information in an illogical order or require users to key information already deducible?
- Have applicable standards been adhered to?
- Can the user explore the system's function without penalty?

- beginner (no knowledge)
- learner (knowledge incomplete, encoded as rules)
- competent (knowledge complete, compiled and not accessible to consciousness)
- expert (knowledge subject to critique and refinement).

As with any sociological evaluation, usability evaluation experiments can be difficult to construct, difficult to analyze and, therefore, potentially expensive. However, a well-tested and highly usable software interface can create a high profile, high quality product. Graham (1995a, page 99) notes that the results of studies at IBM showed that a savings as large as $2 per dollar spent were achieved through thorough usability engineering.

Technique usage

Graham (1995a, pages 417–418) summarizes a number of sources to provide a useful checklist for usability (Table A.23). This list should be used as the main checklist for the usability evaluation.

Deliverables and outputs (post-condition)

Results from usability testing with areas of concern highlighted.

Usage – see Relationship modeling

Use case modeling – see Scenario development

V&V – see Reviews

Versioning (DBMS)   Star rating **

Focus: Handling several versions of information stored
Typical tasks for which this is needed: Design and implement physical database, select database/storage strategy
Related techniques: Configuration management
Input (pre-condition): Existing DB schema
Underpinning concepts: Relational and object database theory

Technique description

The versioning of objects identified in Task: User requirements/Technique: Object retention requirements should be modeled to provide the required functionality. One of the biggest problems with long-lived databases is not just the fact that objects evolve over time and you may wish to access a previous state of an object, but, in addition, that the data schema (i.e. class definition) may also require changing. Only CLOS has a mechanism to support this. If you redefine a class, any resident instances are not lost (as is usually the case) but, instead, when they are next touched upon, an updating method is invoked, which recreates the object according to the old information retained and the new class definition. The mechanism works by storing pointer from old (obsolete) class definitions to the latest class definition. An instance loses fields which are deleted and acquires newly initialized extra fields which were created. The process is instigated automatically but may be customized through meta-methods in the CLOS metaobject protocol. This would allow a user to insert specific initialization routines or even input new values on request.

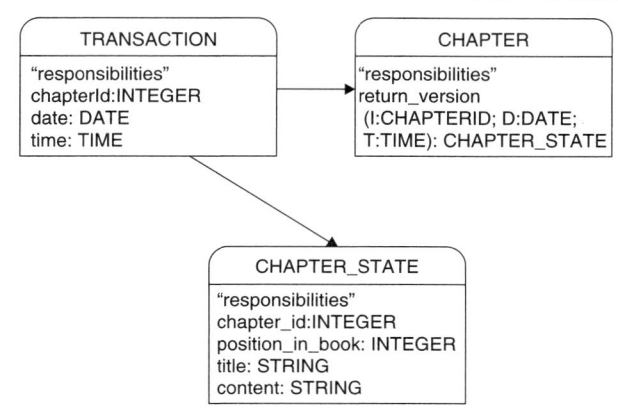

```
                  ┌─────────────────────────┐      ┌──────────────────────────────┐
                  │      TRANSACTION        │      │          CHAPTER             │
                  ├─────────────────────────┤      ├──────────────────────────────┤
                  │ "responsibilities"      │      │ "responsibilities"           │
                  │ chapterId:INTEGER       │─────▶│ return_version               │
                  │ date: DATE              │      │  (I:CHAPTERID; D:DATE;       │
                  │ time: TIME              │      │  T:TIME): CHAPTER_STATE      │
                  └─────────────────────────┘      └──────────────────────────────┘
                              │
                              ▼
                  ┌─────────────────────────┐
                  │      CHAPTER_STATE      │
                  ├─────────────────────────┤
                  │ "responsibilities"      │
                  │ chapter_id:INTEGER      │
                  │ position_in_book: INTEGER│
                  │ title: STRING           │
                  │ content: STRING         │
                  └─────────────────────────┘
```

Figure A.55 An object model of versioning (after Case, 1993).

Technique usage

Versioning needs to be modeled; an example being shown in Figure A.55. For each class to be versioned, there is a generic object class (in Figure A.55 this is the *CHAPTER* class). For each transaction which occurs to change the state of the *CHAPTER* objects, there is a *TRANSACTION* object which provides details about the transaction. Each *TRANSACTION* object is associated with a *CHAPTER_STATE* object which provides the value of the state of the *CHAPTER* object after the transaction occurs. Therefore, each object may have many different states and each state represents a different version of the generic object. To access a particular version of an object, the object identifier and a date or time identifier must be specified. Then the object state which was current at that time can be retrieved.

Deliverables and outputs (post-condition)

A new version of the product together with an inter-version audit trial.

Videotaping   Star rating **

Focus: Requirements elicitation
Typical tasks for which this is needed: Design user interface, evaluate quality, identify user requirements, test, undertake post-implementation review, undertake usability design
Related techniques: Interviews, protocol analysis, record and playback
Input (pre-condition): Users, video equipment, set of questions for interview
Underpinning concepts: Capturing users talking on video permits repeated, detailed evaluation; human communication

350   CORE TECHNIQUES

Technique description

Videotaping is, in terms of principles, aims and procedures, very similar to record and playback (q.v.). All concepts and recommendations there also apply directly in this case. This is true to the extent that the entry could be duplicated exactly with the terms 'record' and 'playback' exchanged for videotaping and 'showing the tape'. As such we refer the reader to that entry.

Technique usage

The only significant difference between Technique: Record and playback and Technique: Videotaping is in the fact that during videotaping an image is also available. The communication channel is thus wider and includes the presentation of visual material by the participants (things such as diagrams, mock-ups, models, rich pictures etc.). As 'a picture is worth a thousand words', this may prove more effective than audiotaping alone. One important aspect that videotaping can capture is the participants' body language.

Deliverables and outputs (post-condition)

Videotape for further analysis for user requirements, perhaps using protocol analysis.

Viewpoints   Star rating *

Focus: Requirements engineering, modeling
Typical tasks for which this is needed: Analyze user requirements, construct the object model, create and/or identify reusable components ('for reuse'), identify CIRTs
Related techniques: Abstraction utilization, relationship modeling
Input (pre-condition): CIRTs and partial design
Underpinning concepts: Different users require different portions of a software system

Technique description

In any group of people involved with the creation or use of a piece of software, there are likely to be many different viewpoints. The viewpoint technique embodies this realization and applies a 'filter' to the overall system which gives particular relevance to the needs of the particular user or user group. So, for instance, individuals may have a data focus, a cost concern or be more interested in how challenging it will be to code or what the reuse prospects are. This means that the properties perceived by an individual *from a given point of view* are (a) only relevant to that point of view and (b) only a subset of the properties

Table A.24 Roles, concerns and representations (after Wirfs-Brock and McKean, 1996).

Role	Concerns and considerations	Proof/representation
User	Tasks supported, usability, performance	Conversations, prototypes
Business analyst	Business process, system context and content, rules, business artefacts, traceability from analysis through to design	Context diagram, object domain model, scenarios, project plan
Customer	Timeline, cost, strategic purpose	Project plan, risk analysis
Data analyst	Legacy protocols, relations, entities (completeness, correctness, access, navigational patterns)	Composition relationships, persistence and retrieval model, context diagram, data interface diagram
Architect	Functional partitions, parallel development, system structure	Context diagram, subsystem diagram, control style, reusable frameworks
GUI design	Ease-of-use, look and feel	Storyboard, visual prototype
Programmer	Technical details, footprint, platform, portability goals, GUI support, server interface layer	Class specifications, subsystems, interaction models, frameworks
Tester	Units of execution, usage, robustness	Scenarios with alternatives and constraints, class and subsystem specs, performance objectives
Trainer/support	Usage, important concepts procedures, principles, facts	Scenarios, business model, context diagram, UI flow and description
Project manager	Team members, communications, skills, resources, effort	Steps and products of design process, progress, effort, scope

of the object (Whitmire, 1997, page 243). These roles, concerns and representations are summarized in Table A.24. A viewpoint thus supports sufficiency (for the present purpose) but does not guarantee completeness.

Traditionally, viewpoint analysis is a requirements elicitation technique which encourages the developer to view the system from the competing viewpoints of different stakeholders. You take extreme viewpoints – e.g. a bank manager wants total security on all accounts held, with no access; whereas a customer wants instant access to money held. This leads to compromise – security via PINs (which slows down the customer a little; but increases the security level a little, also).

This is different again from 'views' in the user sense of restricting access to different aspects of the same object. This can be accomplished by using multiple abstract superclasses (possibly overlapping) which provide a limited interface to the objects concerned (control lies with the client).

More generally, Wirfs-Brock and McKean (1996) describe three different points of view of an object as:

- *usage view*: what is the object's role, its public interface, its context, any restrictions on its use, other objects it relies upon and the information needed for correct and reliable use?
- *extension view*: how can an object be specialized, how is it constructed and on what other objects does its services rely (collaborators)?
- *maintenance view*: how is the object constructed and how can its behaviors be modified/maintained and what impact will making changes have?

At the level of the individual CIRT, Booch (1991, page 39) introduces the notion (actually in terms of abstraction techniques) that different users may have a different perspective. In his much-quoted 'two views of a cat', the owner sees a lovable, strokeable, feedable ball of fur and the veterinarian sees a functioning respiratory and digestive system. The CIRT '*CAT*' should probably cater for both (all) viewpoints in such a way that the CIRT offers two (or more) interfaces. The idea of multiple interfaces or multiple types is described by viewpoints and supporting in OO programming languages such as Eiffel using the selective export facility (Bielak and McKim, 1993) and Java's interfaces; and through design concepts such as the RDD (Wirfs-Brock *et al.*, 1990) notion of contracts. Other notions of multiple viewpoints are discussed by Naja and Mouaddib (1998) and Emmerich (1998) for database modeling.

Technique usage

Identify the relevant viewpoint with your users and encapsulate that knowledge into the software system. Use viewpoint differences for different user groups to create a design strategy to address different security levels and requirements.

In system design, use viewpoints to identify which CIRTs may access which other CIRTs. This can be implemented in, for instance, selective export clauses in Eiffel or via the `public/private/protected` protection for member functions in C++.

In database applications, viewpoints can be used in both these above ways: security and access paths.

Deliverables and outputs (post-condition)

Recommendations on any restrictions of certain user groups to specific CIRTs. Documented multiple interfaces to support various views – as needed.

Visibility analysis   Star rating **

Focus: Detailed design
Typical tasks for which this is needed: Construct the object model
Related techniques: Collaborations analysis, ER modeling, Law of Demeter, package construction

Input (pre-condition): Partial and evolving design
Underpinning concepts: Visibility

Technique description

Visibility analysis generically describes the determination of access paths to objects and methods. There are two related usages of the term 'visibility': both meaning something similar to 'scope', i.e. describing how one object obtains a handle on another in a given execution environment. Visibility analysis is a precursor to determining permanent and temporary inter-object connexions. At a lower level, it concerns which artefacts can be seen across the boundaries of their encapsulating artefact: for example, which operations are visible from outside a class; which classes are visible from the outside of (across the boundary of) a package/cluster/subsystem. This then determines which inter-CIRT communication paths are valid (see Technique: Interaction modeling).

Fusion has a prior design technique for examining the semantics of inter-CIRT coupling called 'visibility analysis', which we discuss as part of the article on visibility in CD: Appendix E. In Fusion (Coleman *et al.*, 1994, page 80), this refers to the construction of a 'visibility graph', in which client–server object relationships are qualified with binary semantic constraints. From these constraints you derive the physical kind of object pointer, argument, or nested sub-object that should be used to implement the relationship.

In Booch (1994), visibility analysis merely refers to the implementation decision itself, rather than a semantic analysis. UML uses the term visibility analysis to describe the same notion as access control in C++ (Stroustrup, 1994, page 211), i.e. the level of external visibility granted to individual attributes or methods. In UML, visibility is marked as either **public** (+), **protected** (#) or **private** (−) – annotations derived from the C++ programming language but also available in Java. In OML, only two levels of visibility are used, as in Smalltalk or Eiffel. These are called public and private, although in reality the private annotation is closely analogous to **protected** in C++. Private in C++ is used to refer to features which are internal and *cannot be accessed directly in sub-classes*. These constraints are depicted graphically in OML by either embedding the artefact within another (private) or placing it straddling the boundary (and hence visible from outside the encapsulation). An example of cluster/package visibility is shown in Figure A.56 which shows classes in a package visible from outside – accomplished by placing them partly inside and partly outside the package boundary (dotted line).

Technique usage

The baseline should be that of non-visibility. This is the basic tenet of OT – that of encapsulation and information hiding. In other words, a conscious decision must be made to allow artefacts to be visible outside its encapsulation. This visibility, however, is vital if that particular operation/class needs to be accessed from beyond the confines of its own encapsulation. Thus, any classes in a package

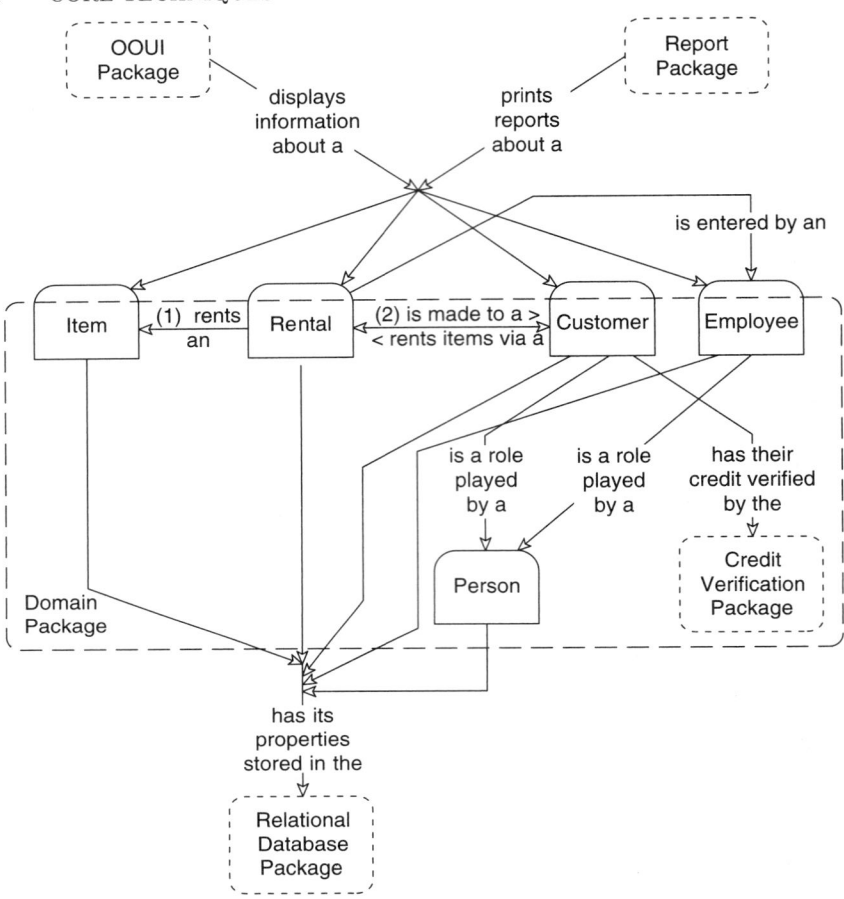

Figure A.56 Packages on an OML package diagram for a rental application (after Firesmith et al., 1997).

that need to receive messages from classes in one or more other package need to be visibility to that other class/package. Any operations or responsibilities that need to be accessible to messages sent by other classes need to be in the interface of the class, i.e. they should belong to the interface/specification – all other operations and responsibilities should be part of the class implementation *only*.

Deliverables and outputs (post-condition)

Use of selected notation (e.g. OML) to depict private, public and possibly protected elements: clusters/package visibility and operation/responsibility visibility.

Table A.25 A portion of the volume analysis for a typical sales CIRT model (after Case, 1993).

Object class	Average number of occurrences	Maximum number of occurrences	Minimum number of occurrences	Growth rate per time period
Customer	6 000	10 000	3 000	5/1 week
Sale	10 000	16 000	4 000	8/1 week
Product	50	80	40	2/1 month
Storage	800	1 600	400	5/1 month
Shop	200	180	220	1/3 months

Visioning (for BPR) – see Envisioning

Volume analysis Star rating ***

Focus: Evaluate amount of information to be handled in DB
Typical tasks for which this is needed: Identify user DB requirements, select database/storage strategy
Related techniques: Access analysis
Input (pre-condition): Database requirements
Underpinning concepts: Database throughput constraints

Technique description

Specifically for database requirements, it is necessary to identify the volume of data that need to be stored in the database. This is based on how many instances are likely for each class, both now and in the future.

Technique usage

For each persistent object, the maximum, minimum and average number of occurrences must be estimated; as well as the number of new occurrences or growth rate in a given time period. These volume figures may be shown on the object model diagram or tabulated separately (Table A.25).

Deliverables and outputs (post-condition)

Quantitative recommendations on the storage volumes likely to be needed (a) initially and (b) at a specified time in the future – in other words, some estimate of the growth rate of data storage needs is required.

Walkthroughs Star rating ***

Focus: Code and design evaluation technique
Typical tasks for which this is needed: Evaluate quality, test
Related techniques: Inspections, reviews, simulation
Input (pre-condition): Design in stable condition
Underpinning concepts: Peer evaluation can find problem areas rapidly

Technique description

Walkthroughs are commonly used to detect design and code defects. There are a number of seemingly similar techniques that are popularly used in relation to software work-products that employ a team of participants to 'examine' the work-product. Whilst superficially they may look similar, depending on the purpose for which this activity is conducted, the process and its outcome can differ dramatically. In terms of software artefact examination techniques, we base our classification on the intent or the primary objective of each technique. To do so, we use the definitions provided by IEEE Std 1028–1988 in which primary objectives of this category of techniques have been enumerated as:

(1) evaluation of project progress
(2) education and examination of alternatives
(3) identification of work-product defects.

Whilst reviews belong to the first and inspections to the third category, walkthroughs relate to the second category of education and examination of alternatives. A walkthrough is a semi-formal examination of a product by a small team of peers led by the product author in which attempt is made to meet a variety of objectives including participant education, examination of alternatives (think tank), examination of readability and modularity problems. Although usually not stated as a primary aim, if a defect is encountered during a walkthrough, it is not ignored.

Technique usage

Whilst many walkthrough techniques exist (e.g. Myers, 1976), few are sufficiently described. The following are techniques that have a reasonably well-defined process model.

IEEE-1028 WALKTHROUGH

Although defect detection is one of the stated aims of IEEE-1028 walkthrough, it seems that the process is mainly used for examination of alternatives and as a process of peer education. Gilb and Graham (1993) state that this walkthrough technique is not precisely defined in the IEEE 1028 standard. The recommended number of participants are reflected to be between two and seven composed of technical peers and the technical leadership of the project. The volume of the material considered although relatively low is still higher than those for the inspection process.

In addition, data collection and retention is optional and change incorporation is left as the prerogative of the work-product producer.

YOURDON STRUCTURED WALKTHROUGH

Specified in Yourdon (1989), this technique is reasonably well defined in that the number and roles of participants, product size, walkthrough duration and management involvement are all specified reasonably precisely.

FREEDMAN AND WEINBURG WALKTHROUGH

Freedman and Weinburg (1982) define a walkthrough process in which a stepwise work-product simulation is conducted using a specifically produced set of inputs. The process conforms with the minimum requirements of the IEEE 1028 standards but is not very precisely defined.

Walkthroughs, as part of requirements engineering (evaluation phase) test that the business object model actually supports all the functionality required by the user. One route is to generate use cases corresponding to the task scripts and evaluate the system functionality in terms of these.

Deliverables and outputs (post-condition)

List of defects.

Web technology – see Internet and web technology

Workflow analysis   Star rating ***

Focus: Management
Typical tasks for which this is needed: Model and re-engineer business process(es)
Related techniques: Gantt chart
Input (pre-condition): Constraints relevant to business processes being used
Underpinning concepts: Document tracking can help improve business processes (including software development processes)

Technique description

Frequent use is made today of the term workflow to indicate the automatic flow of documents from one location to another and keeping track of revisions and authorizations (McGibbon, 1995, page 113).

Technique usage

Workflow analysis supports the tracking of actions as they flow around a business system, together with a discharge of responsibility. The time for processing such requests can thus be monitored as well as the frequency of sending and receiving of messages. This permits analysis of the capacity for processing messages of an individual or role. Such information facilitates optimization of work units within the organization (Kristen, 1995). There are five steps advocated in Kristen (1994):

(1) quantifying the volume and frequency
(2) determine processing time
(3) eliminating redundancy
(4) evaluating responsibilities and authorization and
(5) creating subject-communication models for the SOLL-situation.

Here the aim is to move from the status quo (represented by the German verb 'ist' = is) to what we desire (represented by the German verb 'soll' = should be). Once we know what the workflow *should* be, then we can design the information system to support that pattern of working.

Workflow analysis may be sometimes also be used in the context of BPR (q.v.) and is frequently encapsulated, by use of visualization techniques (q.v.) in a software tool.

Deliverables and outputs (post-condition)

Documented workflow and project plan.

Workshops   Star rating ***

Focus: Use of workshop techniques for rapid elicitation of user requirements
Typical tasks for which this is needed: Develop education and training plan, do user training, identify user requirements
Related techniques: Brainstorming, interviewing, questionnaires, scenario development
Input (pre-condition): Users
Underpinning concepts: Scenarios, Task Scripts and Use Cases

Technique description

Workshops are used in requirements engineering (RE) to complement[†] interviews and may be used for user and trainer training. Graham (1996d) contrasts

---

[†] Unfortunately, they are sometimes used *instead of* interviews.

on-site (cheaper, more likely to get everyone there but subject to frequent interruptions) and off-site (more expensive, better catering, less stressful) locations. He suggests a U-shaped table layout in which everyone can see everyone else together with ample audiovisual support – ranging from sophisticated computer projects equipment to ordinary whiteboards and flipcharts.

A frequent use of workshops in RE is to elicit user requirements as a joint application development (JAD) or rapid applications development (RAD) session – although it should be noted that the word 'rapid' should not be used as an excuse for ill-disciplined prototyping or hacking. While timeboxing uses prototypes as an evolutionary technique to move the build forward through successive iterations, any prototype built during a RAD workshop will almost certainly have to be thrown away – implying that expectations must be managed accordingly.

Technique usage

A workshop usually consists of a preliminary scoping session (to elicit key business objectives, measures of success and priorities) followed by the detailed workshop. The objectives of scoping are (Graham, 1995a, page 365):

- to establish a high level understanding of existing and proposed business processes, the context in which they operate and their goals
- to establish the mission, boundaries and objectives of the project
- to set clear targets, priorities and acceptance criteria for a new system
- to review financial and business justification and identify other benefits
- to complete the activity in a short time via the use of intensive workshop sessions.

A scoping report is produced in this, typically, half- to full-day workshop session. This report then lays the foundation of the workshop itself (often around a week in length) which has as its objectives (Graham, 1995a):

- to produce a detailed statement of system requirements
- to produce and test a set of task scripts in the form of a task object model
- to produce and test a business object model
- to make further recommendations on the resources and equipment required
- to revise development and implementation plans.

Deliverables from the JAD/RAD workshop include a full requirements document which probably includes a context model, a task object model (TOM), a business object model (BOM) and some evaluation of reuse potential. Most importantly, the users' signoff is vital. Since they have played a major role in this collaborative requirements elicitation process, the agreed requirements should be well aligned with their expectations – laying a good basis for the final delivery of a quality software product.

Participants in a workshop include the sponsor, users, the facilitator, the scribe, the project leader and the team members. In addition, observers may attend the workshops (which provides an excellent forum for training) where they may have contributions to make in specific but limited areas of expertise (Graham, 1995a).

Deliverables and outputs (post-condition)

Documented user requirements.

Appendix B
Suites of techniques

Action research Star rating **

Focus: User requirements
Typical tasks for which this is needed: Identify source(s) or requirements, identify user requirements
Related techniques: Rich pictures, soft systems analysis
Input (pre-condition): Research problem
Underpinning concepts: Participating as a member of a team still permits the research to draw valid conclusions

Technique description

Action research is the seeking of an effective method of organizational decision-making which involves the organization as a whole entity in identifying needs, solving problems, laying out plans and implementing decisions. It is directly related to Lewis's Group Dynamics (Lewis, 1947a, b) which is based on and advocates interactions within groups rather than individuals as the basis for study of intra- and inter-organizational action. In other words, it views individuals as they are influenced by and influence social forces such as the decision making process.

Action research is not a scientific research approach in the sense of hypothesis testing. Rather, action research requires the action researcher to use the experience obtained from his or her *own involvement* not only to find logical desirable and defensible improvements to the problem but also as a learning process to improve the interaction (research) process itself (Gilmore et al., 1985).

This implies that action research is inherently an iterative process. Cunningham (1976) provides a model of conducting action research which involves the production of a definite plan of action, fact finding in accordance with that plan, reformulation of the plan on the basis of research results and implementation of the next action to meet the goals of the revised plan. Figure B.1 summarizes this model of the action research approach depicting it as a process.

Based on the above, Hutt and Lennung (1980) define action research as:

362 SUITES OF TECHNIQUES

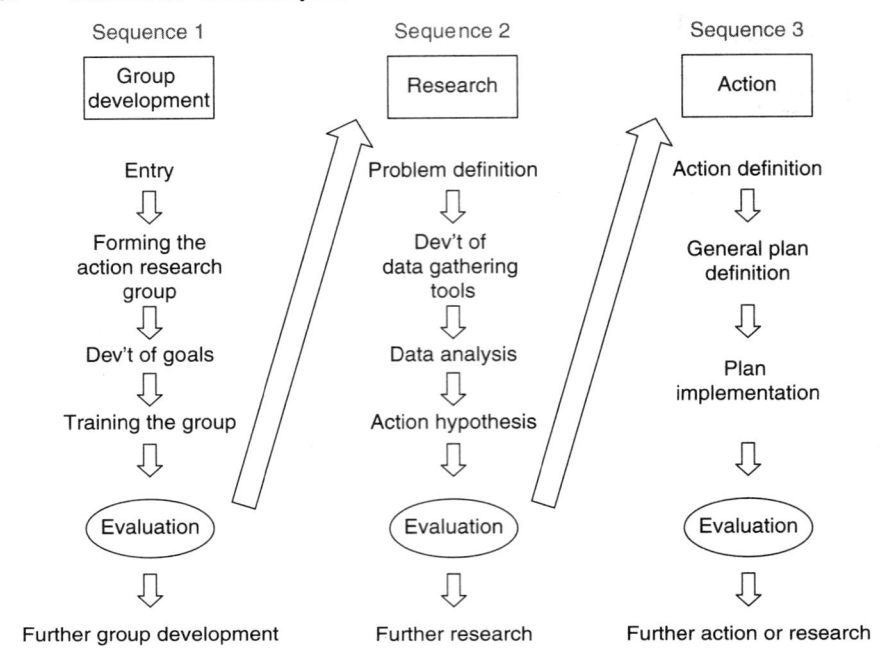

```
Sequence 1              Sequence 2              Sequence 3
┌─────────────┐         ┌──────────┐            ┌──────────┐
│    Group    │         │ Research │            │  Action  │
│ development │         └──────────┘            └──────────┘
└─────────────┘

    Entry             Problem definition        Action definition
     ⇩                      ⇩                        ⇩
  Forming the             Dev't of               General plan
action research        data gathering             definition
    group                  tools
     ⇩                      ⇩                        ⇩
 Dev't of goals         Data analysis               Plan
     ⇩                      ⇩                   implementation
 Training the group    Action hypothesis
     ⇩                      ⇩                        ⇩
 ( Evaluation )        ( Evaluation )           ( Evaluation )
     ⇩                      ⇩                        ⇩
Further group         Further research       Further action or research
 development
```

Figure B.1 Action research viewed as a process (after Cunningham, 1976).

Action research simultaneously assists in practical problem-solving and expands knowledge, as well as enhances the competencies of the respective actors, being performed collaboratively in an immediate situation using data feedback in a cyclical process aiming at an increased understanding of a given social situation, primarily applicable for the understanding of change processes in social systems and undertaken within a mutually acceptable ethical framework.

Other sources of background information to action research include Blum (1955), Beckhard (1969), Steele (1969), Clarke (1972), Warmington (1980) and Whyte and Hamilton (1965).

Technique usage

Action research involves undertaking a piece of research as a member of the team as opposed to being an impartial observer. To set up an action research project, it is first necessary to identify the goal of the research. Perhaps it is to see how well a methodology works in practice; but to do so with a research program that involves you, as researcher, visiting the organization and becoming, either fully or partially, a member of that development team.

In pure science, it is argued that observing and experimenting can be accomplished by an external observer who causes no interference on the system under study (although this has been proven to be incorrect at the quantum level in physics). In action research, a similar experimental program is set up *with the knowledge that* that researcher is, in fact, going to influence, perhaps strongly, the outcome of the experiment. The research goals and particularly the method of analysis must therefore take that knowledge into account.

The information derived from action research can be highly valuable, particularly since the researcher has intimate, first-hand knowledge of the experiment's 'gory details'. However, it is more like a case study in the sense that it is hard to quantify and still harder to draw any sort of generally applicable, never mind statistically valid, conclusions.

Deliverables and outputs (post-condition)

A research plan, information about the problem domain, some potential solutions, further questions.

BPR   Star rating **

Focus: Re-inventing an organization's business processes
Typical tasks for which this is needed: Model and re-engineer business processes
Related techniques: Business process modeling, soft systems analysis
Input (pre-condition): An understanding of existing business, its process(es), environment and goals
Underpinning concepts: BPR Theory

Technique description

Hammer and Champy (1993) define business process re-engineering (BPR) as 'the fundamental rethinking and radical redesign of business processes to achieve dramatic improvements in critical, contemporary measures of performance, such as cost, quality, service and speed'. BPR therefore requires that enterprises take a comprehensive review of their entire existing operations and try to redesign them in a way that serves customers better (Jacobson *et al.*, 1995). The three keywords in the Hammer and Champy definition are 'radical', 're-design' and 'processes'. This implies that BPR:

- Advocates a radical and revolutionary re-orientation of all elements of the business.
  This means that there is a need for an integrated and business centered approach to BPR, i.e. there has to be a central business-oriented purpose, a business strategy, around which BPR is conducted. In addition, the new approach for the implementation of such purpose should represent a fundamentally, and radically better, way of achieving the central purpose than

the current approach. Gaining say a 5 per cent reduction in inventory costs is not what BPR is about; rather, it aims to provide up to a threefold cost reduction. However, Harmon (1998) notes that for many companies a radical approach hasn't worked (and won't work). Nevertheless, companies should still be urged 'to be bold when they redesign process'.

- Requires a re-design of the current business processes.
  This implies in turn that *evolving* the current processes is not a focus of BPR. There is a need for a re-design of business processes either to achieve new goals and purposes or to achieve existing ones much more effectively.
- BPR has a process focus.
  A process is defined as 'the collection of technologies and methods utilized within a particular context by an organization in order to produce a pre-defined outcome' (Younessi and Henderson-Sellers, 1997). This definition implies that there are these three dimensions of methodology, technology and context which underpin a process. The methodological dimension in itself may be modeled or viewed from three distinct perspectives of structure, transformations and causal relationships. As such, a system that is studied in accordance to one or a subset of these dimensions stands a real chance of not having been understood adequately. Such systems are a lot harder to model and improve.

Unlike its predecessors (e.g. traditional corporate re-structuring which focuses primarily on the structural aspects of the business system and to a lesser degree on transformations, i.e. it has a 'structural' approach), BPR has a process approach. By this, we mean that in re-designing the business an appropriate BPR approach considers the business domain in need of redesign as a system that defines a process located in a business setting. This allows a process design approach to the problem which, by incorporating important system elements such as categories of stakeholders (e.g. customers), technologies available or attainable, as well as the current context of the business situation, provides a much richer picture of what there is and what is possible.

We therefore define BPR as: 'taking a business focused, integrated and radical approach to designing a business system that implements a newly devised or aligned organizational strategy to achieve significant business advantage'.

Technique usage

The essential elements of doing business (re-)engineering are as follows.

IDENTIFY AND STATE THE PURPOSE FOR THE BUSINESS ENGINEERING PROJECT

This purpose must be *central, real, clear* and *profit-oriented*. As an example of the importance of this we can note a major insurance conglomerate that went through a business re-engineering exercise which resulted in a significant and measurable improvement of certain of its processes, yet in six months the company was almost bankrupt, the reason being that the areas re-engineered were not central to the business. The purpose must also be stated in terms of measurable entities. Only then can we be assured of its achievement.

USE THE PURPOSE IDENTIFIED TO CLEARLY DEFINE AND MODEL THE PROBLEM SITUATION

Although related, defining the problem is *not* the same as stating the purpose for business process engineering. Here, an investigation into possible contributing factors is conducted and individual opportunities for re-design are identified. Sometimes it is useful to create a model of the present situation. This is done for a number of purposes including: understanding, communication and analysis of the way things are. It must be stated that creation of such a model must not be allowed to stifle creativity, ingenuity, and a revolutionary approach to business process design. This can happen easily if the engineer's views become biased towards the existing way of doing things. In modeling problem situations, object technology will prove beneficial.

COMMENCE ANALYSIS USING THE IDENTIFIED OPPORTUNITIES AND CONTEXT MODELS CREATED

Note that this analysis is possible only if a defined and clear model of the process exists. Ishikawa diagrams, root cause and statistical analysis are among the main tools here. The purpose for this analysis is to identify and separate the common cause from special cause. Once the common and special causes are identified then a decision may be made whether to go for 'gradual process improvement' (i.e. the removal of special causes) or whether a whole new process is needed. If the latter is the case, then we have a design task on our hands.

DESIGN A NEW BUSINESS PROCESS

This new process is aimed to be fundamentally different in its internal characteristics (i.e. the structures, transformations and interactions composing it), yet still fulfil the same purpose as the previous process, only better, and demonstrably so.

MODEL THE NEW PROCESS

One central issue here is how do we capture and communicate this design? The answer is through creating a model of it. This is where object technology becomes an enabler.

IMPLEMENT THE MODEL

Here the business engineer will decide on the performance of various tasks or roles. To do so, a number of considerations such as the vision of the organization, best practices, current technology, funds and human resources available become prominent. Another critical task here is to decide what level of automation and technology to use. In terms of information support technologies, the re-engineered organization is in an enviable position as there is, through the application of object technology, a largely seamless path to the design and implementation of software systems.

Deliverables and outputs (post-condition)

Optimized business model.

Formal methods   Star rating ** (author D. Fowler)

Focus: Formal descriptions
Typical tasks for which this is needed: Construct the object model, evaluate quality
Related techniques: Contract specification
Input (pre-condition): Existing (partial) design
Underpinning concepts: Assertion language, Object-Z

Technique description

Formal specification is the process of creating precise mathematical models of a system. Formal specification languages allow the essential properties of a system to be captured precisely, at a high level. The benefits of using formal methods include: higher quality systems, as the match between computer programs and their specifications can be mathematically verified; a more manageable development process, as a formal requirements specification can be easily compared with the progress which has been made in implementing the system; cheaper, faster development (although the requirements specification phase may be longer, overall implementation time and cost are reduced due to the early identification of specification errors, omissions or ambiguities); their precision offers the potential for greater relevance, assisting in identifying conflicts among the various perspectives that will exist regarding the functional goals of a system; a formally documented requirements specification provides a precise medium for communication, both between specifier and developers and between specifier and clients; and formal specifications can provide a basis for acceptance testing, and also for litigation in the event of legal disputes.

Although formal methods have traditionally been used for the specification of highly technical or scientific systems, the potential which formal methods offer for facilitating the development of more relevant, higher quality software is now becoming recognized within other domains (Hall, 1990; Gerhart, 1990; Barden *et al.*, 1991; Nicholls, 1991; Hinchey and Bowen, 1995), including that of commercial information systems development.

A number of types of formal specification languages exist, built upon different formal logics, each of which are suitable for different applications. Algebraic/axiomatic specification languages describe abstract data types in terms of equations. This makes them useful for specifying prototypical systems since they support executable specifications more easily. Probably the most well known example is OBJ (Goguen, 1978), which has formed the basis for OBJ3 and CafeOBJ (Diaconescu and Futatsugi, 1996).

Perhaps the most widely adopted formal specification languages are Z and VDM. Consequently many of the OO formal specification languages are based on these. VDM++, Z++ and Object-Z belong to the model-based class of object-oriented specification languages in which data models are constructed and operations defined in terms of invariants and pre- and post-conditions. Coleman *et al.* (1994) have incorporated the idea of formal pre-condition and post-condition specifications as part of the Fusion method.

While Object-Z is probably the most mature of the Z-based OO specification languages, there are many other object-oriented formal specification languages based on Z; among them, OOZE (Alencar and Goguen, 1992), MooZ (Meira and Cavalcanti, 1992), Z++ (Lano, 1992) and ZEST (Cusack and Rafsanjani, 1992). Other object-oriented notations not based on Z include Fresco, VDM++ and Object-oriented Petri nets (OPNets: Lee and Park, 1993), which are suited to concurrent system specification. A few notations like HOOD (Heitz *et al.*, 1990) and subsets of Eiffel are aimed at specific languages. Each tend to provide comprehensive support only within their specific environments, with most tending to be focused on program design.

Technique usage

Formal methods are generally suited to large systems development projects, and may be applied to software development at three different levels:

- *Formal specification*: which involves the use of a formal language to create a specification that is less ambiguous and more amenable to formal/informal reasoning.

- *Formal development/verification*: which involves rigorous verification of desirable properties of a formally specified system, and the application of a refinement calculus resulting in executable code.

- *Machine-checked proofs*: in particular, the use of automated theorem provers or checkers which check the proofs for consistency and sound reasoning.

However, it is usually economically infeasible to apply all these stages unless the reliability of a system is truly critical. Although formal correctness proofs can help identify defects in software artefacts (Goldberg and Rubin, 1995, page 126), they are difficult to apply and require trained expert personnel.

Formal specification contributes to the requirements engineering activities. The objective of formal notations is to allow developers to build clear, precise and unambiguous models of what systems should do. Formally defining properties such as the types, attributes, operations and allowable states of the objects and classes in a system ensures a high quality specification of what the system should do (but not *how* it should do it). This precision demands a high level of understanding of the system. It also allows for better validation of the specification with the users (particularly if the users have the formal specification presented to them).

Once constructed, the specification provides a precise statement to the design team of what the system should do, but gives no indication of how this should be done. If it is important to the development of a system, the formal specification can be iteratively refined, to progressively add implementation detail. Each refinement can be proven to embody the functionality present in the higher level specification. If necessary, and if the formal method chosen supports it, this refinement can continue all the way down to program execution.

Metrics collection Star rating **

Focus: Collecting quantitative information for quality assessment and control
Typical tasks for which this is needed: Create and/or identify reusable components ('for reuse'), evaluate quality
Related techniques: Cohesion measurement, complexity measurement, coupling measurement, reuse measurement, statistical analysis of data
Input (pre-condition): Existing artefacts
Underpinning concepts: Measuring provides a quantitative basis for evaluation and improvement

Technique description

It is argued (e.g. Pfleeger *et al.*, 1997) that software engineering can never become a true engineering discipline until there is a solid underpinning of measurement-based theory and a quantitative approach. Measurement theory (e.g. Zuse, 1990) and measurement practice underpin this OPEN technique. Metrics (a.k.a. measures) provide objective and quantitative information on many aspects of software (e.g. designs, codes and processes) and to a variety of users (e.g. developers, managers, end-users, maintainers). Metrics can help a company to benchmark itself against industry norms, document improvements in quality or productivity over time or demonstrate enhanced usability (Constantine, 1997b).

Metrics can be collected for a number of software artefacts and at various scales. Some management aspects of deploying metrics programs are found in Jeffery and Berry (1993) and Hall and Fenton (1997) and in an OO context in

Henderson-Sellers (1995b, 1996). In addition, misuse (or even abuse) of metrics data is all too common (Pfleeger *et al.*, 1997). This is partly due to there being a multi-dimensional nature to both the internal, measurable characteristics and the external, more quality-focused metrics (see e.g. Fenton, 1994 for further discussion). Using a single measure to judge only one aspect of development is doomed to failure. Use of a goal-setting technique like GQM (q.v.) can be a useful precursor to metrics collection.

In selecting metrics, awareness of scales (nominal, ordinal, interval, ratio and absolute) is critical to data analysis; validation scope must be assessed – for example, cyclomatic complexity describes the structural complexity of code in the context of testing; it says nothing about maintainability nor reuse and is not helpful in analysis or cost estimation – wild extrapolations akin to many such statements made in the literature.

Measurement also links to CMM levels. Typically, level 3 organizations will be using metrics effectively; on the other hand, instigating a metrics program in a level 1 company does not automatically lift it to level 3 – although it is part of that maturation process.

Technique usage

Here we systematically summarize the various perspectives: inside a class, external at the class level (i.e. the specification or interface), system level (but ignoring relationships), system level relationships (excluding inheritance) and inheritance coupling (Henderson-Sellers, 1995a).

INSIDE A CLASS

For a coded class with n public methods (those that appear as services in the interface) and, in some languages, m public attributes together with r private methods and s private attributes, a number of intra-class metrics can be calculated. For example, for each of these $n + r$ methods, we can calculate a control flow complexity. This can be accomplished by local application of the cyclomatic complexity for each method, i.e. there must be $n + r$ such values. (Note: these metrics are only collectable once the design has been implemented, i.e. the code exists.) However, since good OO methods are only a few LOC long, the values calculated are probably not very useful.

As well as cyclomatic complexity, we could characterize each method by its size (assuming that a consistent definition for size is used). This gives $n+r$ values in the class for method size, which should be expressed, on a per class basis, in terms of a distribution of method size ($n + r$ values) together with appropriate measures of central tendency. A total method size may also be useful.

For each class, we can also do a straightforward count of total numbers of methods and attributes. This gives one way of representing overall *class size*, S_C, as either (a) a weighted or (b) an unweighted sum of method and attribute sizes.

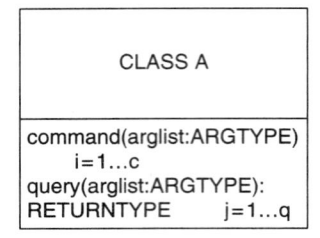

```
                ┌─────────────────────────────┐
                │         CLASS A             │
                ├─────────────────────────────┤
                │ command(arglist:ARGTYPE)    │
                │      i=1...c                │
                │ query(arglist:ARGTYPE):     │
                │ RETURNTYPE      j=1...q     │
                └─────────────────────────────┘
```

Figure B.2 A class offers a number of services in its interface. These may be queries (which return an object) or commands (which don't).

The number of pre-conditions and post-conditions indicate the extent to which the software contracting metaphor (Meyer, 1992c) has been used which infers a reliability value – each method should have both a pre- and a post-condition where the ratios of (number of pre-conditions/number of methods) and (number of post-conditions/number of methods) should both tend to unity. Small values imply less reliability and low robustness.

Cohesion can be measured by the Lack of Cohesion of Methods (LCOM) metric, proposed by Chidamber and Kemerer (1991) and corrected by Henderson-Sellers *et al.* (1996a). Again this is a value that can be calculated *for each class*.

One other metric is needed purely for C++ classes; that is, the number of declared **friend** classes which adds structural (and probably psychological) complexity to the interaction. We class this as internal rather than external for obvious reasons although it is arguably better categorized as a component of inter-CIRT coupling.

External at the class level

The interface (the external view to the class) can be characterized in terms of the total number of services, some of which are queries and some of which are commands (Figure B.2). We see, from the outside, no indication of (internal) size or complexity. We can thus count the total numbers of these commands and queries, possibly weighted by the number of arguments (see Henderson-Sellers, 1996, page 158 for details).

System level but ignoring relationships

System level metrics are often calculated as a simple summation of class metrics. For instance, the total number of classes in a system is an extremely rough measure of system size – one can say that a system containing 1000 classes is likely to be bigger (in all senses of the word) than one with only 20 classes.

We can then look at system-wide averages, assuming we have the appropriate interval or ratio scale, derived from the lower-level measures by evaluating measures of central tendency (mean, mode, median) for the number of commands, queries, methods and other class size measures.

System level relationships but excluding inheritance

System level metrics focus on coupling metrics (q.v.) which count either (a) whether or not there is any reference from class A to class B or (b) how many references exist between all class pairs. One specific type of coupling is inheritance coupling which can be described by a number of different measures (see Technique: Coupling measurement).

Usability metrics

Usability metrics (q.v.) are beginning to emerge (Constantine, 1997b). Three metrics have been proposed:

- essential efficiency
- task consolidation
- task concordance.

These metrics aim to provide quantitative data to assist in evaluating usability in a simple and straightforward manner, based on use-case-type narratives.

Reuse metrics

Reuse metrics (q.v.) attempt to measure design quality in terms of the extent to which inheritance hierarchies are used, both structurally and semantically. Two measures have been proposed by Yap and Henderson-Sellers (1997): the reuse ratio, U, and the specialization ratio, S:

- Reuse ratio, U, which gives an indication of developers inheriting from existing classes, is always less than 1. A value nearer 0 indicates a shallow, broad hierarchy.
- Specialization ratio, S, which also gives an indication of width (large values of S) additionally gives an indication of the extent to which multiple inheritance is used since
    - for a leafy (broad, shallow) structure, $S \gg 1$
    - for lots of multiple inheritance, $S \ll 1$.

Finally, some of these calculations are summarized in an example in Figure B.3. Of the 13 classes, 10 are superclasses and 11 subclasses. Thus $U = \frac{10}{13} = 0.76$ and $S = \frac{11}{10} = 1.1$. There is thus significant reuse but it is still fairly linear implying low use of specialization. The values of NOC_i is $\frac{16}{13} = 1.25$, or $\frac{16}{10} = 1.6$ if the leaf nodes are excluded.

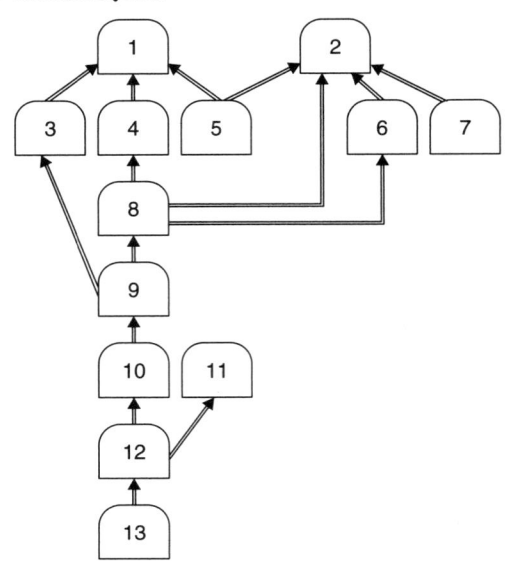

Figure B.3 Example of an inheritance network. Values for various metrics are given in the text (after Henderson-Sellers, 1996).

PROCESS METRICS

McGibbon (1995) suggests that process indicators should be measured, the metrics including:

- Product quality: measured by the number of defects and the number of changes per class subsequent to release of the product.
- Flexibility: measured by the number of enhancements per class and the number of systems reused.
- Time to build: measured in terms of the number of days required to develop a useful set of scenarios.
- Increase of skills: measured in terms of the number of new business areas entered and the increased skills profile of each employee.
- Responsiveness: measured in terms of the number of hours required to enhance the present system.
- Customer satisfaction: measured by the number of complaints (negative) and the number of positive comments (positive).

These process measures have the following desirable properties:

- Quantitative: real figures that can be tracked.
- Responsive: short timescale measurement possible.

- Relevant: key indicators.
- Significant: can substantiate an improvement.
- Understandable: LOC not understandable to end-users.
- Easily obtained: vital to ensure costs of collection don't outweigh benefits of collection.

Soft systems analysis   Star rating *

Focus: User requirements
Typical tasks for which this is needed: Analyze user requirements, identify user requirements
Related techniques: Abstraction utilization, action research, political systems analysis, social systems analysis
Input (pre-condition): Requirements and a realization that a situation is problematic
Underpinning concepts: Phenomenology, hermeneutics, General Systems Theory

Technique description

The objective of every systems study, including those that aim to provide a software product as a part of the solution, should be to improve, in some sense, a real world situation which is deemed to be problematic. To facilitate this, one seeks to model some aspect of that real world situation, or at least develop models which give insight into the real world. Indeed, the world is far too complicated to be fully comprehensible. Any modeling is therefore, by necessity, an extraction of relevant views from the problem situation.

Two interrelated questions arise from this simple observation:

- What is relevant? and
- To whom is it relevant?

In other words: What criteria might one apply to determine relevance, and who determines and applies these criteria?

To experienced systems practitioners this is a real dilemma, one they have been facing since the earliest days of the discipline. The core of the problem is the fact that perceptions are varied; people see different problems when faced with the same situation. Furthermore, people often come up with different solutions to those problems even if they agree on the nature of the problem at hand (Davis, 1988; Curtis, 1990).

This variation of views is manifest in the fact that people see, within a given problem situation, very many system models, each relevant to some viewer's understanding. Which system models are perceived makes the difference between my understanding of the problem situation and yours (Checkland, 1981).

Problem situations and system models are interrelated and complex. To fully appreciate this complexity requires a deeper and better understanding of how models are extracted from problem situations. Any methodology for conducting such a 'systems investigation' can be conceptualized as lying on a continuum between the extreme positions of:

- systematic analysis (hard approach), and
- systemic learning (soft approach).

The lack of complete success of the hard systems approaches to adequately model complex problem situations, particularly those dealing with systems of human activity, led many systems researchers and practitioners to look elsewhere for a solution. During the middle three decades of this century, strides were taken by the likes of Wittgenstein, von Bertalanffy, and Ackoff to define a new world view: one that built upon the systems paradigm. These approaches view systems as intellectual constructs with (among a number of characteristics) a purpose and emergent properties generally supporting that purpose. The work of researchers at the University of Lancaster over the last 20 years has sought to embed the notion of system in a practical problem-solving methodology, now termed 'Soft Systems Methodology (SSM)' (Checkland, 1981; Wilson, 1984; Checkland and Scholes, 1990; Davies and Ledington, 1991).

This alternative approach (soft systems or systemic learning) advocates immersion into the problem situation and conduct of action research (q.v.) and action learning. In other words, the exploration of the situation with a view to learning as much as possible about what it is, why it is there, and how things happen within it, using the intellectual construct of the system to gain insight (Davies and Ledington, 1991). In this endeavor, other people (individuals relevant to the problem situation being studied) will, more often than not, be called upon to assist the systems researcher in his/her fact finding, each inevitably offering their own views. The result of such action learning is a rich understanding of the problem situation which will, in turn, lead to richer and more relevant models of the Universe of Discourse (UoD), without destroying the emergent properties. In fact, this method of study seeks to capture the essence of these emergent properties (Davies and Ledington, 1991). Arising from this enhanced understanding, systemically desirable and culturally feasible changes will emerge and can be actioned.

Technique usage

SSM is traditionally depicted as a seven-stage methodology (Checkland, 1981). However, more recent writings of Checkland and his co-workers depict it in terms of two parallel streams of enquiry (Checkland and Scholes, 1990) although the stages are connected using directional arrows. This does not necessarily imply a sequential flow and iteration is a central feature of the methodology. Each stage is summarized below.

Stage 1: Problem Situation Considered Problematic

A problem situation is a part of reality, our social world of interactions, which has been perceived as problematic by at least one stakeholder (Davies and Ledington, 1991). The initial process undertaken involves a process of discovery using standard fact-gathering methods. Interaction, active learning and action research are the underpinning elements of this stage. To appreciate and analyze the situation as a culture, the techniques of social systems analysis and political systems analysis (q.v.) may be employed.

Stage 2: Problem Expressed

Following (or during, or indeed before a second round of) fact gathering, the analyst collates and attempts to present the problem in a way that makes some sense of the situation, and for the purpose of communicating the findings to others. This can be done in a number of ways: verbally, textually or pictorially. SSM practitioners have found that, of these, the last approach, or at least a combination of the last two approaches, is the most effective. They usually use rich pictures (q.v.) to express their views of the problem situation. More recently, the use of audio and video tapes have also been demonstrated as being useful.

Stage 3: Root Definitions of Relevant Purposeful Activity Systems are Developed

After creating a structured representation of the problem situation, it is possible to define system models which might usefully be evaluated. This constitutes the transition from the real world to the modeling world. This 'disengagement' from the real world is triggered by the formulation of a 'root definition', which expresses the core or the essence of the perception or 'system' to be modeled (Checkland and Scholes, 1990). In terms of modeling, a root definition is a textually based transformational model that expresses how some 'inputs' are transformed into 'outputs'.

A well-structured root definition contains six elements (identified by the mnemonic: CATWOE). These are (Smyth and Checkland, 1976):

- **C**lient(s) or **C**ustomer(s): the beneficiaries or the victims of the system.
- **A**ctor(s): those who carry out the transformation.
- **T**ransformation: the main activity of the system, represented by 'input' being transformed into 'output'.
- **W**orldview: the outlook or view that makes the system meaningful.
- **O**wner: the person or entity who has the authority to abolish the system.
- **E**nvironment: the limitations or restrictions which impinge upon the system.

STAGE 4: CONCEPTUAL MODELS OF THE SYSTEM NAMED IN THE ROOT DEFINITIONS ARE CONSTRUCTED

Once the relevant system has been defined, one must expand the root definition as a series of logically dependent activities required for the transformation to take place within the worldview of the system as described in the CATWOE. These models may be primary-task (dealing with tasks to be performed) or issue-based (dealing with concerns or issues) (Checkland and Wilson, 1980). The model is then pictorially constructed as a network of nodes (activities) and arcs (logical dependencies).

STAGE 5: COMPARISON OF MODELS AND THE REAL WORLD

Through a number of techniques such as informal discussion, formal questioning or model overlay (Checkland and Scholes, 1990), the model is compared with the real world and validated. A new iteration of any one or combination of other stages may result from this validation.

STAGE 6: CHANGES: SYSTEMICALLY DESIRABLE AND CULTURALLY FEASIBLE

A number of recommendations for change will emanate from the debates held in the previous stage. Not all these changes are implementable. We need to decide if they are desirable and culturally feasible. To do this the analyst must look into the cultural nature of the problem situation. The analyst must understand the context in which these changes are recommended. Social system analysis and political systems analysis (q.v.), if performed earlier in the process, will be of immense help here.

STAGE 7: ACT TO IMPROVE THE PROBLEM SITUATION

Once the changes have been narrowed down and agreed upon, implementation should commence. The analyst must bear in mind that the implementation process itself may bring about new problems. Of course, SSM may be used again to study this problem.

Deliverables and outputs (post-condition)

An aligned conceptual model, recommendations, insight into the system, new issues or tasks.

System acceptance Star rating **

Focus: User acceptance of system
Typical tasks for which this is needed: Deliver product to customer, undertake post-implementation review

Related techniques: Acceptance testing
Input (pre-condition): System for client approval
Underpinning concepts: Users should be satisfied with product

Technique description

It has been recognized that the ratio of software to hardware failures in computerized systems is indeed quite high, indicating that the majority of system quality problems have a software origin (Neumann, 1995). In such an environment, procurement and acceptance of software must be conducted very carefully. Indeed, there may be a financial and/or legal consequence if acceptance testing fails, e.g. payment for product not released, product rejected (Baudoin and Hollowell, 1996, page 153).

Similarly to all other products, procurers of software also use a number of criteria to make a selection, or to accept an offer. When accepting software, the customer often makes a selection based essentially on the following criteria, at least at the highest level:

- price
- availability, and
- quality.

System acceptance is an important late stage technique within the development lifecycle involving both the developer and the customer. Often incorporating a series of tests and demonstrations, we define system acceptance as determination of the degree of conformance of the proposed product with the current version of the user requirements as demonstrated by the developer and perceived by the procurer.

System acceptance is, however, often mistakenly equated with 'acceptance testing' which is only a possible subactivity of system acceptance. Whilst system acceptance is (or should be) a lifecycle technique, acceptance testing (q.v.) is one possible approach that may provide some evidence towards the determination of the degree of conformance of software being demonstrated and the intended requirements the software is to fulfil. It is important to note therefore that, to this end, approaches other than testing may also be used. For example, once it is determined that some requirement is to be fulfilled, the conformance of the system with such a requirement may be demonstrated through a formal proof.

It should also be noted that, as a process-oriented technique, system acceptance is fundamentally different in nature to testing in that, whilst testing is conducted with an intent to discover non-conformance (Myers, 1976), acceptance is generally intended to demonstrate conformance.

PREPARING FOR SYSTEM ACCEPTANCE

At the time of system acceptance, it is highly likely that, of the three top-level criteria of price, availability and quality, the first two are already completely or nearly completely satisfied. The central issue of system acceptance is the assessment of the quality of the proposed system. By this we mean that:

- upon presentation of the system to the customer, for acceptance, it is logical to assume that the system is ready to be delivered or nearly so
- if the customers continue to be interested in the product, the financial matters are satisfactorily resolved. Thus the only remaining matter to be decided is that of the quality of the product.

However, as system acceptance is a demonstration of the extent of conformance of software to the requirements, it is important for it to be conducted in an environment that assures both:

- coverage of all important areas of requirement, and
- the establishment of quantitative acceptance success criteria.

To ensure that these are both fulfilled, we recommend an approach that recognizes that the activity of software acceptance is, in fact, identical to that of product quality determination in that they both refer to the degree of satisfaction of the customer with the software product.

Technique usage

The technique described below is a systemically-based system acceptance technique that guides the developer from very early in the development process towards the development of a mechanism that ensures criteria coverage and quantification of success factors. Once the above two goals are satisfied, the customer must evaluate the quality of the system as delivered.

A SIX-STAGE TECHNIQUE FOR SYSTEM ACCEPTANCE

Recognizing quality as a multi-faceted perception held by a variety of stakeholders who might have differing or indeed conflicting goals and objectives, the approach assists in identification of these objectives and their reconciliation, and then assures that they collectively cover the requirements stated. It can also assist in determining requirements that otherwise may remain tacit.

The following is a depiction of the method proposed.

Stage 1: Construct a quality matrix

(1) Identify and name as many relevant systems as possible, where each name is a 'cognitive handle' that allows the identification and communication of a particular coherent and purposeful set of activities (Checkland, 1981). A relevant system name is usually presented in the form of 'A system to be/do/achieve X'. Examples of such definitions are:

- a system to generate birth certificates
- a system to generate reusable components
- a system to provide a uniform computing platform across government agencies.

(2) As the first dimension of the matrix (rows), identify and name, with respect to each relevant system, the stakeholder classes belonging to each of the three role categories of client, actor or owner. Use the following heuristics for such determination:
- clients: are the beneficiaries or victims of the results of the activity being conducted by the system
- actors: those who operate the system
- owners: those with the power to abolish the system.

(3) Discuss and reach agreement with all stakeholders concerned upon the first level (e.g. reliability) and second level (e.g. accuracy) product quality attribute classes that are to form the second dimension of the matrix. In selecting such attributes, we recommend a set that is compatible with the recently emerging IEEE standard of software product quality and/or those promulgated by the ISO standard 9126. These attributes include those of functionality, reliability, usability and maintainability. Each of these attributes may be decomposed into lower level attributes. For example, reliability may be decomposed into sub-attributes of self-containment, accuracy (correctness), completeness, integrity and consistency. (For a comprehensive treatment of this subject see Gillies, 1992.) Do not eliminate an attribute class unless there is solid reason to do so – and one upon which there unanimous agreement.

(4) Iterate between 1, 2, and 3 until all stakeholder classes and their respective product quality attribute classes are determined.

(5) Physically construct the matrix.

Stage 2: Complete the matrix

(1) Within each intersection of the matrix, identify, negotiate and agree, with that particular stakeholder, a number of specific goals that, in his or her view, the software needs to satisfy in order to possess the particular quality attribute under question.

(2) For each such purpose, identify and agree upon a particular set of premises that need to be in place for each aim or purpose to be achieved.
  Relate each of these aims or purposes to a set of requirements in the requirements specification. If some aims or purposes identified above cannot be related to specific extant requirements, then a requirements elicitation technique may need to be (re-)invoked.

(3) Identify a broad number of criteria that, whilst not violating the premises identified in step 2, might assess the capability of the product in its ability to satisfy each requirement identified above.

(4) Negotiate and agree upon a sub-set of the criteria in 3 with at least one criterion per each stated requirement.

(5) Select or devise, and agree upon, a measurement or other means of showing conformance (e.g. formal proof) of each criterion in 4.

(6) Select and agree on a meaningful and measurable level of success for each criterion, consistent and compatible with the measurement devised or selected in 5. For guidance on how to establish 5 and 6, reference may be made to the Technique: GQM and to the work of Fenton (1991).

Stage 3: Test for coverage

(1) Cross-check to see if all requirements from the specification have been represented by criteria selected as a result of multiple application of step 2 of stage 2.

(2) If not, revisit the situation and ask 'Why?'

Stage 4: Document

(1) Document all agreements in an appropriate language. This might require involvement of legal professionals.

(2) Submit the document to configuration management.

(3) Arrange for the document to be signed by the interested parties.

Stage 5: Update

(1) Revise and update by going through at least stages 2, 3 and 4 every time there is an official change to the requirements specification.

Stage 6: Enact

(1) At the time of system acceptance, use the latest version of the acceptance document produced in stage 4, to obtain a list of all requirements the conformance to which is to be demonstrated and the details of the corresponding methods and success criteria for each such demonstration.

(2) Obtain and arrange all resources needed to perform each and every demonstration.

(3) Determine the interdependencies particularly between:
- requirements (e.g. requirement 26 is predicated upon the satisfaction of requirement 32)
- evaluation techniques (e.g. test to demonstrate conformance to requirement 28 requires a structure which is developed when formally proving program Y, the proof of which is a success factor for demonstrating requirement 55)

- physical resources required (e.g. tests for program X and Y both have to run on the same machine and utilize the same peripherals).

(4) Using the information in steps 2 and 3 above, produce a project management activity network (CPM) and a project plan for the system acceptance activity.

(5) Perform each acceptance activity (demonstration, test, analysis, proof, etc.) as stated in the acceptance document and evaluate the results (this should be easy since explicit success factors are available).

(6) Sign off with the customer.

Deliverables and outputs (post-condition)

Recommendation on whether to accept system or not.

TQM   Star rating ***

Focus: Quality
Typical tasks for which this is needed: Evaluate quality
Related techniques: Metrics collection, quality templates
Input (pre-condition): Desire to improve process quality (and hence product quality)
Underpinning concepts: Quality can be managed at the process level

Technique description

TQM is a set of techniques – some might say a philosophy – developed essentially in industrial and commercial environments. It focuses on the concept of quality which it identifies as arising from the process central to the particular project/industry. A quantitative (statistical) study of this central process can highlight improvements which management (but not workers) can make to the system itself. The application of object-oriented ideas to the management of software development is also aimed at improving the quality of the finished product. Indeed, direct parallels between object technology have been drawn (Henderson-Sellers, 1991; Howard, 1992).

TQM advocates the use of measurement to create an environment of continual improvement. Quality is factored into the process rather than as an afterthought, i.e. through quality assessment which is essentially testing after the product is 100 per cent complete. TQM techniques are useful to improve both business processes and software processes where the focus is on the process itself and not on its users. Improvements are incremental. For large jumps in quality improvement a more radical approach, such as BPR, is needed. Yet, eventually, the extent of improvement is assessed in terms of product characteristics (quality) which is user-assessed.

Whilst TQM was a management 'buzzword' of the 1980s and early 1990s, its relevance to objects and in particular to distributed objects is noted by Fingar *et al.* (1997). In a distributed computing system, guaranteed defect-free components are vital. Thus the process support and continuous process improvement espoused in OPEN is recognized as providing a computing environment in which continuous process improvement can become a reality.

Total quality management (TQM) has its origins in seminars presented to the Japanese by American experts after the Second World War. Although seen to be applicable in the Japanese environment, it was doubted for many years whether the Western culture was amenable for the support of the ideas originally proposed by Deming and his colleagues (see e.g. Deming, 1981). However the success of Japanese industry has caused industries in the USA, Europe, Australia etc. to 'think again' and to investigate actively the possible adoption of, for instance, Deming's 'fourteen points'. These points stress the need for continuous quality management not simply at the end of the process, and the full involvement and commitment of all staff who act cooperatively not competitively.

Zultner (1988) examines the interpretation of these fourteen points to software quality engineering. The fourteen points (synopsized in Table B.1) are accomplished, in part, by diagrammatic tools such as Pareto charts, control charts, histograms and scattergrams. The use of quantitative and statistical tools underlines not only point 3, but provide a rationale on which several of the other points are based (e.g. points 2, 4, 5, 6). Education and training are also major factors as are leadership and constancy of purpose, which should be obvious to *all* employees. Enhanced interaction between departments and between workers and management assist in accomplishing a continuous improvement in quality engendered to a significant degree by the pride which all workers can have in their accomplishments. Total quality management, as practiced in commercial organizations, can thus easily be translated to MIS departments and to software development houses (Zultner, 1988).

TQM embodies many of the best parts of old management philosophies but seen from a different angle. For example, although Deming stresses that management by objectives (MBO) must be eliminated, the idea of goal setting is retained in the TQM philosophy with the twist that says that once attained, new goals must be set in order to accomplish gradual and continuous improvement.

In the software industry, plagued by overruns and poor quality, the TQM approach would seem to be a godsend. Indeed, software quality assurance professional groups around the world are rapidly gaining both strength and visibility within the community. In Australia, the Software Quality Association, itself a Special Interest Group of the Australian Computer Society, has run certification courses designed to meet both Australian and international quality standards.

The new 'quality' emphasis is epitomized by 'Joiner's Triangle' (Joiner and Scholtes, 1986) in which quality is represented as being at the top apex of a triangle with supporting vertices of 'scientific approach' or 'data-driven decision-making' and 'implementation by teamwork'. Both these supporting concepts provide a solid support for the attainment of quality. This new quality-focused culture can also be seen as striving for continual improvement, in which frame of

Table B.1 Deming's Fourteen Points (as synopsized in Henderson-Sellers, 1991 from Zultner, 1998).

(1) Create constancy of purpose
(2) Adopt the new TQM philosophy
(3) Evaluate the system objectively and quantitatively
(4) Don't award business on price tag, rather on quality
(5) Aim for constant improvement
(6) Institute on-the-job training
(7) Institute leadership rather than control
(8) Drive out fear (of punishment)
(9) Break down inter-departmental barriers (and rivalries)
(10) Eliminate slogans (which are usually not achievable)
(11) Eliminate numerical goals and objectives (including MBO)
(12) Give workers pride in their work
(13) Institute programs of self-improvement
(14) Involve everyone

reference the vertices of the triangle can be relabeled, more abstractly perhaps, as 'practice' and 'corporate culture' supporting a 'commitment' to the central goal of continual quality improvement.

Focusing on process and not people as TQM does, it takes away blame from the individual and supports a stronger process focus. This can involve a greater demand on audit trails and a large amount of paperwork being generated. Whilst this is not bad in itself, there is a danger that the company may aim to optimize the paperwork without a corresponding improvement in the process being documented. After all it is improved quality that is the goal not a set of documents that purport to document a quality process.

Technique usage

Implementing TQM in a software development organization is no different to doing so in a manufacturing plant. Employees need to be schooled in the fourteen points of Table B.1, to become conversant with the need to quantify and with statistical language. Rather than a technique to accomplish a task, as are many other OPEN techniques, TQM concentrates on the culture of the organization and aligns it with quality-focused ideas above all else.

384   SUITES OF TECHNIQUES

```
Elephant population, Serengeti National Park:
YEAR                    POP.

1980                    30,609
1985                    40,011
1990                    36,109
1995                    42,206
2000                    50,000 *

* figure is an estimate
```

YEAR		POPULATION
2000	🐘🐘🐘🐘🐘🐘	50,000 est
1995	🐘🐘🐘🐘	42,206
1990	🐘🐘🐘	36,109
1985	🐘🐘🐘🐘	40,011
1980	🐘🐘🐘	30,609

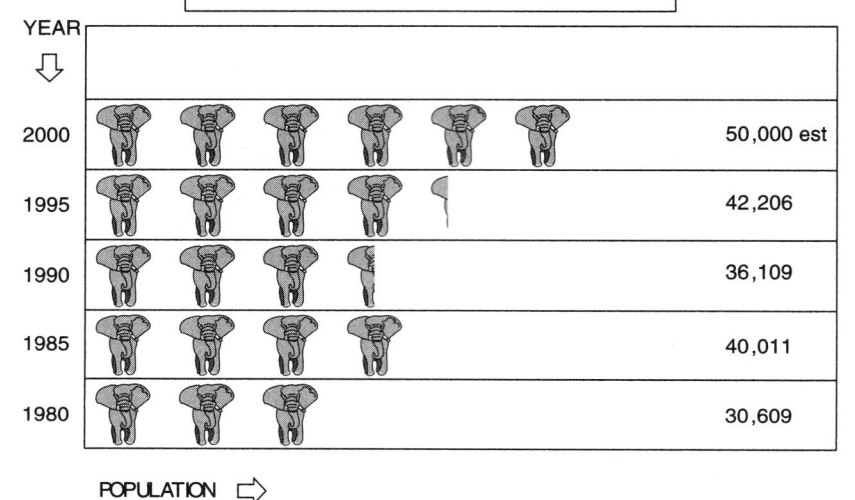

Figure B.4 Comparison of two data presentation techniques: (a) table with numbers and (b) table with symbols.

Deliverables and outputs (post-conditions)

Statistical analyses which can be used to improve the process and hence the product quality. Improved quality of the organizational unit's culture.

Visualization techniques   Star rating **

Focus: Communication, user interface
Typical tasks for which this is needed: Code, construct the object model, design user interface, evaluate quality, undertake architectural design, undertake usability design
Related techniques: Usability measurement
Input (pre-condition): Any artefact which needs visualizing; often data representations

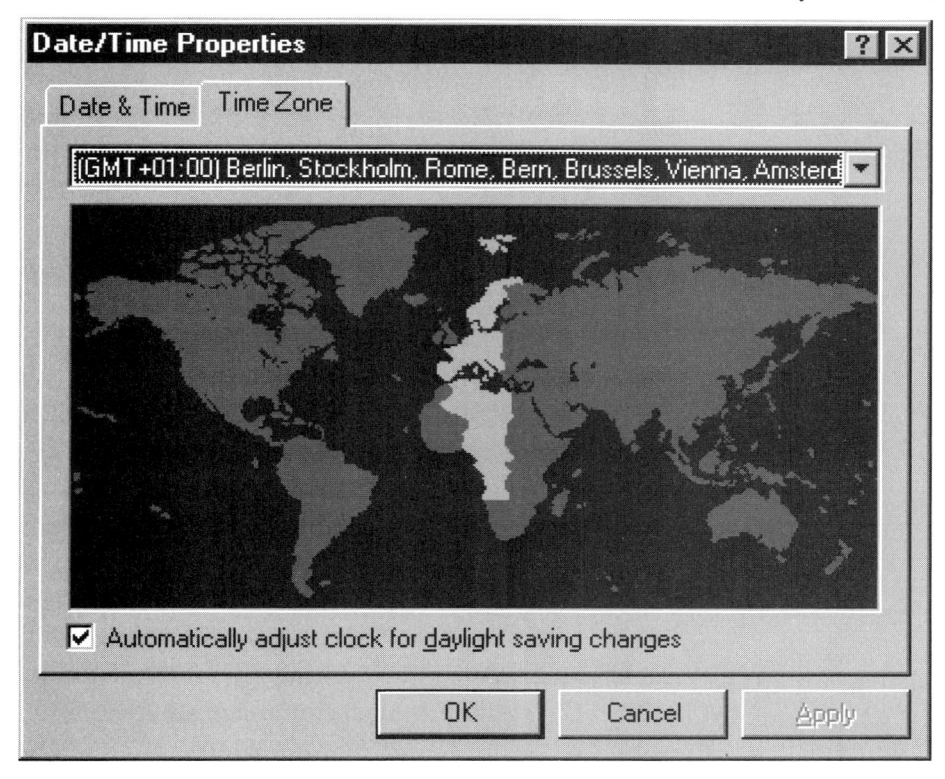

Figure B.5 Map presentation (© Microsoft Corporation).

Underpinning concepts: Pictures are more understandable than tables or words

Technique description

The efficacy of a user's interaction with a software system, among other things, is dependent on how he or she is assisted in visualizing the information that is being presented (Preece *et al.*, 1994). In other words, one very important element of success of any software system, in terms of its usability at least, is how effectively users can visualize the information or what is happening. Visualization techniques assist with this concern.

Human visualization processes are both optical/visual and cognitive. By 'optical/visual' we mean those processes that relate to the functioning of the eyes and the elementary pre-processing performed in the visual system or its interface with deeper cognitive mechanisms. By 'cognitive' we mean those mechanisms which are performed in the brain and manipulate the *results* of a visual observation. Of course, there is no clear dividing line between the two areas. Many processes might clearly fall into one or the other category, but many also

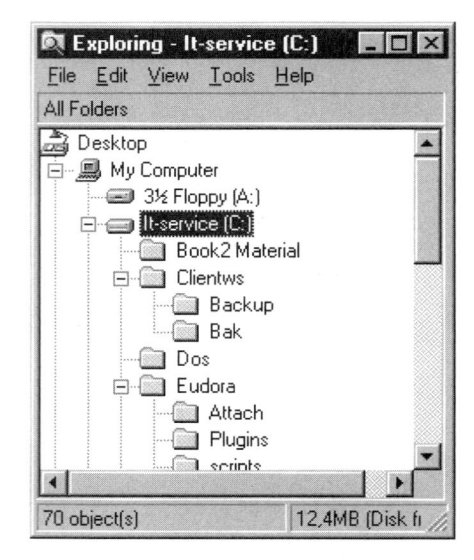

Figure B.6 Example of the folding technique (© Microsoft Corporation).

fall in a grey area in between or can be shown to have distinct elements of both. Nevertheless, we can identify and categorize a number of techniques that *largely* assist one or the other of such processes. We therefore create the two categories of techniques of cognitive assistance and visual assistance.

- *Cognitive assistance*: This category includes examples such as metaphors, cognitive clues and the use of familiar formats.
- *Visual assistance*: This category includes examples such as methods for folding, panning, zooming and the use of dimensions.

Technique usage

This being a practically-oriented book, rather than going into the cognitive details of how or why these techniques work, we will simply present examples of the utilization of these techniques and a brief description of each, and let the reader decide.

COGNITIVE ASSISTANCE TECHNIQUES

Metaphors This is the technique of using the layout and interactions of a familiar setup to the would-be user and replicating it (at least in a stylized fashion) on the computer screen. Examples of metaphors include the desktop metaphor used in the Windows^{TM} from Microsoft Inc. and the oscilloscope metaphor used in many engineering measurement software products.

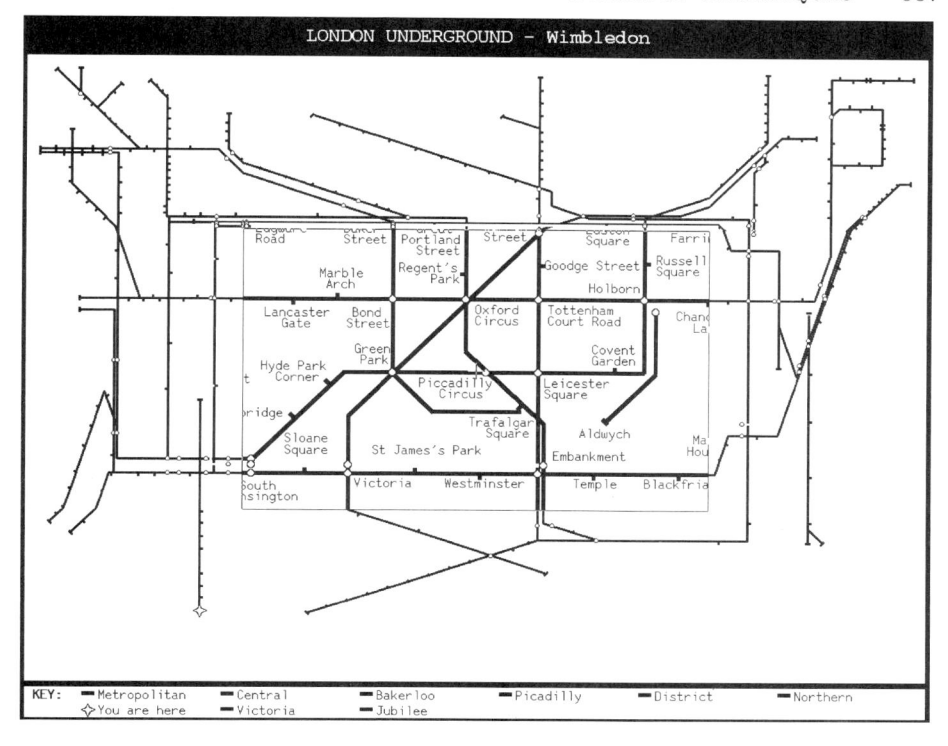

Figure B.7 Bifocal map of the London underground system (after Leung and Apperley, 1994).

Cognitive clues A cognitive clue is similar to a metaphor. It is the process of using a familiar symbol to represent units of what that symbol represents to most humans. Compare the two presentations in Figure B.4. Many people prefer symbolic rendering to arithmetical tables.

Use of familiar formats This is essentially the embodiment of the very logical advice not to 're-invent the wheel'. If it is certain that your audience are already familiar with a specific form of presentation of the data they expect, then present it that way. For example, showing financial accounts on the screen in the familiar T account format rather than two distinct lists of entry. Another example would be the use of a 'graph' to present the continuous change of one variable against another to scientists and engineers.

Use of tables, matrices and maps are amongst other examples of this concept (Figure B.5).

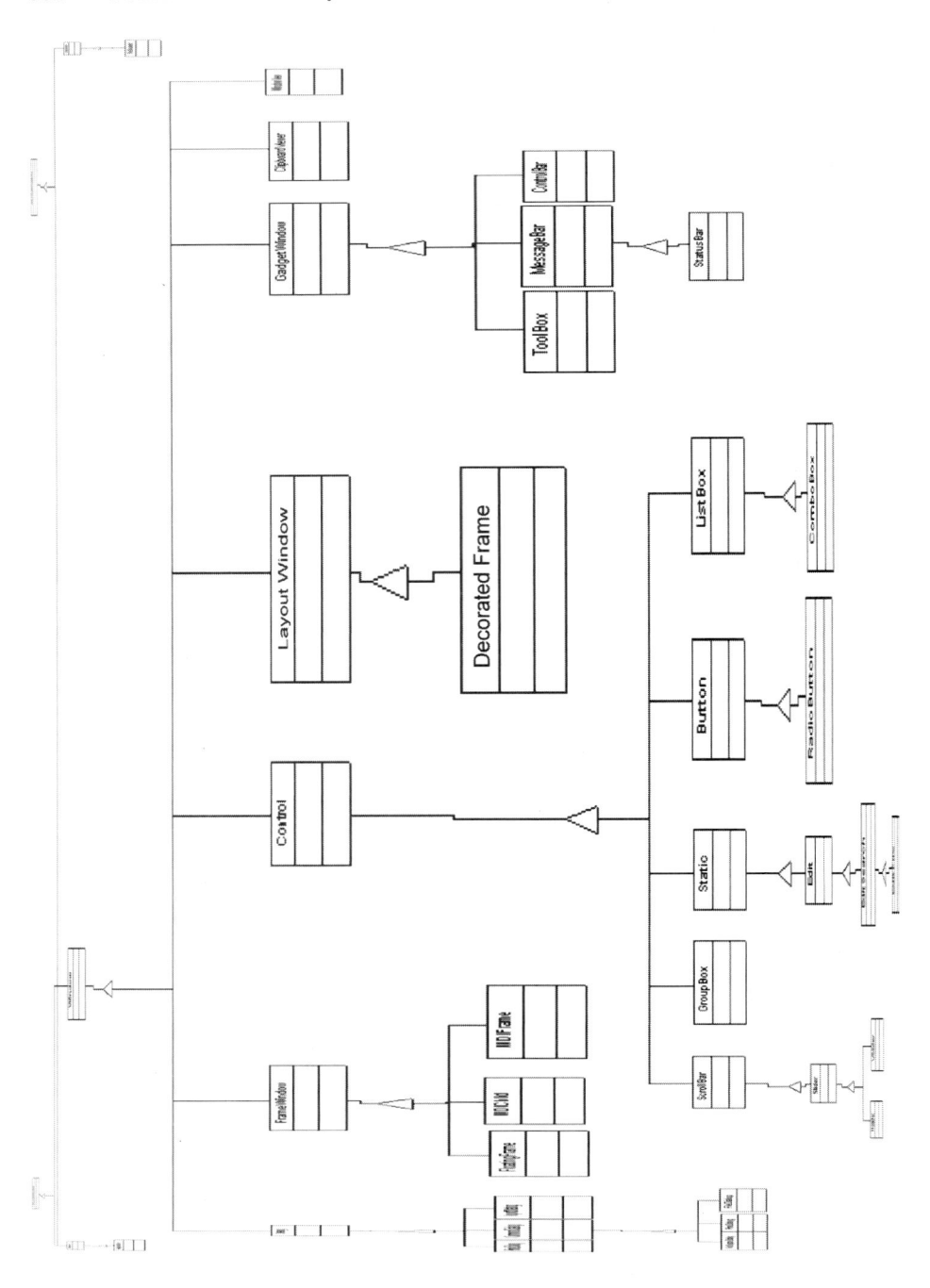

Figure B.8 Fisheye diagram (OMT diagram) (courtesy Y. Leung).

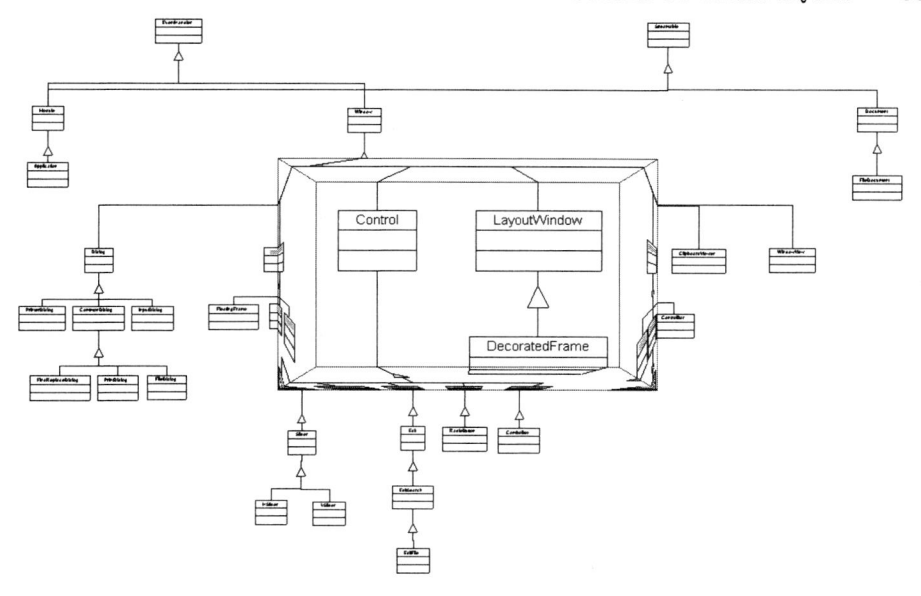

Figure B.9 Bevelled lens example (after Leung *et al.*, 1996).

VISUAL ASSISTANCE TECHNIQUES

Folding Folding is somewhat halfway between the two categories of cognitive and visual. It is the implementation of the cognitive concept of abstraction (q.v.) in a visual manner. The Windows 95, Windows Explorer makes use of this technique (Figure B.6 where (a) is folded and (b) has been unfolded).

Panning Panning is moving a small aperture over a large canvas and displaying those items on the canvas that are under the aperture. The scroll mechanism of Word for Windows is one such example.

Zooming Zooming is the enlargement of a selected section of the canvas so details will be easily viewed. Many computer-aided design (CAD) systems make extensive use of zooming.

Unfortunately, however, there is a problem with panning and zooming. The problem is that if the canvas is too large, we may lose our place on it when we pan or zoom. In other words we may still need visual clues as to what lies beyond the current contents of the aperture so we can move effectively to a new location of our interest. There are a number of ways of assisting with this. Folding is, of course, one possible way. Others include bifocal and fish-eye maps.

Map distortion A *bifocal* map is one in which the entire canvas is displayed on the screen whilst the contents of an aperture or small window are displayed at a higher resolution (Figure B.7). This approach is particularly useful for displaying geographical maps and similar layouts (e.g. as part of a browser for a class library). In certain variations of this technique the majority of the screen 'real estate' is dedicated to the contents of the aperture whilst a small map of the entire canvas and the relative position of the aperture is displayed in a corner of a screen.

A *fish-eye* map (Figure B.8) is an interesting and innovative enhancement to bifocal maps. The basic idea is that the aperture is retained at the centre of the screen, taking up a significant amount of 'real estate'. As one moves away from the border of the aperture and on to the rest of the canvas, the scale of the map grows progressively (various scales are used but the logarithmic scale is popular). Therefore at any one time the entire map is visible, but the points closer to the aperture (which are more likely to be of interest immediately) are shown in greater detail than points far from where we are now. Meanwhile, cognitive continuity is preserved. Other distortion techniques are also possible, e.g. the bevelled lens (Figure B.9) and the document lens (Robertson and Mackinlay, 1993).

Deliverables and outputs (post-conditions)

Better presentation of information.

References

Abbott, R.J. (1983). Program design by informal English descriptions, *Comm. ACM*, **26**(11), 882–894

Abbott, R.J. (1987). Knowledge abstraction, *Comm. ACM*, **30**(8), 664–671

Albrecht, A.J. and Gaffney, J.R. (1983). Software function, source lines of code and development effort prediction: a software science validation, *IEEE Trans. Software Eng.*, **9**(6), 639–648

Alencar, A. and Goguen, J. (1992). OOZE. In *Object Orientation in Z* (S. Stepney, R. Barden and D. Cooper eds), Workshops in Computing, Springer-Verlag, London

Alexander, C. (1979). *The Timeless Way of Building*. Oxford University Press

Anderson, M.Q. and Lievano, R.J. (1986). *Quantitative Management. An Introduction* 2nd edn. Kent Publishing Company, Belmont, CA, 873pp

Andleigh, P.K. and Gretzinger, M.R. (1992). *Distributed Object-Oriented Data-Systems Design*. Prentice Hall Inc., Englewood Cliffs, NJ, 495pp

Anon (1991). *HyperCard Basics*. Apple Computer

Ashworth, C. and Goodland, M. (1990). *SSADM: A Practical Approach*. McGraw-Hill

Bailey, R.W. (1989). *Human Performance Engineering* 2nd edn. Prentice Hall, New Jersey

Baklund, E., Civello, F., Knag, K. and Mitchell, R. (1995). Extending interaction diagrams, *Report on Object Analysis and Design*, **2**(2), 24–33

Baldwin, J.M. (ed.) (1940). *Dictionary of Philosophy and Psychology*. Peter Smith, New York, USA

Barden, R., Stepney, S. and Cooper, D. (1991). The use of Z. In *Z User Workshop, York 1991* (ed. J. E. Nicholls), Workshops in Computing, Springer-Verlag, 99–124

Barnes, B.H. and Bollinger, T.B. (1991). Making reuse cost-effective, *IEEE Software*, **8**(1), 13–24

Barry, D. (1995). On the road to standards, *Obj. Magazine*, **5**(6), 84–86

Basili, V.R. and Rombach, H.D. (1988). The TAME project: towards improvement-orientated software environments, *IEEE Trans. Software Eng.*, **1**(4), 758–773

Baudoin, C. and Hollowell, G. (1996). *Realizing the Object-Oriented Lifecycle*. Prentice Hall, New Jersey, USA, 508pp

Beck, K. and Cunningham, W. (1989). A laboratory for teaching object-oriented thinking, *Procs. 1989 OOPSLA Conference, ACM SIGPLAN Notices*, **24**(10), 1–6

Beckhard, R. (1969). *Organizational Development: Strategy and Models*. Addison-Wesley, Reading, MA, USA

Beedle, M.A. (1997). Pattern based reengineering, *Object Magazine*, **6**(11), 56–70

Bellin, D. and Simone, S.S. (1997). *The CRC Card Book*. Addison-Wesley, Reading, MA, USA, 290pp

Ben-Ari, M. (1990). *Principles of Concurrent and Distributed Programming*. Prentice Hall, 225pp

Berard, E.V. (1993). *Essays on Object-Oriented Software Engineering: Volume 1*. Prentice Hall, Englewood Cliffs, NJ, 352pp

Bezant (1995). *SOMATiK User Guide*. Bezant Object Technologies, 6 St Mary's St, Wallingford, Oxon, OK10 0LE, England

Bielak, R. and McKim, J.C. Jr. (1993). The many faces of a class, *J. Obj.-Oriented Prog.*, **6**(5), 81–85, 95

Bilow, S.C. (1995). Defining and developing user-interface intensive applications with use cases, *Report on Object Analysis and Design*, **1**(5), 28–34

Blanchard, K. and Johnson, S. (1983). *The One Minute Manager*. Willow Books, NY, USA

Blum, F.H. (1955). Action research – a scientific approach, *Philosophy of Science*, **22**, 1–7

Bobrow, D.G. (1989). The object of desire, *Datamation*, **35**(9), 37–41

Bock, C. and Odell, J. (1994). A foundation for composition, *J. Obj.-Oriented Prog.*, **7**(6), 10–14

Booch, G. (1991). *Object-Oriented Design with Applications*. Benjamin/Cummings, Menlo Park, CA, 580pp

Booch, G. (1994). *Object-Oriented Analysis and Design with Applications* (2nd edn). The Benjamin/Cummings Publishing Company, Inc., Redwood City, CA, USA, 589pp

Booch, E.G. (1996). Patterns and protocols, *Report on Object Analysis and Design*, **2**(7), 2–4, 8

Booch, G., and Vilot, M. (1990). Object-oriented design. Inheritance relationships, *The C++ Report*, **2**(9), 8–11

Bowen, J. and Hinchey, M. (1995). 7 more myths of formal methods, *IEEE Software*, **12**(4), 34–41

Bracha, G. and Cook, W. (1990). Mixin-based inheritance, *Proc. ECOOP/OOPSLA '91*, ACM, 303–311

Brachman, R.J. (1985). 'I lied about the trees' or, defaults and definitions in knowledge representation, *The AI Magazine*, **6**(3), 80–93

Brice, A. (1993). Using models in analysis, *Computing*, 27 May 1993, 41

Bruce, K., Petersen, L. and Fietch, A. (1997). Subtyping is not a good 'match' for object-oriented languages, *Proc. ECOOP '97*, LNCS 1241, 104–127

Budd, T. (1991). *An Introduction to Object-Oriented Programming.* Addison-Wesley, Wokingham, UK, 399pp

Buckley, F.J. (1994). Implementing configuration management, *IEEE Computer*, **27**(2), 56–61

Bungard, K. (1993). Client/server computing. Presentation to the Australian Computer Society Object-Oriented Special Interest Group (NSW Branch)

Buschmann, F. (1995). Pattern-oriented software architecture, *Conf. Proc. Object Expo Europe*, 25–29 September 1995, London, England, SIGS Conferences Ltd, 57–66

Buschmann, F., Meunier, R., Rohnert, H., Sommerlad, P. and Stal, M. (1996). *Pattern-Oriented Software Architecture. A System of Patterns.* J. Wiley and Sons, Chichester, UK, 457pp

Butterworth, P. (1991). ODBMS: ODBMSs as database managers, *J. Obj.-Oriented Programming*, **4**(4), 55–57

Campbell, J. (1982). *Grammatical Man: Information, Entropy, Language, and Life.* Simon and Schuster, New York, NY, USA

Canning, P., Cook, W., Hill, W., Olthoff. W. and Mitchell, J. (1989). F-bounded polymorphism for object-oriented programming, *Proc. 4th Int. Conf. Func. Prog. Lang. and Arch.*, Imperial College London, September 1989, 273–280

Cannon, R. (1992). *Lecturing.* HERDSA, NSW, Australia

Cant, S.N., Henderson-Sellers, B., and Jeffery, D.R. (1994). Application of cognitive complexity metrics to object-oriented programs, *J. Obj.-Oriented Programming*, **7**(4), 52–63

Cant, S., Jeffery, D.R. and Henderson-Sellers, B. (1995). A conceptual model of cognitive complexity of elements of the programming process. *Inf. Software Technol.*, **37**(7), 351–362

Card, D. and Glass, R.L. (1990). *Measuring Software Design Quality.* Prentice Hall, Englewood Cliffs, NJ, USA

Cardelli, L. and Wegner, P. (1985). On understanding types, data abstraction and polymorphism, *ACM Computing Surveys*, **17**(4), 471–521

Casais, E. (1998). Re-engineering object-oriented legacy systems, *J. Obj.-Oriented Prog.*, **10**(8), 45–52

Case, T. (1993). Database design for object-oriented systems. Honours thesis, School of Information Systems, University of New South Wales, Australia

Case, T., Henderson-Sellers, B. and Low, G. (1995). Extending the MOSES object-oriented analysis and design methodology to include database applications, *J. Obj.-Oriented Prog.*, **8**(7), 28–34, 56

Case, T., Henderson-Sellers, B. and Low, G.C. (1996). A generic object-oriented design methodology incorporating database considerations, *Annals of Software Engineering*, **2**, 5–24

Cattell, R.G.G. (1991). *Object Data Management.* Addison-Wesley, Reading, MA, USA

Chamberlin, D.D. (1996). Anatomy of an object-relational database, *DB2 Online Magazine*, http://www.db2mag.com/9601cha.htm, Winter 1996

Chambers, C., Ungar, D. and Lee, E. (1989). An efficient implementation of Self, a dynamically-typed object-oriented language based on prototypes, *Proc. 4th ACM Conf. OOPSLA, SigPlan Notices*, **24**(10), 49–70. Reprinted in *Lisp and Symbolic Computation*, **4**(3) (1991), 243–281

Chappell, D. (1997). Making sense of distributed objects, *American Programmer*, **10**(12), 3–7

Checkland, P. (1981). *Systems Thinking, Systems Practice.* John Wiley & Sons Ltd, Chichester, England

Checkland, P. and Scholes, J. (1990). *Soft Systems Methodology in Action.* John Wiley & Sons Ltd, Chichester, England

Checkland, P. and Wilson, B. (1980). Primary task and issue based root definitions in systems studies, *J. Applied Systems Analysis*, **7**, 51–54

Chidamber, S. and Kemerer, C. (1991). Towards a metric suite for object-oriented design, *Proc. OOPSLA'91, Sigplan Notices*, **26**(11), 197–211

Chidamber, S. and Kemerer, C. (1994). A metrics suite for object oriented design, *IEEE Trans. Software Eng.*, **20**(6), 476–493

Chorafas, D.N. and Steinmann, H. (1993). *Object-Oriented Databases.* PTR Prentice Hall, Englewood Cliffs, NJ, USA, 318pp

Clarke, P.A. (1972). *Action Research and Organizational Change.* Harper and Row, London, UK

Coad, P. and Yourdon, E. (1991). *Object-Oriented Analysis* 2nd edn. Prentice Hall, Englewood Cliffs, NJ, 233pp

Coad, P., North, D. and Mayfield, M. (1995). *Object Models. Strategies, Patterns, and Applications.* Yourdon Press, Englewood Cliffs, NJ, USA, 505pp

Cockburn, A. (1997a). Goals and use cases, *J. Obj.-Oriented Prog.*, **10**(5), 35–40

Cockburn, A. (1997b). Using goal-based use cases *J. Obj.-Oriented Prog.*, **10**(7), 56–62

Coleman, D., Hayes, F., Bear, S. (1992). Introducing ObjectCharts or How to Use Statecharts in Object-Oriented Design, *IEEE Transactions on Software Engineering*, **18**(1), 9–18

Coleman, D., Arnold, P., Bodoff, S., Dollin, C., Gilchrist, H., Hayes, F. and Jeremaes, P. (1994). *Object-Oriented Development: the Fusion Method.* Prentice Hall Inc., Englewood Cliffs, NJ, 313pp

Comber, T. and Maltby, J.R. (1994). Screen complexity and user design preference in Windows applications, *OzCHI'94* (S. Howard and Y.K. Leung eds), CHISIG, Ergonomics Society of Australia

Comber, T. and Maltby, J.R. (1995). Evaluating usability of screen designs with layout complexity. In *OzCHI'95* (H. Hasan and C. Nicastri eds), CHISIG, Ergonomics Society of Australia

Constantine, L.L. (1996a). Usage-centered software engineering: new models, methods, and metrics. In *Software Engineering: Education & Practice* (M. Purvis ed.), IEEE Computer Society Press, Los Alamitos, CA, USA

Constantine, L.L. (1996b). Measuring the quality of user interface designs. Paper presented at Software Development '96, San Francisco, 28 March 1996

Constantine, L.L. (1997a). The case for essential use cases, *Object Magazine*, **7**(3), 72–70

Constantine, L.L. (1997b). Efficient objects, *Object Magazine*, **7**(7), 72, 71, 18

Constantine, L.L. (1997c). Visual coherence and usability: a cohesion metric for assessing the quality of dialog and screen designs, *Proc. OzCHI'96*, IEEE Computer Society Press, Los Alamitos, CA, USA

Constantine, L.L. and Henderson-Sellers, B. (1995a). Notation matters: Part 1 – framing the issues, *Report on Object Analysis and Design*, **2**(3), 25–29

Constantine, L.L. and Henderson-Sellers, B. (1995b). Notation matters: Part 2 – applying the principles, *Report on Object Analysis and Design*, **2**(4), 20–23

Constantine, L.L. and Lockwood, L.A.D. (1994). Fitting practices to the people, *American Programmer*, **7**(12), 21–27

Constantine, L.L. and Lockwood, L.A.D. (1998). *Software for Use: A Practical Guide to the Models and Methods of Usage-Centered Design.* Addison-Wesley, Reading, MA, USA

Cook, S. and Daniels, J. (1994). *Designing Object Systems.* Prentice Hall, UK, 389pp

Cooke, M. (1993). *Modeling Auditory Processing and Organisation*, Distinguished Dissertations in Computer Science, Cambridge University Press

Cooper, A. (1995). *About Face: The Essentials of User Interface Design*, IDG Books, 580pp

Coplien, J. (1992). *Advanced C++ Programming Styles and Idioms.* Addison-Wesley, Reading, MA, USA

Cornell, G. and Horstmann, C.S. (1998). *Core Java* 3rd edn, Volumes 1 and 2, SunSoft/Prentice Hall

Cox, K. and Walker, D. (1993). *User Interface Design* 2nd edn. Prentice Hall

Crowe, M.K. (1993). Object systems over relational databases, *Inf. Software Technol.*, **35**(8), 449–461

Cunningham, B. (1976). Action research: toward a procedural model, *Human Relations*, **29**(3), 215–238 New York, NY: Plenum

Curtis, G. (1990). *Business Information Systems: Analysis Design and Practice.* Addison-Wesley, Wokingham, England

Curtis, R. and Wittie, L. (1982). BugNet: a debugging system for parallel programming environments. In *Proc. 3rd International Conference on Distributed Computing Systems*, IEEE Computer Society, 394–399

Cusack, E. and Rafsanjani, G. (1992). ZEST. In *Object Orientation in Z* (S. Stepney, R. Barden and D. Cooper eds), Workshops in Computing, Springer-Verlag, London

Dahl, R.A. (1970). *Modern Political Analysis* 2nd edn. Prentice-Hall, Englewood Cliffs, NJ, USA

Daniels, J. (1997). Object method: beyond the notations, *Object Expert*, **2**(2), 36–40

Davenport, T.H. (1993). *Process Innovation, Reengineering Work through Information Technology.* Harvard Business School Press, Boston, MA, USA

Davies, L. and Ledington, P. (1991). *Information in Action: Soft Systems Methodology.* MacMillan Education, London

Davis, A.M. (1988). A taxonomy for the early stages of the software development life cycle, *J. Systems and Software*, **8**, 297–311

de Champeaux, D. (1991). Object-oriented analysis and top-down software development, *European Conference on Object-oriented Programming 1991, Lecture Notes in Computer Science, No. 512*, Springer-Verlag, Berlin, 360–376

de Champeaux, D. (1997). *Object-Oriented Development Process and Metrics.* Prentice Hall, Upper Saddle River, NJ, USA, 469pp

Demeter (1997). http://www.ccs.neu.edu/home/lieber/what_is_demeter.html

Deming, W.E. (1981). Improvement of quality and productivity through action by management, *National Productivity Review*, Winter 1981/82, 12–22

Deming, W.E. (1986). *Out of the Crisis.* MIT Press

de Paula, E.G. and Nelson, M.L. (1991). Designing a class hierarchy, *Technology of Object-Oriented Languages and Systems: TOOLS5* (T. Korson, V. Vaishnavi and B. Meyer eds). Prentice-Hall, New York, 203–218

Desai, B.C. (1990). *An Introduction to Database Systems.* West Publishing Company, St Paul, 820pp

Desfray, P. (1994). *Object Engineering. The Fourth Dimension.* Addison-Wesley/Masson, Paris, 342pp

De Vaus, D.A. (1996). *Surveys in Social Research* 5th edn, Allen and Unwin, Australia

Diaconescu, R. and Futatsugi, K. (1996). Logical semantics of CafeOBJ, *Research Report IS-RR-96-0024S*, JAIST

Dietrich, W.C., Nackman, L.R. and Gracer, F. (1989). Saving a legacy with objects. In: OOPSLA'90 ACM Conference on Object-Oriented Programming Systems, Languages and Applications (N. Meyrowitz ed.) Addison-Wesley, Reading, MA, USA

Dodani, M. (1994). Semantically rich object-oriented software engineering methodologies, *Report on Object Analysis and Design*, **1**(1), 17–21

Downes, E., Clare, P. and Coe, I. (1991). *Structured Systems Analysis and Design Methodology: Application and Context* 2nd edn. Prentice-Hall

Drake, J.M., Xie, W. and Tsai, W.T. (1992a). Document-driven analysis: description and formalism, *J. Obj.-Oriented Programming*, **5**(7), 33–50

Drake, J., Tsai, W.T., Lee, H.J. and Zualkernan, I. (1992b). A case study to evaluate three object-oriented analysis techniques. Paper presented at *Workshop on Object-Oriented Software Engineering Practice*, Denver, February 1992

D'Souza, D. (1997a). Framework: Java to UML/Catalysis, *J. Obj.-Oriented Prog.*, **10**(5), 10–13

D'Souza, D. (1997b). A clear path to Java, *J. Obj.-Oriented Prog.*, **10**(6), 42–45, 64

D'Souza, D. and Wills, A. (1995). Catalysis – Practical Rigor and Refinement. ICON Computing Inc., Austin, TX, USA, 38pp

D'Souza, D. and Wills, A.C. (1998). *Object-Oriented Development with Catalysis*. Addison-Wesley, in press, 576pp

Duffy, D. (1995). Object-oriented requirements analysis. Part 1: finding abstractions and their relationships, *Report on Object Analysis and Design*, **1**(5), 35–38

Duke, R. and Rose, G. (1998). *Formal Object-oriented Specification Using Object Z*. Academic Press

Duke, R., King, P., Rose, G. and Smith, G. (1991). The Object-Z Specification Language Version 1, Software Verification Research Centre, University of Queensland, Technical Report No. 91-1

Dvorak, J. (1994). Conceptual entropy and its effect on class hierarchies, *IEEE Computer*, **27**(6), 59–63

Edwards, J.M. and Henderson-Sellers, B. (1991). A coherent notation for object-oriented software engineering, *Technology of Object-Oriented Languages and Systems: TOOLS5* (T. Korson, V. Vaishnavi and B. Meyer eds). Prentice-Hall, New York, 405–426

Edwards, J.M. and Henderson-Sellers, B. (1993). Application of an object-oriented analysis and design methodology to engineering cost management, *Journal of Systems and Software*, **23**(2), 123–138

Edwards, J.M. and Henderson-Sellers, B. (1996). An OPEN approach to Mentor: an industrial strength OO software process, pp 218–263 in Volume 1 of *Proc. ObjectWorld '96 Australia* Sydney

Efe, K. (1982). Heuristic models of task assignment scheduling in distributed systems, *IEEE Computer*, **15**(6), 50–56

Embley, D.W., Kurtz, B.D. and Woodfield, S.N. (1992). *Object-Oriented Systems Analysis. A Model-Driven Approach.* Yourdon Press, Englewood Cliffs, New Jersey, USA, 302pp

Emmerich, W. (1998). CORBA and ODBMSs in viewpoint development environment architectures. In *OOIS 97* (M.E. Orlowska and R. Zicari eds), Springer-Verlag, London, UK, 347–360

Ermand, L.D. and Lesser, W.R. (1975). A multi-level organization for problem solving using many, diverse, cooperating sources of knowledge, *Proc. IJCAI-4*, Tbilisi, USSR, 483–490

Ewald, A. and Roy, M. (1998). Microsoft introduce COM+, *Object Magazine*, **7**(11), 17–18

Eysenck, M.W. and Keane, M.T. (1990). *Cognitive Psychology.* Lawrence Erlbaum, UK

Fagan, M.E. (1976). Design and code inspections to reduce errors in program development, *IBM Systems Journal*, **15**(3), 182–211

Farhoudi, Graham, I. and Powell (1997). *Intelligent Agents: An Object-Oriented Approach.* Addison-Wesley, London (in press)

Fenton, N. (1991). *Software Metrics: A Rigorous Approach.* Chapman Hall, UK

Fenton, N.E. (1994). Software measurement: a necessary scientific basis, *IEEE Transactions on Software Engineering*, **20**, 199–206

Fingar, P. (1996). *The Blueprint for Business Objects.* SIGS Books & Multimedia, New York, NY, USA

Fingar, P., Clarke, J. and Stikeleather, J. (1997). The business of distributed object computing, *Object Magazine*, **7**(2), 29–33

Firesmith, D.G. (1993). *Object-Oriented Requirements Analysis and Logical Design: A Software Engineering Approach.* J. Wiley and Sons, New York, 575pp

Firesmith, D.G. (1994). Cluster of classes: a bigger building block, *Report on Object Analysis and Design*, **1**(4), 18–21, 25

Firesmith, D.G. (1995a). Object-oriented regression testing, *Report on Object Analysis and Design*, **1**(5), 42–45

Firesmith, D.G. (1995b). Use cases: the pros and cons, *Report on Object Analysis and Design*, **2**(2), 2–6

Firesmith, D.G. (1996). The PLOOT test pattern language, *Report on Object Analysis and Design*, **2**(7), 53–56

Firesmith, D.G. and Eykholt, E. (1995). *Dictionary of Object Technology. The Definitive Desk Reference.* SIGS Books, NY, USA, 603pp

Firesmith, D.G. and Henderson-Sellers, B. (1998a). Clarifying specialized forms of associations in UML and OML, *J. Obj.-Oriented Prog./ROAD*, **11**(2), May 1998

Firesmith, D.G. and Henderson-Sellers, B. (1998b). Upgrading OML to Version 1.1: Part 1. Referential relationships, *J. Obj.-Oriented Prog./ROAD*, **11**(3), June 1998

Firesmith, D., Henderson-Sellers, B. and Graham, I. (1997). *OPEN Modeling Language (OML) Reference Manual.* SIGS Books, New York, USA, 271pp

Firesmith, D.G., Hendley, G., Krutsch, S.A. and Stowe, M. (1998). *Object-Oriented Development Using OPEN: A Complete Java^{TM} Application.* Addison-Wesley, London

Flanagan, D. (1997). *Java in a Nutshell.* O'Reilly Associates

Foote, B. (1988). *Designing to Facilitate Change with Object-Oriented Frameworks.* Master's thesis, University of Illinois at Urbana–Champaign, IL, USA

Fowler, M. (1996). *Analysis Patterns: Reusable Object Models.* Addison-Wesley, New York, NY, USA, 400pp

Fowler, M. (1997). Personal communication, email sent 15 October

Fowler, M. and Scott, K. (1997). *UML Distilled. Applying the Standard Object Modeling Language.* Addison-Wesley, Reading, MA, 179pp

Freedman, D.P. and Weinburg, G.M. (1982). *Handbook of Walkthroughs, Inspections and Technical Reviews: Evaluating Programs, Projects and Products* 3rd edn. Little, Brown and Co., Boston, MA, USA

Freeman, C. and Henderson-Sellers, B. (1991). OLMS: the Object Library Management System. In *TOOLS 6* (J. Potter, M. Tokoro and B. Meyer eds). Prentice Hall, 175–180

Fung, M., Henderson-Sellers, B. and Yap, L.-M. (1997). A comparative evaluation of OO methodologies from a business rules and quality perspective, *Australian Computer Journal*, **29**(3), 95–101

Furey, S. (1997). Why we should use function points, *IEEE Software*, **14**(2), 28, 30

Gait, J. (1986). A probe effect in concurrent programs, *Software – Practice and Experience*, 225–233

Gale, T. and Eldred, J. (1996). *Getting Results with the Object-Oriented Enterprise Model.* SIGS Books & Multimedia, New York, NY, USA

Galitz, W.O. (1989). *Handbook of Screen Format Design.* QED Information Sciences, Wellesley, MA, USA

Gamma, E., Helm, R., Johnson R. and Vlissides, J. (1995). *Design Patterns: Elements of Reusable Object-Oriented Design.* Addison-Wesley, Reading, MA, 395pp

Garvey, P.R., Phair, D.J., Wilson, J.A. (1997). An information architecture for risk assessment and management, *IEEE Software*, **14**(3), 25–34

Gazdar, G. and Mellish, C. (1989). *Natural Language Processing in Prolog.* Addison-Wesley

Gerhart, S.L. (1990). Applications of formal methods: developing virtuoso software, *IEEE Software*, **7**(5), 6–10

Ghezzi, C., Jazayeri, M. and Mandrioli, D. (1992). *Fundamentals of Software Engineering.* Prentice Hall, NJ, USA

Gibson, E. (1990). Objects born and bred, *Byte*, **15**(10), 245–254

Gilb, T. (1988). *Principles of Software Engineering Management.* Addison-Wesley, Reading, MA, USA

Gilb, T. (1997a). Evolutionary object management, *Object Expert*, **2**(2), 24–29, 72

Gilb, T. (1997b). *The PLanguage Method, a Handbook for Advanced Practical Management and Engineering Methods for Leading Edge Competitiveness; and a Guide to Critical Thinking about Complex Ideas Problems or Systems. Project Language, Process Language, Planning Language* (in preparation: available in draft form on http://www.stsc.hill.af.mil/)

Gilb, T. and Graham, D. (1993). *Software Inspection: Effective Method for Software Project Management.* Addison-Wesley, Reading, MA

Gillies, A. (1992). *Software Quality – Theory and Management.* Chapman and Hall, UK

Gilmore, T., Krantz, J. and Ramirez, R. (1985). Action based modes of inquiry and the host–researcher relationship, *Consultation*, **5**(3), 160–176

Godfrey, R. (1998). Beauty is more than skin deep: behind the pretty (inter)face of human computer interaction, *Proc. SE:E&P'98*, IEEE Computer Society Press, Los Alamitos, CA, USA (in press)

Goguen, J. (1978). Some design principles and theory for OBJ0: A language for expressing and executing algebraic specifications of programs, *Proc. Int. Conf. on Mathematical Studies of Information Processing*, 425–473

Goldberg, A. (1984). *Smalltalk-80: The Interactive Programming Environment.* Addison-Wesley, New York, USA

Goldberg, A., and Robson, D. (1983). *Smalltalk–80: The Language and Its Implementation.* Addison-Wesley, Reading, MA

Goldberg, A. and Rubin, K. (1990). Talking to project managers: organizing for reuse, *Hotline on Obj.-Oriented Technol.*, **1**(10), 7–11

Goldberg, A. and Rubin, K.S. (1995). *Succeeding with Objects. Decision Frameworks for Project Management.* Addison-Wesley, Reading, MA, 542pp

Gomaa, H. (1989). A software design method for distributed real-time applications, *J. Systems and Software*, **9**(2), 81–94

Gossain, S. (1995). Designing object interactions, *Report on Object Analysis and Design*, **1**(5), 39–41, 45

Grady, R.B. and Caswell, D.L. (1987). *Software Metrics: Establishing a Company-Wide Program*. Prentice Hall, Englewood Cliffs, NJ, USA

Graham, I. (1991). *Object-Oriented Methods*. Addison-Wesley, Wokingham, UK, 410pp

Graham, I.M. (1994). *Object-Oriented Methods* 2nd edn. Addison-Wesley, Wokingham, UK

Graham, I.M. (1995a). *Migrating to Object Technology*. Addison-Wesley, Wokingham

Graham, I.M. (1995b). A non-procedural process model for object-oriented software development, *Report on Object Analysis and Design*, **1**(5), 10–11

Graham, I.M. (1996a). Task scripts, use cases and scenarios in object-oriented analysis, *Object-Oriented Systems*, **3**(3), 123–142

Graham, I. (1996b). Requirements engineering as business process modeling, Part II, *Object Expert*, **1**(2), 54–56

Graham, I. (1996c). Linking a system and its requirements, *Object Expert*, **1**(3), 62–64

Graham, I. (1996d). The organization of workshops, *Object Expert*, **1**(6), 52–54

Graham, I. (1997a). Some problems with use cases ... and how to avoid them. In *OOIS '96 Proceedings* (D. Patel, Y. Sun and S. Patel eds), Springer-Verlag London Ltd, London, 18–27

Graham, I. (1997b). 'Smart' software and modern information technology, *Object Magazine*, **7**(2), 24–26

Graham, I. (1997c). The architecture of agents, *Object Magazine*, **7**(7), 26–28

Graham, I.M. and Jones, P.L.K. (1988). *Expert Systems: Knowledge, Uncertainty and Decision*. Chapman and Hall, London, UK

Graham, I.M., Bischof, J. and Henderson-Sellers, B. (1997a). Associations considered a bad thing, *J. Obj.-Oriented Programming*, **9**(9), 41–48

Graham, I., Henderson-Sellers, B. and Younessi, H. (1997b). *The OPEN Process Specification*. Addison-Wesley, London, UK, 314pp

Grosberg, J.A. (1993). Comments on considering 'class' harmful, *Comm. ACM*, **36**(1), 113–114

Gylys, V.B. and Edwards, J.A. (1976). Optimal partitioning of workload for distributed systems, *Proc. Compcon, Fall 1976*, 353–357

Hall, J.A. (1990). Seven myths of formal methods, *IEEE Software*, **7**(5), 11–19

Hall, T. and Fenton, N. (1997). Implementing effective software metrics programs, *IEEE Software*, **14**(2), 55–65

Hammer, M. and Champy, J. (1993). *Reengineering the Corporation: A Manifesto for Business Revolution*. Harper Business, New York

Harel, D. (1987). Statecharts: a visual formalism for complex systems, *Sci. Computer Program.*, **8**, 231–274

Harmon, P. (1997). CORBA and COM: the marketplace perspective, *American Programmer*, **10**(12), 8–15

Harmon, P. (1998). OO BPR, *Cutter Edge*, 17 February 1998

Harrold, M.J. and McGregor, J.D. (1992). Toward a testing methodology for object-oriented software systems. Paper presented at *Workshop on Object-Oriented Software Engineering Practice*, Denver, February 1992

Hart, A. (1989). *Knowledge Acquisition for Expert Systems* 2nd edn. Kogan Page, London, UK

Hawryszkiewycz, I.T. (1991). *Database Analysis and Design* 2nd edn. Macmillan, New York, 574pp

Hawryszkiewycz, I.T. (1994). *System Analysis and Design* 3rd edn. Prentice Hall, Sydney, 490pp

Haynes, P. and Henderson-Sellers, B. (1996). Cost estimation of OO projects. Empirical observations, practical applications, *American Programmer*, **9**(7), 35–41

Haynes, P. and Henderson-Sellers, B. (1997). Bringing OO projects under quantitative control: an output, cash and time driven approach, *American Programmer*, **10**(11), 23–31

Heitz, M., Sneed, I., Derissen, J. and Muller, J. (1990). HOOD, a method to support real-time and embedded system design?, *Proc. Software Engineering Conference*, 923–932

Helgesen, M. and Brown, S. (1995). *Active Listening: Introducing Skills for Understanding*. Cambridge University Press, Cambridge, UK

Hellenack, L.J. (1997). Object-oriented business patterns, *Object Magazine*, **6**(11), 22–32

Henderson-Sellers, A., Henderson-Sellers, B., Pollard, D., Verner, J. and Pitman, A.J. (1995a). Applying software engineering metrics to landsurface parameterization schemes, *J. Climate*, **8**(5), 1043–1059

Henderson-Sellers, B. (1991). Parallels between object-oriented software development and total quality management, *Journal of Information Technology*, **6**(3), 63–67

Henderson-Sellers, B. (1992). Object-oriented information systems: an introductory tutorial, *Australian Computer Journal*, **24**(1), 12–24

Henderson-Sellers, B. (1993). The economics of reusing library classes, *J. Obj.-Oriented Programming*, **6**(4), 43–50

Henderson-Sellers, B. (1995a). Identifying internal and external characteristics of classes likely to be useful as structural complexity metrics, *Proc. OOIS '94*, (D. Patel, Y. Sun and S. Patel eds), Springer-Verlag, New York, USA, 227–230

Henderson-Sellers, B. (1995b). The goals of an OO metrics program, *Object Magazine*, **5**(6), 72–79, 95

Henderson-Sellers, B. (1996). *Object-Oriented Metrics. Measures of Complexity.* Prentice Hall, NJ. USA, 234pp

Henderson-Sellers, B. (1997a). OPEN relationships – composition and containment, *J. Obj-Oriented Prog.*, **10**(7), 51–55

Henderson-Sellers, B. (1997b). Towards the formalization of relationships for object modeling, *Proc. TOOLS Pacific 1997*

Henderson-Sellers, B. (1997c). *A BOOK of Object-Oriented Knowledge* 2nd edn. Prentice Hall, New Jersey, USA, 253pp

Henderson-Sellers, B. (1998). OPEN Relationships – associations, mappings, dependencies and uses, *J. Obj-Oriented Prog.*, **10**(9), 49–57

Henderson-Sellers, B. and Bulthuis, A. (1997). *Object-Oriented Metamethods.* Springer-Verlag, New York

Henderson-Sellers, B. and Edwards, J.M. (1994a). *BOOKTWO of Object-Oriented Knowledge: The Working Object.* Prentice Hall, Sydney, 616pp

Henderson-Sellers, B. and Edwards, J.M. (1994b). Identifying three levels of OO methodologies, *Report on Object Analysis and Design*, **1**(2), 25–28

Henderson-Sellers, B. and Firesmith, D. (1997a). COMMA: Proposed core model, *J. Obj.-Oriented Prog. (ROAD)*, **9**(8), 48–53

Henderson-Sellers, B. and Firesmith, D.G. (1997b). Choosing between OPEN and UML, *American Programmer*, **10**(3), 15–23

Henderson-Sellers, B. and Firesmith, D.G. (1998a). Upgrading OML to Version 1.1: Part 2. Additional concepts and notations, *J. Obj-Oriented Prog./ROAD*, **11**(5), Sept 1998

Henderson-Sellers, B. and Firesmith, D.G. (1998b). *The OML Primer* (in preparation)

Henderson-Sellers, B. and Freeman, B. (1992). Cataloguing and Classification for Object Libraries, *ACM SIGSOFT Software Engineering Notes*, **17**(1), 62–64

Henderson-Sellers, B. and McKim, J.C. jr. (1994). Contracting: What's in it for the supplier? In *TOOLS14* (R. Ege, M. Singh and B. Meyer eds). Prentice Hall, Englewood Cliffs, NJ, 179–186

Henderson-Sellers, B., Fung, M. and Yap, L.-M. (1995b). The role of business rules and quality in methodologies, *Report on Object Analysis and Design*, **2**(4), 10–12, 17

Henderson-Sellers, B., Constantine, L.L. and Graham, I.M. (1996a). Coupling and cohesion (towards a valid metrics suite for object-oriented analysis and design), *Object-Oriented Systems*, **3**(3), 143–158

Henderson-Sellers, B., Graham, I.M., Firesmith, D., Reenskaug, T., Swatman, P. and Winder, R. (1996b). The OPEN heart, *TOOLS 21* (C. Mingins, R. Duke and B. Meyer eds), TOOLS/ISE, 187–196

Henderson-Sellers, B., Graham, I.M. and Firesmith, D. (1997a). Methods unification: the OPEN methodology, *Journal of Object-Oriented Programming (ROAD)*, **10**(2), 41–43, 55

Henderson-Sellers, B., Firesmith, D. and Graham, I.M. (1997b). The benefits of Common Object Modeling Notation, *Journal of Object-Oriented Programming (ROAD)*, **10**(5), 28–34

Highsmith, J. (1997). Messy, exciting, and anxiety-ridden: adaptive software development, *American Programmer*, **10**(4), 23–29

Hinchey, M. and Bowen, J. (eds) (1995). *Applications of Formal Methods*, International Series in Computer Science, Prentice Hall

Horstmann, C.S. (1995). *Mastering Object-Oriented Design in C++*, John Wiley

Howard, R. (1992). What TQM means for OT, *Hotline on Obj.-Oriented Technology*, **3**(11), 13–15

Høydalsvik, G.M. and Sindre, G. (1993). On the purpose of object-oriented analysis, *Proc. OOPSLA '93, SigPlan Notices*, **28**(10), 240–255

Hughes, J.G. (1991). *Object-Oriented Databases*. Prentice Hall, Hemel Hempstead, UK, 280pp

Huitt, W. (ed.) (1992). *Philosophy of Education*, Valdosta State University Press, GA, USA

Humphrey, W.S. (1994). A personal commitment to software quality, *American Programmer*, **7**(12), 2–12

Humphrey, W.S. (1995). *A Discipline for Software Engineering*. Addison-Wesley, Reading, MA, USA

Hutt, M. and Lennung, S. (1980). Towards a definition of action research: a note and bibliography, *Journal of Management Studies*, **17**(2), 241–250

IBM (1997). *Developing Object-Oriented Software. An Experience-Based Approach*. Prentice Hall, Upper Saddle River, NJ, USA, 636pp

Iivari, J. (1991). Object-oriented information systems analysis: a framework for object identification, *Proc. HICSS-92*, IEEE, San Diego, 205–218

Institute of Internal Auditors (1977). *Systems Auditability and Control, Part I, The State of the Art*. IIA, Altamonte Springs, FL, USA

Ipate, F. and Holcombe, M. (1997). An integration testing method that is proved to find all faults, *Int. J. Computer Math.*, **63**, 159–178

Jaaksi, A. (1998). Our cases with use cases, *J. Obj-Oriented Prog. (ROAD)*, **10**(9), 58–65

Jackson, I.F. (1986). *Corporate Information Management*. Prentice Hall International Inc., London, UK, 338pp

Jackson, M. (1975). *Principles of Program Design*. Academic Press, New York, NY, USA

Jacobson, I. (1994). Use cases and objects, *Report on Object Analysis and Design*, **1**(4), 8–10

Jacobson, I. (1995). Formalizing use-case modeling, *J. Obj.-Oriented Prog.*, **8**(3), 10–14

Jacobson, I. (1996). Public communication, ObjectExpo, Sydney, 1996

Jacobson, I., M. Christerson, P. Jonsson and G. Övergaard (1992). *Object-Oriented Software Engineering: A Use Case Driven Approach*. Addison-Wesley, New York, NY, USA, 524pp

Jacobson, I., Ericsson, M. and Jacobson, A. (1995). *The Object Advantage. Business Process Reengineering with Object Technology*. Addison-Wesley/ACM Press, Reading, MA, USA, 347pp

Jacobson, I., Griss, M. and Jonsson, P. (1997). *Software Reuse. Architecture, Process and Organization for Business Success*. Addison-Wesley, Reading, MA, USA, 497pp

Jazayeri, M. (1992). Distributed software design techniques. In *Advances in Object-Oriented Software Engineering* (D. Mandrioli and B. Meyer eds). Prentice Hall, 147–165

Jeffery, D.R. and Berry, M. (1993). A framework for evaluation and prediction of metrics program success, *Proc. 1st Int. Software Metrics Symp.*, IEEE Computer Society Press, Los Alamitos, CA, USA, 28–39

Jeffery, D.R., Low, G.C. and Barnes, M.A. (1993). Comparison of function point counting techniques, *IEEE Trans. Software Eng.*, **19**(5), 529–532

Jenny, C.J. (1977). Process partitioning in distributed systems, *Digest of Papers National Telecommunications Conference '77*, 31:1-1–31:1-10

Johansson, H., McHugh, P.P., Pendlebury, J. and Wheeler III, W. (1993). *Business Process Reengineering – Breakpoint Strategies for Market Dominance*. John Wiley & Sons, Chichester, UK

Johnson, R.E. (1994). An introduction to patterns, *Report on Object Analysis and Design*, **1**(1), 41–43

Johnson, R.E. and Foote, B. (1988). Designing reusable classes, *J. Obj.-Oriented Programming*, **1**(2), 22–35

Joiner, B.L. and Scholtes, P.R. (1986). The quality manager's new job, *Quality Progress*, October 1986, 52–56

Jorgensen, P.C. and Erickson, C. (1994). Object-oriented integration testing, *Comm. ACM*, **37**(9), 30–38

Kathuria, R. and Subramaniam (1996). Assimilation: a new and necessary concept for an object model, *Report on Object Analysis and Design*, **2**(5), 36–39

Keene, S.E. (1989). *Object-Oriented Programming in CommonLisp: A Programmer's Guide to CLOS*, Addison-Wesley

Kelly, G.A. (1955). *The Psychology of Personal Constructs*, W.W. Norton, New York, USA

Kemerer, C. (1993). Reliability of function points measurement: a field experiment, *Comm. ACM*, **36**(2), 85–97

Kendall, E.A., Malkoun, M.T. and Jiang, C. (1997). Multiagent system design based on object-oriented patterns, *J. Obj.-Oriented Prog. (ROAD)*, **10**(3), 41–47

Khoshafian, S. (1993). *Object-Oriented Databases*. John Wiley and Sons, New York, 362pp

Kilian, M. (1991). A note on type composition and reusability, *OOPS Messenger*, **2**(3), 24–32

Kilov, H. (1992). From OSI systems management to an interoperable object model: behavioral specification of (generic) relationships. In *Procs. Third Telecommunications Information Networking Architecture Workshop*, 21–23 January 1992, Narita, Japan, 23-3-1–23-3-8

Kilov, H. (1997). Personal communication, email sent 30 June

Kilov, H. and Ross, J. (1994). *Information Modeling. An Object-Oriented Approach*. Prentice Hall, Englewood Cliffs, New Jersey, USA, 268pp

Kim, W. (1990). Architectural issues in object-oriented databases, *J. Obj.-Oriented Programming*, **2**(6), 29–38

Kim, W. (1995). *Modern Database Systems: the Object Model, Interoperability, and Beyond*. Addison-Wesley/ACM Press, 705pp

Kitchenham, B. (1997). The problem with function points, *IEEE Software*, **14**(2), 29, 31

Kitchenham, B.A. and Linkman, S.J. (1990). Design metrics in practice, *Inf. Soft. Technol.*, **32**(4), 304–310

Kitchenham, B.A. and Walker, J.G. (1986). The meaning of quality. In *Proc. Conf. Software Engineering 86*, 393–406

Kitchenham, B., Pfleeger, S.L. and Fenton, N.E. (1995). Towards a framework for software measurement validation, *IEEE Trans. Software Eng.*, **21**(12), 929–944

Knuth, D.E. (1983). The WEB system of structured documentation, version 2, Stanford University

Knuth, D.E. (1984). Literate programming, *The Computer Journal*, **27**(2), 97–111

Koenig, A. (1994). Thoughts on abstraction, *J. Obj.-Oriented Prog.*, **7**(6), 68–70

Kolewe, R. (1993). Metrics in object-oriented design and programming, *Software Development*, October, 53–62

Kolp, M. and Pirotte, A. (1998). An aggregation model and its C++ implementation. In *OOIS 97* (M.E. Orlowska and R. Zicari eds), Springer-Verlag, London, UK, 211–221

Koontz, R. (1995). Thinking like your business, *Object Magazine*, **5**(1), 50–52

Korson, T. and McGregor, J.D. (1992). Technical criteria for the specification and evaluation of object-oriented libraries, *Software Eng. J.*, **7**(2), 85–94, IEEE

Kristen, G. (1994). *Object Orientation. The KISS Method. From Information Architecture to Information System.* Addison-Wesley, Wokingham, England, 487pp

Kristen, G. (1995). Business engineering, *Report on Object Analysis and Design*, **2**(2), 14–19

Lai, K.W.L. and Guzenda, L. (1991). How to benchmark an ODBMS, *J. Obj.- Oriented Programming*, **4**(4), 12–15

Laird, J.E., Rosenbloom, P.S. and Newell, A. (1986). Chunking in SOAR: the anatomy of a general learning mechanism, *Machine Learning*, **1**(1), 11–46 (reprinted in *Readings in Machine Learning* (J.W. Shavlik and T.G. Dietterich eds), Morgan, Kaufmann, 1990, 555–572

Lakoff, G. (1987). *Women, Fire, and Dangerous Things. What Categories Reveal About The Mind*, Univ. Chicago Press, Chicago, Illinois, USA, 614pp

LaLonde, W., and Pugh, J. (1991). Subclassing $\neq$ subtyping $\neq$ **is-a**, *J. Obj.- Oriented Programming*, **3**(5), 57–62

Lano, K. (1992). Z^{++}. In *Object Orientation in Z* (S. Stepney, R. Barden and D. Cooper eds), Workshops in Computing, Springer-Verlag, London

Lasswell, D. and Kaplan, A. (1950). *Power and Society.* Yale University Press, New Haven, CT, USA

Lavender, R.G. and Schmidt, D.C. (1995). Active object: an object behavioral pattern for concurrent programming, *Pattern Languages of Programming Conference*, Illinois

Lee, Y. and Park, S. (1993). Opnets: an object-oriented high-level petri net model for real-time system modeling, *Journal of Systems Software*, **20**, 69–86

Leffingwell, D. (1997). Calculating the return on investment from more effective requirements management, *American Programmer*, **10**(4), 13–16

Leung, Y.K. and Apperley, M.D. (1994). A review and taxonomy of distortion-oriented presentation techniques, *ACM Trans. Computer Human Interaction*, **1**(2), 126–160

Leung, Y.K., Jeans, D. and Simpson, A. (1996). Interacting with distortion-oriented displays, *Procs. First Asia Pacific Conf. on Computer Human Interaction*, 305–317

Lewis, K. (1947a). Frontiers in group dynamics: pt 1, concepts, methods and reality in social science, social equilibria and social change, *Human Relations*, **1**(1), 5–40

Lewis, K. (1947b). Frontiers in group dynamics: pt 2, channels in group life, social planning, action research, *Human Relations*, **1**(2), 143–153

Li, W. and Henry, S. (1993). Object-oriented metrics that predict maintainability, *J. Sys. Software*, **23**, 111–122

Lieberherr, K.J., Holland, I. and Riel, A. (1988). Object-oriented programming: an objective sense of style, *Procs. OOPSLA '88*, ACM Press, 323–334

Lieberherr, K.J. and Holland, I. (1989). Formulations and benefits of the Law of Demeter, *Sigplan Notices*, **24**(3), 67–78

Loomis, M.E.S. (1993). ODBMS: distributed object databases, *J. Obj.-Oriented Prog.*, **6**(1), 20–23, 88

Lorenz, M. (1993). *Object-Oriented Software Development: A Practical Guide.* Prentice Hall, New Jersey, 227pp

Lorenz, M. and Kidd, J. (1994). *Object-Oriented Software Metrics.* Prentice Hall, New Jersey, 200pp

Low, G.C. and Rasmussen, G. (1998). Partitioning and allocation of objects in distributed application development, submitted to *Object-Oriented Systems*

Low, G., Henderson-Sellers, B. and Han, D. (1995). Comparison of object-oriented and traditional systems development issues in distributed environments, *Inf. Management*, **28**, 327–340

Low, G., Rasmussen, G. and Henderson-Sellers, B. (1996). Incorporation of distributed computing concerns into object-oriented methodologies, *J. Obj.-Oriented Programming*, **9**(3), 12–20

McCabe, T.J. (1976). A complexity measure, *IEEE Trans. Soft. Eng.*, **2**(4), 308–320

McGibbon, B. (1995). *Managing Your Move to Object Technology. Guidelines and Strategies for a Smooth Transition*, SIGS Books, NY, 268pp

McGregor, J.D. (1997). Testing object-oriented components, tutorial presented at ECOOP 1997

McGregor, J.D. and Korson, T. (1993). Supporting dimensions of classification in object-oriented design, *J. Obj.-Oriented Programming*, **5**(9), 25–30

McGregor, J.D. and Sykes, D.A. (1992). *Object-Oriented Software Development: Engineering Software for Reuse*, Van Nostrand Reinhold, New York, USA, 352pp

McHugh, P., Giorgio, M. and Wheeler, W.A., III. (1995). *Beyond Business Process Reengineering: Towards the Holonic Enterprise.* John Wiley and Sons, Chichester, UK, 212pp

McMenamin, S.M. and Palmer, J.F. (1984). *Essential Systems Analysis.* Yourdon Press, Englewood Cliffs, NJ, USA

Mager, R.F. (1968). *Developing Attitude Toward Learning*, Belmont, CA

Marcus, A. (1992). *Graphic Design for Electronic Documents and User Interfaces.* ACM Press, NY, USA

Martin, B.E., Pedersen, C.H. and Bedford-Roberts, J. (1991). An object-based taxonomy for distributed computer systems, *IEEE Computer*, August, 17–27

Martin, J. and Odell, J.J. (1992). *Object-Oriented Analysis and Design.* Prentice Hall, New Jersey, 513pp

Martin, J. and Odell, J.J. (1995). *Object-Oriented Methods. A Foundation.* PTR Prentice Hall, New Jersey, 412pp

Martin, T. (1988). *Information Engineering, Volume 4: Design and Implementation.* Savant, 783–1050

Masotti, G. (1991). EC++: extended C++, *J. Object-Oriented Programming,* **4**(5), 10–20

Mathiassen, L. and Nielsen, P.A. (1989). Soft systems and hard contradictions: approaching the reality of information systems in organisations, *J. Appl. Systems Analysis,* **16**, 75–88

Meira, S. and Cavalcanti, A. (1992). MooZ case studies. In *Object Orientation in Z* (S. Stepney, R. Barden and D. Cooper eds), Workshops in Computing, Springer-Verlag, London

Meunier, R. (1995). The pipes and filters architecture. In *Pattern Languages of Program Design* (J. Coplien and D. Schmidt eds), Addison-Wesley, Reading, MA, USA

Meyer, B. (1988). *Object-Oriented Software Construction.* Prentice Hall, Hemel Hempstead, UK, 534pp

Meyer, B. (1992a). *Eiffel: The Language.* Prentice Hall, New York, 594pp

Meyer, B. (1992b). Design by contract, pp 1–50. In *Advances in Object-Oriented Software Engineering* (D. Mandrioli and B. Meyer eds). Prentice Hall, NY, 214pp.

Meyer, B. (1992c). Applying 'design by contract', *IEEE Computer,* **25**(10), 40–52

Meyer, B. (1994). *Reusable Software: The Base Object-oriented Component Libraries.* Prentice Hall, Hemel Hempstead, UK

Meyer, B. (1997). *Object-Oriented Software Construction* 2nd edn. Prentice Hall, Hemel Hempstead, UK

Meyers, S. (1992). *Effective C++: 50 Specific Ways to Improve your Programs and Designs.* Addison-Wesley

Miller, G. (1956). The magical number seven, plus or minus two: some limits on our capacity for processing information, *The Psychological Review,* **63**(2), 81–97

Milner, R. (1978). A theory of type polymorphism in programming, *Journal of Computer and System Sciences,* **17**, 348–375

Moser, S. (1996). Measurement and estimation of software and software process, PhD thesis, Univ. Berne, Berne, Switzerland

Moser, S. and Cherix, R. (1998). Cost estimation of client/server development projects, submitted to HICSS, January 1998

Moser, S. and Nierstrasz, O. (1996). The effect of object-oriented O-O frameworks on programmer productivity, *IEEE Computer,* **29**(9), 45–51

Moser, S., Henderson-Sellers, B. and Mišić, V. (1997). Measuring object-oriented business models, *Proc. TOOLS 25* (C. Mingins, R. Duke and B. Meyer eds), TOOLS/ISE, Melbourne, 307–316

Moser, S., Henderson-Sellers, B. and Mišić, V. (1998). Cost estimation based on business models, *J. Systems Software* (in press)

Mühlhaüser, M., Gerteis, W. and Heuser, L. (1993). DOCASE: a methodic approach to distributed programming, *Comm. ACM*, **36**(9), 127–138

Murphy, G.C. and Notkin, D. (1996). On the use of static typing to support operations on frameworks, *Object-Oriented Systems*, **3**, 197–213

Murphy, G.C., Townsend, P. and Wong, P.S. (1994). Experiences with cluster and class testing, *Comm. ACM*, **37**(9), 39–47

Myers, G.J. (1976). *Software Reliability: Principles and Practice*. J. Wiley & Sons, USA

Myers, G.J. (1978). *Composite Structured Design*. Van Nostrand Reinhold, Wokingham, UK

Naja, H. and Mouaddib, N. (1998). Viewpoints in object-oriented database. In *OOIS 97* (M.E. Orlowska and R. Zicari eds), Springer-Verlag, London, UK, 81–91

Nerson, J.-M. (1992). Applying object-oriented analysis and design, *Comm. ACM*, **35**(9), 63–74

Nerson, J.-M. (1993). Object-oriented project management, Tutorial at TOOLS11, Santa Barbara, 2 August 1993

Neumann, P. (ed.) (1995). *Computer-Related Risks*. ACM Press/Addison-Wesley, New York, NY, USA, 384pp

NeXT Computer Inc. (1993). *NeXTStep Object-Oriented Programming and the Objective C Language*. Addison-Wesley

Nicholls, J. (1991). Domains of application for formal methods. In *Z User Workshop, York 1991* (J.E. Nicholls ed.), Workshops in Computing, Springer-Verlag, 145–156

Noble, J. and Constantine, L.L. (1997). Interactive design metric visualization: visual metric support for user interface design, *OzCHI'96 Proceedings*, IEEE Computer Society Press, Los Alamitos, CA, USA

Novak, J. and Gowin, D. (1984). *Learning How to Learn*. Cambridge University Press, Cambridge, UK

O'Callaghan, A. (1997a). Object technology migration is not (just) reverse engineering, *Object Expert*, **2**(2), 16–19

O'Callaghan, A. (1997b). Realising the reality, *Application Development Advisor*, **1**(2), 30–33

Odell, J.J. (1992a). Dynamic and multiple classification, *J. Obj.-Oriented Prog.*, **4**(8), 45–48

Odell, J.J. (1992b). What is object state?, *J. Obj.-Oriented Prog.*, **5**(2), 19–21

Odell, J.J. (1993). Specifying requirements using rules, *J. Obj.-Oriented Prog.*, **6**(2), 20–24

Odell, J.J. (1994a). Six different kinds of composition, *J. Obj.-Oriented Prog.*, **6**(8), 10–15

Odell, J.J. (1994b). Power types, *J. Obj.-Oriented Prog.*, **7**(2), 8–12

Odell, J.J. (1997). Personal email communications, July and August 1997

Odell, J.J. (1998). Agents and beyond: a flock is not a bird, *Distributed Computing*, April, 52–54

Odell, J. and Fowler, M. (1995a). From analysis to design using templates, Part I, *Report on Object Analysis and Design*, **1**(6), 19–23

Odell, J. and Fowler, M. (1995b). From analysis to design using templates, Part II, *Report on Object Analysis and Design*, **2**(1), 10–14

Odell, J. and Fowler, M. (1995c). From analysis to design using templates, Part III, *Report on Object Analysis and Design*, **2**(3), 7–10

Odell, J. and Ramackers, G. (1997). Towards a formalization of OO analysis, *J. Obj.-Oriented Prog.*, **10**(4), 64–68

Offen, R.J. and Jeffery, R. (1997). Establishing software measurement programs, *IEEE Software*, **14**(2), 45–53

OMG (1988). Object-oriented analysis and design reference model, draft 7.0 (non-official publication from OOA&D SIG)

OMG (1997a). UML Semantics. Version 1.1, 15 September 1997, OMG document ad/97-08-04

OMG (1997b). UML Notation. Version 1.1, 15 September 1997, OMG document ad/97-08-05

Page-Jones, M. (1995). *What Every Programmer Should Know About Object-Oriented Design*. Dorset House Publishing, New York, 370pp

Page-Jones, M., Constantine, L.L. and Weiss, S. (1990). Modeling object-oriented systems: the Uniform Object Notation, *Computer Language*, **7**(10), 69–87

Pal, P. and Minsky, N.H. (1996). Imposing the Law of Demeter and its variations, paper presented at TOOLS USA, Santa Barbara, CA, August 1996

Pant, Y.R., Henderson-Sellers, B. and Verner, J.M. (1996). Generalization of object-oriented components for reuse: measurements of effort and size change, *J. Object-Oriented Prog.*, **9**(2), 19–31, 41

Parnas, D.L. (1969). On the use of transition diagrams in the design of the user interface for an interactive computer system, *Proc. 24th National ACM Conference*, 379–385

Parsons, J. and Wand, Y. (1997a). Choosing classes in conceptual modeling, *Comm. ACM*, **40**(6), 63–69

Parsons, J. and Wand, Y. (1997b). Using objects for systems analysis, *Comm. ACM*, **40**(12), 104–110

Perry, D.E. and Kaiser, G.E. (1990). Adequate testing and object-oriented programming, *J. Obj.-Oriented Prog.*, **2**(5), 13–19

Petri, C.A. (1962). *Kommunikation mit Automaten*, unpubl. PhD dissertation, University of Bonn

Pfleeger, S.L. (1991). *Software Engineering. The Production of Quality Software* 2nd edn, Macmillan Publishing Co., New York, NY, USA, 517pp

Pfleeger, S.L. and Bohner, S. (1990). A framework for maintenance metrics, *Proc. Conf. on Software Maintenance*, Orlando, FL, USA

Pfleeger, S.L., Jeffery, R., Curtis, B. and Kitchenham, B. (1997). Status report on software measurement, *IEEE Software*, **14**(2), 33–43

Pinto, J.K. and Slevin, D.P. (1986). The project implementation profile: new tool for project managers, *Project Management Journal*, **XVII**(4), 57–70

Plato (1974). *The Republic*, translated by G.M.A. Grube, Hackett, IN, USA

Pree, W. (1995). *Design Patterns for Object-Oriented Software Development*. Addison-Wesley, Reading, MA, USA, 288pp

Pree, W. (1997). Essential framework design patterns, *Object Magazine*, **7**(1), 34–37

Preece, J., Rogers, Y., Sharp, H., Benyon, D., Holland, S. and Carey, T. (1994). *Human Computer Interaction*. Addison-Wesley

Premerlani, W. (1994). Object model transformations, *Proc. Object Expo Europe*, SIGS Books, NY, 237–240

Premerlani, W.J., Blaha, M.R., Rumbaugh, J.E. and Varwig, T.A. (1990). An object-oriented relational database, *Comm. ACM*, **33**(11), 99–109

Putnam, H. (1975). *Mind, Language, and Reality. Philosophical Papers*, vol. 2. Cambridge University Press, Cambridge, UK

Rasmussen, G., Henderson-Sellers, B. and Low, G.C. (1996). An object-oriented analysis and design notation for distributed systems, *J. Obj.-Oriented Prog.*, **9**(6), 14–27

Rational (1993). The Booch Components, V3.0

Rational (1997a). UML Semantics, version 1.0, 13 January 1997 (unpubl.), available from http://www.rational.com

Rational (1997b). UML Notation, version 1.0, 13 January 1997 (unpubl.), available from http://www.rational.com

Ratjens, M. (1993). *The Seminar*, unpubl. book manuscript

Ratjens, M. (1996). The five-minute guide to analysis and design: a recursive, fractal approach, unpubl. manuscript

Reddy, D.R. and Newell, A. (1974). Knowledge and its representation in a speech understanding system. In *Knowledge and Cognition* (L.W. Gregg ed.), Baltimore, 253–285

Reenskaug, T., Andersen, E.P., Berre, A.J., Hurlen, A., Landmark, A., Lehne, O.A., Nordhagen, E., Nêss-Ulseth, E., Oftedal, G., Skaar, A.L. and Stenslet, P. (1992). OORASS: seamless support for the creation and maintenance of object oriented systems, *J. Obj.-Oriented Prog.*, **5**(6), 27–41

Reenskaug, T., Wold, P. and Lehne, O.A. (1996). *Working with Objects. The OOram Software Engineering Manual*, Manning, Greenwich, CT, USA, 366pp

Renouf, D.W. and Henderson-Sellers, B. (1995). Incorporating roles into MOSES. In *TOOLS15*, (C. Mingins and B. Meyer eds). Prentice Hall, 71–82

Rieken, D. (1994). Intelligent Agents, *Comm. ACM*, **37**(7), 18–21

Riel, A.J. (1996). *Object-Oriented Design Heuristics*. Addison-Wesley, Reading, MA, USA, 379pp

Rist, R.S. (1996). Teaching Eiffel as a first language, *J. Obj.-Oriented Prog.*, **9**(1), 30–41

Rist, R. and Terwilliger, R. (1995). *Object-Oriented Programming in Eiffel*. Prentice Hall, Sydney, Australia, 485pp

Robertson, G.G. and Mackinlay, J.D. (1993). The document lens, *Proc. ACM Symposium on User Interface Software and Technology*

Rockart, J.F. (1979). Chief executives define their own data needs, *Harvard Business Review*, Mar/Apr, 81

Rosch, E. and Mervis, C. (1975). Family resemblances: studies in the internal structure of categories, *Cognitive Psychology*, **7**, 573–605

Rosch, E., Mervis, C., Gray, W., Johnson, D. and Boyes-Braem, P. (1976). Basic objects in natural categories, *Cognitive Psychology*, **8**, 382–439

Rotzell, K. and Loomis, M.E.S. (1991). ODBMS: benchmarking an ODBMS, *J. Obj.-Oriented Prog.*, **4**(1), 66–72

Rubin, K. and Goldberg, A. (1992). Object behavior analysis, *Comm. ACM*, **35**(9), 48–62

Rubin, K.S., McClaughry, P. and Pelligrini, D. (1994). Modeling rules using Object behavior analysis and design, *Object Magazine*, **4**(3), 63–67

Rumbaugh, J. (1992). Horsing around with associations, *Journal of Object-Oriented Prog.*, **4**(9), 49–53

Rumbaugh, J. (1994). Getting started: using use cases to capture requirements, *J. Obj.-Oriented Prog.*, **7**(5), 8–12

Rumbaugh, J. (1996). To form a more perfect union: unifying the OMT and Booch methods, *J. Obj.-Oriented Prog.*, **8**(8), 14–18

Rumbaugh, J., Blaha, M., Premerlani, W., Eddy, F. and Lorensen, W. (1991). *Object-oriented Modeling and Design*. Prentice Hall, USA, 500pp

Sakkinen, M. (1988). Comments on 'The Law of Demeter' and C++, *SIGPLAN Notices*, **23**(12), 38

Schank, R.C. and Abelson, R.P. (1977). *Scripts, Plans, Goals and Understanding*. Lawrence Erlbaum Associates, NY, USA

Schmidt, D.C. (1995a). An OO encapsulation of lighweight OS concurrency mechanisms in the ACE toolkit, Technical Report WUCS-95-31, Washington University, St Louis

Schmidt, D.C. (1995b). Using design patterns to develop reusable object-oriented communication software, *Comm. ACM*, **38**(10), 65–74

Schmucker, K.J. (1986). MacApp: an application framework, *Byte*, **11**(8), 189–193

Schatz, S.M. (1993). *Development of Distributed Software: Concepts and Tools.* Macmillan Publishing Company, 209pp

Seidewitz, E. and Stark, M. (1995). *Reliable Object-Oriented Software. Applying Analysis and Design.* SIGS Books, New York, 413pp

Selic, B., Gullekson, G. and Ward, P.T. (1994). *Real-Time Object-Oriented Modeling.* John Wiley & Sons, Inc., New York, 525pp

Shackel, B. (1991). Usability – context, framework, definition, design and evaluation. In *Human Factors for Informatics Usability* (B. Shackel and S.J. Richardson eds), Cambridge University Press, Cambridge, England, 19–40

Sharble, R.C. and Cohen, S.S. (1993). The object-oriented brewery: a comparison of two object-oriented development methods, *ACM SIGSOFT Software Engineering Notes*, **18**(2), 60–73

Shatz, S.M. (1993) *Development of Distributed Software: Concepts and Tools.* Macmillan Publishing Company, 209pp.

Shatz, S.M. and Wang, J. (eds) (1989). *Tutorial: Distributed-Software Engineering*, IEEE Computer Society, Washington DC, USA, 279pp.

Shelton, R.E. (1993). An object-oriented method for enterprise modeling: OOEM. In *Proc. OOP'93, Munich*, SIGS Publications, New York, NY, USA, 61–70

Shepperd, M. (1990). Early life-cycle metrics and software quality modules, *Inf. Soft. Technol.*, **32**(4), 311–316

Shlaer, S. and Mellor, S.J. (1988). *Object-Oriented Systems Analysis: Modeling the World in Data.* Yourdon Press Computing Series, 144pp

Shlaer, S. and Mellor, S.J. (1992). *Object Lifecycles. Modeling the World in States.* Yourdon Press/Prentice Hall, 251pp

Simons, A.J.H. (1995). Mixins: typing the superclass interface, Department of Computer Science, University of Sheffield, Memoranda in Computer and Cognitive Science, CS–95–26

Simons, A.J.H. (1998a). *Object Discovery – a systematic approach to developing object-oriented systems*, Workshop 8, BCS Conference on Object Technology, April 1998

Simons, A.J.H. (1998b). *Object Discovery – a process for developing medium-sized object-oriented applications*, Tutorial 14 presented at European Conf. Object-Oriented Programming (ECOOP), July 1998

Simons, A.J.H. (1999). *Discovery and Invention: object-oriented analysis and design using the Discover Method.* Addison-Wesley, UK

Simons, A.J.H., Low, E.K. and Ng, Y.M. (1994). An optimising delivery system for object-oriented software, *Object-Oriented Systems*, **1**(1), 21–44

Smith, M.D. and Robson, D.J. (1992). A framework for testing object-oriented programs, *J. Obj.-Oriented Prog.*, **5**(3), 45–53

Smyth, D.S. and Checkland, P.B. (1976). Using a systems approach: the structure of root definitions, *Journal of Applied Systems Analysis*, **5**, 75–83

Sommerville, I. (1995). *Software Engineering* 5th edn. Addison-Wesley, UK

Sowa, J.F. and Zachman, J.A. (1992). Extending and formalizing the framework for information systems architecture, *IBM Systems J.*, **31**(3), 590–616

Spivey, J.M. (1988). *Understanding Z: A Specification Language and its Formal Semantics.* Cambridge University Press

Stathis, J. and Jeffery, D.R. (1993). An empirical study of Albrecht function points, in *Measurement – for improved IT management. Proc. First Australian Conference on Software Metrics, ACOSM'93* (J.M. Verner ed.), Australian Software Metrics Association, Sydney, 96–117

Steele, F.I. (1969). Consultants and detectives, *Journal of Applied Behavioral Science*, **5**, 182–202

Steele, G.L. (1986). *The Common Lisp Reference Manual.* DEC/Lucid Press

Stepanov, A. and Lee, M. (1994). *The Standard Template Library.* Hewlett Packard Laboratories

Stone, H.S. and Bokari, S.H. (1978). Control of distributed processes, *Computer*, **11**(7), 97–106

Strachey, C. (1967). *Fundamental Concepts of Programming Languages.* Oxford University Programming Research Group

Strauss, S.H. and Ebenau, R.G. (1995). *Software Inspection Process.* McGraw-Hill, USA

Stroustrup, B. (1991). *The C++ Programming Language* 2nd edn. Addison-Wesley, Reading, MA, USA

Stroustrup (1994). *The Design and Evolution of C++.* Addison-Wesley

Swaminathan, V. and Storey, J. (1997). Domain-specific frameworks. *Object Magazine*, **7**(2), 53–57

Swatman, P.A. (1992). *Increasing Formality in the Specification of High-Quality Information Systems in a Commercial Context*, PhD thesis, Curtin University of Technology, School of Computing, Perth, Western Australia

Taenzer, D., Ganti, M. and Poder, S. (1989). Object-oriented software reuse: the yoyo problem, *J. Obj.-Oriented Prog.*, **2**(3), 30–35

Taivalsaari, A. (1993). Object-oriented programming with modes, *J. Obj.-Oriented Prog.*, **6**(3), 25–32

Taivalsaari, A. (1996). On the notion of inheritance, *ACM Computing Surveys*, **28**(3), 438–479

Taylor, D.A. (1995). *Business Engineering with Object Technology.* John Wiley & Sons Ltd, New York, 188pp

Tennant, R.D. (1981). *Principles of Programming Languages.* Prentice-Hall

Thal, B. and Docker, T. (1995). Project management issues in object-oriented development, *Proc. TOOLS 16* (I. Graham, B. Magnusson, B. Meyer and J.-M. Nerson eds). Prentice Hall, Hemel Hempstead, UK, 207–217

Thomas, D. (1989). What's in an object?, *Byte*, **14**(3), 231–240

Thomas, D. and Jacobson, I. (1989). Managing object-oriented software engineering, Tutorial, *TOOLS '89*, Paris, Nov 13–15 (1989). 52pp

Thomsett, R. (1992). Client and computer professionals, *Professional Computing*, October, 15–19

Thorne, F. (1997). *A software classification scheme for reuse*, MSc Thesis, University of Technology, Sydney, NSW, Australia

Thurston, P. (1993). Object oriented databases, *OOPS Newsletter, No. 17*, British Computer Society, 8–13

Turner, C.D. and Robson, D.J. (1992). The testing of object-oriented programs, Technical Report: TR–13/92, Computer Science Division, School of Engineering and Computer Science, University of Durham, England, 64pp

Turner, J.A. (1987). Understanding the elements of system design. Chapter 4 in *Critical Issues in Information Systems Research*, (R.J. Boland, jr. and R.A. Hirschheim eds), John Wiley, Chichester, 97–111

Ungar, D. and Smith, R.B. (1987). Self: the power of simplicity, *Proc. 2nd ACM Conf. OOPSLA, SigPlan Notices*, **22**(12), 227–241

Unhelkar, B. (1994). Development of a commercial software solution using an OO methodology: a MOSES case study, presented at ObjectWorld '94, Sydney, Sept 1994

Unhelkar, B. (1995a). The MOSES experience, *Obj. Mag.*, **5**(3), 50–55

Unhelkar, B. (1995b). Development of Telerate Currency Options (COPS) using MOSES: a case study, presented as part of Tutorial 51: Merging OOAD methodologies: the COMMA project and its first results, OOPSLA '95, Austin, TX, 15–19 October 1995

Unhelkar, B. (1997). *Effect of granularity of object-oriented design on modeling an enterprise, and its application to financial risk management*, PhD Thesis, University of Technology, Sydney, NSW, Australia

Valaer, L.A. and Babb, R.G. (1997). Choosing a user interface development tool, *IEEE Software*, **14**(4), 29–39

Venema, T. (1992). Client server and DB2, Software AG Canada, presentation in Sydney

Vickers, G. (1965). *The Art of Judgement: A Study of Policy Making*. Chapman and Hall, London, UK, 284pp

Vlissides, J. (1997). Patterns: the top ten misconceptions, *Object Magazine*, **7**(1), 31–33

Waldén, K. and Nerson, J.-M. (1995). *Seamless Object-Oriented Architecture*. Prentice Hall, 301pp

Warmington, A. (1980). Action research: its method and its implications, *Journal of Applied Systems Analysis*, **7**, 23–39

Wertheimer, M. (1958). Principles of perceptual organisation. In *Readings in Perception* (D.C. Beardslee and M. Wertheimer eds), Van Nostrand, NJ, USA

Wheeler, D.A., Brykczynski, B. and Meeson, R.N. jr. (1996). Peer review processes similar to inspections. In *Software Inspection: An Industry Best Practice*, IEEE Computer Society Press

Whitehead, K. (1997). OO methodology issues: what are they and do they matter, *American Programmer*, **10**(3), 4–8

Whitmire, S.A. (1997). *Object-Oriented Design Measurement*. J. Wiley & Sons, Inc., New York, NY, USA, 452pp

Whitten, J., Bentley, L. and Barlow, V. (1989). *Systems Analysis and Design Methods*. Irwin, Boston, MA, 797pp

Whyte, W. and Hamilton, E. (1965). *Action Research for Management*. Irwin–Dorsey, Homewood, IL, USA

Wieringa, R., de Jonge, W. and Spruit, P. (1995). Using dynamic classes and role classes to model object migration, *Theory and Practice of Object Systems*, **1**(1), 61–83

Wilkinson, N. (1994). An informal introduction, *Report on Object Analysis and Design*, **1**(4), 41–43

Wilkinson, N. (1995a). Putting the cards on the table, *Report on Object Analysis and Design*, **1**(5), 46–48

Wilkinson, N. (1995b). *Using CRC Cards: An Informal Approach to Object-Oriented Development*. SIGS Books, New York, NY, USA

Wilkinson, N. (1996). Tools for CRC development, *Report on Object Analysis and Design*, **2**(7), 45–48, 52

Williams, J. (1995). *What Every Software Manager MUST KNOW TO SUCCEED with Object Technology*. SIGS Books, New York, 273pp

Williams, J. (1997). Introduction: patterns, *Obj. Mag.*, **7**(1), 29

Williams R.C., Walker, J.A. and Dorofee, A.J. (1997). Putting risk management into practice, *IEEE Software*, **14**(3), 75–81

Wills, A. (1997). Frameworks and component-based development. In *OOIS'96* (D. Patel, Y. Sun and S. Patel eds), Springer-Verlag, London, 413–430

Wilson, B. (1984). *Systems: Concepts, Methodologies and Applications*. J. Wiley & Sons, Chichester

Wilson, B. (1989). A systems methodology for information requirements analysis. In *Systems Development for Human Progress* (H.K. Klein and K. Kumar eds), Elsevier, Amsterdam, The Netherlands

Winblad, A.L., Edwards, S.D., and King, D.R. (1990). *Object-Oriented Software*. Addison-Wesley, Reading, MA, 291pp

Winston, P.H. (1992). *Artificial Intelligence* 3rd edn. Addison-Wesley

REFERENCES

Winston, M.E., Chaffin, R. and Herrmann, D. (1987). A taxonomy of part–whole relations, *Cognitive Science*, **11**, 417–444

Wirfs-Brock, R. (1994). Adding to your conceptual toolkit: what's important about responsibility-driven design?, *Report on Object Analysis and Design*, **1**(2), 39–41

Wirfs-Brock, R. and McKean, A. (1996). Responsibility-driven design tutorial notes (unpubl.)

Wirfs-Brock, A., and Wilkerson, B. (1989a). Variables limit reusability, *J. Obj.-Oriented Prog.*, **2**(1), 34–40

Wirfs-Brock, R. and Wilkerson, B. (1989b). Object-oriented design: a responsibility-driven approach, *Proc. OOPSLA '89, SigPlan Notices*, **24**(10), 71–76

Wirfs-Brock, R., Wilkerson, B. and Wiener, L. (1990). *Designing Object-Oriented Software*. Prentice Hall, Englewood Cliffs, NJ, 368pp

Wooding, P. (1997). Business frameworks, *Object Magazine*, **6**(11), 50–54

Yang, O., Halper, M., Geller, J. and Perl, Y. (1995). The OODB ownership relationship, *OOIS'94 Proceedings* (D. Patel, Y. Sun and S. Patel eds), Springer-Verlag, 278–291

Yap, L-M. and Henderson-Sellers, B. (1993). ASWEC A semantic model for inheritance in object-oriented systems, *Proc. ASWEC '93*, IREE, Sydney, 28–35

Yap, L-M. and Henderson-Sellers, B. (1997). Class hierarchies: consistency between libraries, *Australian Computer Journal*, **29**(3), 81–94

Younessi, H. (1998). Re-engineering the business process: an object-oriented approach. In *Handbook of Object Technology* (S. Zamir ed.), CRC Press, Boca Raton, FL, USA

Younessi, H. and Henderson-Sellers, B. (1997). Cooking up improved software quality, *Object Magazine*, **7**(8), 38–42

Younessi, H. and Smith, R. (1995). Systemicity and object-oriented approaches to business process re-engineering. In *Proc. 1st Australian Systems Conference*, Edith Cowan University, Western Australia, Australia

Younessi, H., Smith, R. and Grant, D. (1994). Systemicity: a rationale for revisiting object-oriented techniques. In *Proc. 5th Australasian Conference on Information Systems*. Monash University, Victoria, Australia

Younessi, H., Smith, R. and Grant, D. (1995). Towards a systemic approach to object-oriented analysis. In *Proc. 6th Australasian Conference on Information Systems*, Curtin University, Western Australia, Australia

Yourdon, E. (1989). *Structured Walkthroughs* 5th edn. Prentice-Hall

Yourdon, E. (1997). Distributed components in the age of religious wars, *American Programmer*, **10**(12), 24–33

Zachman, J.A. (1987). A framework for information systems architecture, *IBM Systems J.*, **26**(3), 276–292

Zadeh, L.A. (1965). Fuzzy sets, *Information and Control*, **8**, 338–353

Zadeh, L.A. (1973). Outline of a new approach to the analysis of complex systems, *IEEE Trans. on Sys., Man and Cyb.*, **3**(1), 28–44

Zultner, R. (1988). The Deming approach to software quality engineering, *Quality Progress*, November, 58–64

Zuse, H. (1990). *Software Complexity: Measures and Methods*. Walter de Gruyter, Berlin, 605pp

Index

abstract and deferred classes, 45, 91–92, Appendix E (CD)
abstraction, 70, 92–95, Appendix E (CD)
    completion of, 142–143
acceptance testing *see* Testing, acceptance
access analysis, 98–99
access paths, Appendix E (CD)
accidental objects, 106
action research, 361–363
active listening, 99–103
activity grids, 103–105
agents *see* Intelligent agents
aggregation, membership and containment, Appendix E (CD) *see also* Relationships
analysis of judgements, 105–107
application scavenging, 107–110
approval gaining, 110–111, 200
assertion language, Appendix E (CD)
assertions, *see* Contracts
associations, dependency and usage, Appendix E (CD) *see also* Relationships
association class, 43
attributes, 37, 126, 316
audit, 111, 328–329

beta testing *see* Testing, beta
blackboarding, 114–116
BNF lifecycle specification, Appendix E (CD)
BON (Business Object Notation), 46–47, 52, 119–120, 160, 193
BPR, 103–105, 118, 152, 364–367
    theory, Appendix E (CD)
brainstorming, 116–117
business
    process modeling, 117–119, 152
    rules *see* Rules

CATWOE, 376

chainsaw, 74
change management, 148
characteristic, 23
CIRT (class, instance, role or type), 22, 32–33
CIRT indexing, 119–121
class *see* CIRT
    implementation *see* Structure, implementation
    internal design, 121–127 *see also* Design templates
classifier, 38
classification and partitions, 69, Appendix E (CD)
class naming, 127–129
client–server systems *see* Distributed computer systems
clustering (DB), 129–131
clusters *see* Packages
CMM, 86, 370
Coad and Yourdon notation, 45–46
coding
    standards, 127
    style, 81–83
cognitive focus, 94
cohesion, coupling and connascence, Appendix E (CD) *see also* Metrics, cohesion
collaborations, 76, 133–139, Appendix E (CD)
    use of aggregation, 136–137
    use of generalization, 138–139
collapsing of classes (DB), 139–141
color in UIs, Appendix E (CD)
COMMA, 7
COMN (OML's preferred notation), 8–12, 21, 30–36, 50, 307 *see also* OML
Complex Adaptive Systems (CAS) theory, Appendix E (CD)

421

complexity measures, Appendix E (CD) *see also* Metrics, complexity
components, 71, 76, 91, 200–201, 255
composition *see* Aggregation
computer-based training (CBT), 143–145
concept maps, 145–147
concurrency, 50, 83, 188–189, 236, 336
configuration management, 119, 147–150
connascence, Appendix C (CD) *see also* Cohesion, coupling and connascence
containment, Appendix E (CD) *see also* Aggregation, membership and containment; Relationships
context modeling, 150–153
contract-driven lifecycle, 8–12
contracts, 72–74, 195, 197, 310, Appendix E (CD)
CORBA *see* Object request brokers
cost–benefit analysis (CBA), 154
cost estimation, 155–156
    models, Appendix E (CD)
coupling, 135–136 *see* Cohesion, coupling and connascence; Metrics, coupling
CPM charts, 157–158
CRC cards, 53, 158–159, Appendix E (CD)
creation charts, 159–161
critical success factors (CSFs), 161–163
customer training, 163–165

database, 78–79, 237–239
    authorization, 165–167
    clustering, 129–131
    collapsing of classes, 139–141
    fragmentation, 167–168
    indexing, 227–228
    object replication, 257–258
    object retention, 258–259
    product selection, 168
    storage of derived properties, 326–327
    tuning, 341–342
    type selection, 169
    versioning, 348–349
    volume analysis, 355
dataflow modeling, Appendix D (CD)
data presentation, 324–325
defects, 68, 174–177
deferred classes *see* Abstract and deferred classes
delegation, 177–179, Appendix E (CD)

dependency *see* Associations, dependency and usage; Relationships
dependency-based testing *see* Testing, dependency-based
design templates, 18–19, 179–181
diagrams, 47–52
dialog design, 181–186
Discovery method, 15–16, 52
discriminant, 74, Appendix E (CD)
distributed computer systems (DCS), 79, 171–174, 186–189, 262, Appendix E (CD)
    implementation, 220–222
domain analysis, 141–142, 189–190
drop-down boxes, 33–34

encapsulation and information hiding, 71, Appendix E (CD)
envisioning, 152, 190–192
ER modeling, Appendix D (CD)
error messages, 184
event
    charts, Appendix C (CD)
    models, 192–194
exceptions, 194–198
expected value analysis, 198–199

Fagan's inspections *see* Inspections
finite state machines *see* State modeling
Firesmith method, 1–3, 9–12, 77
formal methods, 367–369 *see also* Object-Z
fossil class, 160
frameworks, 108, 109, 199–203 *see also* Idioms, patterns and frameworks
friends, 82
frisbees, 268
function points, Appendix D (CD)
Fusion method, 70, 82, 353
future *see* OOAD, future
fuzzy logic/modeling, Appendix C (CD)

games, 203–206
Gantt charts, 206–207
generalization, inheritance and polymorphism, 208–209, Appendix E (CD) *see also* Relationships
genericity, 209–211, Appendix E (CD)
Gestalt pyschology, 128
god class, 156
GQM (Goal–Question–Metric), 211–213
granularity, 213–214
group problem solving, 214-216

INDEX 423

GUI *see* User interface

HCI, 186, 271
hierarchical task analysis, 216–218
hotspots *see* Patterns
hypergenericity, Appendix C (CD)

idioms, patterns and frameworks,
    Appendix E (CD)
IDL (interface definition language), 83
impact
    analysis, 218–219
    estimation, 219–220
implementation, 81–83
    distributed computer systems
        (DCS), 220–222
    rules, 222–223
    services, 224–225
    structure, 225–227
    using an OOPL, Appendix E
        (CD)
implementation inheritance *see*
    Relationships, implementation
    inheritance
incremental delivery, 6
indexing *see* CIRT indexing
indexing (DB), 227–228
Information Engineering (IE), Appendix
    D (CD)
information hiding *see* Encapsulation and
    information hiding
inheritance *see* Generalization,
    inheritance and polymorphism
    see also Relationships
inheritance hierarchies
    revision of, 295–297
inspections, 228–234
integration testing *see* Testing, integration
intelligent agents, 114, 173, 235–236,
    Appendix E (CD)
interaction
    diagrams, 18, 49–50, 122–123,
        Appendix E (CD) *see also*
        Sequence diagrams
    modeling, 121, 236–237
interactions, 72
interface, 37, 71, 82–83, 256
internet, 239–240
interviewing, 240–245
invariant *see* Contracts
invokes *see* Relationships
iterative development, 11, 317

JAD, 245

Kelly grids, 245–247

Law of Demeter, 83, Appendix C (CD)
layers *see* Collaborations
LCOM *see* Metrics, cohesion
lectures, 247–250
legacy systems, 85, 237–239, 314–315 *see
    also* Wrappers
libraries, 109, 119, 120, 191, 210, 250–253
literate programming, Appendix C (CD)
logic boxes *see* Sequence diagrams, logic
    boxes

mappings *see* Relationships
measurement *see* Metrics
mechanism, 133 *see also* Collaborations;
    Scenarios
membership *see* Aggregation, membership
    and containment; *see also*
    Relationships
mentoring, 254–255
methods, 123–127
method size, 81, 126
metrics, 68, 369–374
    cohesion, 132, 371
    complexity, 142–143
    coupling, 156–157
    process, 374
    reuse 292–293, 364
    thresholds, 332–334
    usability, 343–346, 373
Miller limit, 94, 134
mixin, 255–256,
modeling, 69–78
    languages, 21–52, 85–86
MOSES, 1, 32, 71, 77, 78
M^3P *see* GQM
MVC framework, Appendix E (CD)

naming conventions, Appendix E (CD)
    see also Class naming
navigation *see* Path navigation
normalization, Appendix D (CD)
notation, 30, 31 *see also* BON; Coad and
    Yourdon notation; COMN
    (OML's preferred notation);
    UML

OBA method, 12
object
    replication (DB), 257–258
    request brokers (ORBs), 83, 172,
        Appendix E (CD)
    retention (DB), 258–259

Object-Z, 86, Appendix E (CD) *see also* Formal methods
OMG, 7, 21, 36, 86
OML, 21, 25, 26, 28, 85–86, 189, 193, 208, 236, 307
on-site training *see* Customer training
OOAD
    convergence, 85
    future, 85–86
OOram method, 76
OPEN
    activities, 4–5
    architecture, 3–8
    Consortium, 2, 85
    deliverables, 18–19, 52–55
    home page, 19
    key elements, 3–4
    metamodel, 22–30
    modeling language (OML), 7
    OO principles, 7
    selecting techniques, 57–58
    tailoring matrices, 17, 58
    tasks, 4–5, 12–15
    techniques, 15–18
    underpinning concepts, 22–30
operations, 23
ORBs *see* Object request brokers
ownership modeling, Appendix C (CD)

package, 259–263, Appendix E (CD)
    testing *see* Testing, package
partitions, 74, Appendix E (CD) *see also* Classification and partitions
path navigation, 263–266
patterns, 133, 266–267 *see also* Idioms, patterns and frameworks
peer reviews *see* Reviews
pencil sharpening, 74
Personal Software Process *see* PSP
PERT charts, 267–268
Petri nets, Appendix D (CD)
pistols, 268
PLanguage, Appendix C (CD)
political systems analysis *see* Power analysis
polymorphism *see* Generalization, inheritance and polymorphism
postcondition *see* Contracts
power analysis, 269–270
power types, Appendix E (CD) *see also* Relationships
precedes *see* Relationships
precondition *see* Contracts
priority setting, 270–271

problem solving, 58 *see also* Group problem solving
process modeling *see* business process modeling
programming style *see* Coding style
project management, 67–69, 80
protocol analysis, 271–273
prototypes, 273–274, Appendix E (CD)
    throwaway, 334–335
PSP, Appendix C (CD)
PS–PPS, 205, Appendix C (CD)

quality, 68, 74 *see also* TQM
    templates, 274
qua-types, Appendix C (CD)
query optimization, 263–266, 274–277
questionnaires, 277–279

RAD, 279
    workshops *see* Workshops
record and playback, 280–281 *see also* Videotaping
refactoring, 282–283
refinement, 40, 283–284
regression testing *see* Testing, regression
relational databases, 253–254, Appendix E (CD) *see also* Databases
    compared to objectbases, 169–171
relationships, 25, 287–291
    aggregation, 26, 35, 41–42, 72, 181, 281, 288 *see also* Aggregation, membership and containment
    association, 34, 40–41, 43, 180, 287, 289–290 *see also* Association, dependency and usage
    containment, 26, 36, 72, 288, 290 *see also* Aggregation, membership and containment
    definitional, 28–29, 34
    dependency, 42, 288 *see also* Association, dependency and usage
    directionality, 25–26, 31, 40, 41
    extends, 78
    generalization, 42, 45, 74, 181, 290, 295–297
    implementation inheritance, 29, 74, 208
    inheritance, 42, 181, 290, 295–297
    invokes, 48
    mappings, 72, 287

membership, 35, 72, 288, 290 *see also* Aggregation, membership and containment
meronymic *see* Aggregation; Membership
power types, 289
precedes, 48
referential, 25–29, 34
roles, 181
scenario, 36
specialization, 29, 74,
subclassing, 29, 289
subtyping, 29, 289
transitional, 36
usage, 43, 288–289 *see also* Association, dependency and usage
uses, 78
whole–part *see* Aggregation; Membership
reliability, 291
repeated inheritance, Appendix C (CD)
repertory grids *see* Kelly grids
requirements engineering, 58, 359–360, 367–369
responsibilities and Responsibility-Driven Design, 22, 69–70, 291–292, 316, Appendix E (CD)
reuse, 80, 107, 214, 251 *see also* Libraries
metrics, Appendix E (CD) *see also* Metrics, reuse
reverse engineering, 293–294
reviews, 294–295
rich pictures, 297–298
risk analysis, 298–302
roleplay, 308
roles, 22, 76, 181, 307–308, Appendix E (CD) *see also* Relationships
rules, 309–310, Appendix E (CD)
implementation, 222–223

scenario class diagrams, 19, 48
scenarios, 76, 310–312 *see also* Scenarios, task scripts and use cases
scenarios, task scripts and use cases, 76, Appendix E (CD)
screen
painting, 313–314
scraping, 314–316
scripting *see* Scenarios
seamlessness, 6, 23, 117
selective export, 82–83
semantic net, 48

semiotics, 31–32
SEP *see* software engineering process
sequence diagrams, 122–123
logic boxes, 50
services, 316–318, Appendix E (CD)
implementation, 224–225
simulation, 318
SMART goals, 319
social systems analysis, 320–321
software engineering process (SEP), 4–5, 9, 58
software engineering process architecture (SEPA), 4
soft systems methodology, 374–377
SOMA, 1–3, 9, 77, 103, 162
specialization *see* Relationships, specialization
standards, 321–322
state
machines, Appendix E (CD)
modeling, 322–323
transition diagrams, 50, 52
statistical techniques, 323–325
stereotypes, 29–30, 36, 43–45, 77–78, 325–326, Appendix E (CD)
storyboarding, 327
structure
implementation, 225–227
subclassing a.k.a. whitebox inheritance *see* Relationships
subsystem *see* Package
subtyping a.k.a. blackbox inheritance or specification inheritance *see* Relationships
SVDPI sentences, 217–218
Synthesis method, 1–3
system acceptance, 96, 377–382

task
analysis *see* Hierarchical task analysis
points, Appendix C (CD)
scripts, *see* Scenarios, task scripts and use cases
team
building, 329–330
roles, 107, 303–307
structure, Appendix E (CD)
testing, 9, 68
acceptance, 95–98
beta, 112–114
dependency-based, 179
integration, 234–235
package, 262–263
regression, 284–286

unit, 342–343
  usability, 346–348
textual analysis, 330–331
threads, 335–336
thread safety, 236
thresholds *see* Metrics, thresholds
throwaway prototyping *see* Prototypes
timeboxing, 335
time threads *see* Threads
TQM, 118, 382–384
training, 83–84
  computer-based, 143–145
  customer, 163–165
  trainers, 336–338
traits, Appendix E (CD)
transformations of the object model, 338–340
transitions *see* State modeling; State transition diagrams
triggers *see* State modeling; State transition diagrams

Unified Modeling Language (UML), 7, 21, 36–45, 86, 284
unit testing *see* Testing, unit
usability, 86, Appendix E (CD)
  metrics *see* Metrics, usability
  testing *see* Testing, usability
usage *see* Associations, dependency and usage

use cases *see* Scenarios; Scenarios, task scripts and use cases
user interface (UI), 79, 181–186, 313–314
user requirements, 58, 67
uses relationship *see* Relationships, uses

V&V (verification and validation), 68 *see also* Reviews
variant analysis, Appendix C (CD)
version control, 148
versioning (DB), 348–349 *see also* Record and playback
videotaping, 349–350
viewpoints, 350–352
visibility, 82, 352–354, Appendix E (CD)
visualization, 384–391
volume analysis (DB), 355

walkthroughs, 355–357
web, 239–240
whitebox inheritance *see* Relationships, implementation inheritance
workflow, 357–358
workshops, 358–361 *see also* JAD, RAD
wrappers, 108, 313, Appendix E (CD)

yo-yo effect, 123, 202

Zachman frameworks, Appendix C (CD)